THE ECONOMICS BOOK

Also by Steven G. Medema

*The Hesitant Hand: Taming Self-Interest
in the History of Economic Ideas*

*The History of Economic Thought:
A Reader, 2nd Edition*

*Economics and the Law: From Posner
to Post Modernism and Beyond, 2nd Edition*

Ronald H. Coase

THE
ECONOMICS
BOOK

From Xenophon to Cryptocurrency,
250 Milestones in the History of Economics

Steven G. Medema

STERLING
New York

STERLING
New York

An Imprint of Sterling Publishing Co., Inc.
1166 Avenue of the Americas
New York, NY 10036

ISBN 978-1-4549-3008-2

Distributed in Canada by Sterling Publishing Co., Inc.
c/o Canadian Manda Group, 664 Annette Street
Toronto, Ontario M6S 2C8, Canada
Distributed in the United Kingdom by GMC Distribution Services
Castle Place, 166 High Street, Lewes, East Sussex BN7 1XU, England
Distributed in Australia by NewSouth Books
University of New South Wales, Sydney, NSW 2052, Australia

For information about custom editions, special sales, and premium and corporate purchases, please contact Sterling Special Sales at 800-805-5489 or specialsales@sterlingpublishing.com.

Manufactured in China

2 4 6 8 10 9 7 5 3 1

sterlingpublishing.com

Cover design by Igor Satanovsky

For photo credits, see page 528

For Robert and Sharon Medema, who made it all possible

Contents

Introduction

When asked to define economics, the great economist Jacob Viner once quipped: "Economics is what economists do." In this age, when economists analyze topics as diverse as sumo wrestling and baby names, that definition encompasses the study of pretty much everything. Contemporary economics ranges over anthropology, biology, family life, geography, law, politics, religion, sociology, sports, and beyond. It offers explanations for, and analyses of, behavior across the spectrum of life, consistent with the modern definition of economics as the study of choice in a world of scarce resources. Oh, and yes, economists also study the economy, teach economic theory and methods, provide policy advice, and engage their fellow citizens as public intellectuals.

Viner's one-liner assumes the existence of a person called "an economist," but the role of the professional economist dates back just to the late nineteenth century. Those writing on economic topics prior to that time, including the famed Adam Smith, were educated in other subjects and, at times, not educated at all. These writers were artists, businessmen, government officials, journalists, natural scientists, novelists, philosophers, poets, theologians—virtually anyone capable of writing down his or her own thoughts. Their ideas remain with us not just as topics in university courses but in the principles of modern economics itself.

The history of economics covers much more than the path from past to present. It tells the story of how societies and individuals grappled with the pressing problems of life. For some, that meant trying to understand how to enrich a nation and its people. For others, it meant the pursuit of justice or a reasonable standard of life. For still others, it meant dealing with environmental problems, urban decay, or crime. If economics—broadly defined—is what economists do and have done, then economics has been a variety of things over the centuries.

The earliest economic writers spent relatively little time trying to understand and explain the economy. They focused instead on how to order economic affairs properly. Some, such as Aristotle and Aquinas, analyzed pricing practices to inform their readers of what did or didn't satisfy the dictates of justice according to natural law or God's will. Others, including Thomas Mun and Adam Smith, prescribed ways to increase the wealth of a nation, whether in terms of gold and silver stocks or the production of goods and services. These writers often considered humanity an impediment to its own progress. Unchecked self-interest led to troubles that required firm boundaries on individual action. In the mid-seventeenth century, however, people began trying to understand *how* the economy works: how markets function, what determines prices and incomes, the role of money, what forces cause economic growth and decline. These topics remain at the beating heart of modern economics—even if the explanations for them have changed significantly over time.

Indeed, more than just the explanations have changed. Following a collective desire to make economics more scientific, this once-literary discipline has become highly mathematical, quantitative, and technical. Mathematics allows us to specify more precisely the relationships between variables by creating models to describe them. We derive conclusions from these models, demonstrating that under particular conditions, certain results logically follow. Quantitative methods allow us to test theories with data, probe causal links, measure the magnitude of relationships, and forecast the potential effects of policy changes. Economists have become prognosticators.

Despite their many benefits, however, these tools capture only those factors and forces that lend themselves to mathematical specification or quantification. In many instances, this situation doesn't pose a problem. In others, it results in limitations—either because a model doesn't encompass important facets of reality, or because relevant issues that are difficult to specify in a mathematical framework go unaddressed. Some, including 1991 Nobel Prize recipient Ronald Coase, have suggested that economists ditch the mathematical pyrotechnics and focus on the nitty-gritty of economic reality. But that would be throwing out the baby with the bathwater. Economic reality is as complex as social reality. It requires the use of abstract models to isolate the most important variables that come into play for a given problem. These models, in other words, help economists make sense of the real world. You will encounter a host of these models as you move through this book. Each represents an attempt to capture some aspect of real-life economic or social conditions. What makes an economy grow? How does the number of sellers of a product affect its price? How do laws governing intellectual property affect research and development? How does a change in the money supply affect economic activity? For all their limitations, mathematical models have helped economists find more precise answers—which often influence policymaking—to these questions.

Despite its mathematical precision, there is little that is unambiguous in economic reasoning. U.S. President Harry Truman once demanded that he be sent a one-armed economist, frustrated by the fact that his economic advisers would begin their advice with "On the one hand . . ." only to introduce an entirely different insight with "But on the other hand . . ." soon after. A theory is only as good as the assumptions that underlie it, and economists sometimes disagree about which assumptions pertain to a given situation and thus the conclusions to draw from a particular theory. As a result, the history of economics tells the story of battles over ideas, with implications that ripple through the details of economic theory and the organization of economic activity itself.

The essays you're about to read offer an entry point to this history, allowing you to connect with more than two thousand years of economic insight with minimal effort and to jump from topic to topic as suits your interests. One volume can't do full justice to these individuals, ideas, and events, so the "Notes and Further Reading" section at the end of the book provides a wealth of additional resources should you want to wade more deeply into the history of economics or into specific topics.

A complete list of milestones in economics extends well beyond the 250 enshrined here. For better or worse, this list—to say nothing of the contents of the essays themselves—inevitably reflects my own interests and biases, my own strengths and weaknesses. But it also reflects the book's audience, which ranges from economists and economics students to people with no previous exposure to the subject. My guiding principle has been simple: if I can't explain to my mother (not an economist) a particular point and why it matters in roughly 300 words without putting her to sleep, it falls to the cutting-room floor. If your favorites don't make an appearance, I apologize.

The essays appear in chronological order. Many milestones align easily with a particular year, while others developed over many decades, making it difficult to attach a precise date. My rule, wherever possible, has been to set the date at either the genesis of the idea or at the defining contribution. I have tried to make each essay self-contained, allowing you to sample a particular topic without needing to have read the essays prior to it. The necessity of brevity, though, makes it impossible to define all terms at each step; so, to help you trace people and ideas through time, each essay includes a "See Also" list at the bottom of the page to point you to related milestones. Works originally published in languages other than English typically appear in their English-language titles, and the publication data in the "Notes and Further Reading" section will point you to English translations.

This book explains the people, ideas, and events that define the history of economics. These theologians, statisticians, psychologists, philosophers, mathematicians, historians, and, yes, economists used both primitive and sophisticated methods, working in isolated environments as well as in rich communities of scholarship. A variety of forces shaped their ideas, including world events, the intellectual climate of the day, and even their personal lives. It's virtually impossible to understand the history of ideas fully without paying careful attention to the context within which those ideas developed. This book will arm you with that context and also explain what economists do.

Acknowledgments

It takes many people to make a book like this come together, not least the many fellow historians of economics from whose work I have profited immensely over the years and, specifically, in the preparation of this book. The "Notes and Further Reading" section at the end of the book will give the reader some sense for the extent of my debts. I would also like to thank Mie Augier, Peter Boettke, Antoinette Baujard, Marcel Boumans, Bruce Caldwell, Ross Emmett, Jamie Galbraith, Wade Hands, Kevin Hoover, Herbert Hovenkamp, Joseph Persky, Daniel Rees, Malcolm Rutherford, John Singleton, Keith Tribe, Roy Weintraub, and Buhong Zheng for discussions related to and comments on various essays found in this volume. A special word of thanks goes to Roger Backhouse, my longtime friend and coauthor, who provided extensive amounts of feedback on the contents list, read a number of the essays in draft form and, at least as important, was a regular source of encouragement and commiseration along the way. Needless to say, it is I who bear the responsibility for any errors, infelicities, and the like that remain.

The inter-library loan staff at the University of Colorado Denver's Auraria Library was very helpful in processing a plethora of requests for books found neither among my own holdings nor theirs.

Leah Spiro, my agent at Riverside Creative Management, brought this project to my attention and encouraged me to pursue it. Though I was initially hesitant to put my academic research to one side for a time to work on a book for a more general audience, this project has proven to be at once interesting, challenging, and rewarding. Leah's wisdom, cheerful and encouraging demeanor, and skill at doing those things that agents do are all greatly appreciated.

James Jayo, my editor at Sterling at the inception of this project, provided helpful guidance through the early stages of the writing and revising process. Elysia Liang took over in mid-November 2018 and skillfully shepherded the manuscript through to its finished form. Her careful attention to detail, innumerable suggestions for improving the quality of each essay, and flexibility in the inevitable give-and-take associated with a project such as this have made my life significantly easier and resulted in a book that is much better than it would have been had I been left to my own devices. Linda Liang, the photography editor for this project, has done a wonderful job of locating the many images found in this book, despite the associated challenges. I am also grateful for the efforts of the numerous other individuals on the production team at Sterling, including Michael Cea, Gavin Motnyk, Igor Santanovsky, and Kevin Ullrich.

As usual, the greatest debt of all goes to my wife, Carolyn, who is at once not afraid to tell me when a draft makes no sense, happy to take on the additional family-related burdens that come with approaching deadlines, and willing to overlook the fact that her husband is spending far too much time in his basement office surrounded by stacks of books.

Hesiod's *Work and Days*

Hesiod (c. 750–c. 650 BCE)

Economic activity is as old as human life itself. Primitive societies were subsistence-oriented and people bartered to procure necessary goods. During the Bronze Age, Mesopotamian communities used objects such as cowry shells as money, while coins emerged in the Aegean Sea region around 700 BCE. The development of economic activity brought analyses of how economic life should be structured at the individual and societal levels. Hesiod, a farmer and epic poet living in Boeotia, northwest of Athens, was among the first to explore this, writing *Work and Days*, which combines moral precepts with practical lessons on agricultural management.

Hesiod wrote *Work and Days* in part to reform his ne'er-do-well brother, Perses, who preferred idleness to hard work and was attempting to cheat Hesiod out of his share of the family inheritance. Hesiod acknowledged that life's ultimate goal is "ease and peace," but he explained the impossibility of achieving this by invoking the myth of Prometheus and Pandora. A day's work once provided plenty of food for a year, but man's theft of fire from the gods led Zeus to introduce evil into the world in the form of a jar filled with curses. Hermes offered the jar as a gift to the unknowing Pandora, who, ignoring her brother's warning to never accept gifts from the gods, opened it and released the curses. Now, said Hesiod, "the gods keep man's food concealed, and hard work is necessary to acquire it."

Here we encounter the primitive origins of the fundamental economic problem—scarcity. Work is a necessary response to the scarcity of resources and satisfies basic material needs. For Hesiod, two other points also fuel the drive to work: the social disapproval of laziness (shame), and the desire to emulate others' consumption habits (envy). This emotional drive gives rise to "wholesome" competition, which fosters a work ethic that helps address scarcity. The idea that efficient organization can help humanity surmount resource shortages at the household level lies at the root of economic thinking. Indeed, *oikos*, the Greek word for household, plus *nomos*, meaning custom or law, gives us the etymological roots of economics.

SEE ALSO Plato, Aristotle, and the Golden Mean (c. 380 BCE), Xenophon's *Oeconomicus* (c. 370 BCE), Veblen's *Theory of the Leisure Class* (1899), Pareto Optimality and Efficiency (1906), Scarcity and Choice (1932)

Pandora by British painter John William Waterhouse (1849–1917). Hesiod cited the myth of Pandora, who opened a jar full of evils (mistranslated from the Ancient Greek as "box") to explain why toil was necessary to fulfill even basic human needs.

Pythagoras and Ordering Society

Pythagoras (c. 570–c. 495 BCE)

Modern economics is a highly mathematical and quantitative science. Though most of economists' mathematical and statistical tools have been developed within the last two centuries, the idea that economic and social relationships can be described as mathematical orderings dates way back to ancient Greece.

We know Pythagoras of Samos, the Greek philosopher and mathematician, for developing the theorem in geometry that shows that the square of a right triangle's hypotenuse equals the sum of the squares of its two sides ($a^2 + b^2 = c^2$). But we know little about the man himself, and none of his writings survive. Even so, his influence on the Western intellectual tradition remains significant, deriving largely from the followers who formed around him after he established a school at Kroton, in southern Italy.

Pythagoras sometimes receives credit for introducing weights and measures to the Hellenic world—critical for commerce and exchange—but he and his followers influenced economic thinking more significantly by introducing more logical modes of reasoning into Greek thought. They believed that nature has an underlying mathematical order and that we can ultimately reduce all relationships to numerical form—a view reflected in the Pythagorean motto that "All is number." As a result, math and logic became essential tools for discovering and demonstrating the truths associated with the natural order. The most prominent economics-related example of this influence is Aristotle's analysis of the just price, which relies on mathematical ratios to demonstrate justice in exchange.

Pythagorean reasoning set the stage for the future of economic thinking. Contemporary abstract models of economic activity, using tools ranging from calculus to linear programing to game theory, seem far removed from the simple geometry and numerical relationships utilized by Pythagoras. So, too, does modern econometric analysis, which allows economists to estimate the magnitude of those relations. Yet these complex methods have their roots in the basic Pythagorean notion that economic and other social relationships are best conceptualized as mathematical orderings.

SEE ALSO Plato, Aristotle, and the Golden Mean (c. 380 BCE), Justice in Exchange (c. 340 BCE), The Invention of Calculus (c. 1665), The Econometric Society (1930), Game Theory Enters Economics (1944), Linear Programming (1947)

Pythagoras and his followers believed that all relationships could be expressed in mathematical form. In this line engraving, he is shown seated with one hand on a globe.

PYTHAGORAS.

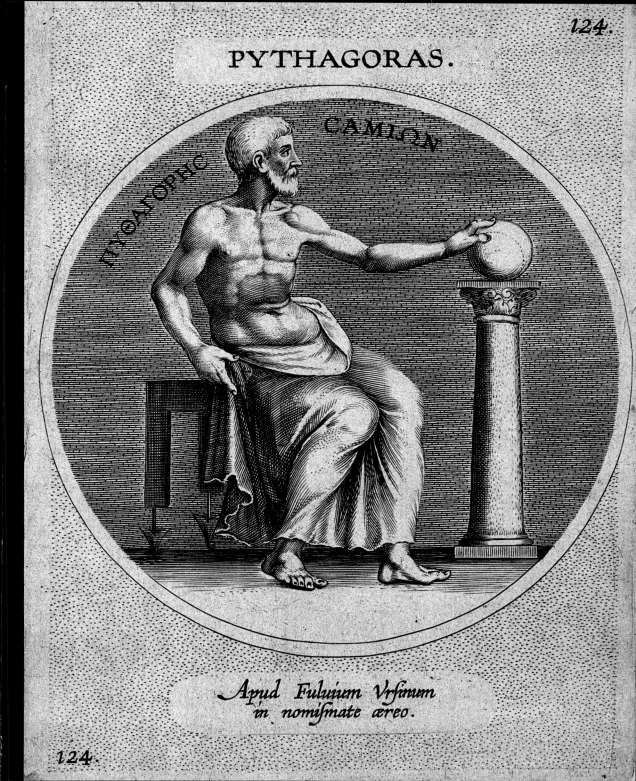

ΠΥΘΑΓΟΡΗΣ CAMION

Apud Fuluium Vrsinum
in nomismate æreo.

Plato, Aristotle, and the Golden Mean

Plato (c. 428–c. 348 BCE), Aristotle (384–322 BCE)

In 594 BCE, Athenian statesman and lawmaker Solon (c. 630–c. 560 BCE) introduced reforms that encouraged commercial enterprise and generated economic growth so significant that Athens achieved a level of wealth not seen again for centuries. What followed, however, were plague, wars, and loss of political independence at the hands of Alexander the Great (356–323 BCE) that saw Athens descend into an equally significant period of social, political, and economic instability. Reacting to this decline, philosophers Plato and his student Aristotle concluded that the pursuit of gain for gain's sake contradicted natural law, leading to war and injustice. Instead, people should work toward achieving a steady state in which individuals have a reasonable standard of living. This was an economic application of the "golden mean," the desirable middle point between the extremes of excess and deficiency.

Both Plato and Aristotle saw economic growth as a danger to society. Plato's ideal state featured common property ownership, while Aristotle supported private property. Plato advocated the specialization of labor, not to promote growth but to achieve a reasonable standard of living with the least effort. He frowned at international trade, too, because traders pursued wealth for its own sake and imported dangerous foreign customs that could contribute to social instability.

Citing the myth of King Midas and his golden touch, Aristotle—who, ironically, had tutored Alexander the Great—believed money shouldn't be an end unto itself but rather a means to an end, used only to acquire needed goods. As such, he condemned retail trade as unnatural because, as he saw it, the retail merchant set money making as his sole purpose and didn't generate any useful products by selling goods produced by others. Usury—defined at this time as any lending of money at interest—looked even more condemnable for similar reasons.

The desire to achieve and remain at an economic golden mean influenced economic thought and practice for two millennia. However, with the renewal of nation-state building and the accompanying drive for economic growth in the 1500s, this aspect of Greek thinking was pushed aside for a more dynamic approach that promised to enrich both the citizens and the state.

SEE ALSO Justice in Exchange (c. 340 BCE), The Just Price (1265), Aquinas on Usury (1265), Smith's *Wealth of Nations* (1776), The Division of Labor (1776)

Midas asked for the power to turn everything he touched to gold, an example of the greed that Aristotle saw as dangerous. Here we see Midas's daughter turned to gold from his touch, nicely illustrating the dangers to which Aristotle pointed.

MIDAS' DAUGHTER TURNED TO GOLD

Xenophon's *Oeconomicus*

Xenophon (c. 430–c. 354 BCE)

One of the first writings on the subject of economics comes from Xenophon, a Greek soldier and philosopher and, like Plato, a student of Socrates. His *Oeconomicus*—the Latin spelling of the Greek word *oikonomikos*, meaning household or estate management—takes the form of a dialog between Socrates and a wealthy young man named Critobulus about what it means to manage household affairs properly.

Influenced by Hesiod's *Work and Days*, Xenophon emphasizes the virtues of hard work, the efficient organization of household activity and production, and the benefits of the division of labor. He conceives of husband and wife as full partners who both contribute to the household estate, emphasizes the importance of agricultural pursuits, and outlines the benefits of education for *all* members of the household, including slaves, to enhance production. He also explores the ethical imperative against gain for its own sake, which dominated the Ancient Greek approach to economic questions, most famously in the writings of Plato and Aristotle.

Xenophon's focus on household organization and management gives his work a very different orientation from most of modern economics, with its focus on markets and growth. But it accurately reflects the economic activity of the day: largely agrarian, and lacking the array of the developed markets that permeate the modern economy. Plenty of merchants in the Hellenic world bought and traded goods, of course, but the household stood at the center of economic life, and the agricultural estate, which provided for many of the needs of the household, functioned as the primary unit of production activity.

Economic analysis today, of course, goes well beyond the art of household management. On the microeconomics side, it examines the behavior of individual consumers of goods and services, the suppliers of labor, and producers of these goods and services, as well as the operation of markets. Macroeconomics, in contrast, examines the determinants of economic aggregates such as inflation, unemployment, and gross domestic product (GDP), along with other determinants of economic growth. However, this micro–macro demarcation is decidedly modern, even if many of the basic questions addressed are as old as economic thinking itself.

SEE ALSO Hesiod's *Work and Days* (c. 700 BCE), Plato, Aristotle, and the Golden Mean (c. 380 BCE), The Division of Labor (1776), Classical Political Economy (c. 1790), The Dismal Science (1849)

A sculpture of the Greek philosopher Xenophon, whose Oeconomicus *provided the etymological root of the word economics as well as the first definition of the subject.*

Justice in Exchange

Aristotle (384–322 BCE)

The influences of Socratic ethics and Pythagorean logic on early economic analysis bear heavily on Aristotle's discussion of exchange in *Nicomachean Ethics*. Focusing on exchange between households, he determines that justice here requires that trades satisfy the dictates of reciprocity. It's unclear exactly what this reciprocity entails, but Aristotle suggests that the usefulness of the goods, plus the labor costs necessary to produce them, form key elements of the equation.

Aristotle illustrates his point by describing an exchange between a cobbler and a builder. Each man receives something of value from the other, and each incurs costs in producing the goods offered. For an exchange to be just, Aristotle posits that the ratios of benefit to cost for each party must be equal. A house provides great benefit to the cobbler, but the cost of producing a pair of shoes is very low. On the other hand, a pair of shoes for the builder provides a relatively small benefit, while the cost of building a house is very high. Given this, the cobbler should provide the builder with many pairs of shoes in return for a house, to satisfy the reciprocity requirement.

Realistically, the builder doesn't need that many shoes, which, Aristotle points out, is one reason for introducing money into the exchange process. When purchasing the house, the cobbler will provide the builder with an amount of money equivalent to many pairs of shoes. Likewise, the builder who wants a pair of shoes won't provide the cobbler with a small portion of a house, but with its monetary equivalent. Money, then, exists to facilitate exchange and helps promote justice within the exchange process.

The concern for justice in exchange was not limited to the Greeks. Indian philosopher Kautilya's *Arthashastra* (c. 300 BCE) emphasized that government should actively promote justice in the marketplace. Considerations of justice are largely absent from modern economic analysis, but they are standard in legal judgments of economic relationships, such as contracts. A truly voluntary exchange, as Aristotle said, will satisfy the dictates of justice—else, the parties would not agree. Given this, a voluntary exchange that is worthy of society's blessing should benefit both parties.

SEE ALSO Plato, Aristotle, and the Golden Mean (c. 380 BCE), The Just Price (1265), Supply and Demand (1767), The Competitive Process (1776)

A cobbler toils in his workshop in this illustrated kylix from Ancient Greece (c. 480–470 BCE). Because the cost of making shoes is low in comparison to building a house, Aristotle argues that the cobbler must exchange many pairs of shoes for a house in order for the exchange to be considered just.

Scholasticism

Albertus Magnus (c. 1200–1280), Thomas Aquinas (1225–1274), Nicholas Oresme (c. 1320–1382), Jean Bodin (1530–1596)

After the death of Aristotle, economic analysis largely faded from view in the Western world. Then, in the late Middle Ages, scholastic thinkers, including Albertus Magnus and St. Thomas Aquinas, resurrected it. Ensconced in the newly forming universities of Europe (Bologna in 1088, Oxford in 1096), these theologian-philosophers focused on interpreting and attempting to reconcile a trinity of classic texts: the Bible, the writings of the early Church Fathers, and the recently rediscovered work of Aristotle. Scholasticism dominated intellectual life in Europe for more than five centuries, from the early twelfth century until the beginning of the Enlightenment.

The scholastics dedicated themselves to outlining a broad theological program, with applications to the Christian life and issues of personal morality. As with Plato and Aristotle, ethics was the driving force behind the analysis. Scholastic writers, such as Aquinas, Nicholas Oresme, and Jean Bodin concerned themselves with appropriate Christian behavior in economic affairs, including pricing practices and monetary arrangements, rather than with understanding the forces governing economic activity.

Their focus on justice in exchange led the scholastics to downplay the pursuit of personal wealth and to decry lending at interest and exchange banking as immoral. As the decades and centuries passed, however, this philosophy collided head-on with emerging market capitalism, aided by the establishment of modern banking, including Italy's famous Medici Bank in 1397 and the development of double-entry bookkeeping. Growing businesses needed to borrow to expand and meet the demand for products, but this could only take place if lenders could charge interest for the use of their money. Likewise, the expansion of international trading necessitated currency exchange, which would be provided only if banks were allowed to make money from that service. Later scholastic writers, such as Johannes Nider of Vienna and Leonard Lessius of Belgium, loosened some of the moral restrictions found in their predecessors' work, recognizing that bankers, like other merchants, deserve to earn a reasonable rate of profit from their activities. Legitimizing these key ingredients of capitalist expansion marked a turning point in societal attitudes toward the activities central to economic growth.

SEE ALSO Plato, Aristotle, and the Golden Mean (c. 380 BCE), The Just Price (1265), Aquinas on Usury (1265), Debasement and Oresme's *De Moneta* (c. 1360), The School of Salamanca (1544), The Quantity Theory of Money (1568)

This illustration from the manuscript of Cantigas de Santa María, *written in thirteenth-century Spain, depicts a banker lending money to a merchant.*

Como a auia aparejou no porto u moraua ō Judeu.

The Just Price

Thomas Aquinas (1225–1274)

Born into the Italian nobility, Thomas Aquinas became one of the most prominent theologians of the Middle Ages. Written in several installments between 1265 and 1274, his *Summa Theologica* remains one of the most important theological treatises ever written. Though its commentaries on economic matters aren't extensive, the passages that do discuss economics stand out for their detailed attempt to derive lessons for economic life by reconciling biblical teachings with Aristotelian ethics and logic.

Like Aristotle, Aquinas emphasized the importance of fairness in exchange. He saw the sale of goods at a just price as a seller's Christian duty. Unlike Aristotle, however, Aquinas was writing during a period of more developed economic activity. With the growth of commercial society, market-based exchange had largely replaced small-scale interpersonal trade. Given this, what determines whether pricing practices in the marketplace conform to the dictates of Christian justice, such as mercy and charity?

For Aquinas, as for Aristotle, trade exists for the benefit of both parties involved. What is given should equal what is received. The price charged in the marketplace, Aquinas argued, will typically satisfy this dictate if it has been established without force or fraud, which of course conflict with Christian principles. Here, price reflects the community's collective estimation of the good's worth. Thus, Aquinas said, the price of cloth at the Fair of Lagny—one of several large annual French merchant markets— should be deemed just, because many sellers are competing to attract customers. Likewise, a good that would normally sell for a low price may justly sell for a much higher price if it is in short supply and people are willing to pay more for it.

Aquinas understood that prices must cover the costs of production, both as a condition of justice and as a requirement for sellers to provide the product. Beyond that, the usefulness of an item determined its market price. This important insight justified how the price of one product could be legitimately higher than another even if the production costs were similar. This also meant that businessmen could justly earn whatever profit the just price generated.

SEE ALSO Justice in Exchange (c. 340 BCE), Scholasticism (c. 1100), Supply and Demand (1767), The Competitive Process (1776)

Thomas Aquinas, depicted in this painted plaque (c. 1870) holding a monstrance and quill.

S·Thomas·Aqiunas· ·II·

Aquinas on Usury

Thomas Aquinas (1225–1274)

Charging interest on loans is standard practice today, but this wasn't always the case. For centuries, the Catholic Church debated usury's propriety and morality. At the center of these debates stood Thomas Aquinas, whose analysis of usury in the *Summa Theologica* formed the basis of the Church's opposition to interest for some 300 years.

The use of debt instruments to finance commerce or personal needs dates at least to Sumeria and was facilitated by emerging banking systems in the thirteenth century. Aquinas acknowledged that the Bible legitimizes usury in some places and opposes it in others, but for him the arguments for its prohibition carried more weight. To defend his position, Aquinas contrasted the lending of a house with lending a bottle of wine. If you lend someone your house for a period of time, it's just to charge rent for its use while still retaining ownership of the house, since the house is not "used up" in this process. But if you lend your neighbor a bottle of wine, you transfer ownership of the wine to her and the wine *is* "used up" when it's consumed. What you expect in return, what justice dictates, is the equivalent: another bottle of wine. To charge more than that runs contrary to justice.

For Aquinas, money was a "consumable," equivalent to the bottle of wine. It provides value only when one is consuming it and is "used up" when you transfer its ownership to another in the exchange process. Thus, charging interest amounted to charging twice for something, once for the use of the thing and once for the thing itself, which conflicts with the reciprocity demanded by Christian justice. In essence, Aquinas didn't perceive any opportunity cost—the value of the best foregone alternative, such as investing it in a business and making profits—associated with lending money. His strictures against charging interest became a part of Church doctrine and, owing to the Church's influence on society, a part of everyday commerce in much of Europe. As a result, credit markets and therefore economic activity there developed more slowly than they would have without this financial restriction.

SEE ALSO Plato, Aristotle, and the Golden Mean (c. 380 BCE), Scholasticism (c. 1100), The Protestant Reformation (1517), The School of Salamanca (1544), The Abstinence Theory of Interest (1836), Opportunity Cost (1889)

A moneylender "dances" with death in this illustration from 1744.

Tod zum Wucherer.

DEin Gold und Geld seh ich nicht an,
  Du Wucherer und gottlos Mann:
Christus hat dich das nicht gelehrt,
Ein schwartzer Tod ist dein Gefehrt.

51

Antwort des Wucherers.

JCh fragt nicht viel nach Christi Lehr:
  Mein Wucher der trug mir vielmehr:
Jetzt bleibt der Leiden all dahinten,
Was hilfft mein Schaben und mein Schinden.

Debasement and Oresme's *De Moneta*

Nicholas Oresme (c. 1320–1382), King Charles V of France (1338–1380)

With the Black Death, incessant warfare, and significant economic instability wreaking havoc during the fourteenth century, the need to finance warfare and defense in an era when tax systems were unreliable, as well as to remedy money shortages, led kings of the time to debase coinage regularly. Debasement involved recalling existing currency, melting it down, and reissuing coins with the same face value but lower precious-metal content. Mints also turned the reserved metal into coins, but the monarch retained this "excess" to finance state expenditures. This process increased the amount of currency in circulation, often leading to severe inflation—a significant economy-wide increase in prices. Because wages typically did not keep up with the increase in the prices of goods, the effects were often severe enough to destabilize the economy.

The problems caused by debasement inspired Nicholas Oresme, a French scholastic philosopher and churchman, to write *De Moneta*, which examined the nature and uses of money through the lenses of moral philosophy and Aristotelian thinking. Oresme harshly condemned debasement, which he considered worse than usury. Its effects went well beyond inflation, impacting, for example, the value of contracts and debt repayment. People paid or repaid in the less valuable, post-debasement money found themselves essentially defrauded, given that these new coins had reduced purchasing power. Observing that debasement caused people to hoard coins with higher precious metal content, Oresme also offered a primitive version of Gresham's Law (bad money drives out good).

Oresme acknowledged that a king had the right to oversee the issuance of currency, but he insisted that this money belongs to the public who uses it and validates its value. As such, a king had no right to alter its precious-metal content without the approval of his citizens. The force of Oresme's arguments convinced King Charles V of France to halt debasement for the remainder of his reign. Even so, debasement's attraction as a source of funds remained powerful enough that it continued to be practiced until paper money replaced precious-metal coins in the 1800s.

SEE ALSO Gresham's Law (1558), John Law and Paper Money (1705), The Gold Standard (1717), Galiani's *Della Moneta* (1751), Cryptocurrency (2009)

After hearing Nicholas Oresme's argument against debasement, King Charles V of France (shown here) ceased the practice.

CHARLES 5.e   DIT LE SAGE,

De Larmessin   Sculp.

ROY DE FRANCE,
et de Bonne, de LV
a la Couronne, en 1364
année, il auoit Espousé
Comencem.t de So. regne,
Entre Charles, C.te de Blois,
de la Bretagne, Mais a la 1.ere
minée, Car le C.te de Blois, fut tué, et
tagne, Ensuitte le duc de Bourbon, et le
Exploits, dans l'Espagne, Soutenant le party
Contre Pierre le Cruel, Roy de Castille, qui estoit Vn
Ses barbares, Impietez, il fut pris par les françois, et
Es chafaut, et henry, fut mis, Sur le trosne, et
le fit connestable de Castille, Charles.V. du Conse
auec l'Angleterre, dont le Roy, Indigne, Entra en
Conestable du Guesclin, l'attaqua cy a propos, qu'il
d'Vne honteuse déroute, Charles.V.e fais.t reflexion
fut Inspire, de tes reduire a trois, et preuoyant les mou
des roys, Voulut par Son Ordonnance de 1375, en Abreger le temps, en fixant la majorite, a 14 ans, On Assure que
le put querir, Enfin Apres Auoir declaré le duc d'Anjou Regent,
Enfans, Ayant mis Ordres aux Affaires de Son Royaume, et
proche Vincennes, Age de 42 ans, en Ayant regné 16.

Fils, de Iean le Bon
xembourg, Succeda
et fut Sacré la mesme
Ieanne de Bourbô, dans le
ny eut de grands troubles,
et Iean, C.te de Monfort, au Suiet
Montfort, fut declaré duc de Bre
Cónestable du Guesclin fir.t de grds
dhenry, fils naturel d'Alphonce de Castille
Apostate et ennemy déclaré du nom Chrestien par
finit malheureus.em.t Sa Vie, lais.t la teste Sur Vn
pour reconnoistre les merites, de du Guesclin
tem, des Estats, rompit le traité de Bretigny, fait
france, Auec Son Armeé, pour la rauager, mais le
fut contraint de se retirer, Suiuy des marques
Sur les Armes de france, des fleurs de lys, S.as nobre
dangereux, qui peuuent Arriuer pend.t la Minorite
ce Prince, fut par l'Ordre du Roy de Nauarre, empoisonne, d'Vn s.y Malin poison, qu'il n'y eut point de remede, qui
les ducs de Berry, et de Bourgogne, tuteurs de Ses
et de Sa maison, il mourut en 1380, au Chasteau de baute

Ibn Khaldun's *Al-Muqaddimah*

Ibn Khaldun (1332–1406)

The Islamic world made many intellectual advances unknown in the West until later times, and economics is no exception. Adam Smith rightly receives credit as the father of modern economics, but many insights ascribed to Smith and his successors appear in the writings of Ibn Khaldun, a Tunisian historian and philosopher. His *Al-Muqaddimah*, written in 1377 as the introduction to his massive history of the Arab and Muslim worlds, contained a wealth of new economic understanding.

Khaldun's approach to the subject was historical, drawing lessons about economic, social, and political organization from the rise and fall of ruling dynasties in North Africa. He emphasized the productive power of the division of labor, the benefits of market-based exchange, and the harmful effects of monopolies and big government. He also used the basic mechanics of supply and demand and the link between the profit motive—the desire for financial gain—and economic prosperity to show the benefits of private enterprise and international trade.

One of Khaldun's most innovative contributions was his theory of the economic cycle. The establishment of a new dynasty, he observed, brings order and urbanization, which facilitates the growth of economic activity, particularly in craft trades such as carpentry and weaving. Population expansion, the division of labor, and the needs of the new government expand the market for goods and services, raising incomes, which fuels further economic expansion. But Khaldun believed this progress had a limit. As standards of living increased, both the population and the ruling dynasty would become complacent, losing the drive that spurred the original economic expansion. The government would levy oppressive taxes, and the dynasty would collapse, bringing economic decline until the emergence of another dynasty.

Unfortunately, Khaldun's insights had little impact even in the Islamic world, where governmental structures and religious norms were not conducive to the dynamic economic development described by Khaldun or by Adam Smith and David Ricardo when their ideas were later introduced into the Islamic world. Yet Khaldun's highly original mind generated observations about economic activity that would only enter the main currents of economic thinking centuries later.

SEE ALSO Supply and Demand (1767), The Division of Labor (1776), Antitrust Laws (1890), Tugan-Baranovsky and the Trade Cycle (1894)

A bust of Ibn Khaldun, located in Casbah of Bejaia, Algeria.

IBN KHALDOUN

The Protestant Reformation

Martin Luther (1483–1546), John Calvin (1509–1564)

Histories of economics often overlook Martin Luther, the German theologian whose protests against the Catholic Church sparked the Protestant Reformation. But like his fellow reformer John Calvin, Luther concerned himself with economic matters. When the Reformation took hold, their ideas steered Protestant nations such as Germany, Holland, Switzerland, and Scotland toward a more commercial society. The economic growth it unleashed even led German sociologist Max Weber to credit Protestantism with the emergence of European capitalist societies in his 1905 book, *The Protestant Ethic and the Spirit of Capitalism*.

Like Aquinas, Luther approved of the market system—as long as it operated within certain limits. He condemned monopolies, unfair trading practices, and speculation. He was willing to tolerate usury only if interest rates remained modest and didn't exploit the disadvantaged. In short, he partially loosened the economic shackles of scholasticism, albeit with suspicion.

Calvin's views on economic matters broadly aligned with Luther's, with one exception. Calvin believed that both church and state should encourage industry and commerce. He promoted a strong work ethic and considered financial rewards for undertaking labor a blessing from God. Calvin resisted the pursuit of gain for its own sake and held that man-made law should prohibit ungodly business practices, such as fraud, just as the Bible does. Unlike most of his predecessors, Calvin was willing to condone the lending of money at interest so long as it remained within moral bounds.

Luther and Calvin grounded their views not in natural law, as the Greeks and Aquinas had done, but in the practice of Christian morality as informed solely by their reading of the Bible. For them, human behavior must adhere to God's will, which meant that the Golden Rule—do unto others as you would have them do unto you—should govern economic relationships. In this sense, these Reformation thinkers represent an early turn toward the assessment of economic activities based primarily on their consequences for everyday life rather than some abstract notion of the "good." Their belief that the growth of wealth offered benefits for both the individual and society would soon become a foundation of economic thinking.

SEE ALSO Plato, Aristotle, and the Golden Mean (c. 380 BCE), Scholasticism (c. 1100), Aquinas on Usury (1265)

A portrait of French theologian and reformer John Calvin (1564).

Mercantile Policies

Jean-Baptiste Colbert (1619–1683), Thomas Mun (1571–1641)

The mercantile system, a term popularized by Adam Smith, describes trade policies commonly practiced in Europe from the sixteenth to nineteenth centuries. These policies, which included taxes on imports, subsidies for exports, and loose immigration policies, were designed to maintain a favorable balance of trade by promoting exports and limiting imports. Whereas imports drained precious-metals stores, exports brought gold and silver that allowed rulers to finance building projects and wars and indicated growing national wealth in the eyes of government officials and the public. For nations lacking access to precious-metals mines, such as England and Holland, trade surpluses were considered essential.

The system originated in France in the late 1530s, when Jean-Baptiste Colbert, the finance minister under Louis XIV, imposed mercantilist policies to strengthen the nation and the king's standing. These trade practices soon spread across Europe. Business owners producing goods for export benefited immensely, whereas the working class and producers of food and materials used to manufacture exported goods suffered—a consequence of keeping production costs low so that exports could compete more effectively on world markets.

Thanks to the invention of the printing press, pamphlets advocating for mercantile policies became influential. Authored by academics, government officials, representatives of business interests, and even cranks, they emphasized these policies' practical consequences, shorn from scholastic moralistic constraints. Thomas Mun, the director of the East India Company, which was established in 1600 and had a monopoly on England's trade with India, was their most prominent advocate; in his *England's Treasure by Forraign Trade* (1664), he argued forcefully for the benefits of a positive balance of trade. Perhaps the mercantilists' most significant innovation was their portrayal of the economy as a separate sphere, one governed by natural laws, which made it possible to assess accurately the consequences of a particular policy.

Mercantilist policies held sway for three centuries, until Adam Smith and others began to convince governments and citizens of the benefits of free trade. The allure of the mercantilist system remains, however, as evidenced by recent U.S. efforts to increase tariffs on imports and so, their supporters claim, increase national economic strength.

SEE ALSO The Balance-of-Trade Controversy (1621), Smith's *Wealth of Nations* (1776), The Theory of Comparative Advantage (1817), The Heckscher–Ohlin Model (1933), The New Trade Theory (1979)

In this seventeenth-century painting (c. 1600–1630), Dutch ships sail from the coast of Mauritius, which was held by the Dutch East India Company from 1638 to 1710. Like its British rival, the Dutch East India Company benefited enormously from mercantile trading policies.

The School of Salamanca

Francisco de Vitoria (c. 1483–1546), Domingo de Soto (1494–1560), Martín de Azpilcueta (1491–1586), Luis de Molina (1535–1600)

In the 1500s, Francisco de Vitoria, a Dominican theologian and philosopher from northern Spain, attempted to reconcile the writings of Thomas Aquinas with new social and economic developments, such as the conquest of the New World and the continued growth of commercial society. De Vitoria, whose influence came primarily through his teaching, became chair of theology at the University of Salamanca in 1526, and a group of theologians gathered around him, establishing a new intellectual tradition. Sometimes called the "Second Scholastic," they became known as the School of Salamanca.

Inspired in part by the precious metals pouring into Europe from the Americas at the time, the greatest contributions of the Salamancans occurred in the monetary realm. They observed how increases in the supply of money led to increases in prices, a relationship that was first formulated in the 1500s and centuries later called the quantity theory of money. They also suggested explanations for exchange-rate determination and offered a justification for charging interest on loans if the lender was giving up profitable business opportunities or incurring significant risk of non-repayment.

The Salamancans had a positive attitude toward the free circulation of resources, including money, goods and services, and people. Their liberal view of the competitive market contrasted sharply with earlier Christian tradition and legitimated economic activity, including pricing practices and banking, without heavy-handed government controls. The Salamancans also made important contributions to the theory of value, rejecting notions that production costs determined the actual price or "just price" of a product. Instead, they argued in favor of a demand-and-supply view, emphasizing that prices generally depend on a buyer's subjective value of a product. They did suggest, however, that the state should regulate the prices of certain necessities, such as bread and meat.

Their work didn't spread far beyond southern Europe, so they had little direct influence on the development of later economic thinking, but the remarkable sophistication of their ideas has led some historians of economics, such as Joseph Schumpeter, to pinpoint the Salamancans as the founders of economic science.

SEE ALSO Scholasticism (c. 1100), Aquinas on Usury (1265), The Quantity Theory of Money (1568), The Velocity of Money (1668), Supply and Demand (1767), The Competitive Process (1776)

A contemporary photograph of the University of Salamanca.

Gresham's Law

Nicholas Oresme (c. 1320–1382), Nicolaus Copernicus (1473–1543), Thomas Gresham (1519–1579)

Named after English financier Thomas Gresham, who in 1558 wrote to Queen Elizabeth I that "good and bad coin cannot circulate together," Gresham's Law holds that bad money drives out good. The idea originated with scholastic theologian Nicholas Oresme and received more extensive development at the hands of astronomer Nicolaus Copernicus, best known for his heliocentric theory of the universe.

Between the mid-1300s and the late 1800s, currency problems plagued Western Europe. Coins with substandard precious-metal content—due to debasement, shaving, or wearing of the coins—circulated with, and had the same face value as, full-weight currency. Full-weight coins had a higher intrinsic value (the amount of precious metal they contained), but they could purchase only the same amount of product as the reduced-weight currency. As a result, people pulled full-weight coins from circulation—hoarding, exporting, or melting them down—and these coins sold for amounts of money that exceeded the face value of the original currency. Many of these problems were noted by Oresme in *De Moneta*.

Gresham's Law also applies to a monetary system, increasingly common in Europe beginning in the thirteenth century, in which two forms of currency, such as gold and silver coins, circulate simultaneously, with face values fixed by the state. If one ounce of gold has twice the value of one ounce of silver, the fixed face values of gold and silver coins must reflect this ratio. Otherwise, shrewd profiteers will pull them from circulation, as above. This insight proved particularly important for bimetallic currency systems of the time, because currency values easily fell out of line with market values. Copernicus noted that, in theory, governments could adjust face values continually to account for changes in market values, but he also recognized the impracticality of doing so.

The removal of good currency from circulation led to financial instability and choked economic activity. Gresham's Law might appear irrelevant in a world in which paper and electronic payments dominate, but we continue to see it in action wherever different forms of legal tender circulate simultaneously, such as Singapore and Zimbabwe, or where both U.S. dollars and the local currency are accepted.

SEE ALSO Debasement and Oresme's *De Moneta* (c. 1360), John Law and Paper Money (1705), The Gold Standard (1717), Galiani's *Della Moneta* (1751), The Price–Specie Flow Mechanism (1752), Cryptocurrency (2009)

These medieval-era coins from fifteenth-century Britain show signs of the clipping and wear that caused problems for metallic currency systems.

The Quantity Theory of Money

Martín de Azpilcueta (Doctor Navarrus) (1491–1586), Jean Bodin (1530–1596)

After European explorers encountered the Americas, an enormous influx of gold and silver poured in from the New World to the Old World. As governments converted more of these precious metals into coins, prices began to increase significantly across Europe.

While Jean Bodin, a French jurist and philosopher, wrote extensively on economic matters at the time and receives credit as being the first thinker to identify this relationship between money supply and price levels, Martín de Azpilcueta preceded Bodin here by a dozen years. Writing in his well-known *Reply to the Paradoxes of M. Malestroit* (1568), Bodin observed that increases in the money supply are likely to cause increases in prices. This insight, refined in numerous ways over subsequent centuries, has come to be known as the quantity theory of money.

At this point in the sixteenth century, theorists assumed that inflation resulted from debasement. They considered the inflow of gold and silver from the New World an unmitigated benefit, increasing both personal and national wealth. The rise of modern nation-states across Europe was putting significant pressure on the public purse with the need to finance wars and fund governmental operations. Bodin's insight, which spread quickly, signaled that this wealth from the New World *wasn't* all good and that governments had to exercise great care when introducing these precious metals into the economy in the form of currency. This all did little, however, to slow the increases in the money supply, with inflationary consequences felt across Europe.

Successively more refined views of the quantity theory of money have remained at the center of economic thinking since the time of Azpilcueta and Bodin, with David Hume, John Locke, Irving Fisher, and Milton Friedman offering prominent explanations of the tight link between the money supply and inflation. John Maynard Keynes and his followers have been among those who are critical of the quantity theory, arguing that increases in the money supply offer the potential to stimulate the production of goods and services and thus boost economic performance.

SEE ALSO Debasement and Oresme's *De Moneta* (c. 1360), The School of Salamanca (1544), Gresham's Law (1558), The Velocity of Money (1668), The Price–Specie Flow Mechanism (1752), Thornton's *Paper Credit* (1802), Wicksell's Cumulative Process (1898), The Phillips Curve (1958), A *Monetary History of the United States* (1963), Cryptocurrency (2009)

Slaves on the island of Hispaniola, which is divided between present-day Haiti and the Dominican Republic, mine precious metals in this illustration, c. 1590–1624, by Flemish engraver Theodor de Bry (1528–1598).

NIGRITÆ IN SCRUTANDIS VENIS METALLICIS
ab Hispanis in Insulas ablegantur.

I

ATtritis & penè absumptis continuo labore Hispaniolæ Insulæ incolis, Hispani aliunde mancipia conquirere cœperunt, quorum ministerio in perfodiendis montibus, venísque metallicis perscrutandis uterentur. Itaque redemptis sua pecunia, & accitis ex Guinea Quartæ Africæ partis Provincia mancipiis Æthiopibus sive Nigritis, illorum porrò opera usi sunt, donec temporis successu quicquid in ea Insula metallicarum venarum inesset, exhaurirent.   Nam ut Lusitani eam Africæ partem, quam ipsi Guineam (incolæ Genni aut Genna appellant) sibi subjectam reddiderant; singulis annis aliquot incolarum centurias exteris nationibus divendebant, quæ mancipiorum vicem supplerent.

A 2   Nigritæ

Empiricism and Science

Francis Bacon (1561–1626), William Petty (1623–1687), Robert Boyle (1627–1691), Christopher Wren (1632–1723), Isaac Newton (1642–1727)

In the seventeenth century, academics increasingly turned away from the authorities of the past, such as the Bible or Aristotle, toward a more scientific approach to knowledge based on observation and experimentation. In England, Francis Bacon made the case for empiricism and induction—the derivation of general conclusions or theories from specific observations, redirecting the scientific process away from deduction—the derivation of logical conclusions from an initial hypothesis. The collective effort to follow Bacon's lead prompted the formation of the Royal Society of London for Improving Natural Knowledge in 1660. This group included architect Christopher Wren, scientists Robert Boyle and Isaac Newton, and William Petty.

Among other roles, Petty was a physician, inventor, surveyor, and demographer—professions that share a strong commitment to quantitative analysis. Petty often assembled vast amounts of data and used what he called "political arithmetick" to answer an array of economic questions. Rejecting the "comparative and superlative words" of other writers, he insisted on expressing his ideas "in terms of number, weight, or measure" and considered "only such causes, as have visible foundations in nature." He used his quantitative methods to compare the value of economic activity in England with that of other nations, and even computed the value of people themselves. In doing so, Petty made critical, albeit primitive, contributions to national accounting, providing estimates of national income that could serve as a basis for taxation and measure economic growth. Economists didn't develop highly accurate methods for such analyses until well into the twentieth century.

Author Jonathan Swift viciously satirized this "political arithmetick" in *A Modest Proposal*. In response to Petty's findings that population growth could remedy Ireland's poverty, Swift suggested that the Irish produce more babies and eat them, providing estimates of the economic benefits of doing so. As Swift's commentary indicates, Petty's data analysis suffered from many flaws due to the primitive data-collection methods of this period and his tendency to draw conclusions that amounted to little more than educated guesses. Nonetheless, that work foreshadowed the centrality of quantitative methods in economic analysis several centuries later.

SEE ALSO The Invention of Calculus (c. 1665), The Gold Standard (1717), Smith's *Wealth of Nations* (1776), Index Numbers (1863), The Econometric Society (1930), National Income Accounting (1934), Natural Experiments (1990)

An engraving of William Petty, 1696.

William Petty. Kn.t

Fellow of the Royall Society

Obijt 16. Dec.r 1687. Anno Ætat: 63.

J. Closterman pinx.

I. Smith fec: et ex:

The Balance-of-Trade Controversy

Thomas Mun (1571–1641), Gerard de Malynes (*fl.* 1586–1641), Edward
Misselden (1608–1654)

1621

In the early 1620s, England's cloth exports fell significantly, causing widespread
unemployment. The most common explanation for this at the time pointed to a shortage
of money resulting from imbalanced exchange rates. Gerard de Malynes, a merchant
and government official, argued that the Mint had undervalued English currency relative
to its precious-metals content, resulting in coins worth more than their face value. This
imbalance meant that England received less money for its exports and paid more for
its imports, resulting in a net outflow of gold and silver. To resolve the crisis, Malynes
championed using exchange-rate controls to increase the currency's value.

Thomas Mun and Edward Misselden, both employed by major trade merchants,
argued against this strategy and instead advocated the "balance-of-trade doctrine."
Malynes and others, they contended, had it backward: the relationship between the value
of exports and the value of imports determined currency values and bullion flows—not
the other way around. To slow the outflow of gold and silver, England needed to reduce
imports of unnecessary goods, whether luxuries from the Orient or manufactured goods
that could be produced domestically, and increase its exports by ensuring that its goods
competed more effectively on world markets. This required both increased government
support, such as subsidies, for exporting industries and a *lower* exchange rate.

Misselden and Mun didn't dispute that England's currency shortage posed a
problem, but for them the issue wasn't a decline in "wealth," as represented by gold and
silver currency, but the lack of financial resources to facilitate production and exchange.
If English companies were sufficiently competitive, the resulting exports would generate
the needed gold and silver bullion.

This debate made clear the tight relationship between money and economic
activity, showing how the value of money turned on the basic forces of demand and
supply. The view of money as financial capital rather than something to be accumulated
also revealed how money facilitates production and trade. Modern debates on trade
echo similar themes, with economists arguing for free trade to a public often inclined to
favor export promotion and import restriction.

SEE ALSO Mercantile Policies (1539), Gresham's Law (1558), Supply and Demand (1767), The Theory
of Comparative Advantage (1817), The Heckscher–Ohlin Model (1933), The Stolper–Samuelson Theorem
(1941), The Factor-Price Equalization Theorem (1948)

*Two men weave cloth on a loom in this sixteenth-century woodcut illustration. Cloth was one of Britain's most
important exports during this period.*

Tulipmania

In the seventeenth century, Holland was an economic powerhouse. The Dutch East India Company, founded in 1602, was the world's first publicly traded company and a major player in foreign trade. Amsterdam was home to the world's first stock exchange, also established in 1602, and, along with the Bank of Amsterdam, it facilitated economic growth. Tulipmania, the Dutch tulip bubble that began in 1636 and lasted until February 5, 1637, developed soon after Dutch ambassador Ogier de Busbecq introduced the exotic flower from the Ottoman Empire to Western Europe. A financial bubble occurs when speculative demand drives the price of a product well above its typical value. When the bubble bursts, prices fall markedly and those who purchased the good at much higher prices sustain significant losses.

By virtue of their scarcity, tulips instantly became a luxury good, and the rarest varieties, with white or yellow streaks running through their petals, commanded astronomical prices. Each bulb, however, took many years to cultivate. Their limited availability, delayed maturation, and skyrocketing prices drew speculators. These speculators helped create a futures market, allowing people to buy and sell contracts for bulbs available at the end of the growing season and furthering the frenzy. One particular bulb, the Viceroy, sold for several times the value of a house. The bubble finally burst when speculators, who had purchased bulb contracts hoping to sell them at a profit when prices rose, found that they couldn't attract buyers at the higher prices they wanted. When buyers realized that the prices far exceeded the real value of these bulbs, demand and prices collapsed. Those who had purchased contracts at high prices could sell them only at a substantial loss—if at all—leaving many investors penniless.

Recent economic research has questioned certain aspects of the "bubble" story. Those who subscribe to the efficient markets hypothesis— that asset prices always accurately reflect all available information—argue that dramatic price swings associated with tulipmania and other bubbles, such as the South Sea Bubble of the early 1700s and the Dot-Com and housing bubbles in the early 2000s, have a rational basis in factors such as production costs and the desirability of the goods.

SEE ALSO John Law and Paper Money (1705), The Efficient Markets Hypothesis (1965), The Great Recession (2007), Cryptocurrency (2009)

Above: *A drawing of a tulip with striped petals, 1677. These cultivars commanded the highest prices during the height of Tulipmania.* **Main image:** *This seventeenth-century Flemish painting shows a man selling tulip bulbs.*

1651

Hobbes's *Leviathan*

Thomas Hobbes (1588–1679)

In seventeenth-century England, social and religious customs failed to hold envy, greed, and malice in check. Seeking to redress the abuses of power committed by King Charles I (1600–1649), Parliament declared war on the crown, and the English Civil War raged for nine bloodstained years. Philosophers and theorists began calling into question the basic principles that organized civil society. In the final year of the struggle for dominance between crown and Parliament, Thomas Hobbes offered the most influential and controversial response to these conditions.

In *Leviathan*, his magnum opus on statecraft and political science, Hobbes argues that civil society is possible only if a strong government enacts and enforces laws that secure social order. Negative passions of human nature, such as vanity and greed, too often rule people's thoughts and actions, causing various kinds of destruction when left unchecked. The absence of government leaves humanity in the "state of nature," as Hobbes called it, where the primary right is self-preservation—a right that can justify virtually any act, including preemptive violence against others. A scarcity of resources makes conflict inherent in this state of nature, to the point where society will descend into a "war of all against all" and human life famously becomes "solitary, poor, nasty, brutish, and short." The implications for the economy are straightforward: because people cannot enforce their property or contract rights, they have no motive to work or produce goods and there is little prospect for economic growth.

Hobbes proposed a solution, however. A social contract would establish a sovereign—an individual or an assembly of individuals—given absolute authority to make and enforce laws. According to Hobbes, the optimal form of this government is monarchy. This absolute authority, which Hobbes portrayed as the biblical beast Leviathan, would allow the government, through fear and force where necessary, to curb the human passions that wreak such havoc in the state of nature. Hobbes's analysis proved highly controversial, particularly in advocating the restoration of a strong monarchy, but it clearly established the necessity of a strong central government of some variety for economic order, particularly through its role in securing property and contracts.

SEE ALSO Locke's Theory of Property (1690), Mandeville's *Fable of the Bees* (1705), Smith's *Wealth of Nations* (1776), *Homo Economicus* (1836)

The frontispiece of the first edition of Leviathan *featured this illustration by French artist Abraham Bosse, who offers a detailed rendition of Hobbes's absolute monarch.*

Rent and the Theory of Surplus

William Petty (1623–1687)

Before the nineteenth century, officials struggled to establish stable methods for taxing income. Roaming tax collectors more closely resembled corrupt shakedown artists, and taxes on features such as windows and chimneys did little more than change construction habits. In the mid-1600s, Sir William Petty, working on behalf of the English crown, found a more dependable tax base: rent, or the income that landowners received from leasing their lands. Food is always in demand, and this demand increases with the population. Because more land is brought into cultivation as the demand for food increases, landowners thus can expect their rents to grow over time, making them a steady ongoing source of tax revenue.

Writing in his *Treatise of Taxes and Contributions* (1662), Petty defined rent as the income that remained after a tenant farmer deducted the costs of production, such as workers' wages and replacement of tools and materials. He attributed this income to the productivity of the land and considered it a pure surplus because, unlike with labor, machinery, and materials, the production process didn't consume the land. In fact, land could generate a steady amount of rent year after year without requiring the landlord to do much of anything to sustain it.

Petty's theory, however, didn't explain adequately why this surplus should accrue to the landlord rather than the tenant. After all, the surplus wouldn't exist without tenant farmers applying or paying labor to work the land. David Ricardo, Thomas Robert Malthus, and others later answered this question by drawing on the Malthusian theory of population: as the population expands, the demand for food rises and with it food prices. Competition among tenant farmers for the right to cultivate the best lands and produce food to meet this demand allowed landlords to extract more surplus and thus accrue more rent. This theory of rent explained the origins of the landlords' share of the national income and justified its taxation—something that rulers were often loath to do because they relied on the political support of these powerful landowners. But it also provided the framework through which economists for two centuries viewed the contribution of land itself to the value of the products that it generated.

SEE ALSO The Physiocrats (1756), The *Tableau Économique* (1758), The Malthusian Population Theory (1798), Diminishing Returns (1815), The Labor Theory of Value and the Theory of Exploitation (1867), The Single Tax (1879)

A farmer meets his patron in this woodcut, 1517.

The Equalization of Returns

William Petty (1623–1687)

Sir William Petty's belief that rent, the income that landowners received from their lands, represented a pure surplus of output, provided a useful starting point for establishing a tax system. The question then became how to value land income for tax purposes, especially if tenants used the land to create different products. To answer this question, Petty formulated the notion of the equalization of returns—that the financial returns to production inputs such as land, labor, and machinery will tend to be equal across their various employments.

Petty suggested in his *Treatise of Taxes and Contributions* (1662) that, if 100 men worked for ten years growing grain and another 100 men worked for ten years mining silver, the resulting surpluses likely will be identical. This comparison offers a nice illustration of Petty's scientific and statistical turn of mind, both because a group of 100 men will account for variations in productivity across miners and because the ten-year time period allows for yearly variations in harvests due to, say, changing weather conditions. So how, then, do these returns tend to even out? The answer is that if the surplus gained from farming falls below the surplus gained from mining, production will shift from farming to mining. This adjustment will decrease relative returns in the mining sector and raise those in agriculture until the surpluses once again come into balance. Given this equalization, Petty concluded that the rent accruing to the owners of an acre of land should be identical, regardless of what that land's tenants are producing. The value of the silver could then determine the value of any other output.

Petty fully understood that the equalization of returns represented only a tendency and that the vagaries of life could change the rates of return at any point in time. In the late nineteenth century, British economist Alfred Marshall would distinguish between short-run and long-run values, which provided an explanation for how the tendency toward equalization of returns works itself out over time.

SEE ALSO Rent and the Theory of Surplus (1662), Turgot's *Reflections* (1766), Smith's *Wealth of Nations* (1776), The Competitive Process (1776), Diminishing Returns (1815), The Time Horizon (1890), The Stolper–Samuelson Theorem (1941), The Factor-Price Equalization Theorem (1948)

A man carries a sack of grain in this engraving (1698) by Dutch artist Jan Luyken (1649–1712). Petty observed that the returns from production in different sectors of the economy, such as farming and mining, will tend to be equal.

The Invention of Calculus

Isaac Newton (1642–1727), Gottfried Wilhelm Leibniz (1646–1716)

Economics didn't become a mathematical science until the late nineteenth century, but the seeds of this transformation began growing in the second half of the seventeenth century when Isaac Newton and Gottfried Wilhelm Leibniz independently developed "infinitesimal calculus." This branch of mathematics covers motion and change and, in retrospect, it's easy to see why it became a key tool of economic analysis. After all, economics looks at how changes in prices affect the demand for goods, how changes in the amount of labor employed affect the production of products and services, and how changes in government spending affect national output and income.

Scientists applied the principles of calculus to physics and astronomy almost immediately after its creation. Economics, however, had to wait its turn for more than a century. Some argue that Swiss mathematician Daniel Bernoulli's 1738 use of calculus to compute the expected profit or loss from a game qualifies as an economic application. In 1772, Italian mathematician, astronomer, and physicist Paolo Frisi may have been the first to apply calculus to an overtly economic problem in his discussion of the price-determination process. Far more important and ultimately influential were the calculus-based contributions made in the nineteenth century by Augustin Cournot, Johann von Thünen, and Hermann Gossen, whose work collectively anticipated key pieces of the analysis associated with the marginal revolution that began in the 1870s and its emphasis on individual responses to incremental changes in economic incentives.

The invention of calculus also offers a noteworthy example of an early dispute over the priority of discovery. Newton developed this branch of mathematics first, but he had a habit of not publishing ideas not yet worked out to his satisfaction. Leibniz developed the mathematical system nearly a decade later but published first. The question of whom to credit led to a major breach within the European mathematical community, not healed until the early nineteenth century, and has its parallels in modern economics in the debates over who should be given credit for innovations in theories related to monopolistic competition and general equilibrium analysis.

SEE ALSO Bernoulli on Expected Utility (1738), Thünen's *Isolated State* (1826), Cournot's *Researches* (1838), Gossen's Two Laws (1854), The Marginal Revolution (1871), Linear Programming (1947)

A portrait of Isaac Newton by English painter James Thornhill (1675–1734), completed in the early eighteenth century.

The Velocity of Money

Josiah Child (c. 1630–1699), John Locke (1632–1704)

In 1668, England's Parliament discussed a proposal to lower the maximum legal interest rate from 6 percent to 4 percent. Josiah Child, a merchant and author of *Brief Observations Concerning Trade and Interest of Money*, supported this move, asserting that the trade histories of continental European countries proved that those with lower interest rates, such as Holland, saw greater economic prosperity.

John Locke, then secretary to the chancellor of the exchequer, argued against Child. For him, the determining factor of the interest rate is the amount of money needed to facilitate trade at a point in time, relative to the supply of money. Lowering the maximum interest rate would reduce the supply of funds that people would lend, thereby restricting the amount of money available for business investment and choking off prosperity. A low rate of interest thus *resulted from* prosperity, with people having large amounts of money to lend, rather than *causing* it.

So, just how much money should a nation have in circulation to properly facilitate the exchange process? According to Locke, the answer depends not just on the quantity of money itself but also on "the quickness of its circulation"—that is, how often money changes hands. A given amount of money could support either more or less economic activity, depending on this "velocity," as it later came to be called. Because it would cause lower returns, a government-mandated reduction in the interest rate would reduce the cost of holding on to funds, leading to a decline in velocity and, by extension, in the demand for products. The result? Economic contraction and increased unemployment.

This concept of velocity also provided an important addition to the quantity theory of money—the relationship between money and prices. The greater the velocity with which money circulates, the greater will be the pressure that a change in the supply of money exerts on prices. It is not changes in the money supply alone that lead to inflation or deflation, but rather the interaction of those changes with the circulation's velocity.

SEE ALSO Debasement and Oresme's *De Moneta* (c. 1360), The School of Salamanca (1544), The Quantity Theory of Money (1568), The Balance-of-Trade Controversy (1621), The Price–Specie Flow Mechanism (1752), Thornton's *Paper Credit* (1802), Wicksell's Cumulative Process (1898), The Phillips Curve (1958), *A Monetary History of the United States* (1963), Cryptocurrency (2009)

This illustration shows the English philosopher John Locke, who developed the concept of velocity to describe the rate at which money changes hands in an economy.

Locke's Theory of Property

John Locke (1632–1704)

In *Leviathan*, Thomas Hobbes described the state of nature as a "war of all against all." But English philosopher John Locke, writing in the second of his *Two Treatises of Government* (1690), saw nature as somewhat more harmonious because "The state of Nature has a law of Nature to govern it." One of these laws, reason tells us, is that a person shouldn't harm others or their property. This raises the question of what legitimately constitutes a person's property. If the law of nature ordains that the Earth's resources belong to *all*, Locke said, what allows any individual to claim any of those resources as private property? His answer: the application of labor. The act of employing labor on something unowned—say, by cultivating an unowned parcel of land—provides ownership rights to that thing. These property rights, he said, exist in nature in and of themselves, but people come together through a social contract to form a government to enforce them. Civil society exists, then, to protect property.

Locke didn't consider these property rights unlimited. People shouldn't claim more than they can consume or put to productive use. Doing so results in spoilage or waste, which runs contrary to the laws of nature. However, the existence of money allows one to accumulate unlimited amounts of property without spoilage. One person justly can acquire massive amounts of land and grow food far beyond what he or she ever could hope to consume, by exchanging that food for money, which doesn't spoil, and putting the food into the hands of others who can eat it. For Locke, the introduction of money justifies both unlimited accumulation and inequality. Ironically, his theory found favor both with the emerging capitalist class and later with socialists, who viewed his ideas as a foundation for a labor theory of value, the idea that the value of a product is determined by the amount of labor used in its production.

SEE ALSO Hobbes's *Leviathan* (1651), Smith's *Wealth of Nations* (1776), The Labor Theory of Value (1821), The Labor Theory of Value and the Theory of Exploitation (1867)

Peasants toil in this sixteenth-century engraving by Hans Schäufelein. According to Locke, the application of labor to unowned land confers property rights.

Laissez-Faire

Pierre le Pesant, sieur de Boisguilbert (1646–1714), Adam Smith (1723–1790)

The term *laissez-faire* is typically associated with the view that government shouldn't interfere with private behavior, particularly in the marketplace. The laissez-faire maxim dates to seventeenth-century France and was popularized by Pierre de Boisguilbert, a regional government administrator. His *Le Detail de la France* (1695) repeatedly invoked the phrase "laisse faire la nature" (let nature run its course) in its passionate critique of French finance minister Jean-Baptiste Colbert's mercantilist policies, which ranged from trade restrictions to an edict requiring that all craftsmen be members of guilds. Boisguilbert believed that government interference in business, even if well intentioned, would always make matters worse, as evidenced by the poor living conditions that resulted under Colbert's policies.

Adam Smith's name would later be most closely associated with the idea of laissez-faire, even though he didn't use the term in print. Smith provided strong statements in *Wealth of Nations* about the benefits of individual liberty, arguing that if people are allowed to apply their capital and labor where they see fit, economic growth will naturally follow. He acknowledged that individual liberty would only work to the best interests of society if framed in an appropriate structure of laws, customs, and morals, but he ultimately believed that individual liberty would produce better outcomes than any ruling body. This belief was further reinforced in his invocation of the "invisible hand," a force that channeled the individual pursuit of self-interest to the best interests of society.

While Smith was well aware of the ways that individual liberty could benefit economic growth, it was not until the nineteenth century that these ideas became tightly linked. Even here, laissez-faire was not seen as an entirely beneficial approach. The English classical economists who built on Smith's work identified significant problems with laissez-faire policies, ranging from low wages to under-investment in scientific research. Since that time, many significant battles within economics, and within the realm of economic policy, have been waged over the possibilities and limitations of laissez-faire and the appropriate role for government within the economic system.

SEE ALSO Mandeville's *Fable of the Bees* (1705), The Physiocrats (1756), Smith's *Wealth of Nations* (1776), The Invisible Hand (1776), Classical Political Economy (c. 1790), Pigou's *Wealth and Welfare* (1912), Externalities and Market Failure (1958)

In the late seventeenth century, the French government banned the import of foreign lace to protect the skilled craftsmen who created this luxury product, an example of which is shown here. Pierre de Boisguilbert used the phrase "laisse faire la nature" to condemn such protectionist policies.

John Law and Paper Money

John Law (1671–1729)

John Law, a Scot who spent much of his adult life in France to avoid a murder charge back home, was a man of banking and finance. Law rejected the quantity theory of money, which linked the supply of money to inflation, believing that an increase in the quantity of money would stimulate the demand for goods and increase employment and output.

For Law, money's specific form didn't matter. As paper was far cheaper than gold and its quantity easier to regulate, Law described it as the ideal monetary medium in his book *Money and Trade Considered* (1705). Unlike coins, however, paper money had no independent value and so was viewed with great suspicion. It had long been used in China beginning with the Tang Dynasty (618–907), but over-production caused severe inflation and led to its elimination in the fifteenth century.

Nonetheless, Law persuaded France to adopt his ideas. He established, in 1716, the *Banque Générale*, which issued notes that could be converted to gold, pay taxes, and finance the national debt. Two years later, Law's bank was nationalized as the *Banque Royale*, and the link between the notes and gold was removed as precious metals lost their status as legal tender. Meanwhile, Law formed the Compagnie des Indes (also known as the Mississippi Company), which acquired exclusive rights over much of France's international trade and its tax collection, in exchange for refinancing the government's debt. The Company issued new shares of stock to fund these debt obligations. Law's marketing skills led the price of these shares to climb rapidly—from 500 francs to 10,000 francs during 1719 alone. The French government printed a massive amount of notes to support this bubble. Attempts to control the resulting inflation led to a selloff of the stocks and banknotes. Law's paper-money system collapsed, resulting in widespread financial ruin and hostility toward paper money. Though paper money gained more acceptance in the nineteenth century, it wasn't until the twentieth that economists such as Irving Fisher and John Maynard Keynes convinced others that paper currency not backed by gold could effectively manage payments and promote economic stability.

SEE ALSO The Quantity Theory of Money (1568), Tulipmania (1636), Thornton's *Paper Credit* (1802), The Bullionist Controversy (1810), The Efficient Markets Hypothesis (1965), The Great Recession (2007)

Alarmed speculators, discovering that they could not convert their paper banknotes into gold and silver, gathered in the streets when the Mississippi bubble burst in 1720.

Mandeville's *Fable of the Bees*

Bernard Mandeville (1670–1733)

Over the centuries, economists have wrestled mightily with a very basic question: Does the behavior of a self-interested individual promote, or hinder, the interests of society at large? The Ancient Greeks, the Scholastics, and the mercantilists were convinced that self-interest had significant negative ramifications for economic activity and required government restraints, but the tide began to turn when Bernard Mandeville outlined the benefits of self-interested behavior in *The Grumbling Hive: or, Knaves Turn'd Honest*, published in 1705.

In this 433-line poem, Mandeville explained why private vices were necessary for a society to flourish economically, using a tale of a thriving beehive. The hive's success came despite the fact that vices such as cheating, greed, and vanity seemed to characterize economic and social life. This gave rise to great complaint among some within the hive; but when the gods eliminated vice, competitive behavior among the bees weakened to such an extent that industry eventually collapsed. The thriving hive became a shadow of its former self. The lesson drawn from this tale was that self-interest provides the basis for robust economic activity, and that attempts to weed it out of society will be harmful. Over the next twenty-four years, Mandeville expanded his analysis with commentaries explaining the lessons of the poem, under the title *The Fable of the Bees*, which ultimately reached its final form in 1729.

The Fable of the Bees generated a good deal of controversy, due largely to its perceived implications for morality—that behavior widely regarded as vice could, in fact, be virtuous and should be encouraged. Yet Mandeville had identified an important paradox. Take, for example, the vice of pride—one of several noted in *The Fable*. Though typically frowned upon in discussions of ethical behavior, Mandeville tells us that absent vanity, there would be no motivation to impress the people around us, which would have severe implications for industries ranging from fashion to housing and for the employment that these motivations support.

SEE ALSO Plato, Aristotle, and the Golden Mean (c. 380 BCE), Scholasticism (c. 1100), Mercantile Policies (1539), Laissez-Faire (1695), Pigou's *Wealth and Welfare* (1912), Public Goods (1954), Externalities and Market Failure (1958), The Free-Rider Problem (1965)

An ink-and-wash drawing of a bustling beehive from the early seventeenth century. Bernard Mandeville composed a poem about a beehive to depict how vices, such as greed, can bring economic success.

The Gold Standard

Isaac Newton (1642–1727)

Though best known for his pioneering work in physics, Sir Isaac Newton served as Warden of the Royal Mint in England from 1696 until 1699, and then as Master of the Mint from 1699 until his death in 1727. Appointed by King William III (1650–1702) through the influence of his friend John Locke, Newton dove into his work at the Mint. He used his scientific expertise to establish far more precise systems of weights and measures, soon replicated around the world, to increase the quality of England's coinage. Just as important were the steps he took to stabilize the English currency, which unintentionally put England on the gold standard.

A gold standard links the value of a country's currency to gold, setting a fixed rate at which the currency can be converted into gold bullion, typically measured in ounces. Known today as a system for valuing paper currency and fixing the value of one nation's currency in terms of another's, it was originally used to establish the relative values of gold and silver coins in the bimetallic currency systems that dominated Europe prior to the widespread use of paper money. It also fixed exchange rates and seemed to provide a safeguard against extreme inflation, since the money supply could only expand at the rate of gold supplies.

Silver coins had long been the dominant form of currency in England—hence the name "pound sterling" as the basic unit of British currency—while gold coins were more prevalent on the continent. Oscillations in currency markets led Newton to revalue the gold guinea in terms of silver, but he considerably undervalued the silver coins. This resulted in a substantial outflow of silver from England, as an ounce of silver could purchase more gold on the continent than it could in England. Silver coins thus effectively disappeared from circulation—Gresham's Law in action—putting England on a de facto gold standard in 1717 that was legally formalized a century later. Other countries followed suit throughout the nineteenth century, and the gold standard remained the basis for national and international monetary systems until the early 1970s.

SEE ALSO Debasement and Oresme's *De Moneta* (c. 1360), Gresham's Law (1558), John Law and Paper Money (1705), Galiani's *Della Moneta* (1751), Thornton's *Paper Credit* (1802), The Bullionist Controversy (1810), The Bretton Woods Agreement (1944), Flexible Exchange Rates: The End of Bretton Woods (1971), Cryptocurrency (2009)

A diagram of a coining press and dies found in the Tower of London, 1800. Until 1812, the Tower of London was the site of the Royal Mint, where most British coins were made.

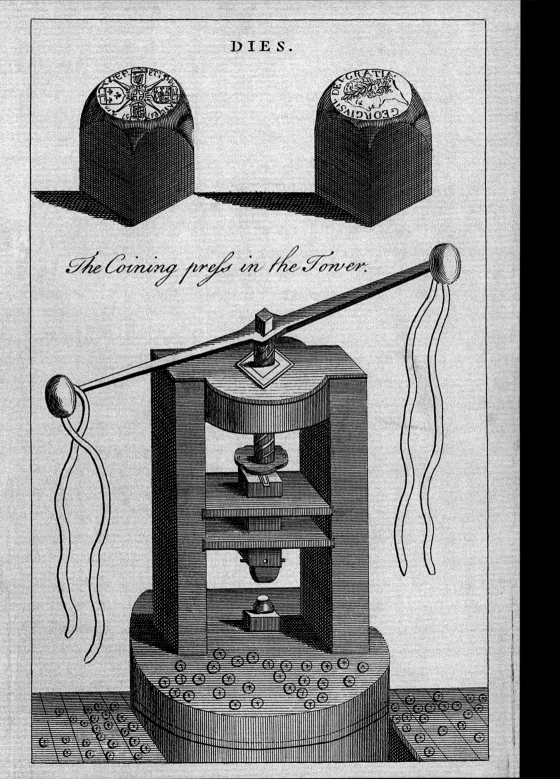

DIES.

The Coining press in the Tower.

The Scottish Enlightenment

David Hume (1711–1776), Adam Smith (1723–1790)

The Scottish Enlightenment, typically dated to 1718 with the publication of Gershom Carmichael's *Supplements and Observations* on the writings of German philosopher Samuel Pufendorf, provides the context for the two most influential pieces of eighteenth-century economic thinking: David Hume's analysis of money, including the price–specie flow mechanism, and Adam Smith's magisterial treatise *Wealth of Nations*. Emerging several decades after Enlightenment ideas had influenced English and Continental thinking through the work of Isaac Newton, John Locke, René Descartes, Galileo Galilei, and Gottfried Leibniz, the Scottish variant had its own distinct features. Scottish Enlightenment thinkers were suspicious of the rationalism advocated by Descartes and others; instead, they saw empirical methods and historical analysis as surer ways of discovering the laws and essential truths that governed natural and social orders and how people could manipulate these orders to promote progress.

This social and historical approach led these Enlightenment thinkers to formulate the "four stages theory," which described how society had progressed through several stages. Each stage was an improvement on the one before it, especially in terms of social organization and economic productivity. Because people could learn to use natural resources and adapt to changing circumstances, economic organization moved from hunter-gatherer systems (the first stage) to pastoral farming, agrarian life, and finally an exchange economy, with the legal system evolving along the way to facilitate these changes. Political organization and legal structures—the analyse of which were still very much tied to philosophy—were seen as inseparable from economic concerns. In fact, Adam Smith's *Wealth of Nations* evolved out of lectures on jurisprudence that he gave at the University of Glasgow.

Though philosophy was at the heart of the Scottish Enlightenment, it impacted the arts, architecture, the natural sciences, rhetoric, and poet. Its influence crossed over to the European continent and the American colonies, with both Voltaire and Benjamin Franklin praising the gifts Scottish Enlightenment thinking had offered to life and thought.

SEE ALSO The Invention of Calculus (c. 1665), The Velocity of Money (1668), Locke's Theory of Property (1690), The Gold Standard (1717), The Price–Specie Flow Mechanism (1752), Smith's *Wealth of Nations* (1776)

A contemporary photo showing a nighttime view of the University of Glasgow, a major intellectual hub during the Scottish Enlightenment.

Bernoulli on Expected Utility

Daniel Bernoulli (1700–1782)

During the eighteenth and nineteenth centuries, many economic writers believed that the price of a good was largely determined by production costs. But some contended instead that the perspective of the buyer, or of a community of buyers, was the fundamental factor. Swiss mathematician Daniel Bernoulli, the son and nephew of famous mathematicians Johann and Jacob Bernoulli, offered the most compelling explanation for this stance.

Bernoulli resolved the St. Petersburg Paradox, named after the *Commentaries of the Imperial Academy of Science of St. Petersburg*, the journal in which it first appeared in 1738. Suppose that an individual can play a coin-flip game for a fixed fee. The player receives a payoff of $2 if heads appears on the first coin flip; the payoff doubles for each successive appearance of heads, and the game ends when tails appears. The probability of winning $2 is ½, the probability of winning $4 is ¼, and so on. The expected value (EV) of the game—the probability-weighted average of all possible outcomes—then, is $EV = \frac{1}{2}(2) + \frac{1}{4}(4) + \frac{1}{8}(8) + \frac{1}{16}(16) + \ldots = \infty$. Though the expected value of this game is infinity, most people wouldn't want to pay more than $20 to play. Why?

Bernoulli's answer was that the value that people place on a good is not determined by its price, but by the "utility," or happiness, that it provides. This utility depends on individual circumstances—the greater a person's income, the lower the utility received from additional income. A poor person, then, is more likely than a millionaire to make the effort to clip coupons or to pick up a dollar bill from the sidewalk. Similarly, the amount that a poor individual would risk on this game will be lower than the amount offered by a rich individual, and even the rich man is unwilling to pay anything close to the game's expected value. Bernoulli thus anticipated some key insights of the marginal revolution, which developed a utility-based approach to individual economic behavior. He also provided the basis for later work by John von Neumann, Oskar Morgenstern, and others on expected utility and the economics of risk.

SEE ALSO Galiani's *Della Moneta* (1751), Diminishing Returns (1815), Gossen's Two Laws (1854), The Marginal Revolution (1871), Jevons's *Theory of Political Economy* (1871), Game Theory Enters Economics (1944)

Daniel Bernoulli's famed St. Petersburg Principle *is named for the Russian city in which the journal that published his findings was based. The Church of the Savior on Spilled Blood, one of the notable landmarks in St. Petersburg, is pictured here.*

Galiani's *Della Moneta*

Ferdinando Galiani (1728–1787)

Ferdinando Galiani was one of the leading minds of the Italian Enlightenment. Though educated with the intention of joining the Catholic Church, Galiani quickly turned his attention to economics. In 1751, in his early twenties, he completed his most important work, *Della Moneta* ("On Money"). His sympathies were with mercantilism; he saw international trade as a zero-sum game with inevitable winners and losers, and he advocated debasing currency to improve the balance of trade. However, the key contribution of *Della Moneta* is the development of a subjective theory of value—the idea that the value of a good is determined by the worth individuals place on it, rather than being inherent in that good.

Galiani lived in an age during which money consisted primarily of gold and silver coins, which were typically valued based on their precious-metal content. Taking a very different line, he argued that the value of money is actually determined by the amount of commodities it can purchase. He rejected the notion that any object had intrinsic value, whether determined by production costs or otherwise. Value, he claimed, is a "ratio" of utility and scarcity. It is utility, the capacity of a good to make one happy, that governs the demand for a good; and its scarcity relative to this demand determines its value.

According to Galiani, the value of gold and silver coins should be determined no differently than that of any other good. Gold and silver have value because they are scarce, and their utility comes from their beauty, as evidenced by their use in jewelry and decoration. Because gold and silver are valuable, the value of coins will reflect the amounts of gold and silver embodied in them. Thus, gold and silver are used as money because they are valuable, and not valuable because they are used as money. Though Galiani's work was influential in Italy during his lifetime and served as a springboard for the Italian utilitarian tradition, it was only with the marginal revolution of the 1870s that his insights about subjective value became a centerpiece of economic thinking.

SEE ALSO Mercantile Policies (1539), The Balance-of-Trade Controversy (1621), Bernoulli on Expected Utility (1738), Supply and Demand (1767), The Law of Demand (1820), The Marginal Revolution (1871), Menger's *Principles of Economics* (1871)

Ferdinando Galiani's subjective theory of value explained that precious metals, such as the gold used to create these earrings (1700–1800s), had value because they were scarce and gave their owners the pleasure of having beautiful objects.

The Price–Specie Flow Mechanism

Richard Cantillon (1680–1734), David Hume (1711–1776)

Mercantilists argued that governments should strive for a positive balance of trade, or an excess of exports over imports. David Hume challenged this view in his essay "Of the Balance of Trade," which appeared in his *Political Discourses* (1752). Hume is best known for his contributions to philosophy, history, and politics; but his writings on money and trade informed the views of Adam Smith and the American Federalists of the eighteenth century and the Keynesians and monetarists of the twentieth. Hume saw labor and commerce as a key source of national strength and opposed the mercantilist view that money is wealth. For Hume, money is merely "the oil which renders the motion of the wheels [of trade] more smooth and easy."

One mercantilist argument in favor of a positive balance of trade was that it would increase the nation's precious-metals stock, since payments received for exports took the form of gold and silver bullion. This additional bullion could be put into circulation as money, or specie, which in turn would stimulate trade. Hume believed that these benefits were temporary. If the inflows of gold and silver from a continuous trade surplus were turned into coins, the supply of money would grow, leading to ever-increasing prices. As the prices of domestic goods rose, the demand for lower-priced imports would increase, thereby harming the balance of trade. Wages, and thus production costs, would also rise and increase the price of goods sold abroad. Exports would then fall, further reducing the trade surplus, perhaps even making it negative. This link between the money supply, the price level, and the trade balance became known as the price–specie flow mechanism.

In short, Hume found the mercantilist position inconsistent. If a country wanted a continuously positive balance of trade, the only way to do so under a gold and silver–based currency system was to prevent bullion from entering into circulation as money. Instead, it should be stored for an emergency, such as war. Hume opposed paper money, the supply of which could easily be increased, leading to more imports and diminished domestic production without the accompanying benefit of increased gold and silver stocks.

SEE ALSO Mercantile Policies (1539), The Quantity Theory of Money (1568), The Balance-of-Trade Controversy (1621), Galiani's *Della Moneta* (1751), Cantillon's *Essay on the Nature of Trade* (1755), The Phillips Curve (1958), The Natural Rate of Unemployment (1967), The New Classical Macroeconomics (1972)

An eighteenth-century engraving of David Hume.

Cantillon's *Essay on the Nature of Trade*

Richard Cantillon (1680–1734)

William Petty wasn't the only person to quantify economic relationships during the seventeenth and eighteenth centuries. In England in 1697, Gregory King (1648–1712) created some of the first richly detailed summaries of international trading activity, while Charles Davenant studied the relationship between corn prices and output levels. However, the most systematic use of quantitative analysis to inform economic thinking during this period came from the Irishman Richard Cantillon. We know little about Cantillon's life, beyond the fact that he made both a fortune as a speculator and many enemies in the process. Legend has it that he was murdered in his bed by his valet, who then burned down his house.

Sometime around 1730, Cantillon penned *An Essay on the Nature of Trade in General*, which is widely regarded as the first comprehensive treatise on economics. Published twenty years after his death, its contents range from price determination and monetary analysis to income distribution. Cantillon also distinguished himself with his "general" or abstract theoretical approach. Unlike other writers at the time, he attempted to describe how the economic system actually works—not how it *should* work—informing his theories with detailed data that he gathered on his many travels. His analysis reflected the same scientific, empirical spirit that informed William Petty's writings; but, unfortunately, Cantillon's extensive collection of data has been lost to history, likely burned along with his house.

Most importantly, Cantillon's *Essay* analyzed how goods and payments flow through the economy. He offered a primitive version of the "circular flow" model to describe these movements, highlighting the interdependence between the various sectors of the economy and also between production and income. By using his model to trace the flow of money through the economy, Cantillon also demonstrated how growth in the money supply, particularly relevant given the large influx of gold and silver from the Americas that had been going on for two centuries by that time, could lead to increases in either output or inflation. Cantillon's analysis of these flows influenced François Quesnay's construction of the *Tableau Economique* in the late 1750s, and today the "circular flow" diagram is a common sight in introductory economics textbooks.

SEE ALSO Empiricism and Science (1620), The Price–Specie Flow Mechanism (1752), The *Tableau Économique* (1758), Tugan-Baranovsky and the Trade Cycle (1894), The Circular Flow Diagram (1933)

The title page of Richard Cantillon's An Essay on the Nature of Trade in General *in French.*

ESSAI
SUR LA NATURE
DU
COMMERCE
EN GÉNÉRAL.

TRADUIT DE L'ANGLOIS.

en réalité composé par de Cantillon

A LONDRES,
Chez FLETCHER GYLES;
dans Holborn

M. DCC. LV.

Rousseau's "Political Economy"

Jean-Jacques Rousseau (1712–1778)

French philosopher Jean-Jacques Rousseau stands with Thomas Hobbes and John Locke as one of the great seventeenth- and eighteenth-century theorists of the social contract. His essay "Political Economy," written in 1755, provided a framework for the subject that pervaded economic thinking for more than a century and remains influential today.

For Rousseau, the essence of political economy was the "wise and legitimate" governing of the state "for the common good." This required three things: First, government authorities should rule according to the "general will" of society, securing life, liberty, and property through an enlightened system of laws that its citizens would willingly follow. Second, the authorities should ensure that each "particular will" is in agreement with the general will; this virtuous governance allows individual members of society to believe that government authorities are acting in the interest of *all* rather than pursuing their own gain or that of a particular social class. Finally, the government should provide for "public needs," protecting property, promoting social order, and ensuring that enough opportunities exist for people to procure subsistence through work. If the authorities govern according to these principles, the law will command voluntary obedience—in contrast to Thomas Hobbes's vision of government, which must forcefully rule with absolute authority to prevent society from falling into chaos and conflict.

Rousseau's definition of "political economy" provided the foundation for discussions of the subject throughout the next century. It is perhaps most prominently reflected in Adam Smith's own description of political economy as "a branch of the science of a statesman or legislator." Rousseau brought the "political" element into "political economy," establishing the subject as a policy science meant to inform the decisions of kings, princes, and legislative bodies. As such, it was overtly prescriptive: it didn't seek merely to uncover the laws underlying economic relationships; it also turned these relationships into lessons about governing wisely.

SEE ALSO Hobbes's *Leviathan* (1651), Locke's Theory of Property (1690), Supply and Demand (1767), Smith's *Wealth of Nations* (1776), Classical Political Economy (c. 1790), The Law of Demand (1820), Scarcity and Choice (1932)

A vintage print of Jean-Jacques Rousseau seated outdoors.

The Physiocrats

François Quesnay (1694–1774), Victor de Riqueti, Marquis de Mirabeau (1715–1789)

The mercantilist policies instituted by Jean-Baptiste Colbert, the French finance minister under Louis XIV, severely hampered the development of agricultural production in France. Restrictions on the export of agricultural goods kept domestic food prices low, allowing manufacturers to pay lower wages. These low wages, combined with a tax system that exempted many wealthy landowners, made life incredibly difficult for much of the citizenry, particularly the working class. Agricultural profits languished due to the backward farming methods used at the time. These low profits prevented farmers from investing in agricultural improvements and implementing the large-scale cultivation methods practiced elsewhere in Europe.

Physiocracy, the first true "school" of economic thought, emerged as a response to these conditions. Though the original spark came from the Marquis de Mirabeau in his book *L'ami des Hommes* (1756), it was François Quesnay, the physician to the royal mistress, Madame de Pompadour, who stood at the head of the physiocrats and built a system of economic analysis around agriculture. At the center of Quesnay's system was the concept of the "net product"—revenue with the costs of production deducted. The physiocrats believed that only agriculture generated a net product, meaning that mercantilist policies, which promoted manufacturing at the expense of agriculture, crippled economic growth and prosperity. They advocated undoing the mercantile system and replacing it with policies that promoted agricultural production and development. The net product generated from increased agricultural output would provide the capital for further agricultural development and a source of tax revenue that would reduce the burden on the lower classes.

Though the physiocrats counted some of the most prominent people in France among their members and influenced Americans including Benjamin Franklin, Thomas Jefferson, and James Madison, their program of economic reform failed to gain significant traction. The twin influences of Adam Smith's *Wealth of Nations* and the Industrial Revolution soon swept these ideas aside, as each demonstrated—one theoretically and the other practically—that both manufacturing and agriculture could contribute mightily to economic growth.

SEE ALSO Rent and the Theory of Surplus (1662), The *Tableau Économique* (1758), The Industrial Revolution (1760), Smith's *Wealth of Nations* (1776)

A portrait of François Quesnay, one of the founders of physiocracy.

The *Tableau Économique*

François Quesnay (1694–1774)

Economics is now—and has been since the 1950s—a science that uses models. At the most basic level, a model is a representation of economic relationships that simplifies many features of reality into a set of variables that you can manipulate. Economic models offer a way to analyze how changes in key variables affect economic relationships or outcomes.

French physician François Quesnay developed the first economic model, the *Tableau Économique*, or economic table, in 1758 to depict the flow of resources through the French economy. Using graphing techniques and numbers, the *Tableau* expressed a physiocratic view of the economy, assuming that it consisted of two sectors, agriculture and manufacturing, and three classes of individuals: landlords, farmers, and manufacturers and artisans. Reflecting the basic premise of physiocracy, agriculture was the only sector that generated a net product. According to Quesnay, it was possible to receive a 100 percent return on all money flowing into agriculture if farmers adopted modern cultivation techniques, such as plows pulled by horses rather than cattle. On the other hand, manufacturing was assumed to be "sterile"—the value of its output equaled the value of the inputs that went into production—and thus didn't produce net product.

With its wonderful system of zig-zags, the *Tableau* demonstrated how investment in agriculture, spending on agricultural products, and adopting policies designed to promote agriculture would increase net product. Reinvestment of this surplus in agriculture would continue to push the system upward. In contrast, corresponding investment, spending, and promotion of manufacturing would cause net product to drop and thus lead to economic decline.

The *Tableau* produced these results only because the model assumed the very thing it was meant to prove—that only agriculture generates a net product. But its message against mercantilism—that growth could come via investment and export trade in agriculture—had a significant influence on Adam Smith. Its visual representation of economic growth also foreshadowed modern input–output analysis by illuminating how the flows of resources into different sectors of the economy contribute to national output.

SEE ALSO Rent and the Theory of Surplus (1662), Cantillon's *Essay on the Nature of Trade* (1755), The Physiocrats (1756), Smith's *Wealth of Nations* (1776), Input–Output Analysis (1941)

The table from François Quesnay's Tableau Économique *offers a visual representation of how resources were thought to flow through the French economy and of the net product (seen in the middle column) generated by agriculture.*

TABLEAU ÉCONOMIQUE.

Objets à considérer, 1º trois sortes de dépenses; 2º leur source; 3º leurs avances;
4º leur distribution; 5º lurs effets; 6º leur reproduction; 7º leurs rapports
entr'elles; 8º leurs rapports avec la population; 9º avec l'Agriculture; 10º avec
l'industrie, 11º avec le commerce; 12º avec la masse des richesses d'une Nation.

DÉPENSES. PRODUCTIVES *Relatives à l'Agriculture, &c.*	DÉPENSES DU REVENU, *l'Impôt compris, se partagent a la Classe productive et a la Classe Stérile.*	DÉPENSES. STÉRILES *Relatives à l'Industrie, &c.*
Avances annuelles *pour produire un revenu de 2000.tt sont 2000.tt*	**Revenu** *Annuel de*	**Avances annuelles** *pour les Ouvrages des Dépenses Stériles sont*
2000.tt produisent net	2000.tt	1000.tt

Productions   *moitié passe icy*   **Ouvrages, &c.**

1000.tt	s.	d.	reproduisent net	1000.tt	s.	d.	1000	tt s. d.
500	"	"	reproduisent net	500			500	
250	"	"	reproduisent net	250		"	250	"
125		"	reproduisent net	125		"	125	"
62	10	"	reproduisent net	62	10	"	62	10 "
31	5	"	reproduisent net	31	5	"	31	5 "
15	12	6	reproduisent net	15	12	6	15	12 6
7	16	3	reproduisent net	7	16	3	7	16 3
3	18	2	reproduisent net	3	18	2	3	18 2
1	19	1	reproduisent net	1	19	1	1	19 1
0	19	6	reproduisent net	0	19	6	0	19 6
0	9	9	reproduisent net	0	9		0	9
0		6	reproduisent net	0	5			
0	2	6	reproduisent net	0	2	6	0	2 6
0	1	3	reproduisent net	0	1	3	0	1 3
0	0	8	reproduisent net	0	0	8	0	0 8

Total 2000.tt s. d.　　　　Total 2000.tt s. d.　　　　Total 2000.tt s. d.

Il n'est pas nécessaire de s'attacher à l'intelligence de ce Tableau avant la lecture des 7. pre-
miers chapitres, il suffit à chaque chapitre de faire attention à la partie du Tableau qui y a rapo.

The Industrial Revolution

Economic thinking has always been a reflection of economic life. Given that the economy had been wrapped up in agriculture, small-scale manufacturing, and regional trading for thousands of years, it is no surprise that economic thinking revolved around these aspects of economic activity. But beginning in 1760, a series of inventions in Britain transformed economic life. The creation of the spinning jenny by James Hargreaves in 1764 and the power loom by Edmund Cartwright in 1785 kick-started a boom in textile production. James Watt's development of the steam engine in 1769 transformed manufacturing and paved the way for large-scale railway transport in the early 1800s. The advent of electronic telegraphy in the 1830s made communication instantaneous rather than a days- or weeks-long process.

Though the Industrial Revolution played out over eighty years, the changes that it sparked happened at a breakneck pace. The move from hand tools to mechanized mass production brought tremendous economic growth. New machinery generated mind-boggling increases in output capacity and lowered production costs dramatically. Items ranging from clothing to household goods became much more affordable for the common man, and even Karl Marx acknowledged the benefits of these developments. However, these benefits didn't come without costs. While the middle and upper classes expanded, conditions for the working class deteriorated. Low wages, poor working conditions, child labor in factories, and the displacement of labor by machinery made life challenging for the average worker. Overcrowded and often unsanitary living conditions in urban industrial areas made day-to-day living even more difficult.

Though the effects of the Industrial Revolution on economic thinking arrived slowly, it ultimately led to two major changes: First, it called into question the agricultural basis that grounded so much of economic thinking, though the importance of agriculture continued to dominate economic analysis well into the nineteenth century. Second, its effects on the working class led economists to become much more actively involved in questions of social-economic policy.

SEE ALSO The Physiocrats (1756), Classical Political Economy (c. 1790), The Malthusian Population Theory (1798), Diminishing Returns (1815), The Machinery Question (1817), Marx's *Das Kapital* (1867), *Lectures on the Industrial Revolution* (1884)

James Hargreaves's spinning jenny, shown in this illustration from 1811, allowed textile workers to spin eight spindles of thread at a time.

WOOLLEN MANUFACTURE.

SPINNING JENNY.

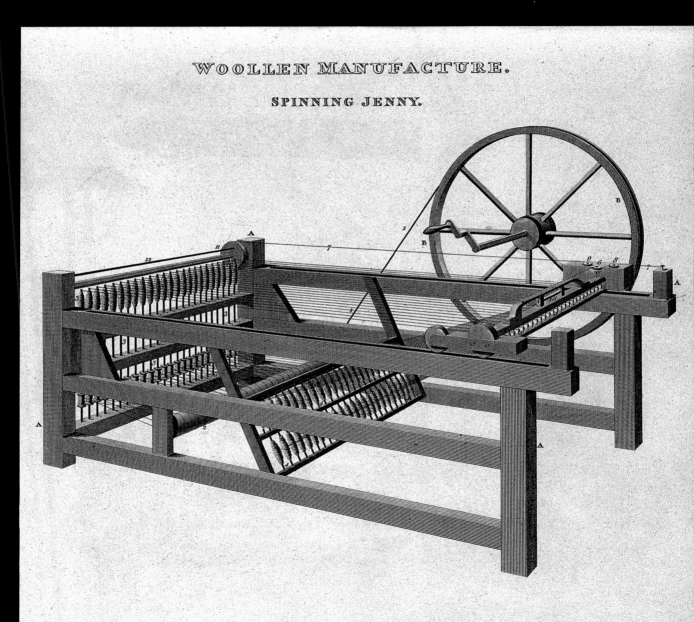

Published as the Act directs, 1811, by Longman, Hurst, Rees, Orme and Brown, Paternoster Row, London.

Turgot's *Reflections*

Anne Robert Jacques Turgot (1727–1781)

Jacques Turgot was a government official who eventually became the controller-general of finances for France. In this position, he liberalized trade and attempted to bring fiscal order to the government's messy affairs, particularly by reforming the tax system to make it more efficient and lessen its burden on the lower classes. Though strongly influenced by the physiocrats, particularly with respect to the economic importance of agriculture, Turgot was very much his own man and considered manufacturing a key to growing national wealth.

In his *Reflections on the Formation and Distribution of Wealth*, Turgot developed a theory of capital that offered a great leap forward from William Petty's insight. Petty observed that the returns on investments in different production inputs will tend toward equality, but Turgot argued that returns on investments of capital will ultimately vary rather than equalizing. He pointed out that a person can use accumulated capital in several ways. She can purchase land to earn rent, invest in a business to earn profit, or lend her funds to earn interest. Though capital flows from areas of lower to higher return, the rates of return on these investments differ thanks to factors such as relative risk. For example, investment in agriculture in a place where harvests are steady will generate a lower return than investment in a business because its failure could destroy one's entire investment. The overall level of returns in the economy as a whole will also rise and fall in response to attitudes toward saving money. When more people are saving instead of spending, capital will be plentiful and returns on it will be lower.

With these insights, Turgot offered a comprehensive explanation for how the forces of supply and demand affect the returns on money or financial capital—interest, profits, and rent. When supply is plentiful relative to demand, the price or return will tend to be lower; when the demand is high relative to supply, the price or return will tend to be higher. The factors that affect the prices of goods and services influence money and capital in similar ways.

SEE ALSO Rent and the Theory of Surplus (1662), The Equalization of Returns (1662), Bernoulli on Expected Utility (1738), Galiani's *Della Moneta* (1751), The Physiocrats (1756), Supply and Demand (1767), Böhm-Bawerk's *Capital and Interest* (1884)

Anne Robert Jacques Turgot is depicted seated at his desk in a drawing from 1840.

Supply and Demand

James Steuart (1707–1780)

In 1767, Sir James Steuart's *Inquiry into the Principles of Political Economy* introduced the term *political economy* into the English lexicon and offered the first systematic treatise on the subject. A Scot who supported the Jacobite rebellion against the English crown, Steuart's views were shaped both by the Scottish Enlightenment and by the Continental influences that he encountered during his exile after the Scottish defeat in the Battle of Culloden.

Steuart's *Principles* is best known for explaining how the relationship between demand and supply determines prices at any given point in time. Steuart described demand as an inverse relationship between the price of the good and the quantity that people wish to purchase. The demand for a good stimulates production and thus increases the supply of the good. The price that results will depend on the degree of competition on both the demand and supply sides of the market. Extensive competition among buyers on the demand side will cause the price to increase, while greater competition among sellers will result in a lower price. This "double competition," as Steuart called it, sets upper and lower bounds on the price of a good, with "vibrations" of competition on the demand side driving up price for a time and subsequent "vibrations" of competition between sellers pushing it down again in response. In this sense, the movement of prices over time is a function of the forces of supply and demand—forces that are much greater than those of any individual.

Though Steuart's analysis took economic thinking to new heights by explaining price determination in this way, it was eclipsed by Adam Smith's *Wealth of Nations*, which was published only nine years after Steuart's treatise. Smith's work targeted what he considered the mercantilist errors found in Steuart's analysis, such as the view of international trade as a zero-sum game and a preference for state-controlled monopolies. Ironically, Smith accomplished this in part by utilizing the very demand-and-supply framework that Steuart had pioneered.

SEE ALSO Mercantile Policies (1539), The Scottish Enlightenment (1718), Galiani's *Della Moneta* (1751), Smith's *Wealth of Nations* (1776), The Competitive Process (1776), The Law of Demand (1820), The Demand–Supply Model (1890)

The title page of Sir James Steuart's treatise on Inquiry into the Principles of Political Economy, *which explores the relationship between—and first used the term—"supply and demand."*

A N
I N Q U I R Y
INTO THE
PRINCIPLES OF POLITICAL OECONOMY:
BEING AN
ESSAY ON THE SCIENCE
O F
Domestic Policy in Free Nations.

IN WHICH ARE PARTICULARLY CONSIDERED

POPULATION, AGRICULTURE, TRADE, INDUSTRY, MONEY, COIN, INTEREST, CIRCULATION, BANKS, EXCHANGE, PUBLIC CREDIT, AND TAXES.

By Sir JAMES STEUART, Bart.

Ore trahit quodcumque potest atque addit acervo.   HOR. Lib. 1. Sat. 1.

IN TWO VOLUMES.

VOL. I.

LONDON:
Printed for A. MILLAR, and T. CADELL, in the Strand.
MDCCLXVII.

Smith's *Wealth of Nations*

Adam Smith (1723–1790)

Adam Smith's *An Inquiry into the Nature and Causes of the Wealth of Nations* is a cornerstone in the history of economics. It is both a work about economic theory, describing how Smith envisioned the workings of a competitive market process, and a polemic against mercantilism. In many ways, Smith's treatise provided the basic framework for virtually all subsequent thinking about the market system.

Smith was a Scottish moral philosopher who, in his own day, was better known for *The Theory of Moral Sentiments* (1759), a book that examined the motives for human behavior, than for *Wealth of Nations*. Though the former book spoke to the broad range of human motivations, *Wealth of Nations* zeroed in on the effects of self-interested behavior, which Smith believed dominated decision-making in the economic realm. Smith's genius lay not so much in developing specific economic concepts but in knitting together various ideas that were "in the air" into a wide-ranging analysis of economic activity. His building blocks were the division of labor, capital accumulation, and competitive exchange. He wove these concepts together to argue that freedom of trade on the broadest possible scale would best promote the growth of national wealth. Smith used this analysis to attack mercantilist policies that impeded economic growth by elevating manufacturing over other industries, facilitating the creation of monopolies, subsidizing exports, and limiting imports. While this mercantilism enriched the businessmen, the low wages and higher prices that resulted hurt the working class.

In addition to forming the basis for nineteenth-century classical political economy and, indeed, for much of economics as we know it today, *Wealth of Nations* also provided what many consider to be a foundational defense of individual liberty, the market system, and limited government, making Smith one of history's foremost expositors of the competitive market system's virtues. Yet Smith's analysis is not without its critics. He paints a picture of a smoothly operating economy, absent excessive government interference, when in reality the economy's adjustment processes are sometimes anything but smooth and the benefits of economic growth are not always as universal as Smith implied.

SEE ALSO Mercantile Policies (1539), Laissez-Faire (1695), The Division of Labor (1776), The Competitive Process (1776), The Invisible Hand (1776), Productive and Unproductive Labor (1776), Classical Political Economy (c. 1790)

A statue of Adam Smith at the University of Glasgow's Adam Smith Business School, which was named in honor of the famed moral philosopher and political economist.

The Division of Labor

Adam Smith (1723–1790)

Specialization in a particular task makes the worker more proficient at it and increases output. The origins of this idea trace back to Greek philosopher Xenophon (c. 370 BCE), but Adam Smith made this division of labor the linchpin of economic growth. To illustrate its power, he invoked the example of a pin-making factory in *Wealth of Nations* (1776). Left to his own devices, a single worker may not be able to make even a single pin in a day and certainly couldn't produce more than twenty. With the division of labor, workers perform specific tasks and make use of specialized machinery, meaning that a group of ten workers may produce as many as 48,000 pins in a day! According to Smith, the invention of machinery itself is, in fact, the effect of the division of labor, as workers develop ways to work more efficiently and "inventor" becomes a separate occupation.

The specialization associated with the division of labor was the key to enhancing a country's productivity and the accumulation of financial capital needed to encourage economic growth. However, specialization leaves a dairy farmer with an enormous supply of milk and very little of the other products he requires. Given this, Smith explained, the division of labor will only occur where people can exchange the goods that they produce for those produced by others. The larger the market for a product, the greater the incentive to specialize.

For Smith, international trade is simply the division of labor across countries, an insight that he used to make his case against mercantilism. Mercantilist policies limiting imports and promoting exports impeded the exchange and flow of resources to their most valuable uses. By removing these barriers and taking advantage of the division of labor across countries, output would increase and prices would fall, generating a "universal opulence" which "extends even to the lowest ranks of the people." Smith's argument began to turn the tide against barriers to free trade, aided by David Ricardo's subsequent elaboration of the theory of comparative advantage. Though governments today remain tempted to turn to protectionist policies, Smith's insights about the benefits of free trade have become a staple of growth-oriented economic thinking.

SEE ALSO Mercantile Policies (1539), The Theory of Comparative Advantage (1817), The Heckscher–Ohlin Model (1933), The Stolper–Samuelson Theorem (1941), The Factor-Price Equalization Theorem (1948)

An illustration from Denis Diderot's (1713–1784) Encyclopédie, 1751–1766, showing pin-makers at work and the machinery they use. Adam Smith is thought to have drawn on this illustration when he observed that the division of labor allowed workers who specialize in one aspect of the pin-making process to be more productive than workers who were tasked with creating an entire pin from start to finish.

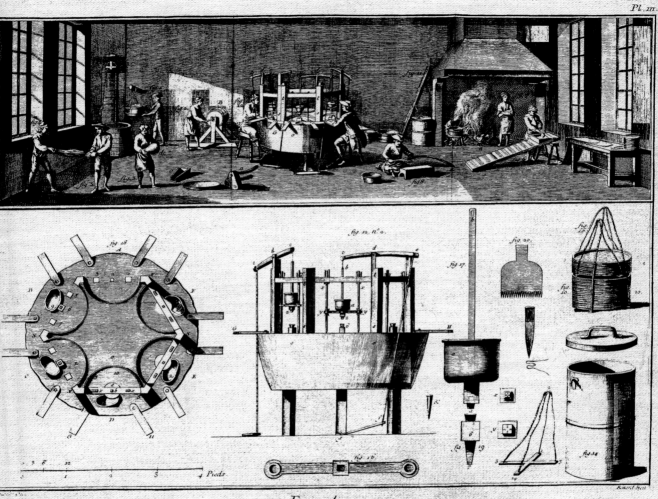

Pl. III.

Epinglier

The Competitive Process

Adam Smith (1723–1790)

To make his case in *Wealth of Nations* (1776) that a freely operating competitive market system is superior to mercantilist and physiocratic policies, Adam Smith had to describe how these markets would operate if left to their own devices. For Smith, the starting point was the "natural price"—the price just high enough to keep resources in their present employment. If labor, capital, and land are receiving their natural price, then the goods that they produce will also sell at this sum.

The "market price"—the price that exists in the marketplace at any point in time— may be above or below the natural price; but, thanks to competition, market prices are "continually gravitating" toward it. If the market price of hats (an example used by Smith) rises above the natural price, the returns to the land, labor, and capital used to produce hats will also rise above their natural rates. This will cause resources to flow to hat production as new hat makers enter the market seeking those higher returns. The increased supply of hats then causes their market price to fall back to the natural price. If the price falls below the natural price, this dynamic is reversed as makers leave the market in search of better opportunities; when the supply of hats decreases, the market price is driven up to its natural level.

According to Smith, prices will remain above the natural level only if there is some sort of monopoly, whether that results from a trade secret, exclusive control over a resource necessary to produce a good, or an exclusive franchise conferred by the government. It was the last of these that particularly concerned Smith, as it was a common mercantilist policy that benefited the businessman at the expense of the consumer, who was left to deal with the reduced availability of goods and higher prices. The competitive process, in contrast, would cause resources to flow to the production of goods most valued by consumers. The forces of competition would ensure that these goods were provided at the natural—rather than the higher monopoly—price.

SEE ALSO Mercantile Policies (1539), Supply and Demand (1767), Smith's *Wealth of Nations* (1776), Walras's *Elements of Pure Economics* (1874), The Demand–Supply Model (1890)

A collection of fashionable hats, 1876. As Smith observed, the prices of hats, like those of many goods, are determined by the forces of competition.

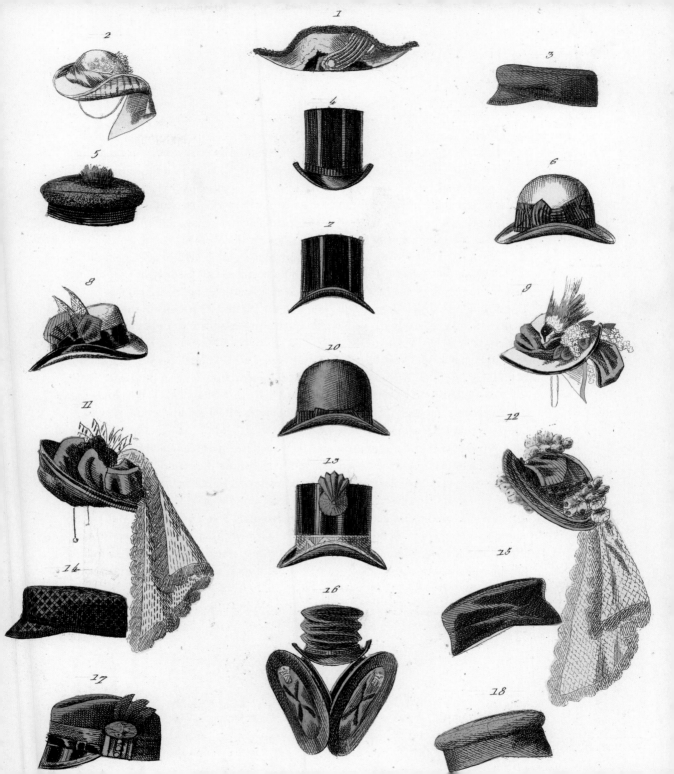

The Invisible Hand

Adam Smith (1723–1790)

In economic writings before Adam Smith, you'll notice a common theme: the perception that individuals shouldn't be left to their own devices. Their actions often didn't promote the best interests of society as a whole, whether that be justice, as in the case of the Ancient Greeks and the Scholastics; the accumulation of gold and silver bullion, as with the mercantilists; or the growth of net product, as advocated by the physiocrats. These groups believed government action, ranging from price controls to import restrictions, was needed to restrain practices that worked against society's interest.

No one did more to alter this perception than Smith in *Wealth of Nations* (1776). His notion of the "invisible hand" has become shorthand for the market system's potential to promote the best interests of society as a whole. Smith argued that by employing his capital where it will yield him the greatest return, the businessman would also yield the greatest return to the nation—the invisible hand would translate his self-interest to society's best interests.

But what is this "invisible hand?" We have no idea. Though many associate Smith with the idea of the "invisible hand," he used the term only once in this book. Some have argued that it is the hand of God. Others have proposed that it is the competitive pricing system, and still others believe it is the state, which establishes the laws that allow the market to function.

Whatever Smith's meaning, people have used the invisible hand to justify laissez-faire policies that minimize the government's role within the economic system. This is a bit ironic, in that there is a strong case to be made that Smith was anything but a laissez-faire economist. He advocated government interventions ranging from legal limits on interest rates to the public provision of primary-school education to help ward off the mind-numbing effects of the specialization associated with the division of labor. For Smith, the market system will only operate in society's best interests if embedded within an appropriate framework of laws, customs, and morals, making government essential to its success.

SEE ALSO Plato, Aristotle, and the Golden Mean (c. 380 BCE), Aquinas on Usury (1265), Mercantile Policies (1539), Laissez-Faire (1695), Mandeville's *Fable of the Bees* (1705), Smith's *Wealth of Nations* (1776)

The Eye of God, the Hand of God, and the Sacred Heart *by C. Savini after the Italian engraver Salvardi. Some have interpreted Adam Smith's concept of the invisible hand to be the hand of God.*

Amore e Fiducia nella sua amabiliſſima providenza

Dio vede tutto

Dio può tutto

Dio ci ama

C. Savini.

Dal Salvardi in Bologna.

Productive and Unproductive Labor

François Quesnay (1694–1774), Adam Smith (1723–1790)

Adam Smith's *Wealth of Nations* (1776) provided a blueprint for economic growth that remains central to modern economics. However, there is one aspect of his thinking that has not stood the test of time: his conception of the things that do and do not contribute to economic growth.

About two decades earlier, François Quesnay and his physiocrat followers claimed that only the agricultural sector was productive; the sole way to use labor resources productively was to devote them to agricultural pursuits. Smith used different criteria to differentiate between productive and unproductive labor. For Smith, productive labor contributed to the stock of national output by generating a "vendible commodity." Forms of employment that generated no such output were considered unproductive because they didn't produce additional value or promote accumulation of the capital that fueled economic growth. For example, the work performed by civil servants, the military, lawyers, clergy, entertainers, and professors fell in this category. Spending money on these unproductive professions, rather than saving and investing it or buying tangible goods, harmed the economy.

These distinctions between productive and unproductive labor had important policy implications. The market process didn't always allocate labor resources to productive uses, however defined. Thus, both Quesnay and Smith argued that the government needed to encourage the productive employment of labor and discourage the unproductive. That said, the government was a part of the problem as well, given its support for unproductive activities.

The influence of utilitarianism pushed aside these distinctions in the nineteenth century, defining productive labor as any work that generates utility for which people are willing to pay, whether it involves actors performing in a play or construction workers building a house. However, you could justly argue that the distinction between unproductive and productive labor continues today, as some measures of economic activity, such as gross domestic product (GDP), fail to account for the value of household labor, including cooking and cleaning.

SEE ALSO The Physiocrats (1756), The *Tableau Économique* (1758), Smith's *Wealth of Nations* (1776), Utilitarianism (1789), Veblen's *Theory of the Leisure Class* (1899), National Income Accounting (1934)

Mezzetino (c. 1718–1720), by the French painter Antoine Watteau (1684–1721), shows the character after whom this painting is named playing a guitar. Mezzetino appeared in theatrical comedies in Italy during this time. Both François Quesnay and Adam Smith would have considered such performances an example of unproductive labor.

Utilitarianism

Jeremy Bentham (1748–1832), John Stuart Mill (1806–1873)

The earliest economics thinkers, including Aristotle and Aquinas, saw economics as a branch of ethics and evaluated economic outcomes, laws, and policies based on ethical considerations. Even with the move by David Ricardo and others to establish economics as a separate science outside of moral philosophy, economists sought to offer ethical grounding for policy. It was utilitarianism that came to play that role.

The utilitarian approach, as laid out by the Englishman Jeremy Bentham in his *An Introduction to the Principles of Morals and Legislation* (1789) and subsequently expanded by John Stuart Mill and others, suggested that individuals are ruled by the twin forces of pleasure and pain. People will seek the former and attempt to avoid the latter to increase their "utility"—their pleasure, or satisfaction. Bentham further argued that the goodness of individual actions and the laws and policies set by government should be judged by the utility they provide to society as a whole. This standard for evaluation is reflected in the utilitarian dictum "the greatest good for the greatest number." Gone, then, was the idea that actions should be evaluated against some intrinsic scale of right or wrong.

Bentham's utilitarianism fundamentally influenced economic thinking in two ways: First, by making individual calculations of pleasure and pain the centerpiece of his system, Bentham helped ground economics in the belief that individuals pursue their self-interest, as emphasized by Adam Smith two decades earlier. Second, the utilitarian notion of the greatest good for the greatest number provided the basis for policies that would serve the interests of society as a whole rather than simply those of the politically powerful classes. British philosopher and economist John Stuart Mill, a disciple of Bentham, made this the basis for economic policy evaluation in his highly influential *Principles of Political Economy* (1848), a book that dominated economics instruction for more than fifty years. For Mill, utilitarian analysis could reveal where government intervention could improve on the economic outcomes associated with laissez-faire, the limitations of which were becoming increasingly evident by the mid-nineteenth century.

SEE ALSO Plato, Aristotle, and the Golden Mean (c. 380 BCE), Laissez-Faire (1695), Smith's *Wealth of Nations* (1776), Classical Political Economy (c. 1790), Mill's *Principles of Political Economy* (1848), Jevons's *Theory of Political Economy* (1871), Ordinal Utility (1893), Pigou's *Wealth and Welfare* (1912), The Hicks–Allen Consumer Theory (1934), Revealed Preference Theory (1938)

In 1817, Jeremy Bentham catalogued different sources of pleasure and pain using a series of tables.

TABLE OF THE SPRINGS OF ACTION:

…ving the several Species of PLEASURES and PAINS, of which Man's Nature is susceptible: together with the several Species of *Interests*, *Desires*, and *MOTIVES*, respectively corresponding to them: and the several Sets of Appellatives *Neutral*, *Eulogistic* and *Dyslogistic*, by which each Species of *MOTIVE* is wont to be designated: to which are added EXPLANATORY NOTES and OBSERVATIONS, indicative of the Applications of which the Matter of this TABLE is susceptible, in the Character of a *Basis* or *Foundation*, of and for the Art and Science of MORALS, otherwise termed ETHICS,—whether *PRIVATE*, or *PUBLIC alias* POLITICS—(including LEGISLATION)—*THEORETICAL*, or *PRACTICAL alias* DEONTOLOGY—*EXEGETICAL alias EXPOSITORY* (which coincides mostly with *THEORETICAL*), or *CENSORIAL*, which coincides mostly with DEONTOLOGY: also of and for PSYCHOLOGY, in so far as concerns ETHICS, and HISTORY (including BIOGRAPHY) in so far as considered in an *ETHICAL* Point of View.

No. I. PLEASURES AND PAINS,

—of the TASTE*—the* PALATE*—the alimentary canal—of* INTOXICATION.

Corresponding *Interest*,

Interest of the PALATE—Interest of the BOTTLE.

Corresponding *MOTIVES*—with NAMES,

…NEUTRAL: viz.	—II. EULOGISTIC: viz.	—III. DYSLOGISTIC: viz.	
…unger. …ed of food. …ant of food. …sire of food. …ar of hunger. …irst, …ought. …ed, want, desire of the means of …nching, relieving, …ting, &c. thirst. …nanition.	*Proper, none.* *Improper.* 1. Love of the pleasures of the social board—of the social bowl, or glass—of good cheer—of good living—of the good goddess—of the jolly god, &c.	1. Gluttony. 2. Gulosity. 3. Voracity. 4. Voraciousness. 5. Greediness. 6. Ravenousness. 7. Liquorishness. 8. Daintiness. 9. Love, appetite, craving, hankering, propensity, eagerness, passion, rage—of, for, to, and after—cramming, stuffing, de-	vouring, gormandizing, guttling, &c. 10. Drunkenness. 11. Ebriety. 12. Intoxication. 13. Sottishness. Love &c. (*as per Col.* 3.) of &c. drink, liquor—drinking, tippling, toping, boosing, guzzling, swilling, soaking, sotting, carousing—junketting, revelling, &c.

No. II. PLEASURES AND PAINS,

—of the sexual appetite, or of the sixth Sense.

Corresponding *Interest*,

SEXUAL INTEREST.

Corresponding *MOTIVES*—with NAMES,

NEUTRAL: viz.	—II. EULOGISTIC: viz.	—III. DYSLOGISTIC: viz.	
…*-worded, none.* …*-worded,* …l desire.	None.	1. Venery. 2. Lust. 3. Lechery. 4. Lewdness. 5. Lustfulness.	6. Libidinousness. 7. Lecherousness. 8. Salacity. 9. Salaciousness. 10. Venereal desire.

No. III. PLEASURES AND PAINS,

—of SENSE, *or of the* SENSES*: viz. generically or collectively considered.*

Corresponding *Interest*,

Interest of SENSE—of the senses:—SENSUAL INTEREST.

Corresponding *MOTIVES*—with NAMES,

NEUTRAL: viz.	—II. EULOGISTIC: viz.	—III. DYSLOGISTIC: viz.	
…*-worded, none.* …*-worded,* …cal want, need, …gency, necessity—…re, appetite.	None.	1. Sensuality. 2. Luxury. 3. Carnality. 4. Debauchery. 5. Intemperance. 6. Luxuriousness. 7. Voluptuousness.	8. Love, appetite, craving, &c. (*as per No. I. Col.* 3.) of, for, to, and after—sensual pleasure, enjoyment, gratification, indulgence, &c. See note (*b*). *Synonyms to pleasure.*

No. IV. PLEASURES AND PAINS,

…*ed from the matter of* WEALTH.—PLEASURES *of possession—acquisition—affluence—opulence.* PAINS *of privation—loss—poverty—indigence.*

Corresponding *Interest*,

PECUNIARY INTEREST. Interest of the PURSE.

Corresponding *MOTIVES*—with NAMES,

—I. NEUTRAL: viz.	—II. EULOGISTIC: viz.	—III. DYSLOGISTIC: viz.	
…*-worded, none.* …*-worded,* …sire, want, need, hope, …spect, expectation—of the …ans of subsistence, of com…ence, plenty, abundance, …es, opulence;—of profit, …uisition, &c. …r, apprehension—of loss, …uniary damage, want, pe…y, poverty, impoverish…nt, indigence. …sire, &c.—of maintaining, …serving, improving, mend…, bettering, meliorating, …ancing—a man's condi…n, situation, station, posi…—in life, in society, in … world, &c.	1. Economy. 2. Frugality. 3. Thrift. 4. Thriftiness. 5. Desire, hope, prospect, expectation—of thriving. 6. Prudential regard, care, attention, for, and to a man's pecuniary concerns, property, income, estate, livelihood, subsistence.	1. Parsimony. 2. Parsimoniousness. 3. Penuriousness. 4. Closeness. 5. Stinginess. 6. Niggardliness. 7. Miserliness. 8. Nearness. 9. Dirtiness.	1. Covetousness. 2. Cupidity. 3. Avarice. 4. Rapacity. 5. Rapaciousness. 6. Corruption. 7. Corruptness. 8. Venality. 9. Love, appetite, &c. (*as per No. I. Col.* 3.) lust, greediness—of, for, to and after—money, gain, lucre, pelf—hoarding, flint-skinning, scraping, &c.

No. V. PLEASURES AND PAINS,

—of POWER, *influence, authority, dominion, governance, government, command, rule, sway, &c.; —of governing, commanding, ruling, &c.*

Corresponding *Interest*,

Interest of the SCEPTRE.

Corresponding *MOTIVES*—with NAMES,

—I. NEUTRAL.	—II. EULOGISTIC.	—III. DYSLOGISTIC.	
1. Ambition. 2. Aspiringness. 3. Desire, &c. as per No. IV. Col. 1. of *power* &c. as above; of promotion, preferment, advancement; of exaltation, aggrandisement, ascendancy, preponderancy, superiority; of rising in the world, &c.	*Single-worded, none.* *Many-worded,* 1. Honest, becoming, praiseworthy, laudable, honourable, generous, noble, virtuous—ambition.	1. Ambition. 2. Love, appetite, craving, hankering, eagerness, greediness, thirst, lust, rage, passion—for *power*, &c. (as per Col. 1.) 3. Spirit of faction, turbulence, intrigue.	4. *Self-regarding* or *dissocial* moral qualities, liable to be *manifested* in the *exercise* of power, and *productive* of the *abuse* of it;—and wont to be spoken of in the character of MOTIVES. 1. Tyranny. 2. Tyrannicalness. 3. Despotism. 4. Despoticalness. 5. Arbitrariness. 6. Imperiousness. 7. Dictatorialness. 8. Domineeringness. 9. Magisterialness. *And see No. VIII. Col.* 4.

No. VI. PLEASURES AND PAINS,

—of CURIOSITY.

Corresponding *Interest*,

Interest of the SPYING-GLASS.

Corresponding *MOTIVES*—with NAMES,

—I. NEUTRAL.	—II. EULOGISTIC.	—III. DYSLOGISTIC.	
1. Curiosity. 2. Inquisitiveness. 3. Love of novelty. 4. Love of experiment. 5. Desire of information.	*Single-worded, none.* 1. Love, desire, appetite, thirst, rage, passion, for knowledge, learning, instruction, literature, science; useful information; the arts, &c. 2. Laudable curiosity.	1. Inquisitiveness. 2. Pryingness. 3. Impertinence. 4. Meddlesomeness.	5. Idle, vain, busy, prying, impertinent—curiosity, inquisitiveness.

No. VII. PLEASURES AND PAINS,

—of AMITY: *viz.* PLEASURES *derivable from the* good-will, *thence from the* free services, *of this or that individual.*—PAINS *derivable from the* loss *or* non-acquisition *of ditto.*

Corresponding *Interest*,

Interest of the CLOSET.

Corresponding *MOTIVES*—with NAMES,

—I. NEUTRAL.	—II. EULOGISTIC.	—III. DYSLOGISTIC.	
Single-worded, none. *Many-worded,* 1. Desire, wish, want, need, hope, prospect, expectation—of obtaining, gaining, acquiring, procuring,—partaking of, sharing in—enjoying, retaining, securing—the good opinion, favourable opinion, good-will; good offices, services; help, aid, assistance, support, co-operation; vote; interest; favour, patronage, protection, countenance, recommendation—of this or that *individual.*	*Single-worded, none.* *Many-worded,* Honest, &c. (*as per No. V. Col.* 2.) desire, &c. (*as per No. VII. Col.* 1.). I. NEUTRAL *continued.* 2. Fear, apprehension, dread—of losing, forfeiting, forgoing—the favour, good opinion, &c. as above. 3. Desire, &c. of ingratiating a man's self with him, of recommending a man's self to him, to his favour, &c. as above;—of obtaining, &c. a place in his favour.	1. Servility. 2. Slavishness. 3. Obsequiousness. 4. Cringingness. 5. Abjectness. 6. Meanness. 7. Sycophantism. 8. Toad-eating.	9. Propensity, readiness—to fawn, cringe, truckle to, humour, flatter—this or that individual. 10. Desire, hope, &c. of insinuating, worming a man's self, creeping, into the good graces of the individual in question; of currying favour with him.

No. VIII. PLEASURES AND PAINS,

—of the MORAL *or* POPULAR *sanction: viz.* PLEASURES *of* REPUTATION, *or good repute:* PAINS *of* BAD REPUTATION, *or ill-repute.*

Corresponding *Interest*,

Interest of the TRUMPET.

Corresponding *MOTIVES*—with NAMES,

—I. NEUTRAL.	I. NEUTRAL *continued.*	—II. EULOGISTIC.	—III. DYSLOGISTIC.
Single-worded, none. *Many-worded,* 1. Desire, &c. (*as per No. VII.*)—of obtaining, &c. the good-will, &c., thence the eventual services, &c. of *the public at large*, or a more or less considerable, though not liquidated, portion of it. 2. Fear, &c. (*as per No. VII. Col.* 2.) of losing, &c. the good opinion, &c. of ditto.	3. Fear, or sense—of shame, disrepute, opprobrium, reproach, dishonour, disgrace, ignominy, infamy, odium, unpopularity; of ill, evil, bad—repute, report, or fame; of an ill, &c. name; of bad reputation, bad character: of being disgraced, dishonoured, &c. 4. Sense of propriety, decorum, honour, dignity; moral rectitude, moral duty.	1. Honour. 2. Conscience. 3. Principle. 4. Probity. 5. Integrity. 6. Uprightness. 7. Rectitude. 8. Honesty. 9. Heroicalness. 10. Honest, becoming, laudable, virtuous, pride: a proper degree of pride. ☞ Conscience *and* Principle *belong also*	1. Vanity. 2. Vainness. 3. Ostentation. 4. Fastidiousness. 5. Vain glory. 6. False glory. 7. False honour. 8. Pride. 9. False pride. 10. Self-sufficiency. 11. Loftiness. 12. Haughtiness. 13. Assumingness. 14. Arrogance. 15. Overbearingness. 16. Insolence. *And see No. V. Col.* 4.

to Nos. IX. and X.: so likewise Probity &c.: *and these last belong to No. XIV, in so far as depends upon the* LEGAL SANCTION.

No. IX. PLEASURES AND PAINS,

—of the RELIGIOUS SANCTION.

Corresponding *Interest*,

Interest of the ALTAR.

Corresponding *MOTIVES*—with NAMES,

—I. NEUTRAL.	—II. EULOGISTIC.	—III. DYSLOGISTIC.	
1. Religion. 2. Religiousness. 3. Sense of religious duty. 4. Religious zeal, fervour, ardour. 5. Fear of God. 6. Hope from God. 7. Love of God.	1. Piety. 2. Devotion. 3. Devoutness. 4. Godliness. 5. Holiness. 6. Sanctity. 7. Righteousness. 8. Pious, godly, holy, sacred—&c. zeal, fervour, ardour, &c.	1. Superstition. 2. Bigotry. 3. Enthusiasm. 4. Fanaticism. 5. Sanctimoniousness. 6. Hypocrisy. 7. Affectation of, pretension to—religion,	&c.—piety, &c.—*as above, Col.* 2. 8. Religious prejudice. 9. Religious frenzy. 10. Religious intolerance.

No. X. PLEASURES AND PAINS,

—of SYMPATHY.

Corresponding *Interest*,

Interest of the HEART: *viz. more or less expanded, expansive, comprehensive—in proportion to the* number *of the persons, whose welfare is the object of the* desire.

Corresponding *MOTIVES*—with NAMES,

—I. NEUTRAL.	—II. EULOGISTIC.	II. EULOGISTIC *continued.*	—III. DYSLOGISTIC.
I.—*towards this or that determinate INDIVIDUAL—* 1. Sympathy. 2. Fellow-feeling. 3. Good-will. 4. Friendship. 5. Personal attachment, affection, regard, kindness, tenderness, fondness. II.—*towards this or that DOMESTIC, or other comparatively PRIVATE circle—* 1. Family, domestic, parental, social, attachment, &c.—*as above.* III.—*towards the POLITICAL community at large—* 1. National attachment. 2. National zeal. IV.—*towards MANKIND at large—* 1. Sympathy, fellow-feeling, good-will, regard, kindness—for or towards—mankind, the human species, the race of men, &c.—in general.	(*Mostly names of permanent moral qualities.*) I.—*towards this or that INDIVIDUAL—* 1. Kindness. 2. Goodnature. 3. Amicableness. 4. Complacency. 5. Benignity. 6. Tenderness. 7. Loving-kindness. 8. Affability. 9. Courteousness. 10. Urbanity. 11. Pity. 12. Compassion. 13. Commiseration. 14. Charity. 15. Mercy. 16. Clemency. 17. Long-suffering. 18. Forbearance. 19. Humanity. 20. Kindheartedness. 21. Tenderheartedness. 22. Goodness of heart. 23. Gratitude.	II.—*towards this or that comparatively PRIVATE circle*—no otherwise than as above. III.—*towards the POLITICAL community, or nation, at large—* 1. Patriotism. 2. Public spirit. 3. Public zeal. 4. Love of country. IV.—*towards MANKIND at large—* 1. Philanthropy. 2. General, universal, all-embracing, all-comprehensive—benevolence, beneficence, kindness, &c.—(*See Col.* 1. *and* 2.)	I.—*towards this or that INDIVIDUAL—* 1. Partiality. 2. Favouritism. 3. Partial attachment, &c.—(*See Col.* 1. *and* 2.) II.—*towards this or that comparatively PRIVATE circle—* 1. Family partiality. 2. Party attachment, favour, affection, prejudice, prepossession zeal, spirit, rage, madness. 3. Spirit of faction. 4. Corporation spirit. III.—*towards the POLITICAL community at large—* 1. Nationality. 2. National partiality, prejudice, prepossession. IV.—*towards MANKIND at large—* None.

No. XI. PLEASURES AND PAINS,

—of ANTIPATHY*—of ill-will—of the* IRASCIBLE APPETITE: *including the* PLEASURES *of* revenge, *and the* PAINS *of* unsatisfied vindictiveness.

Corresponding *Interest*,

Interest of the GALL-BLADDER.

Corresponding *MOTIVES*—with NAMES,

—I. NEUTRAL.	—II. EULOGISTIC.	—III. DYSLOGISTIC.	
1. Antipathy. 2. Dislike. 3. Aversion. 4. Displeasure. 5. Anger. 6. Wrath. 7. Exasperation. 8. Resentment. 9. Indignation. 10. Incensement.	*Single-worded, none.* *Many-worded,* 1. Just, proper, legitimate, justifiable, warranted, well-grounded, due, becoming, laudable, praise-worthy, commendable, noble, dignified—displeasure, indignation, resentment.	I.—*Specially derived and directed affections—* 1. Ill-will. 2. Ill-humour. 3. Animosity. 4. Spite. 5. Malice. 6. Hatred. 7. Hate. 8. Abhorrence. 9. Abomination. 10. Detestation. 11. Execration. 12. Rage. 13. Fury. 14. Rancour. 15. Revenge. 16. Vengeance. 17. Envy. 18. Jealousy.	II.—*Abstract moral qualities—* 19. Spleen. 20. Ill-nature. 21. Waspishness. 22. Maliciousness. 23. Malignity. 24. Malignancy. 25. Venomousness. 26. Cruelty. 27. Barbarity. 28. Savageness. 29. Brutality. 30. Ferocity. 31. Vindictiveness. 32. Vengefulness. 33. Obduracy. 34. Obdurateness. 35. Implacability. 36. Callousness. 37. Unjust, improper, &c.—asperity, harshness, rigour, severity, antipathy, &c. (*See Col.* 2. *and* 3.)

No. XII. PAINS,

—of LABOUR*—toil—fatigue.*

Corresponding *Interest*,

Interest of the PILLOW.

Corresponding *MOTIVES*—with NAMES,

—I. NEUTRAL.	—II. EULOGISTIC.	—III. DYSLOGISTIC.	
Single-worded, none. *Many-worded,* 1. Love of ease. 2. Aversion to labour. 3. Fear, apprehension, dread—of toil, fatigue, over-exertion, over-working, over-straining.	*None.*	1. Indolence. 2. Laziness. 3. Sloth. 4. Slothfulness. 5. Sluggardliness. 6. Sluggishness. 7. Self-indulgence. 8. Idleness.	9. Listlessness. 10. Torpidness. 11. Torpidity. 12. Segnity. 13. Tardiness. 14. Dilatoriness. 15. Procrastination. 16. Slowness. 17. Lenitude. 18. Drawlingness.

No. XIII. PAINS,

—of DEATH, *and* BODILY *Pains in general.*

Corresponding *Interest*,

Interest of EXISTENCE—of bodily, corporal, personal, SELF-PRESERVATION—safety—security.

Corresponding *MOTIVES*—with NAMES,

—I. NEUTRAL.	—II. EULOGISTIC.	—III. DYSLOGISTIC	
		I. Transient EMOTIONS.	*II. Permanent QUALITIES.*
1. Self-preservation. 2. Self-defence. 3. Self-protection. 4. Desire of, regard to, or for—personal safety, security. 5. Fear, apprehension—of pain, suffering, &c. 6. Fear of death. 7. Love of life.	*Properly belonging to this head, none.* *Borrowed from the habitudes of the INTELLECTUAL faculty—* 1. Prudence. 2. Circumspection. 3. Forecast. 4. Foresight. 5. Cautiousness. 6. Vigilance. 7. Prudential care.	1. Dread. 2. Terror. 3. Appalment. 4. Consternation. 5. Dismay. 6. Tremor. 7. Trepidation.	1. Timidity. 2. Timorousness. 3. Pusillanimity. 4. Faint-heartedness. 5. Chicken-heartedness. 6. Cowardice. 7. Poltroonery.

No. XIV. PLEASURES AND PAINS,

Of the SELF-REGARDING *class, generically or collectively considered:*—(i. e. of all the above sorts, except Nos. X. and XI.)

Corresponding *Interest*,

SELF-REGARDING Interest.

Corresponding *MOTIVES*—with NAMES,

—I. NEUTRAL.	—II. EULOGISTIC.	—III. DYSLOGISTIC.	
Single-worded, none: except in so far as those in No XII. may here be applicable. 1. Personal interest. 2. Self-regarding interest.	*None: except in so far as those in No. XIII. may here be applicable.*	1. Self-interest. 2. Selfishness.	3. Interestedness. 4. Self-interestedness.

Classical Political Economy

Thomas Robert Malthus (1766–1834), Jean-Baptiste Say (1767–1832), David Ricardo (1772–1823), John Stuart Mill (1806–1873)

Dominating economic thinking from around 1790 until the marginal revolution of the 1870s, classical political economy is typically characterized as the body of economic analysis that developed out of Adam Smith's *Wealth of Nations*. Its leading practitioners include T. R. Malthus, David Ricardo, Jean-Baptiste Say, and John Stuart Mill, among others. Like every other "school" of economic thought, the classical economists didn't agree on everything, making it difficult to pin down an explicitly classical approach to any particular economic question. This is nowhere more evident than in the debate over whether Karl Marx should be placed in the classical camp; although he was perhaps the most violent critic of classical economics, his theories relied heavily on elements of Smith and Ricardo.

Two important trends arose during this period. The first is the separation of economic thinking from the questions of moral philosophy that had loomed so large in previous centuries. The classical economists focused more on developing a science that could explain how the economy operated as it experienced significant industrial and commercial development. This new breed of political economists also occupied themselves fleshing out the details of Smith's framework, from wage and price determination and the role of money in the economy to the effect of machinery on production. They expanded some pieces in new directions and, at times, challenged and modified others.

The second distinguishing feature was its political element. Classical political economy was a policy-driven discipline aimed at compiling a body of knowledge that could inform governmental decision-making. Though often caricatured as staunch proponents of laissez-faire, the classicals are best characterized as pragmatic reformers, convinced of the general virtues of a market economy but increasingly cognizant of its warts. They devised proposals for combating unemployment and its effects, to provide services that the market appeared to provide in less than ideal amounts, and to stabilize the monetary system. They did so both through their writings and, for some, direct involvement in the policy process, as with David Ricardo's service as a member of Parliament and Nassau Senior's role in reforming Britain's Poor Laws.

SEE ALSO The Malthusian Population Theory (1798), Say's Law (1803), Diminishing Returns (1815), Ricardo's *Principles of Political Economy and Taxation* (1817), The Political Economy Club (1821), The Abstinence Theory of Interest (1836), Mill's *Principles of Political Economy* (1848), The Marginal Revolution (1871)

An etching of the House of Lords in session, 1809. Many classical political economists took an active role in policy debates, including David Ricardo, who held a seat in Parliament from 1819 until his death in 1823.

The Malthusian Population Theory

Thomas Robert Malthus (1766–1834)

When Thomas Robert Malthus penned his *Essay on Population* in 1798, he questioned the common view that a large and growing population was important for national and economic strength. But Malthus also challenged utopian socialists such as William Godwin, who believed the abolition of private property would improve the human condition, reducing sexual passion and thus population growth. Instead, Malthus contended that such growth was inevitable and would bring nothing but misery and vice.

Malthus's argument was built on two basic assumptions: the need for food, and the constancy of "the passion between the sexes." The latter would cause the population to double every generation, but because new lands being brought into cultivation were inferior to already-cultivated lands, the food supply would grow much more slowly. Without checks on population growth, the population would soon outstrip the food supply—a result sometimes referred to as the "Malthusian trap."

Malthus believed that nature had built-in checks to population growth. The reasonable man, he explained, will forgo or delay marriage if conditions don't allow him to support a family without lowering his station in life. While this "preventative check" curbs population growth until conditions improve, it leads men to gratify their sexual desires through vice—though he later allowed that "voluntary restraint," or abstinence, could also limit population growth. A second check on population growth, the "positive check," resulted from the misery to which the population's pressure on the food supply contributed. Deaths due to war, disease, famine, and the like would be sufficient, Malthus said, to keep the population from outstripping the food supply, but society would continually bump up against these limits, making living conditions difficult. In short, there was no utopia.

Malthus's theory of population became a fundamental building block of classical political economy, grounding everything from theories of income distribution to the law of diminishing returns. Though advances in agricultural productivity, which Malthus did not foresee, and changing societal attitudes toward birth control have alleviated overpopulation concerns in some areas of the world, Malthus's theory continues to influence discussions of the world's resources, as well as environmental debates.

SEE ALSO Classical Political Economy (c. 1790), Diminishing Returns (1815), The Stationary State (1815), *Illustrations of Political Economy* (1832), The Dismal Science (1849), The Iron Law of Wages (1862), The Wages Fund Controversy (1866), Resources for the Future and Environmental Economics (1952)

Thomas Malthus believed that ever-increasing population growth would make daily life incredibly difficult, especially as the population strained against the limits of its food supply.

Thornton's *Paper Credit*

Henry Thornton (1760–1815)

Early writings on monetary theory paid little attention to the role and influence of banks, which led to serious problems when a series of financial crises hit Britain during the 1790s. Over the preceding century, paper notes, issued by banks and backed by gold and silver, had become increasingly common forms of currency. Fearing that these crises would lead to bank failures and make their notes worthless, panicked depositors tried to convert their paper banknotes to gold and silver at small banks around the country, causing the precious-metal reserves held by the Bank of England on behalf of these small banks to drop sharply. In response, the Bank halted payments in gold and silver, which only worsened the panic.

In 1802, Henry Thornton, a successful banker and member of Parliament, identified the crux of the problem in *An Inquiry into the Nature and Effects of Paper Credit of Great Britain*. He explained how the public's confidence in the banking system directly affects such crises. If people had confidence in the banking system, they wouldn't rush to withdraw their funds. By putting a stop to gold and silver payments rather than continuing to lend freely to credit-worthy borrowers, and perhaps even increasing its lending, the Bank had pursued the wrong course. The Bank of England was not then a "central bank," as we think of it today. Instead of serving as an overseer of the country's banking system and monetary policy, it served as a backstop that provided liquidity to smaller banks when needed. Thornton's proposal made it the "lender of last resort," responsible for preventing monetary crises, one of the key roles played by today's central banks, such as the Federal Reserve in the U.S.

The sweep of Thornton's *Inquiry* runs well beyond the panic of the moment. He analyzed how variations in money supply affect domestic and international economic activity, emphasizing how the money supply, interest rates, prices, and the velocity of circulation are linked. His work remained unsurpassed in its influence until the writings of economists such as Irving Fisher and Knut Wicksell in the late 1800s.

SEE ALSO The Velocity of Money (1668), John Law and Paper Money (1705), The Price–Specie Flow Mechanism (1752), The Bullionist Controversy (1810), The Real Rate of Interest (1896), Wicksell's Cumulative Process (1898), The Federal Reserve System (1913), Cryptocurrency (2009)

The Bank of England is depicted as the Old Lady of Threadneedle Street in this 1797 political cartoon by James Gillray (1756–1815). William Pitt (1708–1778), Britain's prime minister at the time, is shown stealing gold from her pockets, a reference to the real-life Pitt's attempt to finance a war with France using the Bank's gold. This move depleted the Bank's reserves, forcing it to suspend the conversion of paper notes into bullion.

Say's Law

Jean-Baptiste Say (1767–1832), James Mill (1773–1836)

French economist Jean-Baptiste Say was one of the most important Continental economic thinkers during the first half of the eighteenth century. In his *Traité d'économie politique*, published in 1803, he formulated an idea that came to be known as "Say's Law." While Englishman James Mill formulated the theory around the same time, it became most closely associated with Say.

Say's Law says that "supply creates its own demand," meaning that the production of goods generates sufficient income to purchase everything that has been produced. This implies that there can never be an overproduction of goods or a shortage of aggregate demand. In short, Say's Law would seem to rule out the possibility of recessions, which often result from decreased demand for goods relative to their supply.

Most classical economists, including David Ricardo, took Say's Law as gospel, and it remained a central tenet of economic thinking until John Maynard Keynes published his *General Theory* in 1936. T. R. Malthus was an exception, and his critique of Say's Law set off a raging debate. Malthus acknowledged that the production of goods generated incomes sufficient to purchase them, but insisted that if too much of that income was saved and invested in production, rather than being devoted to consumption, supply could easily exceed demand, leading to a glut of goods on the market. This would result in falling prices, reduced profits, and increased unemployment. With less aggregate income available for purchases, this decrease in demand would spread across the economy.

In time, it was recognized that Say's Law might hold in the long run but not in the short run. Keynes's quip that "in the long run we are all dead" neatly captures the importance of considering both timeframes. Malthus's spotlight on these short-run concerns led Keynes to bemoan the fact that Malthus's position had not won the day in his debate with Say and his followers, and the Great Depression of the 1930s made clear that this short run could be very long indeed.

SEE ALSO Classical Political Economy (c. 1790), Underconsumption (1804), The Time Horizon (1890), Tugan-Baranovsky and the Trade Cycle (1894), The Great Depression (1929), Keynes's *General Theory* (1936)

A fishmonger shows his catch of the day to a shopper in The Fish Market *in Antwerp, 1827, by Flemish painter Ignatius Josephus van Regemorter (1785–1873). According to Say's Law, the supply of goods creates the demand for them, ensuring that there can never be a deficiency of overall demand.*

Underconsumption

James Maitland, Eighth Earl of Lauderdale (1759–1839), Thomas Robert Malthus (1766–1834), J. A. Hobson (1858–1940)

Neither Adam Smith's *Wealth of Nations* nor Say's Law—that supply creates its own demand—explained economic downturns or what to do about them. A set of theories based on the principle of underconsumption, the inability to sell goods at prices sufficient to cover costs or to sell them at all, evolved to fill this gap. French economic thinker Barthélemy de Laffemas first mentioned underconsumption in 1598, but it wasn't until 1804 that the Eighth Earl of Lauderdale took a deep dive into the subject.

Many theories about underconsumption attribute its cause to a lack of demand. This lack of demand leads to cutbacks in production and layoffs, which worsens the problem by reducing aggregate income in the economy. Though proponents of these theories were labeled "underconsumptionists," the root of the trouble here was actually over-saving. Over-saving not only reduced consumption, but also increased output because much of those savings were invested. Too much frugality, then, could have the unintended effect of putting the economy into a recession.

The solution to underconsumption involved decreasing savings and increasing consumption. Given that the working class devoted virtually all of their income to consumption, over-saving was seen as a problem caused by the upper classes. Lauderdale and Malthus thought income redistribution an ideal solution. Malthus also advocated that the wealthy devote more of their income to unproductive expenditures— employing additional servants or attending plays and concerts—which would reduce their savings and direct money to those who would spend it.

Underconsumption theories attracted the attention of a few economists—including J. A. Hobson, who built a theory of economic fluctuations, or business cycles, around underconsumption in the early 1900s. However, they never dominated the economic conversation because of the grip of Say's Law and because of the value that economists placed on savings. It wasn't until the publication of John Maynard Keynes's *General Theory* in 1936 that a different demand-side explanation for downturns emerged.

SEE ALSO Smith's *Wealth of Nations* (1776), Say's Law (1803), Tugan-Baranovsky and the Trade Cycle (1894), Unemployment (1896), Luxemburg's *Accumulation of Capital* (1913), The Oxford Approach to Welfare (1914), Keynes's *General Theory* (1936)

In The Toilet *(1830), by Dutch painter Jan Lodewijk Joxis, a maid helps a woman get dressed. Thomas Robert Malthus believed that it was possible to avoid underconsumption if the wealthy spent more on "unproductive" activities, such as hiring domestic help.*

The Bullionist Controversy

Henry Thornton (1760–1815), David Ricardo (1772–1823)

The Bank of England suspended the conversion of banknotes into bullion in 1797 as its gold stock diminished. This decision launched a lengthy debate, culminating in 1810, over the question of whether these notes should be freely convertible. The "bullionists," who favored convertibility, argued that if banks weren't required to convert notes to bullion on demand, they would have an incentive to issue notes whose value exceeded their gold holdings. This would increase the money supply, leading to inflation. British financier and political economist David Ricardo cited the rising price of gold as evidence that exactly this had occurred. Given this, the bullionists concluded that banks couldn't be trusted to properly issue banknotes and that sound policy demanded a return to full convertibility.

The "antibullionists," however, believed that the market would impose a natural brake on the issuance of notes. Because demand was limited by the needs of commerce, any notes issued had to finance productive economic activity—an idea known as the "Real Bills Doctrine." No one, they argued, would borrow money without planning to use it for a productive purpose. As such, the price of bullion was unrelated to the supply of banknotes.

It was economist and parliamentarian Henry Thornton who resolved the controversy and demonstrated the error of the Real Bills Doctrine. He contended that the demand for banknotes depended on the relationship between the rate of profit and the rate of interest on notes. If the former exceeded the latter, people would borrow money hoping to capitalize on the price differential, since the profits that money could earn when invested in a business would exceed the interest on the loan. This borrowing would expand the supply of banknotes and drive up prices. If interest costs exceeded the rate of profit, the dynamic would be reversed.

Thornton played a major role in drafting a parliamentary report adopting the bullionist position, restoring convertibility gradually over the next decade. His depiction of the relationship between money, interest, and prices anticipated elements of Knut Wicksell's model of the "cumulative process," which formalized the link between the money supply and the price level.

SEE ALSO The Quantity Theory of Money (1568), John Law and Paper Money (1705), The Gold Standard (1717), Thornton's *Paper Credit* (1802), Wicksell's Cumulative Process (1898), Cryptocurrency (2009)

In Midas, Transmuting all, into Paper *(1797) by James Gillray, British prime minister William Pitt sits on top of the Bank of England and transforms its gold reserves into paper notes. This political cartoon criticizes Pitt's decision to suspend the convertibility of banknotes into gold in 1797.*

MIDAS, Transmuting all into GOLD PAPER.

History of Midas.— The great Midas having dedicated himself to Bacchus, obtains from that Deity, the Power of changing all he Touched.
Apollo fixed Asses Ears upon his head, for his Ignorance.—& although he tried to hide his disgrace, with a Regal Cap, yet the very Sedges which grew
from the Mud of the Pactolus, whisper'd out his Infamy, whenever they were agitated by the Wind from the opposite Shore.— Vide Ovid's Metam.

Utopian Socialism

Claude-Henri de Saint-Simon (1760–1825), Robert Owen (1771–1858),
Charles Fourier (1772–1837)

By ushering in the transition from agrarian society to industrial capitalism, the Industrial Revolution brought significant social and economic upheaval and greater inequality. Socialism emerged as one reaction against these disruptions and offered the possibility of organizing social and economic life on more egalitarian terms. Early modern forms of socialism—dubbed "utopian socialism" by Karl Marx—didn't embody a consistent set of principles. Nonetheless, many socialist thinkers envisioned a society in which collective ownership or control would replace private property and competitive materialistic impulses gave way to harmonious living.

French social theorist Claude-Henri de Saint-Simon saw an industrialized society as the ideal. This society had private property, but a small group of scientific, industrial, and engineering experts would plan its organization based on the belief that science and technology offered solutions to nearly any societal problem. Welsh industrialist Robert Owen authored the first significant book in this tradition, A *New View of Society* (1813), and founded a textile factory in New Lanark, Scotland, where working and living conditions vastly surpassed those of typical industrial towns and workers could access welfare programs. He subsequently spearheaded a short-lived experiment to create a utopian cooperative society in New Harmony, Indiana, before turning his attention to worker cooperatives and labor unions. French mathematician Charles Fourier proposed a society that was composed of small cooperative associations and emphasized personal relationships. Individuals in this society would work on tasks that interested them, negating the mind-numbing repetition resulting from the division of labor. His ideas spawned a few communities in Europe and America and had a profound impact on philosopher Étienne Cabet, whose vision for communism (a term that Cabet coined) inspired Marx.

The difficulties of implementing these ideals, such as infighting and administrative problems, proved to be utopian socialism's undoing. Yet utopian socialism's legacy lives on in small communities around the world and in modern organizational management, through attempts to humanize the workplace and empower workers.

SEE ALSO The Division of Labor (1776), *The Communist Manifesto* (1848), Mill's *Principles of Political Economy* (1848), The Socialist Calculation Debate (1920)

This illustration from 1838 shows Robert Owen's vision for his socialist community in New Harmony, Indiana.

Diminishing Returns

Thomas Robert Malthus (1766–1834), David Ricardo (1772–1823), Robert Torrens (1780–1864), Edward West (1782–1828)

First recognized by A.-R.-J. Turgot in 1766 and developed simultaneously in 1815 by T. R. Malthus, David Ricardo, Edward West, and Robert Torrens, the law of diminishing returns tells us that if producers add more units of one input, such as labor, to a fixed amount of other inputs, the additions to output will eventually begin to decline. Land, as Malthus described in his *Essay on Population*, exemplifies this principle: Because fertility varies across different areas, the best lands are cultivated first. As cultivation expands, the additional output per acre will begin to fall. When combined with the knowledge, derived from William Petty, that rates of return tend to be similar across different types of resources, it became clear that if the returns to land fall, so will the returns to other inputs.

The law of diminishing returns demonstrates how events influence the development of ideas. France's blockade of Britain during the Napoleonic Wars limited food imports and led to a significant expansion of domestic agriculture. With less-fertile lands being brought under the plow, production costs and food prices crept upward. When the blockade ended in 1814, food began flowing into the country again, but British farmers, who had to grapple with these higher production costs, couldn't compete with the cheaper imports. Ricardo, Malthus, West, and Torrens used the principle of diminishing returns to explain the source of this problem and argue *against* limiting imports because higher food prices would keep wages artificially high, increase costs for British producers throughout the economy, make exports less competitive, and diminish economic growth.

You can apply the law of diminishing returns beyond production to explain why the third slice of pizza doesn't add as much satisfaction as the second or why, beyond some point, additional hours of study generate progressively smaller increases in test scores. This law, though, is often misinterpreted as suggesting that an activity should cease once the point of diminishing returns is reached. Were that the case, people would almost never eat that second or third slice of pizza.

SEE ALSO The Equalization of Returns (1662), Classical Political Economy (c. 1790), The Malthusian Population Theory (1798), The Stationary State (1815), Gossen's Two Laws (1854), The Falling Rate of Profit (1857), The Iron Law of Wages (1862)

This 1858 painting by British artist John Linnell shows farmers harvesting wheat. Napoleon's blockade caused the price of wheat in Britain to jump nearly 60 percent in 1807–1810.

The Stationary State

Adam Smith (1723–1790), David Ricardo (1772–1823)

According to Adam Smith, an economy that harnessed the division of labor (particularly through international trade), facilitated the accumulation of capital, and allowed the competitive market to channel that capital to its most productive uses could thrive and flourish. In the end, though, he sounded a pessimistic note. Profitable investment opportunities would eventually dry up, causing capital accumulation to slow and ultimately cease. Any further extension of the division of labor would grind to a halt. The result? Persistent economic stagnation—a stationary state.

In the first half of the nineteenth century, David Ricardo and John Stuart Mill drew on the Malthusian population principle and the theory of diminishing returns to refine this notion of a stationary state—with even grimmer implications. Diminishing returns in agriculture would cause food prices to rise and increase competition to farm the best lands, reducing agricultural profits to a minimum. Because returns to different sectors tend to equalize, profits in manufacturing would fall commensurately. Capital accumulation and thus economic growth would come to a standstill, while a growing population would ensure that wages would continually hover at subsistence levels. The solution, for Ricardo, was free trade. By exporting manufactured goods and using the proceeds to import food from countries—such as America—where the worst effects of diminishing returns had yet to manifest themselves, England could put off the arrival of the stationary state.

The theory of the stationary state shares important similarities with Karl Marx's theory of crisis and the inevitable collapse of capitalism. Both suggest that there are inevitable limits to capitalism's ability to sustain economic growth and provide reasonable standards of living. Fortunately, these dim prospects have not been realized. Ricardo, Mill, and other economists of the period didn't recognize the massive role that forces such as technological change and education would play in expanding possibilities for economic growth, an oversight that wouldn't be remedied until the twentieth century.

SEE ALSO The Equalization of Returns (1662), Classical Political Economy (c. 1790), The Malthusian Population Theory (1798), Diminishing Returns (1815), The Theory of Crisis (1867), The Harrod–Domar Growth Model (1939), The Solow–Swan Growth Model (1956), Endogenous Growth Theory (1986)

Two women operate large looms in this undated colored lithograph. David Ricardo believed that free trade would delay the onset of the stationary state in Britain by allowing it to export manufactured items, such as cloth, in exchange for food.

Conversations on Political Economy

Jane Marcet (1769–1858)

Prior to the 1880s, writings on economics focused more on influencing public opinion than on influencing other "economists." However, these writers' definition of "the public" was limited, consisting primarily of influential men who served as heads of state, religious leaders, and policymakers. British writer Jane Marcet expanded this audience by writing a series of books to educate women in the sciences. Each work featured a conversation between a young female pupil, Caroline, and her teacher, Mrs. Bryant, a format that Marcet saw as more beginner-friendly than a lecture. *Conversations on Political Economy*, published in 1816, was the book that covered the basics of political economy, including the ideas of Adam Smith, T. R. Malthus, and David Ricardo.

As an educated woman who moved in the intellectual and literary social circles of the time, Marcet knew well the advantages of an education in the sciences, including political economy. Mrs. Bryant informed Caroline that "The science of political economy is intimately connected with the daily occurrences of life," from shopping to current events. Ignoring its basic principles "may lead us into serious practical errors," especially when talk on the streets, newspapers, and even poetry spread misconceptions and false information about the subject. *Conversations on Political Economy* took the reader through the key topics featured in economic writings of the period. Marcet explained how the division of labor and the accumulation of capital increases national wealth and covered the determination of prices, income distribution across different social classes, and the significance of international trade.

Though Marcet's original motivation for these "conversations" was to educate women about the new science of political economy, the books gained a wide audience and were translated into many languages. Indeed, the degree to which Marcet and Harriet Martineau, another "popularizer" of economic ideas, spread economic knowledge remained unsurpassed until Paul Samuelson penned what would become the most influential introductory textbook in history shortly after World War II.

SEE ALSO Smith's *Wealth of Nations* (1776), Classical Political Economy (c. 1790), The Malthusian Population Theory (1798), Ricardo's *Principles of Political Economy and Taxation* (1817), *Illustrations of Political Economy* (1832), Samuelson's *Economics* (1948)

Jane Marcet gained fame for her popular introductory books on subjects ranging from chemistry to political economy.

The Machinery Question

Thomas Robert Malthus (1766–1834), David Ricardo (1772–1823),
John Barton (1789–1852)

Adam Smith's analysis of the division of labor assumed that labor and machinery were complementary: the development of new machinery would make labor more productive and increase the demand for labor. In 1817, John Barton challenged this view, arguing that machinery did little more than displace labor and posed a grave threat to the working classes. David Ricardo expressed a similar viewpoint in the third edition of his *Principles of Political Economy* (1821).

Barton and Ricardo's line of thinking resonated with the working class in England. With the mechanization of textile manufacturing and the emergence of technological advances such as power looms, demand for skilled labor plummeted. The ranks of workers competing for unskilled jobs swelled, depressing wages and causing significant bouts of unemployment. The Luddites, a secretive group of English textile workers opposed to new technology, tried to turn back the clock by attacking factories and destroying machines in industrial regions such as Nottinghamshire and Lancashire.

In contrast, T. R. Malthus argued that machinery lowered costs and prices, stimulating increased demands for goods. This, along with the new employment opportunities created by the manufacturing of this machinery, would absorb displaced labor. Though this viewpoint didn't resonate with the working classes, it found favor with many economic thinkers because it fit in with their belief that a market economy adjusts quickly to reemploy available resources.

The machinery question is one example of how economic analysis during this period was limited by the failure to understand that the effects of economic decisions or events may be very different in the short run and the long run. Barton and Ricardo's view is certainly relevant in the short run, as seen when new inventions created surges in unemployment in nineteenth-century England or robots replace factory workers today. Meanwhile, the positive effects described by Malthus tend to manifest themselves only in the long run, which often offers little comfort to the displaced workers.

SEE ALSO Ricardo's *Principles of Political Economy and Taxation* (1817), *Illustrations of Political Economy* (1832), The Labor Theory of Value and the Theory of Exploitation (1867), The Theory of Crisis (1867), The Time Horizon (1890), Luxemburg's *Accumulation of Capital* (1913), Creative Destruction (1942)

Luddites destroy machinery at a textile factory in this 1844 engraving. In response to such vandalism, the British government had made machine-breaking a crime punishable by death in 1812.

Ricardo's *Principles of Political Economy and Taxation*

David Ricardo (1772–1823)

David Ricardo was a British financier, political economist, and, from 1819, member of Parliament. First exposed to economics when he picked up a copy of Adam Smith's *Wealth of Nations* on a trip to Bath, he began contributing to economic debates in 1809 and figured prominently in both the bullionist controversy over whether paper money should be freely convertible into gold and the debate over the Corn Laws, which restricted grain imports. In 1817, with the encouragement of his good friend James Mill, he released a full-blown treatise on economics, *Principles of Political Economy and Taxation*.

Ricardo made important contributions to the analysis of prices, income distribution, international trade, and public debt. Taking issue with Smith's theory of value, he attempted to reestablish the basis of price in the amounts of labor needed to produce each good, a concept known as the labor theory of value. He used his good friend Malthus's theories of population growth and diminishing returns to land to develop a new theory that describes how income is distributed among landowners, capitalists, and workers. An ardent proponent of free trade, Ricardo developed the theory of comparative advantage to explain its benefits. He also argued that debt-financed government spending had no effect on demand in the economy, as consumers would respond by saving more now to pay off the debt obligation through taxes in the future. In the 1970s, American economist Robert Barro made this proposition, known as "Ricardian equivalence," a key feature of the new classical macroeconomics. Perhaps the most distinctive feature of the *Principles*, though, was Ricardo's method of analysis. At once abstract and analytically rigorous, Ricardo's book reads more like a work in modern economics than any other work published in English up to the marginal revolution in the 1870s.

Ricardo's insights were so influential that nineteenth-century classical economics is often referred to as "Ricardian economics." But Ricardo's efforts didn't end with his writings. As a member of Parliament, he devoted his efforts to educating his colleagues on the basic principles of political economy and supporting free-trade policies.

SEE ALSO Smith's *Wealth of Nations* (1776), Classical Political Economy (c. 1790), The Bullionist Controversy (1810), The Machinery Question (1817), The Theory of Comparative Advantage (1817), The Labor Theory of Value (1821), The Falling Rate of Profit (1857), The Iron Law of Wages (1862), The Wages Fund Controversy (1866), The Marginal Revolution (1871), The New Classical Macroeconomics (1972)

David Ricardo, featured in this 1888 engraving, emerged as one of the most influential classical economists, making many contributions on subjects ranging from international trade to the determinants of land rents.

Engraved by W. Holl.

D. RICARDO.

From an Engraving by Hodgetts after the Picture
by T. Phillips, R.A.

The Theory of Comparative Advantage

David Ricardo (1772–1823)

Adam Smith might have been the most influential advocate of free trade, but his discussion of its merits left some questions unanswered. Smith implicitly assumed that people would specialize in goods they produce better than others and then trade with others for the goods they need. But what if you, or your country, are superior to everyone else in every production activity? Are there then still any benefits to be gained from trade? David Ricardo answered yes, through what became known as the theory of comparative advantage.

Ricardo's theory is laid out in the chapter "On Foreign Trade" in his *Principles of Political Economy* (1817). Suppose that in England, a unit of labor can produce one bottle of wine or one unit of cloth, while a unit of labor in Portugal can produce six units of wine or three units of cloth. The opportunity cost of producing a unit of cloth in England is one bottle of wine, whereas the opportunity cost of a unit of cloth in Portugal is two bottles of wine. England has a comparative advantage in producing cloth because it can do so at the lower opportunity cost. Portugal has a comparative advantage in producing wine because its opportunity cost is only one-half unit of cloth there, versus one unit of cloth in England. These countries will generate more wine and more cloth if each produces according to its comparative advantage, specializing in the good that it can make at the lowest opportunity cost. Free trade between these countries will then allow each country to have more of both goods than they would without specialization.

Though his theory appears counterintuitive, as it suggests that even the strongest producers can gain from international trade, Ricardo's conception of comparative advantage nudged policymakers away from protectionist policies and toward freer trade. While modern theories of international trade have advanced Ricardo's insights in multiple ways, including describing the very rare conditions in which the law of comparative advantage may not hold, it remains the foundation of the economist's approach to international trade, one that is ignored at a nation's economic peril.

SEE ALSO The Division of Labor (1776), Ricardo's *Principles of Political Economy and Taxation* (1817), Opportunity Cost (1889), The Heckscher–Ohlin Model (1933), The New Trade Theory (1979)

This contemporary photo shows a vineyard in Portugal's Douro Valley. To explain the theory of comparative advantage, David Ricardo described how Portugal would specialize in wine production because its opportunity cost for making wine is lower than in other countries.

The Law of Demand

Thomas Robert Malthus (1766–1834)

The law of demand is perhaps the most fundamental idea of economics. At the most basic level, it states that the amount of a product that people wish to purchase will vary inversely with the good's price. Though this essential insight is nearly as old as economic thinking itself, economists didn't begin to seriously study the concept of demand and its underpinnings until the nineteenth century.

In *An Investigation of the Cause of the Present High Price of Provisions* (1800), T. R. Malthus provided the first significant leap forward by measuring demand using the price that people are willing to pay for a good. Twenty years later, in his *Principles of Political Economy*, he then introduced the concept of "intensity of demand" to explain why this price changes with variations in supply. A consumer's intensity of demand reflects the amount that she is willing to sacrifice, or pay, to obtain a commodity. The greater this intensity of demand, the higher the price that she is willing to pay. If supplies fall, those with greater intensities of demand will bid up the price. Because only those with the greater intensities of demand will be willing to pay this higher price, theirs are the only demands that will be satisfied. However, increased supplies can be sold only if those with less-intense demands can also purchase the good. This is possible only if the price drops to a level that these individuals are willing to pay.

Though Malthus provided a theoretical foundation for the law of demand, he didn't explain *why* some individuals have greater intensities of demand and some less. Some classical economists made these differences turn on income—the rich being willing to pay more than the poor—but this provided only a very partial answer. The answer to this question would have to wait until the marginal revolution, when a new theory of choice would portray consumer behavior as an effort to maximize utility and link the individual's willingness to pay for a good to the additional utility received from it.

SEE ALSO Supply and Demand (1767), Utilitarianism (1789), Classical Political Economy (c. 1790), The Marginal Revolution (1871), Jevons's *Theory of Political Economy* (1871), The Demand–Supply Model (1890)

For Thomas Robert Malthus, intensities of demand, the extent to which consumers desire a particular good, determine the good's price.

The Political Economy Club

James Mill (1773–1836), Thomas Tooke (1774–1858)

One sign that political economy was coming into its own as a subject was the formation of the Political Economy Club in 1821. This London-based club was the brainchild of Thomas Tooke, a British merchant, statistician, and economist, and brought together individuals dedicated to "promoting the knowledge of Political Economy" and free trade. Its founding members included the leading economic minds in Britain at the time, including David Ricardo, T. R. Malthus, Robert Torrens, and James Mill, as well as political figures, civil servants, and journalists. Jane Marcet, Nassau Senior, John Stuart Mill, F. Y. Edgeworth, William Stanley Jevons, and Alfred Marshall were among those who later became members. The Political Economy Club was just that—a club— with membership limited to thirty until 1847 and thirty-five thereafter. In this sense, it was unlike (and to some extent replaced by) the professional societies that formed in Britain and America toward the end of the century.

The Club's meetings followed the strict format laid down by James Mill in its original set of rules. Each gathering addressed a question submitted in advance by one of the members. That member would begin the meeting with an opening statement, and discussion would ensue. In time, these opening statements grew into the reading of full-length papers, some of which were subsequently published in article or pamphlet form. The topics ran the gamut from particulars of economic theory to the policy issues of the day. Members contemplated the validity of the Malthusian population principle, the relationship between money supply and inflation, trade restrictions, and child labor, among other subjects.

The records of the meetings reveal a less-than-harmonious environment. Most questions sparked vociferous debate, and even the leading economic theorists had substantially different takes on the answers to many of the questions. But it was through these debates that the leading practitioners of classical political economy worked out a number of its principles, making the club, in economist D. P. O'Brien's words, a "vital hub" of economic thinking in England.

SEE ALSO Classical Political Economy (c. 1790), *Conversations on Political Economy* (1816), The Abstinence Theory of Interest (1836), Mill's *Principles of Political Economy* (1848), Jevons's *Theory of Political Economy* (1871), Edgeworth's *Mathematical Psychics* (1881), The Professionalization of Economics (1885), Marshall's *Principles of Economics* (1890)

The first meeting of the Political Economy Club was held at the home of Swinton Holland in Russell Square, London, pictured here.

The Labor Theory of Value

David Ricardo (1772–1823), James Mill (1773–1836), Karl Marx (1818–1883)

The attempt to explain the value, or price, of a good is a consistent thread running through the history of economics. While the earliest economic thinkers, such as Aristotle and Aquinas, were concerned with the ethical questions that came with setting a "just price," subsequent writers wrestled with how prices are actually determined. Between the seventeenth and late nineteenth centuries, many writers, including William Petty, Adam Smith, David Ricardo, James Mill, and, perhaps most prominently, Karl Marx, pinpointed labor as the fundamental determinant of value.

The labor theory of value posits that the relative prices of any of two goods depend on the relative quantities of labor used to produce them. If it takes ten hours of labor to produce a pair of shoes and five to produce a shirt, the price of a pair of shoes will be double that of a shirt. In a world where manual labor is the only input, this makes a good deal of sense. But what about the machinery and materials also used to produce the product? According to the labor theory of value, these things are merely embodied labor; the amount of labor embodied in machinery and materials will factor into these relative prices just as manual labor does.

Ricardo, in his *Principles of Political Economy and Taxation*, was the first to formulate a sophisticated labor theory of value, one that applied to both manual labor and production processes that incorporated machinery. James Mill seized on Ricardo's formulation and became one of its most important advocates, but many classical economists continued to follow Adam Smith's view that overall costs of production, rather than quantities of labor, determined prices. A few decades later, Marx made the labor theory a central element of his analysis of capitalism, including his prediction of its inevitable collapse. With the advent of the marginal revolution, which emphasized the importance of consumer demand in price determination, labor- and cost-based theories of value ultimately gave way to explanations grounded in the twin forces of demand and supply.

SEE ALSO Justice in Exchange (c. 340 BCE), The Just Price (1265), Smith's *Wealth of Nations* (1776), Classical Political Economy (c. 1790), Ricardo's *Principles of Political Economy and Taxation* (1817), The Theory of Crisis (1867), The Marginal Revolution (1871), Marshall's *Principles of Economics* (1890)

According to labor theory of value, the price of these tailors' services is determined by their labor time and the labor time embodied in their tools and materials.

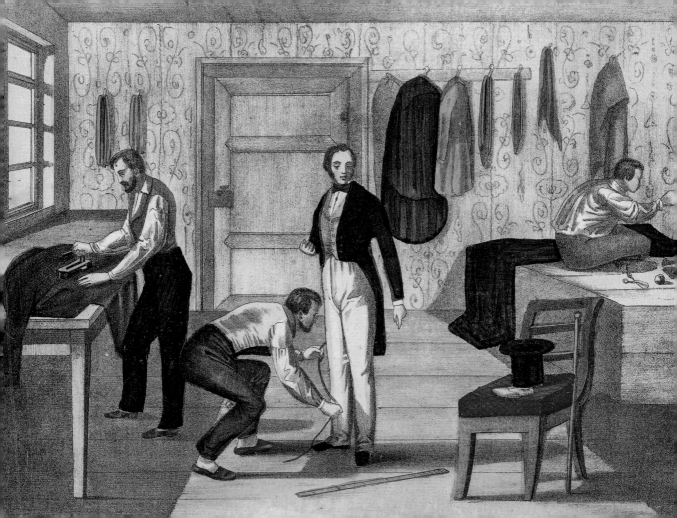

Thünen's *Isolated State*

Johann Heinrich von Thünen (1783–1850)

Though the classical approach to economics dominated Great Britain and America for much of the nineteenth century, economic thought on the European Continent was much more diverse. As a result, Continental thinkers developed several ideas that anticipated much later findings associated with the marginal revolution, emphasizing the role of benefit-cost analysis in consumer and producer decision-making. One such contribution came from Johann Heinrich von Thünen, a German landowner whose major work, *The Isolated State*, was published in three parts between 1826 and 1863.

Thünen developed location theory, using calculus to examine the optimal geographic location for specific industries in an agricultural society where the quality of the land is uniform and transportation costs are the only relevant variable. If the landowners' goal is to maximize the rent received from their land, the different production sectors should be positioned in a series of concentric circles around a city. Dairy and more perishable food items should be cultivated on the land closest to town, with timber, which is expensive to transport due to its weight, grown in the second ring. Cattle, which require large plots of land but can be walked to market, would be raised in a ring beyond that. While empirical evidence provides some support for Thünen's theory, he deserves more credit for the attention he brought to the study of economic geography, which has become an important component of analyzing international trading relationships.

Thünen's calculus also helped him discover that he could determine the contribution of different production inputs by measuring the increase in output associated with adding another unit of one input. He then demonstrated that the payment for each additional input will typically equal the additional value that it contributes to the output. Later refined further by John Bates Clark, this insight, now known as the marginal productivity theory of distribution, helps us understand how wages, interest, profits, and returns to land are determined within a competitive market system, and why they may be higher in some sectors than in others.

SEE ALSO The Invention of Calculus (c. 1665), Classical Political Economy (c. 1790), The Marginal Revolution (1871), Clark's *Distribution of Wealth* (1899), The Hotelling Model of Locational Choice (1929), The New Trade Theory (1979)

A diagram from Johann Heinrich von Thünen's The Isolated State, *showing the different sectors of production organized in concentric rings. Thünen posited that such an arrangement would maximize landowner rents.*

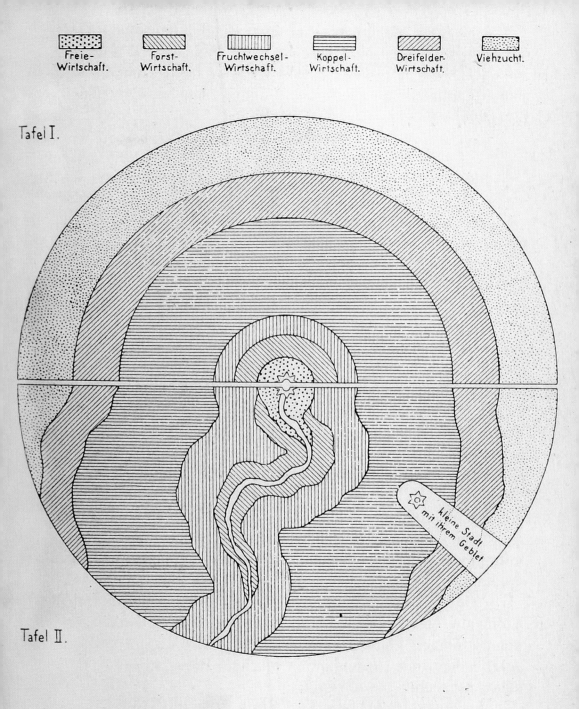

Freie-Wirtschaft. Forst-Wirtschaft. Fruchtwechsel-Wirtschaft. Koppel-Wirtschaft. Dreifelder-Wirtschaft. Viehzucht.

Tafel I.

Tafel II.

kleine Stadt mit ihrem Gebiet

1 5 10 15 20 40 Meilen

25*

The French Engineering Tradition

Claude Louis Marie Henri Navier (1785–1836), Jules Dupuit (1804–1866)

The long tradition of French engineer–economists began with King Louis XV's (1710–1774) creation of the *Ecole Nationale des Ponts et Chaussées*, the famed training ground for French civil engineers, in 1747. Its most famous members included Henri Navier, Augustin Cournot, Charles Minard, and Jules Dupuit. These French engineers distinguished themselves by analyzing social issues alongside engineering questions. The link between engineering and economics was in some ways a natural one. The construction of public works such as roads and bridges raised questions about how to finance them and whether it was worthwhile to provide such infrastructure.

To answer these questions, engineers needed to measure and analyze these projects' benefits and costs. Articles by Navier in 1830 and Dupuit in 1844 outlined innovative techniques that allowed engineers to evaluate projects through this lens. These new techniques quantified the trade benefits of a new project and measured consumer surplus, the difference between the price paid for a good and the price the consumer is willing to pay. They also assessed costs beyond those for labor and materials, such as the reduced consumption resulting from taxes used to finance a new road. It was particularly important to accurately measure the trade benefits from roads and bridges to justify their construction costs. Engineers considered how new infrastructure would facilitate commerce and, in turn, increase tax revenue, potentially making them self-financing. But they also needed to acknowledge that some of this commerce would have occurred without the public works in question, albeit at a higher transportation cost. There was much debate during the mid–nineteenth century about managing the challenges of estimating trade impacts and quantifying the benefits to consumers, but the need to solve immediate practical problems facilitated innovations in economic analysis.

By measuring both benefits and costs, the engineers rejected the notion that the economic value of a good is given solely by its production cost, a central tenet of classical economics. Their contributions foreshadowed important insights associated with the marginal revolution, including the concepts of marginal utility (the satisfaction that a consumer receives from an additional unit of a good) and consumer surplus.

SEE ALSO Classical Political Economy (c. 1790), The Labor Theory of Value (1821), Cournot's *Researches* (1838), Consumer Surplus (1844), The Marginal Revolution (1871), Cost–Benefit Analysis (1958)

A group portrait of the engineers, officials, and workers involved with the construction of the Lessart Viaduct, which runs across the Rance River in northwestern France (1879). This was one of many projects spearheaded by engineers who studied at the Ecole Nationale des Ponts et Chaussées.

Illustrations of Political Economy

Harriet Martineau (1802–1876)

While Jane Marcet did more than any other writer to facilitate the spread of economic ideas to the educated classes, it was Harriet Martineau who brought economic knowledge to the masses. Born to the family of a respected textile manufacturer, Martineau was forced to help support the family when its business failed in the late 1820s. She turned to writing and, inspired by Marcet, penned a series of fictional essays called *Illustrations of Political Economy* (1832). The *Illustrations* educated readers about the operation of a market system. Believing that "Example is better than precept," Martineau didn't merely want to present her audience with a statement of foundational principles, but to explain them "in a familiar, practical form" through stories. Each tale emphasized how these principles could help readers understand the world around them.

Martineau's stories often explore why the working class had a difficult situation in life. She explains how the Malthusian population principle, in which population growth threatens to outstrip the available food supply, together with the advance of machinery, pushes down wages and increases unemployment. Her stories were anything but callous; Martineau's sympathy for the working class stands out in her writings. The *Illustrations* also stand out for Martineau's portrayal of women as rational economic agents and for describing the ways in which changing economic conditions affected the lives of women and children.

Martineau's decision to wed fiction to political economy rather than simply writing a layman's explanation of economic theory was in part a reaction to the social norms of the period: non-fiction wasn't seen as an appropriate genre for the female writer unless she focused on household affairs. Fiction was the more "proper" vehicle that allowed Martineau to express her views on social-economic policy and reach a broad audience. In fact, sales of her *Illustrations* outstripped those of Charles Dickens. Martineau was also a staunch abolitionist. Though this earned her the ire of many Americans in the late 1830s, her books on American social life, the product of a two-year visit to the United States, contained pioneering contributions to sociology.

SEE ALSO Classical Political Economy (c. 1790), The Malthusian Population Theory (1798), *Conversations on Political Economy* (1816), The Machinery Question (1817), Samuelson's *Economics* (1948)

Harriet Martineau, shown here in this 1879 engraving, used stories to teach her readers about the principles of political economy in her Illustrations of Political Economy.

The Abstinence Theory of Interest

Nassau William Senior (1790–1864)

Though prohibitions on lending money at interest had largely disappeared by the end of the sixteenth century, the practice remained controversial into the nineteenth. The capitalist's profits were similarly suspect, and the labor theory of value, which suggested that labor is the source of all value, didn't help the cause. David Ricardo had justified interest and profits as a return to the risk taken by the capitalist, but this explanation fell short. If there were no risk involved, rates of interest and profits should be zero, yet almost no one would be willing to lend or invest for no return. It was Nassau W. Senior, Oxford's first professor of political economy and architect of the British Poor Law, who provided an explanation, one that portrayed capital as a cost of production, on a par with labor.

In *An Outline of the Science of Political Economy* (1836), Senior argued that the accumulation of capital is possible only because capitalists choose to abstain from present consumption and devote a share of their income to investment. This abstinence imposes a cost on the capitalist. Interest and profits serve as a necessary reward for incurring that cost, just as wages are a return for working. Senior's use of the word "abstinence" as a synonym for "waiting," though, was unfortunate. It came during a period when the capitalist class in Britain enjoyed very high living standards, even as they accumulated and reinvested capital, while the working class lived at or near subsistence levels. It is no surprise that Senior's image of a rich man's "abstinence" became the object of derision.

Though later superseded by more nuanced theories developed by Eugen von Böhm-Bawerk, Irving Fisher, John Maynard Keynes, and others, the abstinence theory of interest offered the first explanation for the *scarcity* of capital. It had long been recognized that capital enhances production, but this alone couldn't explain its value. By focusing on the opportunity costs of accumulating capital, Senior could outline why its use must always command a price greater than zero, even when there is no risk.

SEE ALSO Turgot's *Reflections* (1766), The Labor Theory of Value and the Theory of Exploitation (1867), Böhm-Bawerk's *Capital and Interest* (1884), The Real Rate of Interest (1896), Keynes's *General Theory* (1936)

This cartoon lampoons the idea of the British's wealthy classes practicing "abstinence" and depicts an aristocratic woman choosing to be "frugal" by leaving the powder off her wig.

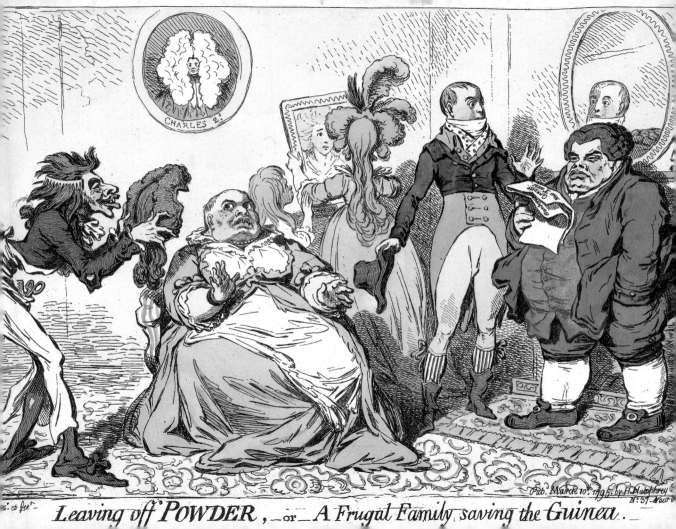

CHARLES 2.

Leaving off POWDER, — or — A Frugal Family saving the Guinea.

Pub. March 10th 1795. by H.Humphrey

Nº 37. New

Homo Economicus

John Stuart Mill (1806–1873)

Economics distinguishes itself from other social sciences with its reliance on a creature called "*homo economicus,*" or "economic man." Though first portrayed as an extremely selfish individual, *homo economicus* has evolved to some extent to designate a person who makes decisions based on calculations of benefits and costs. He is often assumed to be rational, and deliberation forms a key feature in his decision-making process.

Homo economicus may be considered an outgrowth of the utilitarian tradition that forms the foundation of modern economics. It isn't unusual to credit Adam Smith for introducing *homo economicus,* largely because he built his economic system around the belief that individuals pursue their self-interest in the marketplace; but John Stuart Mill solidified something approaching the modern definition in an 1836 essay, "On the Definition of Political Economy; and on the Method of Investigation Proper to It." He wrote, "Political Economy presupposes an arbitrary definition of man, as a being who invariably does that by which he may obtain the greatest amount of necessaries, conveniences, and luxuries, with the smallest quantity of labour and physical self-denial with which they can be obtained in the existing state of knowledge." Critics of classical economics, including John Ruskin, took issue with this depiction of man for offering a misguided, narrow view of human nature. The origins of the labels "economic man" and "*homo economicus*" are more obscure. We find them in several works published during the 1880s, including Henry Sidgwick's influential *Principles of Political Economy* (1883) and Charles Devas's *The Groundwork of Economics* (1883). The latter uses the Latin variant that later became commonplace.

This rational economic agent became a fundamental building block of economics, demanding goods and services as a utility-maximizing consumer, and producing products and using productive resources as a profit-maximizing producer. The post–World War II period saw the economic man take his place as a creature whose habits extend to all areas of life, a transformation that helped expand the domain of economics far beyond its original boundaries.

SEE ALSO Smith's *Wealth of Nations* (1776), Utilitarianism (1789), The Dismal Science (1849), Scarcity and Choice (1932), The Economics of Discrimination (1957), The Rational Voter Model and the Paradox of Voting (1957), Public Choice Analysis (1962), The Economics of Crime and Punishment (1968), The Economic Analysis of Law (1973), Behavioral Economics (1979)

Philosopher and political economist John Stuart Mill, shown here, created one of the first descriptions of the rational creature known as homo economicus.

JOHN STUART MILL, M.P.

The Positive–Normative Distinction

John Stuart Mill (1806–1873), John Neville Keynes
(1852–1949), Lionel Robbins (1898–1984)

Virtually from the start, economics has involved both *positive* analysis, which develops theories and uses empirical tools to analyze economic activity, and *normative* analysis, which draws conclusions about what "should be" done based on economic insights. English lawyer Nassau Senior and philosopher-economist John Stuart Mill first brought this positive–normative distinction into economics in 1836, with Mill providing an in-depth analysis in his essay "On the Definition of Political Economy; and on the Method of Investigation Proper to It."

Mill, like Senior, distinguished between the findings of science (for example, free trade promotes growth) and the advice based on these findings (governments should pursue free trade). The science of political economy, he argued, attempts to establish laws and uniformities using facts or deductions derived from assumptions. Policy advising is not a proper part of the science; instead, it is an "art," one that determines the appropriate goals to pursue and how best to attain them. John Neville Keynes, father of John Maynard Keynes, added further nuance in 1891 by describing the "art" of economics as the proper use of positive economics to pursue normative, policy-oriented goals.

Lionel Robbins brought the positive-normative distinction home most forcefully in his *Essay on the Nature and Significance of Economic Science* (1932). Economic science, Robbins said, offers tools for evaluating alternative courses of action. But making a choice among those alternatives involves value judgments, and there is nothing in economic science that provides a basis for such judgments. This didn't mean economists couldn't take positions on policy issues; they simply couldn't wrap their positions in the cloak of "economic science."

The idea that economic science cannot address normative questions represented a stark break from the past, when ideological, ethical, and value judgments were central to economic thinking. This didn't, however, rob economics of its policy relevance. Instead, it forced economists to clarify that their policy recommendations came not from "economic science," but from value judgments about the merits of policy consequences—who gains, who loses, and how much—revealed by that scientific analysis.

SEE ALSO Scarcity and Choice (1932), Logical Positivism (1938), The "Methodology of Positive Economics" (1953)

Coalbrookdale by Night (1801) by French painter Philippe Jacques de Loutherbourg shows night workers tending a roaring furnace. For John Stuart Mill, the laws of production that govern such work can be considered positive statements, while questions about how the resulting wealth should be distributed belong to the normative realm.

Cournot's *Researches*

Antoine Augustin Cournot (1801–1877)

Some of the first modern mathematical approaches to economic questions arrived with the publication of Antoine Augustin Cournot's *Researches on the Mathematical Principles of the Theory of Wealth* in 1838. Cournot was a French mathematician and philosopher of science who spent much of his career in university administration. He made excursions into economics at multiple points over the years, but it was his first work, the *Researches*, that had the greatest influence.

The defining feature of Cournot's masterpiece was the way he explained the principles of political economy in mathematical form, primarily through the use of calculus. The book is best known today for its analysis of oligopoly—a market dominated by a small number of sellers—but Cournot's analysis included other innovations. He posited demand as an inverse relationship between quantity and price. He had an inkling that demand elasticity, or sensitivity to a change in a good's price, can vary for different products, which has important implications for how changes in market conditions, such as higher production costs, affect consumption and production. Cournot was also the first to depict demand and supply and observe how taxes on goods affect markets using graphs, providing a visual illustration of this relationship and making the analysis more precise. His most significant contribution, though, was his work on market structure. He began by studying a monopolistic market and showed how the output of goods in the market changes as you add more producers to the model. His analysis of the two-firm case—now known as Cournot duopoly—inspired Edward Chamberlin's theory of monopolistic competition, which explored competition in a market with a large number of firms selling different versions of the same basic product. John Nash and others used the Cournot duopoly as a springboard for applying non-cooperative game theory to economic questions.

Cournot's extensive use of calculus led to the book's neglect, as very few economic writers of that era could understand the mathematics. It wasn't until the pioneers of the marginal revolution referenced his work decades later that the broader economics community took notice.

SEE ALSO The Invention of Calculus (c. 1665), The Marginal Revolution (1871), The Bertrand Model (1883), The Demand–Supply Model (1890), Elasticity (1890), *The Theory of Monopolistic Competition* (1933), The Stackelberg Model (1934), Non-Cooperative Games and Nash Equilibrium (1950)

An undated photo of Antoine Augustin Cournot, one of the first to describe economic principles using advanced mathematics.

The German Historical School

Wilhelm G. F. Roscher (1817–1894), Karl Knies (1821–1898), Gustav Schmoller (1838–1917), Werner Sombart (1863–1941)

Concerns about its abstract methods led some to advocate for a more historically informed approach to economics. The German Historical School, which dominated academic economics in Germany during the second half of the nineteenth century, provided the most well-developed alternative to the classical view.

The members of the German Historical School were, first and foremost, economists, but the historical approach dates to the publication of historian and social scientist Wilhelm Roscher's *Outline of Lectures on Political Economy* (1843), with Gustav Schmoller, Karl Knies, and Werner Sombart playing leading roles in subsequent generations. Roscher largely rejected the classical economists' use of deductive logic to search for economic laws that could be generalized for any circumstance. Instead, he and his followers emphasized the role of place and time and studied the influence of the evolutionary forces. They highlighted how the economic present is conditioned by the economic past and published extensive studies of economic history. Historical and statistical analysis, rather than deductive reasoning, offered the tools for understanding the economic system. The historical economists, particularly the second generation headed by Schmoller, also criticized the laissez-faire leanings of classical economics. They favored greater governmental intervention to promote national economic development, seeing mercantilist policies, often perceived as tools for building national strength at the time, as an example of beneficial government intervention.

The historical school influenced much of Europe and had its greatest impact in Germany, where the school's members served as influential university chairs and their students dominated its civil service. The school's influence spread to England and America as well. In the late nineteenth and early twentieth centuries, English historical economics grappled with both classical and Marshallian economics, whose theories revolved around individual maximization and the logic of supply and demand. Many leading American economists of this period, particularly among those associated with the institutionalist school, had been educated in German universities and pursued research and policy agendas in keeping with the historical school's approach.

SEE ALSO Classical Political Economy (c. 1790), The Marginal Revolution (1871), Marshall's *Principles of Economics* (1890), The Economics Tripos at Cambridge (1903), Mitchell's *Business Cycles* (1913), Institutional Economics (1919), *Legal Foundations of Capitalism* (1924)

Members of the German historical school were found in academic institutions throughout Germany, including the University of Berlin (shown here in 1890), where Gustav Schmoller and Werner Sombart held professorships.

Consumer Surplus

Jules Dupuit (1804–1866)

For centuries, the question of "value" was a vexing problem for economists. Concepts such as "intrinsic value" (value that is inherent in the good), "value in use" (the value of the good when used or consumed), and "value in exchange" (the price that the good commands on the market) were scattered throughout the economics literature. But what *is* the value of a good to the person who consumes it? And how might we measure the total value that a good provides to all those who consume it?

Jules Dupuit made the first sophisticated effort to measure these consumer valuations in *De la mesure de l'utilite des travaux publics* (1844). A distinguished French civil engineer, he wanted to quantify the *benefits* of public works projects, such as roadways, to determine whether they were worthwhile, rather than simply comparing projects based on their costs, which was the standard practice. Because their utility isn't directly measurable, he decided to use monetary values as an approximation but recognized that price alone wasn't sufficient to capture a good's worth to its users.

Dupuit suggested that the net benefit received from a good could be measured by the difference between the price that consumers are willing to pay for a good and the price that they actually pay for it. In a graph of a demand curve, this is the area below the curve and above the market price. He called this "*utilité relative*," later dubbed "consumer surplus" by Alfred Marshall.

Dupuit understood that a new roadway would reduce transportation and other production-related costs for goods, leading to lower prices. This would both benefit existing consumers and raise consumption, which in turn increases the total surplus. To determine whether a project should move forward, Dupuit said, one needed to estimate the total increase in consumer surplus that it generated and compare this with the cost of the project. Dupuit also showed how this approach can be used to measure the reduction in the surplus associated with a price increase caused by a tax. His technique remains a standard method for analyzing tax policy to this day.

SEE ALSO The French Engineering Tradition (1830), Marshall's *Principles of Economics* (1890), Pareto Optimality and Efficiency (1906), Pigou's *Wealth and Welfare* (1912), The Kaldor–Hicks Efficiency Criterion (1939)

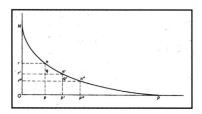

Above: *To evaluate public-works projects such as this, Dupuit calculated how they increased consumer surplus, which is represented graphically as the area below the demand curve and above the price. This demand-curve graph is a facsimile of one drawn by Dupuit.* **Main image:** *Jules Dupuit supervised the construction of Paris's sewer system. This map (1836) shows where the underground tunnels would be built.*

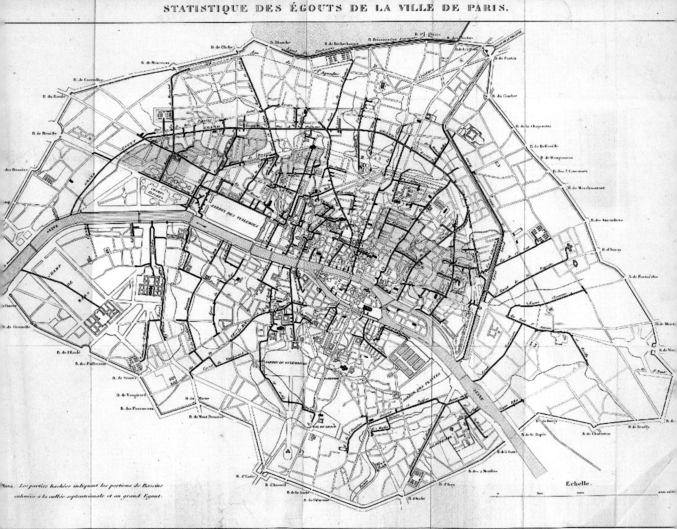

STATISTIQUE DES ÉGOUTS DE LA VILLE DE PARIS.

Échelle.

Nota. Les parties hachées indiquent les portions de Bassins
enlevées à la vallée septentrionale et au grand Égout.

The Communist Manifesto

Karl Marx (1818–1883), Friedrich Engels (1820–1895)

Karl Marx was a German-trained philosopher powerfully influenced by the ideas of Georg Wilhelm Friedrich Hegel. Unable to secure an academic appointment in Germany because of his radical views, he turned to journalism and eventually political economy. Marx's exposure to classical economics came via his friend, supporter, and eventual collaborator Friedrich Engels, an industrialist with business interests in Germany and England. With Engels, Marx wrote the *Communist Manifesto*. The tract was commissioned in 1848 by the Communist League, a secret labor association dedicated to overthrowing the wealthy ruling class and eliminating private property and social classes.

Where prevailing economic thinking rosily portrayed capitalism's potential to bring economic growth, the *Manifesto* depicted its overthrow and replacement by socialism. The *Manifesto* is grounded in Marx's theory of historical materialism. History, here, is a story of class struggle, and each stage of history is defined by the organization of production. In the capitalist stage, the proletariat, which encompasses the working class, grapples with the bourgeoisie, the owners of capital who exploit the wage earners to maximize the profits gained from production. The proletariat will eventually recognize their oppression and overthrow the capitalists through revolution, ushering in a classless society. The state would wither away, as it was no longer needed to enforce the hierarchical economic relationships of capitalism.

Though Marx and Engels concluded their book with a call to action—"Working Men of All Countries, Unite!"—the *Manifesto's* initial influence was relatively small. Their efforts to differentiate their approach from existing brands of socialism was offputting, especially to utopian socialists who advocated cooperation and gentle persuasion to achieve their ends. In the 1870s, renewed interest in Marx's ideas led to numerous translations and voluminous sales of the *Manifesto*. The spread of Marxism in the decades following the Russian Revolution of 1917 made the book required reading in many parts of the world. Its critique of capitalism and its vision for a more egalitarian society have made it relevant to those who see capitalism benefiting the few at the expense of the many, giving the *Manifesto* a place among the classics of Western political thought.

SEE ALSO Utopian Socialism (1813), Marx's *Das Kapital* (1867), The Labor Theory of Value and the Theory of Exploitation (1867), The Theory of Crisis (1867), Luxemburg's *Accumulation of Capital* (1913)

Karl Marx and Friedrich Engels collaborated on many projects, including The Communist Manifesto. *Here, they are portrayed reviewing the proofs for* Neue Rheinische Zeitung, *a daily newspaper they founded with other members of the Communist League.*

Mill's *Principles of Political Economy*

John Stuart Mill (1806–1873)

John Stuart Mill, the son of economist James Mill, was one of the towering intellects of the nineteenth century. His *Autobiography*, with its descriptions of his unusual and even tortured childhood, is a classic work in the genre. A student of Jeremy Bentham, he made contributions to philosophy that were even more influential than his economic writings and gained fame for his writings on liberalism, a school of thought that promoted individual freedom.

Mill's *Principles of Political Economy* (1848) set the tone for economic thinking for the next several decades, remaining a reference and a source of textbook instruction into the twentieth century. It expansively developed, updated, and at times corrected the Ricardian system on topics including demand and supply analysis, international trade and finance, economic growth, and the theory of wages.

Where David Ricardo was extremely abstract, Mill carefully led readers through the basic principles of economics and their application to social problems. Using Ricardo's theory of comparative advantage as a springboard, he outlined how the gains from trade were divided based on one nation's demands for imports relative to another's. Mill also put utilitarianism at center stage, focusing policy concerns on the promotion of "welfare." Though convinced that the pursuit of self-interest benefited society economically, he pointed to areas where government action could remedy the market system's limitations. He explained that the laws of production may be fixed, but those of distribution are not. This made it possible for sound economic policies to forestall the arrival of the stationary state, in which economic growth ceases, and to offer reasonable living conditions once it did arrive. He advocated for the regulation of natural monopolies, a term he coined to describe monopolies that arise due to technological factors or other circumstances that make it difficult for other producers to enter the market. He also examined situations where the effects of individual actions, such as negligence and scientific discovery, spill over on others or on society as a whole. In this, Mill's treatise highlights how the classical approach to economic policy had evolved over the past half-century and how its initial laissez-faire leanings progressively weakened.

SEE ALSO Utilitarianism (1789), Classical Political Economy (c. 1790), The Stationary State (1815), Ricardo's *Principles of Political Economy and Taxation* (1817), The Wages Fund Controversy (1866), The Benefit Principle of Taxation (1896), Pigou's *Wealth and Welfare* (1912), External Economies and Diseconomies (1912), Externalities and Market Failure (1958).

The title page of the sixth edition of Mill's Principles, *the most comprehensive exposition of classical political economy. It became the textbook of choice for economics professors into the twentieth century.*

PRINCIPLES

OF

POLITICAL ECONOMY

WITH

SOME OF THEIR APPLICATIONS TO SOCIAL PHILOSOPHY.

BY

JOHN STUART MILL.

IN TWO VOLUMES.

VOL. I.

SIXTH EDITION.

LONDON:
LONGMAN, GREEN, LONGMAN, ROBERTS & GREEN.
MDCCCLXV.

The Dismal Science

Thomas Carlyle (1795–1881), John Ruskin (1819–1900)

Karl Marx was the most famous opponent of classical political economy, but many figures associated with Romanticism during the nineteenth century also disapproved of it. Britain's most prominent arts and literary figures, including Samuel Taylor Coleridge, Robert Southey, Thomas Carlyle, Charles Dickens, and John Ruskin, opposed its materialist emphasis on productivity and growth. With its seeming support for the factory system and its long hours, low wages, and poor working conditions, political economy appeared to lead society to poverty. Its grounding in individualist utilitarianism and T. R. Malthus's grim prediction that the world's population would continually bump up against its food supply was contrary to the Romantics' belief in human perfectibility. Small wonder, then, that political economy became known as "the dismal science." Though the term first appeared in Carlyle's "Occasional Discourse on the Negro Question" (1849), where he complained that political economy offered no defense of slavery, it eventually became associated with Malthus's dismal prognostications.

Among these Romantic critics, it was Ruskin who had the most enduring legacy. Ruskin found inspiration in Carlyle, who criticized classical economists for promoting the production of wealth without considering the accompanying political and ethical obligations. Critical of political economy's pretensions to science, Ruskin found fault with its claims that natural economic laws somehow justified laissez-faire policies and impoverished conditions. Political economy's depiction of the "economic man," praise for the division of labor, and individualistic approach to social organization didn't sit well with him either. For Ruskin, man is essentially moral and social rather than selfishly materialistic. The value of a good shouldn't be related to the costs of production or the pricing of the marketplace, but to its ability to support life. In Ruskin's words, "There is no wealth but life. Life, including all of its powers of love, of joy, and of admiration."

Though these Romantic critiques resonated with the working classes, they found little support among upper-class readers. Even so, Ruskin's ideas in particular powerfully influenced subsequent heterodox economists including Arnold Toynbee and J. A. Hobson, as well as founders of the British Labour Party.

SEE ALSO Classical Political Economy (c. 1790), The Malthusian Population Theory (1798), *Homo Economicus* (1836), *Lectures on the Industrial Revolution* (1884), The Oxford Approach to Welfare (1914), Galbraith's *The Affluent Society* (1958)

A portrait of Thomas Carlyle, the essayist who first labeled economics "the dismal science" (1879).

E. HADER pinxit 1879. Gesetzlich geschützt

T. Carlyle

Phot. u. Verl. v. Sophus Williams, Berlin W.

Gossen's Two Laws

Hermann Heinrich Gossen (1810–1858)

A one-time civil servant who dabbled in the insurance business, Rhinelander Hermann Heinrich Gossen authored a wide-ranging treatise, *Die Entwickelung der Gesetze des menschlichen Verkehrs* (1854), believing that he would revolutionize social science as Copernicus had the natural sciences. In the process, Gossen made important contributions to the theory of consumer behavior, which few would seriously analyze until the late nineteenth century.

Gossen's first major conclusion was that devoting additional resources to an activity yields progressively smaller amounts of additional pleasure. This insight, which harkens back to Daniel Bernoulli's theory of expected value and his claim that the pleasure from additional income falls as income increases, is known as "Gossen's first law," or the law of diminishing marginal utility.

Using his first law, Gossen developed his "second law," which describes what happens when an individual has optimized her use of resources. This optimal use occurs when the additional utility, or pleasure, received from allocating a unit of a resource for one activity is identical to the pleasure received from allocating that same unit to any other activity. An individual has maximized her utility, for example, when the last dollar spent on clothing generates the same utility increase as the last dollar spent on food; if it doesn't, she could continue to increase her utility by spending less money on a good that provided lower utility and more money on a good that gave higher utility. In accordance with Gossen's *first* law, these incremental increases in pleasure will eventually become equal via those spending adjustments.

Gossen had anticipated by nearly two decades the main findings of W. S. Jevons, whose theory of consumer behavior, including the principle of diminishing marginal utility, underpins the modern theory of demand. But because of the limited circulation of Gossen's book, almost no one was aware of his contribution. In fact, Gossen took it out of print himself not long after its publication. It was only when Jevons was given a copy and acknowledged Gossen's priority in the second edition of his own book that his name and two laws became more widely known in the field.

SEE ALSO The Invention of Calculus (c. 1665), Bernoulli on Expected Utility (1738), Diminishing Returns (1815), Jevons's *Theory of Political Economy* (1871), The Demand–Supply Model (1890), Revealed Preference Theory (1938)

Gossen's two laws explain how the interaction of utility and price determines a shopper's purchases, such as her choice of hats from the wide selection of styles featured in this nineteenth-century advertisement.

CHAPEAU en paille manille ou paille de riz, garni d'une ruche de mousseline de soie plissée, guirlande de roses formant aigrette et nœud de ruban moiré sur le côté **17.50**

CHAPEAU en paille légère, la passe garnie de pavots de soie coquillée et de ruban moiré formant nœud sur le côté, aigrette de feuillage.

Prix.. **21** fr.

CHAPEAU en paille anglaise, garni mousseline plissée, fleurs en soie et ruban satin, aigrette de feuillage sur le côté.... **8.50**

CHAPEAU en paille de soie, la passe garnie d'une ruche de taffetas plissé, cache-peigne en pareil et aigrette de pavot soie avec feuillage................ **23** fr.

TOQUE forme nouvelle, le bord recouvert d'un tissu pailleté, la calotte en taffetas plissé, garni d'une aigrette de fleurs et la passe entourée d'un joli feuillage...... **14.50**

CHAPEAU forme élégante en paille fine, avec bord fantaisie, garni d'un joli ruban moiré envers satin, aigrette de pavots soie sur le côté, la passe relevée par un nœud de ruban avec fleurs

Prix. **25** fr.

CHAPEAU en paille de riz fine, garni d'un joli ruban moiré et d'un panache de plumes autruche qualité extra. **15.75**

CHAPEAU canotier en paille satin avec ou sans fond verni noir, plumes couteaux sur le côté................. 2.95 et **2.45**
En paille manille .... 4.75 et 3.90

CHAPEAU pour fillette, la calotte évidée, garni d'un joli nœud de taffetas tout soie
A la Samaritaine...... .... **8.75**

The Falling Rate of Profit

Karl Marx (1818–1883)

In *Wealth of Nations*, Adam Smith theorized that the rate of profit in a capitalist economy tends to fall. This principle remained a centerpiece of economic thinking through much of the nineteenth century, but there were disagreements about why this fall would occur. Smith believed that competition would eventually cause profitable new investment opportunities to dry up. David Ricardo pointed to diminishing returns in agriculture, which meant that returns in manufacturing would also decrease, as the rate of profit in all industries tends to equalize. Unlike Smith and Ricardo, Karl Marx offered an explanation that centered on the forces of competition and technological progress.

Writing in his *Grundrisse* (1857), Marx described two forms of labor: living labor, which comes from workers, and "dead" labor, which is embodied in machinery and materials. For Marx, living labor creates all new value, including the "surplus value" that becomes the capitalist's profit. The competitive pressures of capitalism create the need to increase the productivity of labor. The development of new technology can accomplish this, but this new machinery displaces labor. As the share of living labor in the production process falls, so too does the surplus from production and the profit flowing to the capitalist. Other factors, such as cheaper production inputs made available from international trade, could increase the rate of profit, but these effects were temporary and couldn't stop the downward trend. For Marx, the falling rate of profit was "the most important law in political economy," as it kindled both technological progress and the swelling unemployment that would lead to the violent overthrow of capitalism.

Empirical evidence, such as the fact that average business profits have remained strong over time, and modern theories of economic growth have largely discredited this theory, but it attracted attention in the nineteenth century because of the rapidity with which machines were displacing labor. For the classical economists, the falling rate of profit was the force behind the eventual onset of the stationary state. For Marx, however, the falling rate of profit contained the seeds of his theory of crisis and the end of capitalism.

SEE ALSO Rent and the Theory of Surplus (1662), Smith's *Wealth of Nations* (1776), Classical Political Economy (c. 1790), The Stationary State (1815), The Machinery Question (1817), Ricardo's *Principles of Political Economy and Taxation* (1817), The Theory of Crisis (1867), The Harrod–Domar Growth Model (1939), The Solow–Swan Growth Model (1956), Endogenous Growth Theory (1986)

The equipment shown in this 1957 photo of an iron foundry, taken a century after Marx wrote his Grundrisse, *is an example of the kind of machinery that can displace workers as capitalists attempt (futilely, Marx said) to safeguard their profits.*

The Iron Law of Wages

Ferdinand Lassalle (1825–1864)

Ricardian economics offered dim prospects for the laboring classes. Though wages could grow in times of prosperity, Ricardo and other nineteenth-century classical economists believed that they would fall back to subsistence levels, thanks to the significant ongoing population growth predicted by T. R. Malthus and diminishing returns in agriculture. German socialist Ferdinand Lassalle called this dynamic the "iron law of wages," also known as the subsistence theory of wages, using it as a rationale to replace capitalism. Lassalle, though, was no Marxist. Marx completely rejected the Malthusian population principle and believed that capitalism was destined for destruction. Lassalle argued instead for political reforms that would extend voting rights to all, rather than merely the landed class. Voters could then create pressure for policies that would bring structural changes to the economy. Lassalle, in particular, wanted the state to help establish producer cooperatives. These cooperatives would allow workers to receive a share of their employers' profits in addition to their wages, offering them the prospect of achieving a reasonable standard of living.

It's possible to argue that Lassalle misunderstood Malthus and Ricardo's views about wages. Though they believed that capitalism would push wages to subsistence levels, they didn't consider *physical* subsistence as the relevant minimum. Instead, they proposed a *psychological* notion of subsistence. As incomes rose during good times, people would develop tastes for nicer things, which would elevate their standard of what constituted "subsistence." When wages once again began to fall, they would not be willing to supply their labor for less than this minimum. Thus, if wage increases could be sustained for long periods of time, the minimum level to which wages could eventually fall would actually leave the laboring classes with a reasonable standard of living.

You can hear echoes of the iron law of wages in today's debates over the minimum wage. In times of economic prosperity, the legal minimum is often irrelevant, as strong demand for labor boosts wages above this level, but when the demand for labor weakens, wages are pushed toward that minimum. Concerns about whether the minimum wage provides for an adequate standard of living have become flashpoints for political controversy.

SEE ALSO Smith's *Wealth of Nations* (1776), Classical Political Economy (c. 1790), The Malthusian Population Theory (1798), The Stationary State (1815), Ricardo's *Principles of Political Economy and Taxation* (1817), *Illustrations of Political Economy* (1832), The Wages Fund Controversy (1866)

According to the iron law of wages, the wages of workers, such as these women employed in a coal mine in late nineteenth-century France, will be forced down to the subsistence level in the long run.

Index Numbers

William Stanley Jevons (1835–1882)

William Stanley Jevons is best known for developing a utility-based theory of consumer choice, but he was also an accomplished statistician. In 1863, he sought to determine whether recent discoveries of gold in California and Australia had reduced its value. At the time, there was no method for determining such variations. Had increased gold supplies caused its price to fall relative to other goods, or did factors affecting markets for other goods cause their prices to rise relative to gold? Developing a fixed measure that would allow them to differentiate between a change in the value of goods and general changes in the price level had mystified economic thinkers for two centuries.

Jevons started with the premise that the value of gold is given by the amount of other goods that it could purchase. A change in the purchasing power of gold over time would indicate a change in its value. To show that the purchasing power of gold had weakened, Jevons needed to see if prices had risen on average. Using data gathered from magazine articles and newspapers, he assembled information about prices for thirty-nine products, including copper, timber, wool, and beef, from 1845 to 1862. Jevons calculated the ratios of the prices between the base year and the year in question for each product. He then took the geometric mean, which better accounts for the potentially vast differences in prices across different goods when computing an average value of these ratios. This single number would show the change in the average price of these products from one year to another. With this calculation, Jevons showed that on average, prices had risen by nine percent, meaning the value of gold had fallen by an equivalent amount following these new gold discoveries.

Economists and statisticians such as Étienne Laspeyres, Hermann Paasche, and Irving Fisher soon developed price indices that used more sophisticated statistical techniques to better measure inflation and deflation. John Maynard Keynes, writing seventy years later, said that Jevons's contribution moved the subject forward more than all subsequent efforts combined and provided the inspiration for much of the work that followed, including the consumer price index.

SEE ALSO Empiricism and Science (1620), The Marginal Revolution (1871), Jevons's *Theory of Political Economy* (1871), National Income Accounting (1934), The Consumer Price Index (1946)

A *table from* William Stanley Jevons's A Serious Fall in the Value of Gold Ascertained and Its Social Effects Set Forth (1863), *showing the average prices of various commodities in the mid-1800s. Jevons used these data to determine whether the purchasing power of gold had changed.*

Of the Average Yearly Prices.

·hly prices obtained as described in the above list, the simple arithmetical mean prices fc
·ulations were made to prevent error. The following table was thus prepared, and fo

TABLE showing the Average Price of each of 39 chief Commodities, during each of the Years 1845-62.

845.	1846.	1847.	1848.	1849.	1850.	1851.	1852.	1853.	1854.	1855.	1856.	1857.	1858.	1859.	
9·06	59·39	59·69	59·46	59·64	59·97	60·98	60·53	61·42	61·54	61·39	61·34	61·78	61·30	61·98	
7·0	94·8	90·5	77·5	79·7	80·5	84·8	90·2	115·0	121·0	118·3	132·4	136·1	118·8	131·4	1
7·8	91·5	96·8	85·2	83·6	85·1	84·9	96·7	116·0	126·0	126·0	118·3	123·3	108·2	109·5	1
8·5	19·0	18·7	16·9	15·8	17·7	17·3	17·8	23·9	23·9	23·4	25·1	24·3	22·3	22·5	
5·0	191·5	194·5	144·0	124·8	118·0	111·4	124·0	185·0	198·3	171·3	181·1	168·4	143·7	140·2	1
6·2	100·4	95·8	82·5	74·7	70·6	66·5	72·6	96·7	116·0	100·8	114·2	106·5	90·2	76·2	
4·3	31·6	30·2	29·5	32·0	32·4	32·0	29·1	35 6	33·1	33 4	37·3	39·4	33 3	32·9	
8·8	30·7	36·7	32·6	32·0	30·3	28·1	29·0	37·5	47·5	44·0	42·5	44·3	39·6	45·2	
4·8	24·6	26·3	23·1	26·4	32·0	31·7	27·8	29·5	35·9	39·5	37·0	38·0	31·2	28·6	
0·4	43·7	48·6	46·8	33·9	37·5	38·2	39·1	50·4	64·2	57·0	54·4	58·6	52·0	55·3	
6·4	6·6	6·0	4·8	4·6	4·9	5·7	5·4	6·4	7·5	8·5	10·5	13·6	11·1	11·2	
1·7	11·0	10·4	10·3	9·6	9·5	10·0	9·6	12·2	13·5	13 5	14·5	19·3	15·1	15·6	
6·0	85·0	85·3	73 3	67·3	61·5	60·0	59·6	78·2	82·0	80·5	72·1	71·8	64·2	68·4	
8·70	8·08	7·46	6·69	6·28	6·69	6·73	6·42	7·26	8·23	7·71	8·89	8·71	8·75	7·15	
4·1	4·0	4·0	3·4	3·4	3·9	4·6	4·9	6·4	6·0	4·1	4·4	4·8	5·0	4·6	
$4\frac{3}{8}$	$4\frac{7}{8}$	$6\frac{3}{8}$	$4\frac{1}{4}$	$5\frac{1}{8}$	$7\frac{1}{4}$	$5\frac{3}{4}$	$5\frac{3}{8}$	$5\frac{3}{8}$	$5\frac{3}{8}$	$5\frac{3}{4}$	6	$7\frac{1}{4}$	$6\frac{1}{4}$	$6\frac{1}{2}$	
$6\frac{3}{8}$	$7\frac{3}{8}$	$7\frac{5}{8}$	6	$5\frac{1}{2}$	$7\frac{7}{8}$	$7\frac{1}{2}$	7	7	7	7	$7\frac{1}{8}$	$8\frac{3}{4}$	$8\frac{1}{4}$	$8\frac{3}{8}$	
3	$3\frac{3}{8}$	$4\frac{1}{2}$	$3\frac{1}{4}$	$3\frac{7}{8}$	$5\frac{1}{8}$	4	$3\frac{3}{4}$	$3\frac{1}{2}$	$3\frac{1}{2}$	$3\frac{7}{8}$	$4\frac{3}{8}$	$5\frac{3}{8}$	$4\frac{3}{4}$	$4\frac{3}{4}$	
5·6	15·3	13·5	10·5	11·6	13·3	13·9	15·0	17·8	13·9	13·8	17·6	20·2	15·3	18 6	
2·8	11·9	10·1	10·2	10 5	11·8	13·0	12 6	13 5	13·6	12·5	17·3	22·4	16·4	15·8	
6 2	49·3	49·7	39·1	36·9	41·5	44 5	46·9	(48 3)	(57·5)	(54·8)	53·2	54·9	55·4	70·8	
8·8	32·5	38·2	32·0	30·1	30·8	29·2	31·7	37·4	58·5	47 0	35·7	34·1	29·5	29·2	
0·8	54·7	69·7	50·5	44·3	40·3	38·5	40·7	53·3	72·4	74·7	69·2	56 3	44·2	43·7	
1·7	32·7	44·2	31·5	27·7	23·4	24·7	28·5	33·2	36·0	34·7	41·1	42·1	34·7	33·5	
2·5	23·7	28·7	20·5	17·5	16·4	18·6	19·1	21 0	27·9	27·4	25·2	25·0	24·5	23·2	
2·3	35·0	49·0	30·4	26·2	23·3	25·5	29·8	35·0	45·8	45·7	45·0	38·3	32·3	32·3	
9·0	38·9	50·5	36·7	30·6	26·8	28·6	32 3	40·1	47·3	46·5	43·9	43·0	41·9	42·3	
8·7	49·0	51·4	39·2	31·5	27·2	27·2	30·6	38·5	45·6	43·3	41·6	41·3	42·9	39·7	
2·3	69·4	61·0	64·0	62·0	61·1	68·0	70·0	86·6	80·2	87·7	90·4	68·5	69·6	72·1	
6·5	94·5	81·5	85·5	79·5	73·5	76·0	81·5	98·0	101·5	107·0	107·5	89·5	89·5	93·5	
8·4	32·7	30·8	26·6	27·9	25·0	24·3	27·1	31·4	34·4	26·6	26·9	27·4	28·5	28·0	
0·7	40 6	47·3	43 4	38·8	37·3	35·9	36·4	44·4	49·2	49·7	50·4	50·4	50·2	51·4	
7·4	50·8	52·6	52 0	43·7	42·3	42·6	42·6	50·9	50 3	50·9	54 1	58·8	53·9	57·2	
6·8	51·6	53·9	52·2	45·8	42·8	38·8	38·5	45·1	46·7	47·4	52·4	54·6	44·1	48·8	
6·7	82·9	87·8	81·3	63·2	69·9	75·1	74·2	90·6	98·9	100·4	105·3	106·9	107·6	106·5	1
2·5	34·2	28·5	23·7	25·7	26·0	25·4	22·8	24·7	22·9	26·3	29·3	37·3	27·7	26·5	
3·06	2·93	3·93	3·27	2·53	2·46	2·49	2·17	3·10	4·38	3·71	3·38	4·25	3·53	3·43	
9·9	9 2	9·0	7·7	8 6	10·9	10·6	8·6	11·5	11·7	9·0	8·9	13·2	10·3	12·8	
3·4	3·0	3·0	2·8	3·1	3·6	3·3	3·9	4·3	4·8	5·0	5·2	5·2	5·0	4·5	

* Average of first nine months.

The Wages Fund Controversy

Thomas Robert Malthus (1766–1834), William Thomas Thornton (1813–1880), Francis D. Longe (1831–1910)

Classical economists believed that the forces of supply and demand determined the prices of products, but their views on wage determination went in an entirely different direction. Adam Smith believed that the total pool of wages available in the economy was determined by the wages fund, the share of accumulated capital that an employer set aside to pay his workers. This view reflected how wages were paid in agrarian societies; landowners used proceeds from the previous season's crop sales to fund their workers' salaries during the next growing season.

Nineteenth-century economists, including David Ricardo, T. R. Malthus, and John Stuart Mill, later wedded Smith's notion of the wages fund to Malthus's prediction of rapid population growth to create a new theory. Because the wages fund has already been established when a new production period begins, wages will depend on the size of the population; the average wage would equal the wages fund divided by the working-age population. Though economic growth could raise the wages fund from year to year, population growth would force wages downward toward subsistence levels—what Ferdinand Lassalle labeled the Iron Law of Wages. This law formed a powerful argument against labor unions, as the fixed size of the fund meant that there wasn't enough money for wage increases. Indeed, Mill saw population control as perhaps the only way to move working-class wages above their meager levels.

In 1866, Francis Longe and W. T. Thornton published a pamphlet that challenged the wages-fund doctrine. Longe and Thornton argued that wages in many industries, such as retail and manufacturing, actually came from ongoing revenues, meaning that the funds available for wages could vary and that unions could justifiably demand higher wages. Mill famously acknowledged the validity of this challenge and recanted his support for the wages-fund doctrine. This left economics without a well-developed theory of wage determination for more than thirty years until John Bates Clark offered a new theory in 1899. Clark's theory, which stated that a worker's wages are determined by the value of the output she produces, became the basis for modern analysis of wage determination.

SEE ALSO Smith's *Wealth of Nations* (1776), The Malthusian Population Theory (1798), Ricardo's *Principles of Political Economy and Taxation* (1817), Mill's *Principles of Political Economy* (1848), The Iron Law of Wages (1862), Clark's *Distribution of Wealth* (1899)

This 1851 etching, inspired by Thomas Robert Malthus's writings on population growth, shows an overcrowded London.

Marx's *Das Kapital*

Karl Marx (1818–1883)

Karl Marx envisioned the violent overthrow of capitalism and its replacement by communism, where the tools of production and returns to production belong to all, but his *Communist Manifesto* and mid-century revolutionary movements across Europe failed to bring about this change. He then embarked on a deeper study of political economy, the culmination of which was *Das Kapital: Kritik der politischen Ökonomie*. Originally conceived as a six-volume work, Marx was able to publish only the first volume, in 1867, before his death sixteen years later, leaving his friend and collaborator, Friedrich Engels, to arrange the publication of volumes II and III from Marx's notes.

Marx's goal in *Das Kapital* was "to lay bare the economic law of motion of modern society." An economic determinist, he believed that the economic environment at each stage in history conditioned life and thought, a view called historical materialism. Here, economic conditions shaped tastes, attitudes, and actions, laws and political organization, and even the individual psyche. For Marx, classical economics was simply an outgrowth of and apology for the capitalist environment. Even capitalists themselves could hardly be blamed for exploiting their workers, since this was the only option under capitalism. Though he believed capitalism would destroy itself, he considered it to be a beneficial force, as it increased productivity manyfold and paved the way for a higher standard of living when communism arrived.

As its subtitle indicates, *Das Kapital* is a "critique of political economy" and a response to Smith, Ricardo, and Mill's work. It lays out Marx's theories of value and distribution, production, money and interest, and capital accumulation, among other topics. Although he reached very different conclusions about the path of capitalism than did his contemporaries, he drew heavily on the classical tradition, leading some to consider Marx, its harshest critic, to be the last of the great classical economists. *Das Kapital*'s influence has been enormous. It inspired the communist economic systems in the former Soviet Union and beyond and the development of welfare systems in capitalist countries, and it informs both evolutionary theory and concerns about artificial intelligence, with its enormous labor-saving potential.

SEE ALSO Smith's *Wealth of Nations* (1776), Classical Political Economy (c. 1790), Ricardo's *Principles of Political Economy and Taxation* (1817), *The Communist Manifesto* (1848), Mill's *Principles of Political Economy* (1848), The Labor Theory of Value and the Theory of Exploitation (1867), The Theory of Crisis (1867), Luxemburg's *Accumulation of Capital* (1913)

Karl Marx vividly described the forces underpinning capitalism and traced capitalism's path toward destruction in his groundbreaking book, Das Kapital.

The Labor Theory of Value and the Theory of Exploitation

Karl Marx (1818–1883)

Karl Marx criticized many aspects of classical political economy in *Das Kapital* (1867), but he agreed with a number of classical writers on the labor theory of value. For Marx, labor was both the essence of commodities (they are, in effect, crystallized labor) and the source of all value. Any surplus arising from production naturally belongs to the worker who provides the labor, but the capitalist is able to use his power in the labor market to secure this surplus for himself. Marx formulated his theory of exploitation to explain how this occurs.

In a capitalist society, the laboring classes rely on the capitalists to equip them with the tools of production. To receive wages, workers must offer their labor to capitalist employers. Though six hours of labor per day may be sufficient for the worker to provide a living for himself and his family, which Marx called "necessary labor," the capitalist can compel him to work ten hours per day as a condition for employment. These additional four hours are what Marx labeled "surplus labor." The capitalist provides the worker with an income sufficient for subsistence, keeping the remainder of the value generated by that worker—the surplus—for himself as profit.

Though growing demand for labor puts upward pressure on wages, this drives the capitalist to replace workers with machinery to remain competitive in the marketplace. This displacement of labor creates a growing "reserve army of the unemployed," which reinforces the capitalist's power to dictate terms to labor. If a worker doesn't like the wage offered, there are many unemployed workers who will gladly accept the job on the available terms. This pushes wages toward the subsistence level. For Marx, the surplus population that Thomas Malthus described in his *Essay on Population* wasn't in fact a surplus of people, but instead a "surplus" of labor power created by the inherent dynamics of capitalism from which the capitalists benefited. This aspect of Marx's theory continues to resonate as perceptions that the middle class is disappearing and concerns about the increasing concentration of wealth have become topics of serious discussion and debate.

SEE ALSO Rent and the Theory of Surplus (1662), Classical Political Economy (c. 1790), The Malthusian Population Theory (1798), The Labor Theory of Value (1821), *The Communist Manifesto* (1848), Marx's *Das Kapital* (1867), Luxemburg's *Accumulation of Capital* (1913).

For Marx, capitalists reaped their profits by exploiting the working class, a dynamic that is depicted in this Victorian-era cartoon.

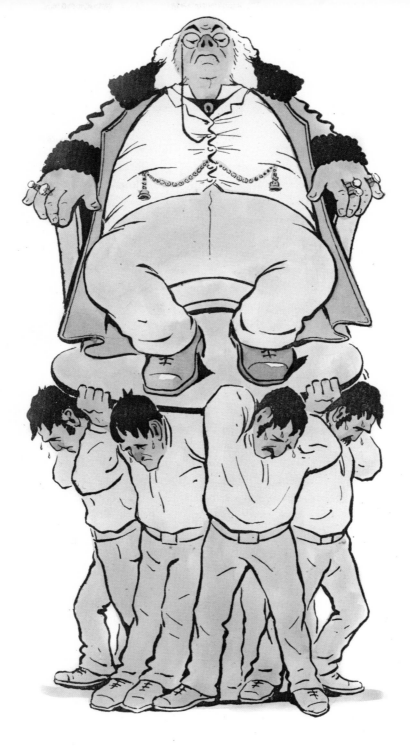

CAPITAL & LABOUR.

The Theory of Crisis

Karl Marx (1818–1883)

Most economists today believe that a market economy, backed by sound economic policies, can continue to grow indefinitely, with some ups and downs along the way. But this wasn't always the case. Adam Smith and the classical economists envisioned an eventual end to the economic growth process and the onset of a persistent stationary state. Marx's view of history led to an even more dramatic conclusion: increasingly severe crises that would lead to the eventual replacement of the capitalist system by communism.

Though Marx's *Das Kapital* (1867) didn't paint a clear picture of how capitalism would meet its end, he described two particular dynamics at work. First, because the parts of a fully evolved capitalist system are often highly dependent on one another, the effects of downturns in some sectors of the economy spread quickly. This would result in increasingly severe and frequent business cycles—repeated periods of economic expansion and contraction.

The second force at work is the increasing concentration of capitalist production. As the market becomes dominated by a smaller number of increasingly large firms, growing unemployment and the deteriorating situation of those who remain employed spread "misery, oppression, slavery, degradation, exploitation." The working class will eventually revolt against their capitalist masters. "The knell of capitalist private property sounds," and "the expropriators are expropriated," ushering in communism. Under communism, the people would collectively own the means of production, including land and factories, and have free access to any goods they need.

For Marx, the capitalist system and the larger natural laws governing the course of history made this violent overthrow of capitalism inevitable. Efforts to improve working conditions, such as laws promoting higher wages, would be ineffective at best and potentially would even hasten capitalism's demise by further encouraging employers to replace labor with machinery.

In time, however, Marx's followers, observing capitalism's staying power, modified his theory, believing that income redistribution allowed capitalists to placate the laboring class and keep the revolution at bay. Even so, some would argue that recent corporate outsourcing and wage stagnation resonate with Marx's understanding of the capitalist dynamic, helping socialist ideas gain popularity in today's political sphere.

SEE ALSO Smith's *Wealth of Nations* (1776), Classical Political Economy (c. 1790), Say's Law (1803), Underconsumption (1804), The Machinery Question (1817), The Falling Rate of Profit (1857), Tugan-Baranovsky and the Trade Cycle (1894)

Marx's depiction of the end of capitalism was compelling to many, but it also was a target of criticism. This cartoon depicts the views of his detractors, who believed that communism would destroy a system that seemed to bring prosperity.

VOL. XIII.—No 317.

APRIL 4, 1883.

Price, 10 Cents.

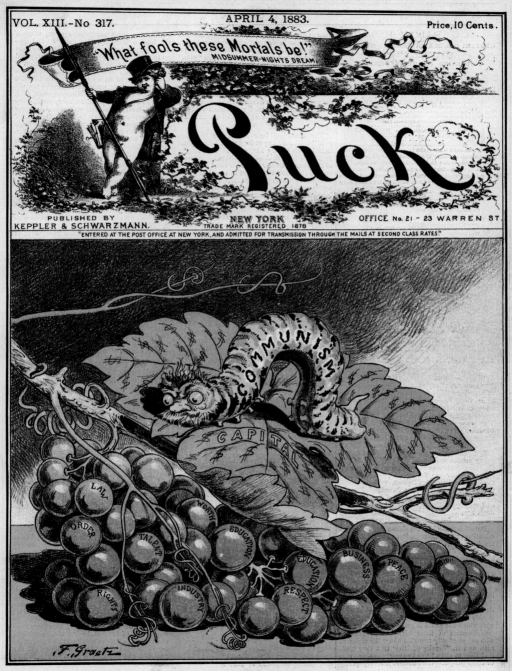

"What fools these Mortals be!"
MIDSUMMER-NIGHTS DREAM.

Puck

PUBLISHED BY
KEPPLER & SCHWARZMANN.

NEW YORK
TRADE MARK REGISTERED 1878

OFFICE No. 21 - 23 WARREN ST.

"ENTERED AT THE POST OFFICE AT NEW YORK, AND ADMITTED FOR TRANSMISSION THROUGH THE MAILS AT SECOND CLASS RATES."

A DESTRUCTIVE WORM.

The Marginal Revolution

Léon Walras (1834–1910), William Stanley Jevons (1835–1882), Carl Menger (1840–1921), Alfred Marshall (1842–1924), John Bates Clark (1847–1938)

When the Political Economy Club of London met in 1876 to celebrate the centenary of *Wealth of Nations*'s publication, its members suggested that the great work of developing political economy into a science was largely finished. But this optimism masked discontent among a new generation of thinkers. Though not entirely dismissive of classical thinking, they had a growing sense that classical political economy lacked the precision of other scientific fields and, at times, pointed in the wrong direction, whether in its explanation of price determination or its advocacy for laissez-faire policies. By 1876, a different approach to many central questions in economics was under way.

Known as the "marginal revolution," this transformation began in the 1870s with W. S. Jevons's *The Theory of Political Economy* offering the opening salvo (1871). Scholars including Jevons, Carl Menger, Léon Walras, Alfred Marshall, and John Bates Clark constructed a theoretical framework based on the maximizing choices of individual consumers and producers. Often employing calculus, which was now more widely understood, their work highlighted the influence that even marginal, or infinitesimal, changes in incentives will have on individuals' production and consumption decisions and market activity. In doing so, it provided greater depth of insight into many central economic questions, from wage and price determination to how producers and consumers respond to changes in market conditions.

The extent to which this marginalist approach was truly revolutionary is a matter of some debate among modern historians. Scholars such as Augustin Cournot, Johann Heinrich von Thünen, and Hermann Heinrich Gossen had anticipated several of these developments, and even those who directly developed this new approach were divided on how far it deviated from the classical tradition. What emerged, though, was a new foundation for the basic economics of demand and supply that, with its grounding in mathematical logic, put economics on firmer scientific footing and laid the foundation for contemporary economic analysis.

SEE ALSO The Invention of Calculus (c. 1665), Smith's *Wealth of Nations* (1776), Classical Political Economy (c. 1790), The Political Economy Club (1821), Thünen's *Isolated State* (1826), Gossen's Two Laws (1854), Jevons's *Theory of Political Economy* (1871), Menger's *Principles of Economics* (1871), The Austrian School (1871), Walras's *Elements of Pure Economics* (1874), Marshall's *Principles of Economics* (1890), Clark's *Distribution of Wealth* (1899)

The marginal revolution shifted the focus of economic analysis, moving the field toward questions about the decisions that individual consumers and producers make in the marketplace.

Jevons's *Theory of Political Economy*

William Stanley Jevons (1835–1882)

William Stanley Jevons inaugurated the marginal revolution in Britain with his book *The Theory of Political Economy*, published in 1871. Jevons, whose interests also included meteorology and chemistry, sought to put economics on a more scientific footing, combining differential calculus and other mathematical methods with utilitarianism to theorize about individual behavior in the marketplace. He is best known for deriving the conditions for when consumers have maximized their utility. What matters to consumers is the "final degree of utility" (now called marginal utility) received from a good. For utility to be maximized, the ratio of the marginal utilities received from two goods must be equal to their relative prices—the equivalent of Gossen's second law.

For Jevons, the most important result of this analysis was a new theory of value. He demonstrated that the relative prices of any two goods will be determined strictly by the marginal utilities that consumers receive from each of those goods. He saw this as evidence that the production costs play no direct role in determining goods' prices; classical theories of value, which cited labor and costs as the main price determinants, needed to be replaced. Using the framework of marginal utility, Jevons also offered one of the earliest theories of labor supply. An additional hour of work generates positive utility because an individual can use income earned from work to purchase goods, as well as negative utility from the labor itself. The worker will supply additional hours of labor as long as the increase in utility gained from working is greater than the cost in utility.

The Theory of Political Economy was written in haste and is less well developed than other classic texts of the marginal revolution. Because of this, Jevons's theory of price determination fell short in several respects, such as his insistence that production costs don't significantly affect prices. The work of Marshall, Walras, and others would supersede Jevons's theory. Even so, his basic economics of utility maximization remains at the heart of today's theory of consumer behavior, and his insistence that economics become a mathematical science set the tone for the marginal revolution.

SEE ALSO The Invention of Calculus (c. 1665), Bernoulli on Expected Utility (1738), Utilitarianism (1789), The Labor Theory of Value and the Theory of Exploitation (1867), The Marginal Revolution (1871), Walras's *Elements of Pure Economics* (1874), Marshall's *Principles of Economics* (1890), Ordinal Utility (1893), The Hicks–Allen Consumer Theory (1934)

William Stanley Jevons, a leading figure of the marginal revolution, sketched out a theory of consumer behavior rooted in the calculus of utility maximization.

Menger's *Principles of Economics*

Carl Menger (1840–1921)

Like W. S. Jevons, Carl Menger, a professor at the University of Vienna, was a harsh critic of the classical theory of value, which proposed that value was determined by the costs of production. His *Principles of Economics*, published in 1871, attempted to remedy this perceived shortcoming by proposing a subjective theory of value, one that made the prices of goods depend on consumers' desires for the products.

Unlike Jevons, Menger eschewed both mathematics and references to utility, formulating his analysis in terms of "unmet needs" and the "intensity of desire" to fulfill those needs. He hypothesized that individuals will allocate their income across goods in a way that fulfills the greatest unmet need. The value of any good, therefore, is determined by the amount of satisfaction that the consumer would lose if the final unit of the good were unavailable. This result is analytically very similar to Jevons's theory that the ratio of the "final degree of utility" to price will be equal for all goods that a consumer purchases. Plus, it allowed Menger to solve a problem that had perplexed economists for centuries: the diamond-water paradox, which asks why diamonds are so much more valuable than water yet so much less essential to life. Because diamonds are very scarce, the consumer's unmet need is great, meaning that an additional diamond is highly valued. Water, in contrast, is plentiful relative to unmet need, and thus additional amounts of water would command a low price.

Menger also used this theory to explain the value of inputs into the production process. Inputs, he argued, receive their value from the goods that they help to create. The value of a shoemaker, for example, is given by the satisfaction lost by consumers if he didn't produce shoes. In the end, then, all value in the economy is derived from consumers' subjective valuations of the goods they consume. That value, in turn, resides in the minds of consumers and so cannot be ascertained outside the marketplace. This subjective approach to value became a central tenet of the Austrian School, with Menger revered as one of its founders.

SEE ALSO Utilitarianism (1789), Classical Political Economy (c. 1790), The Marginal Revolution (1871), Jevons's *Theory of Political Economy* (1871), The Austrian School (1871), The *Methodenstreit* (1883), The Socialist Calculation Debate (1920), Hayek's "Use of Knowledge in Society" (1945)

Carl Menger's subjective theory of value explains why diamonds, such as this 38-carat stone from Indonesia, are considered more valuable than water.

The Austrian School

Carl Menger (1840–1921), Eugen von Böhm-Bawerk (1851–1914), Friedrich von Wieser (1851–1926)

The publication of Carl Menger's *Principles of Economics* in 1871 marks the beginning of the "Austrian" School of economics, so named because its origins lay in Vienna. The school's most prominent early members included Menger, Eugen von Böhm-Bawerk, and Friedrich von Wieser. With Böhm-Bawerk and Wieser's influence on subsequent generations of students, including Ludwig von Mises and Friedrich von Hayek, a true "school" of thought emerged. Its members advanced the development of marginal analysis but, at the same time, pushed it in a different direction from that proposed by other marginalist thinkers.

While many classical and modern economists believe that value is measurable, reflected in prices and costs, the Austrian School adopts a "subjectivist" approach: they insist that only the individual knows the value that she places on a good, and market prices simply reflect the aggregation of these subjective values. These individual subjective values, in turn, are governed by opportunity cost, a concept later developed by von Wieser that denotes the individual's perception of what is sacrificed in pursuing a particular course of action. It is impossible for external observers to discern these opportunity costs or the values that individuals place on goods.

The Austrians' subjectivism left them suspicious of government interference in the marketplace. Markets develop to bring order out of the actions of disparate individuals, and competition typically ensures that market outcomes align with individual interests. The Austrians acknowledge that forces such as uncertainty cause markets to work imperfectly, but because government authorities cannot know individuals' exact valuations and costs, even policies designed to improve market performance are problematic.

Though aspects of Austrian thinking, such as the importance of opportunity costs and Böhm-Bawerk's theory of capital, have influenced or worked their way into modern mainstream economics, its subjectivist approach failed to carry the day. Unlike the objectivist approach of W. S. Jevons, Léon Walras, and Alfred Marshall, it didn't lend itself to mathematical analysis, and many thought it couldn't offer the type of scientific precision that they considered essential for sophisticated economic thinking.

SEE ALSO The Marginal Revolution (1871), Menger's *Principles of Economics* (1871), The *Methodenstreit* (1883), Böhm-Bawerk's *Capital and Interest* (1884), Opportunity Cost (1889), Marshall's *Principles of Economics* (1890), The Socialist Calculation Debate (1920), Knight's *Risk, Uncertainty, and Profit* (1921), Hayek's *Road to Serfdom* (1944), Hayek's "Use of Knowledge in Society" (1945)

A photochrome of the University of Vienna, where many of the founders of the Austrian school studied, worked, and taught.

Walras's *Elements of Pure Economics*

Léon Walras (1834–1910)

Léon Walras was a French economist who spent much of his academic career at the University of Lausanne, Switzerland, after his father, also an economist, and Augustin Cournot encouraged him to join the profession. In 1874, his contribution to the marginal revolution, the *Éléments d'Économie Politique Pure*, or *Elements of Pure Economics* in English, took economic theorizing to a level of sophistication not seen before. What differentiated the *Éléments* from other works by W. S. Jevons, Carl Menger, Alfred Marshall, and Cournot was its "general equilibrium" approach.

Walras explicitly accounted for the interdependence of markets, explaining how an alteration in demand in one market affects not just price and output in that market, but prices and quantities in other markets as well. These "secondary" effects then have their own supply- or demand-influencing effects across markets. For example, a shortage of steel not only drives up the price of steel, but impacts markets for products that use steel in their manufacturing process, steel substitutes, and the labor market for steel workers. The economic system will only settle down to a new equilibrium when prices have adjusted to equate supplies and demands in all markets simultaneously. This is the "general" equilibrium. Walras imagined that this equilibrating process was accomplished by utility-maximizing consumers making their demands known and by profit-maximizing producers generating supplies in response to a set of prices called out by a metaphorical "auctioneer," who continually adjusts prices until equilibrium is achieved across markets.

Despite Walras's groundbreaking contribution, he had little influence on economic analysis in the English-speaking world until well into the twentieth century. The lack of an English translation of the *Éléments*, and its sophisticated mathematics put it beyond the reach of most economists. Meanwhile, Marshall and his disciples insisted that *partial equilibrium* analysis, which looks at individual markets in isolation, was a sufficient framework for studying most economic problems. As economic analysis became increasingly mathematical after World War II, Paul Samuelson, Kenneth Arrow, Gérard Debreu, and others brought the Walrasian approach to the center of economic theorizing, giving Walras the recognition and influence that had eluded him during his lifetime.

SEE ALSO Cournot's *Researches* (1838), The Marginal Revolution (1871), Marshall's *Principles of Economics* (1890), The Fundamental Theorems of Welfare Economics (1943), *Foundations of Economic Analysis* (1947), Proving the Existence of a General Equilibrium (1954), Debreu's *The Theory of Value* (1959)

An excerpt from Elements of Pure Economics. *Despite the groundbreaking nature of Léon Walras's work, its initial impact was limited because most scholars at the time found his mathematical approach too difficult to understand.*

Théorème de l'équilibre général.

---

108. Les m ($m-1$) quantités totales $D_{a,b}=M$, $D_{b,a}=N$,
$D_{a,c}=P$, $D_{c,a}=Q$, $D_{a,d}=R$, $D_{d,a}=S$, $D_{b,c}=F$, $D_{c,b}=G$,
$D_{b,d}=H$, $D_{d,b}=J$, $D_{c,d}=K$, $D_{d,c}=L$ ... étant déterminées
mathématiquement, comme il vient d'être dit, l'échange se fera,
sur le marché, suivant les équations :

$$(1)\ \frac{v_b}{v_a}=\frac{M}{N}=\mu,\quad (2)\ \frac{v_c}{v_a}=\frac{P}{Q}=\pi,\quad (3)\ \frac{v_d}{v_a}=\frac{R}{S}=\rho,$$

$$(4)\quad \frac{v_c}{v_b}=\frac{F}{G},\quad (5)\quad \frac{v_d}{v_b}=\frac{H}{J},\quad (6)\quad \frac{v_d}{v_c}=\frac{K}{L}.$$

Or, en divisant les équations (2) et (3) par l'équation (1), et
l'équation (3) par l'équation (2), il vient

$$\frac{v_c}{v_b}=\frac{NP}{MQ}=\frac{\pi}{\mu},\quad \frac{v_d}{v_b}=\frac{NR}{MS}=\frac{\rho}{\mu},\quad \frac{v_d}{v_c}=\frac{QR}{PS}=\frac{\rho}{\pi};$$

d'où, par la comparaison avec les équations (4), (5) et (6), on
tire

$$\frac{F}{G}=\frac{NP}{MQ}=\frac{\pi}{\mu},\quad \frac{H}{J}=\frac{NR}{MS}=\frac{\rho}{\mu},\quad \frac{K}{L}=\frac{QR}{PS}=\frac{\rho}{\pi}.$$

Ces équations sont des équations de condition dont il importe
essentiellement de préciser le sens. Elles signifient que μ, π et
ρ étant les quantités de (A) qui s'échangent contre 1 de (B),

The Single Tax

Henry George (1839–1897)

Many critiques of political economy targeted the vast wealth disparities that accompanied industrial capitalism. By the latter third of the nineteenth century, two percent of the population controlled thirty percent of national wealth and an even larger share of property in the United States, while nearly half the population had no wealth at all and very little property. Henry George, an American journalist and political economist, captured the public imagination when he proposed a radical restructuring of the tax system to address inequality. At that time, taxes were levied mostly on goods, property, and imported products; there was no permanent federal income tax in America until 1913.

In his book *Progress and Poverty* (1879), George rejected Malthusian-based explanations for low wages and unemployment, which pinned these problems on excessive population growth. The true culprit was the concentration of land in the hands of the few. Control of land and its resources allowed landowners to secure the return from the land for themselves. These returns often comprised much of the value of the goods produced on this land and promoted widespread land speculation. Many landowners preferred to let their property sit unused, to cash in on increasing land values, rather than putting it to use.

For George, land was a public trust, and its returns belonged to the public. He thus proposed that the government levy a tax equal to 100 percent of the unimproved value of land. Because the tax wouldn't apply to increases in value associated with landowner improvements, the landowners would retain the returns resulting from any enhancements they made. This tax, unlike taxes on income and goods, wouldn't reduce the incentive to improve the land's productivity; moreover, tax revenue would provide enough funding for government operations, sparing the working classes from any need to pay taxes.

George's proposal attracted tremendous public support in both the U.S. and Great Britain. Nearly a century later, even Milton Friedman, who was skeptical of many tax schemes, suggested that George's single tax was preferable to most others. Though it was never put into practice, Georgism, as it is frequently called, continues to attract support today.

SEE ALSO Rent and the Theory of Surplus (1662), The Physiocrats (1756), The Malthusian Population Theory (1798), Ricardo's *Principles of Political Economy and Taxation* (1817), The Benefit Principle of Taxation (1896), Optimal Taxation (1971), Supply-Side Economics (1974)

Henry George's proposal to enact a single tax on the value of unimproved land offered part of the inspiration for this nineteenth-century cartoon, which depicts George as a knight spearing a dragon representing landlordism.

HENRY GEORGE AND THE DRAGON.

Edgeworth's *Mathematical Psychics*

Francis Ysidro Edgeworth (1845–1926)

Francis Ysidro Edgeworth, an Irishman educated at Trinity College, Dublin, and at Oxford, made several important contributions to economics and statistics in the late nineteenth century. In his book *Mathematical Psychics*, published in 1881, Edgeworth, like W. S. Jevons, focused on applying mathematics to the study of utility. He paid particular attention to the exchange of goods, or bartering, between a pair of economic agents. Edgeworth believed that Jevons had oversimplified the exchange process, leading him to conclude wrongly that the same forces that explain price determination in a competitive market setting also apply to bargaining among small numbers of agents.

Edgeworth demonstrated that there is a number of potential bargains that can improve the utility of both agents, just as there is a range of possible sale prices that will make both you and your car dealer better off. Through successive rounds of bargaining, or what Edgeworth called "recontracting," they eventually exhaust the available gains from exchange. Edgeworth emphasized that there is a variety of potential equilibrium points, lying along what he called the "contract curve." The particular equilibrium that the agents ultimately reach will depend on how this bargaining plays out. Thus, it isn't possible to determine the relative prices of the bartered goods and the amount each agent consumes outside the context of a competitive market, where prices are determined by forces beyond the individual's control, rather than by bargaining.

Edgeworth's analysis in *Mathematical Psychics* made many groundbreaking contributions, especially by introducing the concept of indifference curves, which show different combinations of goods that provide a consumer with a specific level of utility. British economist Alfred Marshall praised the work, saying that it showed "clear signs of genius," and its influence contributed to Edgeworth's appointment as the first editor of *The Economic Journal* in 1891. Subsequent work on the theory of international trade, taxation, and monopoly pricing illustrated Edgeworth's capacity for making important theoretical contributions across the economic spectrum. Nonetheless, some of the most important implications of *Mathematical Psychics* lay dormant for decades, until the development of game theory provided economists with tools to reach more definitive conclusions about the outcomes of bargaining.

SEE ALSO Jevons's *Theory of Political Economy* (1871), Economics Journals (1886), Ordinal Utility (1893), Indifference Curves (1906), The Hicks–Allen Consumer Theory (1934), Game Theory Enters Economics (1944), Non-Cooperative Games and Nash Equilibrium (1950)

One of the graphs that appear in Mathematical Psychics. *This book featured several innovative visual representations of economic concepts, including the contract curve and the indifference curve.*

FIG. 1.

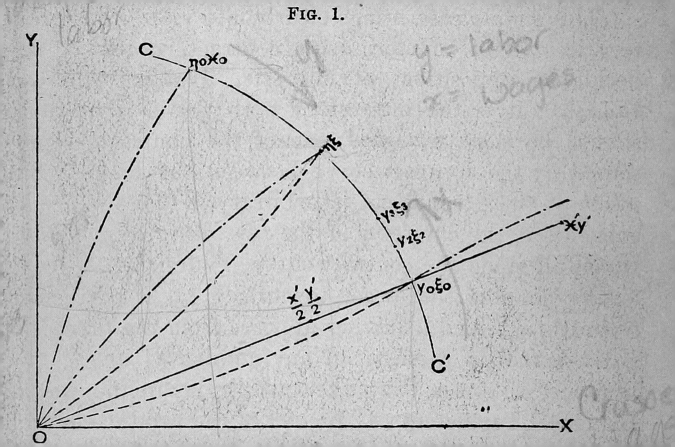

La Scienza della Finanze

Maffeo Pantaleoni (1857–1924), Antonio de Viti de Marco (1858–1943), Ugo Mazzola (1863–1899)

As a policy science, economics relies on the political process to put its insights into action. Rulers, legislators, and voters help translate economic policy ideas and ideals into real-world economic policies. Despite this, economic theory had largely ignored the policymaking process until the late nineteenth century, when a group of Italian economists, including Maffeo Pantaleoni, Antonio de Viti de Marco, and Ugo Mazzola, constructed theories that took government operations into account. This new field of analysis was known as *la scienza della finanze*—the science of (public) finance.

Pantaleoni's "Contribution to the Theory of the Distribution of Public Expenditure" (1883) described the challenge of creating a government budget as an optimal allocation problem, akin to that of W. S. Jevons's consumer, who tries to maximize utility given a budget. The government must weigh the marginal benefits of offering public goods and services against the marginal costs of the taxes used to finance them. To provide these goods at efficient levels, it must supply a quantity that equates marginal benefit and marginal cost.

Mazzola and de Viti de Marco, meanwhile, described the political process as an exchange between the government and its citizens. The state supplies public goods at prices determined by tax payments, while consumers demand public goods in the same way that they demand groceries or clothing. If the political process functions like a smoothly operating market, the interaction between this supply and demand will result in efficient taxation levels and quantities of public goods.

Not all these scholars arrived at such an optimistic view of the state. Amilcare Puviani and Giovanni Montemartini argued that the propensity of legislators to exaggerate benefits and disguise costs, and to manipulate the political process to serve their self-interest, made it difficult to achieve efficient outcomes. Though *La Scienza della Finanze* had little influence outside Italy, its insistence that economic policy analysis incorporate the workings of the political process helped inspire modern public choice analysis, an economic approach to politics that portrays legislators, bureaucrats, and voters as self-interested utility maximizers rather than benevolent public servants.

SEE ALSO Jevons's *Theory of Political Economy* (1871), Walras's *Elements of Pure Economics* (1874), The Benefit Principle of Taxation (1896), The Rational Voter Model and the Paradox of Voting (1957), Public Choice Analysis (1962)

A photo of the Piazza del Campidoglio in Rome, the city where Antonio de Viti de Marco taught public finance (1890).

174. P. Z. - ROMA. PIAZZA DEL CAMPIDOGLIO.

The Bertrand Model

Joseph Bertrand (1822–1900)

In 1883, some forty-five years after its publication, a French mathematician named Joseph Bertrand released a review of Augustin Cournot's *Researches into the Mathematical Principles of the Theory of Wealth*. In addition to criticizing Cournot's work harshly, he challenged Cournot's analysis of duopoly, a market consisting of two sellers. The "Bertrand model" subsequently became, along with Cournot's model, one of the pillars of modern oligopoly theory. It is also perhaps the only instance in which a book review has made a major contribution to economic theory.

Cournot's analysis demonstrated that a duopolistic market will have higher prices and lower output than a highly competitive market. He assumed that firms compete on output, producing the number of units that maximizes their profits given the amount they expect the other firm to produce. The sum of the firms' outputs falls short of the output that results in a market with many competitive firms, resulting in higher-than-competitive prices. Bertrand came to a different conclusion, arguing that if the two firms compete on price, which he considered a more common real-life scenario, the market will actually replicate the competitive outcome. Bertrand's reasoning is very simple. Suppose that Company A is a monopolist selling bottled water for $2 and that a bottle costs $1 to produce. Company B has an incentive to enter the market and charge $1.95, stealing all the customers for itself. Company A can then respond by cutting its price to $1.90, and this price-cutting process continues until the price falls to a level just sufficient to cover costs, the same result reached if there were many sellers competing in the market.

Though Bertrand thought he had refuted Cournot's findings, he had done no such thing. Their different conclusions turned on whether the firms make prices or outputs their strategic choice variable. Bertrand, however, did provide the first illustration that firms operating in a market with few sellers have many strategic choices for maximizing their profits and will not necessarily charge higher-than-competitive prices. This insight came more fully into view with the introduction of game theory into economic analysis in the twentieth century.

SEE ALSO Cournot's *Researches* (1838), The Hotelling Model of Locational Choice (1929), The Stackelberg Model (1934), Game Theory Enters Economics (1944), Non-Cooperative Games and Nash Equilibrium (1950)

A drawing of Joseph Bertrand, who was a professor at the prestigious Collège de France and held the position of permanent secretary at the Paris Academy of Sciences for twenty-six years.

BERTRAND
Secrétaire perpétuel
de l'Académie
des Sciences.

The *Methodenstreit*

Gustav Schmoller (1838–1917), Carl Menger (1840–1921)

For some two centuries, economic discourse has wrestled with an uneasy tension between abstraction and realism. On one side, abstract theoretical analysis makes it possible to effectively analyze a complex economic reality. On the other, there is the view that abstract, deductive modeling pushes aside too many aspects of that reality to shed light on economic problems. At times, the tension between these contrasting perspectives has come to a head and exploded into full-blown controversies, as seen with Carl Menger's publication of *Untersuchungen über die Methode der Socialwissenschaften, und der politischen Ökonomie insbesondere* in 1883.

Menger's book launched the *Methodenstreit*, a "method dispute," which pitted Menger and other members of the Austrian School against Gustav Schmoller, who penned a scathing review of Menger's book, and the German Historical School. The Austrian School believed that progress in economic analysis could only come about by developing theories that are based on deduction and that rely on a basic set of assumptions. Logic would illuminate relationships and help assess how changing conditions affect economic activity and performance. The historical economists rejected the idea that deductively based theories could provide significant insights across time, place, and circumstance. Theories must be constructed inductively, based on detailed historical and data analysis.

The effects of the *Methodenstreit* went well beyond the decade-long debates in the academic literature. Gustav Schmoller, the leader of the German Historical School and the most powerful figure in German economics, used his influence to exclude members of the Austrian School from faculty positions in German universities. As a result, Germany felt the influence of the marginal revolution much later than did many other European countries. In the end, however, it was Austrian thinking that had the greater long-run influence, as the historical method faded away while the deductive approach of the Austrians became the preferred method of economic analysis. That said, opposition to abstract, deductive analysis has not disappeared from economics, and critics of the discipline have suggested that the Great Recession was due in part to the disconnect between economic theories and the real world.

SEE ALSO The German Historical School (1843), The Marginal Revolution (1871), Menger's *Principles of Economics* (1871), The Austrian School (1871).

A bust of Gustav Schmoller (1907), who clashed with Carl Menger on whether theories based on deductive reasoning from a set of assumptions could offer useful economic insights.

Lectures on the Industrial Revolution

Arnold Toynbee (1852–1883)

Like Germany, England developed a historical approach to economics during the late nineteenth century. The most influential piece of scholarship to come out of this approach was Arnold Toynbee's *Lectures on the Industrial Revolution*, a set of lectures delivered to undergraduate modern history students at Oxford University in 1881–82 and published posthumously in 1884. Toynbee's work offered a sweeping indictment of how economic life and thought had transformed during the eighteenth and nineteenth centuries, popularizing the term "industrial revolution" within the English lexicon. His lectures historicized this important transition, while also advocating for social reform. In fact, it was a desire to fix what he considered a broken system that led Toynbee to economics in the first place.

Toynbee depicted the invention of the steam engine and Smith's *Wealth of Nations* as the main drivers of change and upheaval, some of which was beneficial but much of which he considered harmful. He observed how competition became the ethos of the marketplace and, echoing Karl Marx, how machine production and competitive markets began alienating labor from ownership. Influenced by John Ruskin, he dismissed both classical economics, which he labeled a "cruel, inhuman, [*sic*] infant killer," and its laissez-fare leanings because they seemed to support ruthless industrialization. To come to grips with the workings of capitalism, Toynbee believed it was essential to use the past to understand both the present and the future. Historical methods were the only means for anyone to gain the insights needed to develop policies and reforms that he believed were necessary to address the ills of the Industrial Revolution, including low wages, poor working conditions, widespread unemployment, and squalid living conditions. Classical economics, he said, had no answer for these.

Toynbee's writings were wildly popular with the general public but had only a small impact on economics at the time. However, his reformist attitude and the attention that he called to the plight of the working class led to the founding of many philanthropic organizations, including London's Toynbee Hall, which is dedicated to alleviating poverty.

SEE ALSO The Industrial Revolution (1760), Smith's *Wealth of Nations* (1776), Classical Political Economy (c. 1790), The German Historical School (1843), The Dismal Science (1849), Marshall's *Principles of Economics* (1890), The Economics Tripos at Cambridge (1903)

Arnold Toynbee was deeply concerned with the human cost of the Industrial Revolution, as machinery displaced workers and offered only a low standard of living to those who could find work, a concern also captured in this cartoon from an 1851 issue of Punch.

SPECIMENS FROM MR. PUNCH'S INDUSTRIAL EXHIBITION OF 1850.

(TO BE IMPROVED IN 1851).

Fabian Socialism

George Bernard Shaw (1856–1950), Beatrice Webb (1858–1943), Sidney Webb (1859–1947), H. G. Wells (1866–1946)

Founded in 1884, the Fabian Society emerged from the growing interest in socialism in Great Britain during the late 1800s. Its members included some of the leading minds of the late Victorian era, including social reformers Sidney and Beatrice Webb, playwright George Bernard Shaw, and writer H. G. Wells. Though committed socialists, the Fabians staunchly opposed the sort of violent social and political change described by Karl Marx, preferring instead to work through local government organizations and the labor union movement—Beatrice Webb coined the term "collective bargaining"—to gradually transform capitalism to socialism.

The Fabians had a profound influence on British economic and social life. They founded the London School of Economics in 1895, utilizing a bequest left by one of its members to promote the spread of Fabian ideas and "the betterment of society." In 1913, the Webbs established the *New Statesman* magazine; though no longer associated with the Fabian society, it remains an important voice of the British left. The Society's members were also active in the formation of, and remain affiliated with, the British Labour Party.

The Webbs were the heart and soul of the Fabian movement. In their writings, they argued that Britain should move away from what they considered the outdated, laissez-faire oriented ideas of classical political economy. Their proposals for reforms drew from studies on the harm caused by industrialization, the English Poor Laws (the welfare system of the time), and international policy. The writings of the Webbs and other Fabians offered ideas for a minimum wage, regulation of work hours, universal health care, and a national education system. Not all of their proposed reforms were so attractive, however. Like many intellectuals of the period in Britain and the U.S., a number of the early Fabians were attracted to eugenics—including sterilization—as a mechanism for improving the quality of the population. Though Fabian reform efforts brought only modest success during their lifetimes, the welfare system established in Britain following World War II embodied many of the reforms advocated by the Webbs a half-century earlier.

THE SITE OF
17 OSNABURGH STREET
WHERE
THE
FABIAN SOCIETY
WAS FOUNDED
IN 1884

SEE ALSO Classical Political Economy (c. 1790), Utopian Socialism (1813), *The Communist Manifesto* (1848), Marx's *Das Kapital* (1867), The Theory of Crisis (1867), The Oxford Approach to Welfare (1914), Supply-Side Economics (1974)

Above: *A plaque commemorates the site in London where the Fabian Society was founded.*
Main image: *Beatrice and Sidney Webb were two of the most prominent figures of the Fabian Society.*

Böhm-Bawerk's *Capital and Interest*

Eugen von Böhm-Bawerk (1851–1914)

One of the most important figures in the early Austrian School was Eugen von Böhm-Bawerk, a professor at the Universities of Innsbruck and Vienna and a civil servant. His *Capital and Interest*, released in 1884, is best known for outlining a theory of production and exchange that accounts for how the passage of time affects the value of a good.

According to Böhm-Bawerk, people have a positive rate of time preference: they value income and goods in the present more highly than in the future. To defer the satisfaction of consuming a good, they will demand a premium that compensates them for postponing their consumption. This premium takes the form of interest.

To explain why interest plays an important role in production, Böhm-Bawerk introduces the concept of "roundaboutness." Capital, he explained, increases output from a given amount of land and labor. However, this capital lengthens the time it takes to generate revenue. Ten fishermen might catch ten fish in a day if they used their hands, but if a capitalist ordered boats and nets and equipped those ten fishermen with this capital, they might catch 500 fish. Manufacturing the boats and nets takes time, which comprises the roundabout part of the production process, because in that same period the capitalist could use her money for other productive purposes. Because people value the present more highly than the future, individuals will only use financial capital to fund these roundabout processes if they receive interest payments on their investments.

Böhm-Bawerk's theory of time preference was an important ingredient in Knut Wicksell's cumulative process analysis, which links interest rates, the money supply, and the price level. It also offered an influential argument against Karl Marx's labor theory of value. Even if the value of boats and nets could ultimately be reduced to the value of the labor that created them, the additional fish they would catch wouldn't exist without the roundabout methods of production made possible by the capitalist. Because these methods require interest payments, which is a cost of producing the good, roundaboutness leads to a price that exceeds labor value, illustrating that the capitalist's return is not due simply to the exploitation of labor.

SEE ALSO Aquinas on Usury (1265), The Protestant Reformation (1517), The Abstinence Theory of Interest (1836), The Labor Theory of Value and the Theory of Exploitation (1867), The Austrian School (1871), The Real Rate of Interest (1896), Wicksell's Cumulative Process (1898)

Eugen von Böhm-Bawerk introduced the concept of "roundaboutness" to describe production processes that need a longer time to be completed, such as the manufacture of the boats and nets used to increase the catch of the tuna fishermen in this painting (c. 1860) by the French artist Félix Ziem (1821–1911).

The Professionalization of Economics

The last two decades of the 1800s saw economics, like many other subjects, become professionalized as an academic discipline in Great Britain and the United States. The days when philosophers and well-educated laymen such as Adam Smith and David Ricardo could make fundamentally important contributions to the subject were fading into the past. Going forward, specialized economists would dominate the field, and programs to train new generations of these specialists, such as the Cambridge Economics Tripos, became increasingly common in universities.

The emergence of professional societies catering to economists demonstrated the field's growing importance and increased its prestige. The American Economic Association (AEA) was formed in 1885 to provide "encouragement of economic research" and "perfect freedom of economic discussion." It aimed to expand academic economics and promote the use of economic knowledge in policy debates, without taking a stance on any particular set of doctrines or policies—a position that it continues to hold today. In 1890, the desire in Great Britain to have a society comparable to the AEA led to the creation of the British Economic Association, later renamed the Royal Economic Society (RES), "to promote the study of economic science."

Like many professional societies, both the AEA and the RES grappled with a host of issues in their formative years, especially pertaining to membership. Should they be "learned" societies of academic economists, or should they include members from the general population? In the end, both of these groups opted for open membership, allowing anyone with an interest in the subject to join. Even so, academic economists dominated both societies from the start, and their conferences and publications continue to target an academic audience.

As the field of economics and the number of economists expanded over the next century, many new professional societies emerged. Some of these, such as the Society of Labor Economists and the History of Economics Society, cater to academic sub-specialties, while others, such as the National Association for Business Economics and the National Association of Forensic Economics, support economists working in business and consulting.

SEE ALSO The Political Economy Club (1821), Economics Journals (1886), The Economics Tripos at Cambridge (1903)

Portraits of five early presidents of the American Economic Association: Richard E. Ely (top left), Jeremiah W. Jenks (top right), Simeon N. Patten (bottom right), John Bates Clark (bottom left), and Frank W. Taussig (center).

EX-PRESIDENTS OF THE AMERICAN ECONOMIC ASSOCIATION.

Richard E. Ely, University of Wisconsin.　　　　　　　Jeremiah W. Jenks, Cornell University.

Frank W. Taussig, Harvard University.

John B. Clark, Columbia University.　　　　　　　Simeon N. Patten, University of Pennsylvania.

Economics Journals

The earliest economic writings typically consisted of short passages found in much larger treatises on subjects such as philosophy and theology, or were found in small pamphlets exploring a particular policy-related question. As scholars began to develop larger and more detailed frameworks for economic analysis in the eighteenth and nineteenth centuries, they turned to book-length treatises to share economic knowledge. By the early twentieth century, however, the academic journal quickly became the favored medium for disseminating new economic knowledge.

The first new journals—the *Quarterly Journal of Economics*, published by the economics faculty at Harvard University, and *Publications of the American Economic Association* (later the *American Economic Review*)—launched in 1886. These were followed in short order by *The Economic Journal* (1890), published by the Royal Economic Society, and the *Journal of Political Economy* (1892), published by the economics faculty at the University of Chicago. Over the course of the next century, this literature grew from a handful of journals to several hundred, many of them focused on narrow subfields, such as monetary economics, public finance, and labor economics. These journals were by no means the first to specialize in economic subjects. The physiocrats' journal, *Éphémérides du Citoyen* (1765), the *Journal des Économistes* (1841), and *Zeitschrift für die Gesamte Staatswissenschaft* (1844) all significantly predate their modern brethren. However, the most influential work of this time appeared in book form.

It took another half-century for journals to fully supersede book-length works as the outlet for important contributions to the field. Nonetheless, the rise of journals as forums for scholarship signaled a shift in economics research toward more narrowly drawn problems. It also reflected the desire to transmit the latest advances more quickly to the growing profession, bypassing the lengthy gestation process required to bring a book-length work to publication. In this, as in its rigorous methods of analysis, economics adopted practices already prevalent in the more prestigious natural sciences.

SEE ALSO The Physiocrats (1756), The Professionalization of Economics (1885)

The table of contents page from the inaugural volume of The Quarterly Journal of Economics, *one of the first economics journals.*

THE

QUARTERLY JOURNAL

OF

ECONOMICS

VOL. I   *OCTOBER 1886*   No. I

CONTENTS

PUBLISHED FOR HARVARD UNIVERSITY

BOSTON
GEORGE H. ELLIS 141 FRANKLIN STREET
1886

Opportunity Cost

Friedrich von Wieser (1851–1926)

You may have heard that "there ain't no such thing as a free lunch." The phrase originated in the late nineteenth century as a response to American saloons offering a "free" lunch to attract drinking customers. Many now use the phrase to convey the idea that nothing in life is really free, a sentiment encapsulated in the economic theory of "opportunity cost."

The traditional economic approach to costs, sometimes referred to as the "real costs" approach, holds that the prices actually paid for consumer goods or the inputs required to produce the goods provide an accurate measure of their cost. Austrian economist Friedrich von Wieser, writing in his book on *Natural Value* in 1889, took a very different approach—one in keeping with the subjectivist approach to value espoused by the Austrian School. Wieser, who succeeded Carl Menger as a professor at the University of Vienna, argued that the true cost of an activity reflects the value of the next-best option that was sacrificed to pursue the chosen activity. That lunch is not really "free," then, because you have to forgo doing something else with your time to take advantage of the promotion. Wieser called this the "alternative cost," but it soon became known as the "opportunity cost." For Wieser, all value is ultimately determined by utility. Thus, opportunity cost equals the utility sacrificed when an individual pursues one course of action rather than another, which Wieser called "marginal utility." This reversed the classical view that costs determine prices, suggesting instead that *utility determines costs*.

This relationship between marginal utility and opportunity cost shifted the foundation of economic analysis from the more general concepts of supply and demand to the principles of scarcity and choice which underlie them. Scholars including Philip Wicksteed and Lionel Robbins used this relationship to revamp the definition of economics as a discipline and broaden the scope of economic analysis during the first third of the twentieth century.

SEE ALSO Utilitarianism (1789), Classical Political Economy (c. 1790), The Marginal Revolution (1871), Jevons's *Theory of Political Economy* (1871), Menger's *Principles of Economics* (1871), The Austrian School (1871), Scarcity and Choice (1932)

Saloon owners used free lunches to entice hungry customers to buy drinks at their establishments. American artist Charles Dana Gibson drew three patrons enjoying their meal.

Marshall's *Principles of Economics*

Alfred Marshall (1842–1924)

Alfred Marshall's *Principles of Economics*, published in 1890, is the capstone book among the pioneering works of the marginal revolution and perhaps the most influential writing published during that period. As professor of political economy at the University of Cambridge, Marshall shaped the future direction of economics through his writings, particularly his *Principles*, and by the force of his personality. As a result of his influence, Cambridge remained the center of the economics universe for many years.

Marshall defined economics as "a study of mankind in the ordinary business of life." This study "examines that part of individual and social action which is most closely connected with the attainment and with the use of the material requisites of well-being." His *Principles* had a practical focus that reflected this: though a skilled mathematician, Marshall presented his ideas using an intuitive and graphical approach that could be grasped by the layman, relegating the mathematics to the book's appendices.

Marshall's *Principles* developed and further refined the tools that economists since the time of Adam Smith have used to study basic economic problems, but it also brought us many concepts that have become central to modern economics. He created a model that explained the workings of demand and supply, developed the concept of elasticity, showed the importance of distinguishing between the short run and the long run when making economic forecasts, and examined how increasing the level of production can provide cost advantages, a concept known as economies of scale. These tools allowed Marshall to offer new insights into how a market system operates and to evaluate the benefits and costs of economic policies via the use of consumer surplus analysis.

The rebirth of general equilibrium analysis and the development of game theory in the twentieth century revealed certain limitations in Marshall's framework, which focused on individual markets in isolation and ignored the possibility that sellers in a marketplace could strategize to increase profits. Yet, the simple and elegant approach of his *Principles* was key to many of the advances in economics over the last century and continues to inform economists' research and teaching.

SEE ALSO Smith's *Wealth of Nations* (1776), The Marginal Revolution (1871), Walras's *Elements of Pure Economics* (1874), The Demand–Supply Model (1890), Ceteris Paribus (1890), Elasticity (1890), The Time Horizon (1890), Pigou's *Wealth and Welfare* (1912), Game Theory Enters Economics (1944), Non-Cooperative Games and Nash Equilibrium (1950), Supply-Side Economics (1974)

Alfred Marshall (pictured here in 1921) not only introduced key economic concepts, such as the demand–supply model and elasticity, but made them accessible to a general audience.

The Demand–Supply Model

Alfred Marshall (1842–1924)

The concepts of supply and demand are as old as economic thinking itself, but an in-depth understanding of how they determine market prices and producers' output had to wait until economists had the mathematical and graphical tools developed during the marginal revolution. Using British engineer Fleeming Jenkin's graphical analysis of demand and supply from 1870 as a springboard, Alfred Marshall developed the model more fully in *Principles of Economics* (1890).

For centuries, economic thinkers had debated whether prices were determined by demand, with sellers charging the highest price consumers would be willing to pay, or by the costs of production, with sellers responding to competition and charging lower prices to attract buyers for their products. Marshall argued that each perspective was misguided, noting "We might as reasonably dispute whether it is the upper or the under blade of a pair of scissors that cuts a piece of paper, as whether value is governed by utility or cost of production." He admits that you could still use your scissors if you hold one blade still and move the other, but he ultimately concludes that cutting, like price determination, depends on the interaction of two forces. He depicted this interaction in the now-famous diagram of demand and supply curves.

With the demand–supply model, Marshall explored how the forces that change demand and supply affect prices and the quantities of goods bought and sold when the market is in equilibrium. It soon became clear that this model could help analyze economic policies, allowing economists to treat taxes, subsidies, regulations, and the like as variables that influenced demand and supply.

In a big-picture sense, Marshall made his most important contribution by demonstrating how this model could be fruitfully applied to *all* markets, including those for labor, capital, and money. In this way, he provided a unifying framework for a vast swath of economic analysis. His basic model of demand and supply remains at the core of economic thinking, infusing everything from introductory economics textbooks to the models used by the Federal Reserve to manage monetary policy.

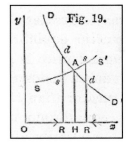

SEE ALSO Supply and Demand (1767), The Wages Fund Controversy (1866), The Marginal Revolution (1871), *Ceteris Paribus* (1890), Elasticity (1890), The Time Horizon (1890), Chamberlin's *The Theory of Monopolistic Competition* (1933), *The Economics of Imperfect Competition* (1933), The Chicago School (1946)

Above: *Marshall used the graph shown here to illustrate his demand–supply model.* **Main image:** *Alfred Marshall illustrated the interaction of supply and demand by comparing them to the blades of scissors.*

Ceteris Paribus

Alfred Marshall (1842–1924)

Alfred Marshall's model of demand and supply, laid out in his *Principles of Economics* (1890), posits that the quantities of a product demanded by consumers and supplied by sellers are a function of its price at a given point in time. All other variables that could affect demand and supply, such as incomes, production costs, and the number of buyers and sellers, are assumed to be constant. Marshall captured this assumption with the term *ceteris paribus*, a Latin expression meaning "other things equal," or constant.

An analysis using this assumption is static rather than dynamic because it ignores the passage of time and, unlike an analysis of general equilibrium, examines just a single market, or a handful of markets. Marshall's "partial equilibrium" approach thus doesn't account for feedback effects (that changes in prices and quantities in one market can affect those in other markets). However, he didn't see these limitations as shortfalls. For Marshall, the *ceteris paribus* assumption was a necessary abstraction for dealing with the complexities of economic reality. "The forces to be dealt with are," he said, "so numerous that it is best to take a few at a time and to work out a number of partial solutions as auxiliaries to our main study." It isn't that these other forces don't matter; but to see, for example, how a change in consumer incomes or a sales tax affects a market, we must hold them constant for the purposes at hand. Marshall didn't consider this approach unusual or unique to economics. He called it a "scientific device," one that people have used since the beginning of time to deal with complex problems.

Marshall didn't see an analysis based on *ceteris paribus* as an end point, either. As you continue your economic analysis, you can loosen certain assumptions, eventually reaching a point where you discover effects related to general equilibrium and the passage of time. Today, economists continue to use Marshall's *ceteris paribus*–based approach, particularly when studying situations where feedback effects across markets are relatively unimportant or when their focus is confined to one particular market.

SEE ALSO Walras's *Elements of Pure Economics* (1874), Marshall's *Principles of Economics* (1890), The Demand–Supply Model (1890)

Alfred Marshall's concept of ceteris paribus *allows economists to use supply-and-demand analysis to gauge how a decrease in the demand for one of the goods in this California general store will affect its price if the prices of the other goods remain constant.*

Elasticity

Alfred Marshall (1842–1924)

The law of demand tells us that the quantity of a product that people wish to purchase will vary inversely with its price. However, to analyze the effects of price changes, it's important to understand how sensitive this quantity is to changes in price. The sensitivity of demand to price changes can depend on many factors, including the number of substitutes for the good and the time period under consideration. It's also important to know how the quantity supplied of a good will respond to price changes and the magnitude of the relationship between demand and consumer incomes. Indeed, statistician Ernst Engel noted in 1857 that the proportion of income spent on food tends to fall as income rises—an insight known as Engel's Law.

In his *Principles of Economics* (1890), Alfred Marshall introduced the concept of elasticity to capture these relationships. Marshall explained that when demand for a good is more price-elastic, the amount demanded will change more drastically when there is a price change; a good with a price-inelastic demand is one for which the quantity demanded isn't very sensitive to price changes. Goods with many substitutes, or alternatives, will typically have elastic demands. If the price of orange juice rises, many people will switch to other fruit juices or beverages. Gasoline, on the other hand, has fairly inelastic demand because most vehicles can only run on one type of fuel; in fact, gasoline consumption barely budges when price rises by a percentage point or two. This all assumes that there aren't other variables, such as the prices of other goods, changing simultaneously—an application of Marshall's *ceteris paribus* assumption; otherwise, any observed demand changes can't be attributed solely to changes in the good's price.

Developments in econometrics, the application of statistical techniques to economic data, have allowed economists to make precise estimates of elasticity values. These estimates have facilitated economic forecasting and policy analysis and are often used to predict the effects of tariffs on the demand for imported goods and how proposed increases in the minimum wage will affect the demand for labor and employment rates.

SEE ALSO Supply and Demand (1767), The Law of Demand (1820), Cournot's *Researches* (1838), Marshall's *Principles of Economics* (1890), The Demand–Supply Model (1890), *Ceteris Paribus* (1890), The Cobb–Douglas Function (1928), The Econometric Society (1930), Haavelmo's "Probability Approach" (1944)

The price elasticities of demand for the goods showcased on this page from the October 1, 1916 issue of the New York Tribune *vary widely. For example, gold jewelry and grand pianos have more elastic demand than do coffee and shoes.*

The Time Horizon

Alfred Marshall (1842–1924)

John Maynard Keynes once famously quipped that "in the long run we are all dead." His message underscored the importance of making corrections to market systems in the short term, even if the system may correct some of its own problems with time. Prior to the late nineteenth century, most economists didn't recognize that the time period under scrutiny could impact market outcomes so significantly. Many aspects of classical economics, such as Say's Law and T. R. Malthus's views on the machinery question, make sense if you think about how market forces work themselves out over an extended period of time; but when you start considering their effects in the short term, very different outcomes manifest themselves.

Alfred Marshall offered the first in-depth explanation of the time horizon's importance in his *Principles of Economics* (1890). His distinction between the "short run" and the "long run" is often considered his most important innovation. The "short period" is one in which some productive inputs are fixed, limiting a firm's ability to adjust its output in the most cost-effective fashion when market conditions change. In the "long period," firms can adjust any input, giving them more flexibility in responding to changing market conditions, and firms can enter or exit the market.

These different timeframes allow us to observe how changes in the demand for a good affect the market equilibrium's price and output, or how an increase in the money supply affects the price level, over a specific period. For example, an increase in the demand for new homes can push their prices up significantly in the short run, when the supply of housing is relatively fixed; but as home builders expand their production in response to these higher prices, home prices tend to fall somewhat. The long-run effect on home prices, then, isn't as extreme as the short-run effect. When combined with Marshall's *ceteris paribus* assumption, attention to the time horizon allows us to separate the effects of long-run forces from the more immediate effects of short-run disturbances.

SEE ALSO Classical Political Economy (c. 1790), Say's Law (1803), The Machinery Question (1817), The Marginal Revolution (1871), Marshall's *Principles of Economics* (1890), *Ceteris Paribus* (1890), The Phillips Curve (1958), The Natural Rate of Unemployment (1967)

Advances in refrigeration and transportation have significantly increased the range of possible short-run supply adjustments for perishable goods, such as the cuts of meat featured The Meat Market *(1819) by British painter James Pollard.*

Antitrust Laws

In the late nineteenth century, the United States witnessed the rise of monopolies, especially in oil and steel industries. In some sectors, such as manufacturing, economies of scale allowed large firms to produce products at lower costs, driving smaller firms out of the industry. In others, businesses colluded to fix prices and divide markets or monopolized markets through mergers or unfair pricing practices. Standard Oil, for example, conspired with railroads to secure shipping prices far below those available to its competitors, allowing it to crush its rivals and control oil prices.

Public outcry against these practices led to laws that would rein in monopolies. In 1890, Congress passed the Sherman Antitrust Act, a "comprehensive charter of economic liberty aimed at preserving free and unfettered competition as the rule of trade." The act outlawed collusion and attempts to monopolize an industry through the creation of trusts, a set of independent companies that are managed by a single board of trustees and effectively operate as a single company. In 1914, Congress passed two additional pieces of legislation to strengthen the government's power to curb the growth of monopolies. The Clayton Act prohibited mergers that could substantially impede competition; outlawed tying contracts, which require a buyer purchasing one product from a company to purchase another unrelated product; and made price discrimination, the practice of charging different prices for the same product to different buyers when there are no differences in production costs, illegal. The Federal Trade Commission Act banned deceptive trading practices and established the Federal Trade Commission to protect consumers and promote competition, alongside the Antitrust Division of the U.S. Department of Justice.

The U.S. government has won lawsuits against—or secured favorable out-of-court settlements with—companies including Standard Oil, Kodak, AT&T, and Microsoft and prohibited numerous proposed mergers that it considered anticompetitive. Though antitrust enforcement exemplifies how government intervention can promote competition, economists don't always agree on when the emergence of monopoly power should be restricted. In fact, we typically find them testifying on both sides of an antitrust case, because it is often difficult to separate competitive from anticompetitive behavior.

SEE ALSO The Competitive Process (1776), Institutional Economics (1919), *Legal Foundations of Capitalism* (1924), The Economic Analysis of Law (1973)

President Theodore Roosevelt (1858–1919) gained a reputation as a "trust-buster" for breaking up monopolies using the Sherman Antitrust Act. In this 1906 cartoon, he is drawn wrestling with snakes representing John D. Rockefeller (1839–1937), the head of Standard Oil, and Senator Nelson W. Aldrich (1841–1915).

VOL. LIX. No. 1525.   PUCK BUILDING, New York, May 23, 1906.   PRICE TEN CENTS.

"What Fools these Mortals be!"

Puck

Entered at N. Y. P. O. as Second-class Mail Matter.

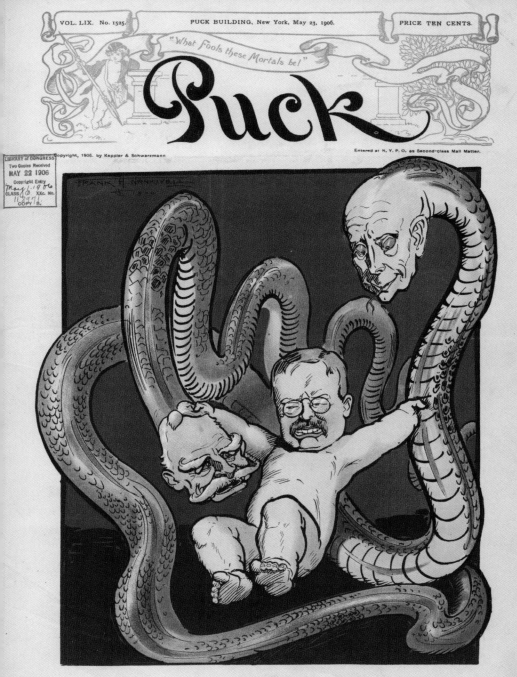

THE INFANT HERCULES AND THE STANDARD OIL SERPENTS.

Ordinal Utility

Vilfredo Pareto (1848–1923), Andreas Voigt (1860–1940)

In the late nineteenth century, economists including W. S. Jevons, Léon Walras, and F. Y. Edgeworth melded calculus with Jeremy Bentham's utilitarian approach to human behavior, which suggests that individuals seek to increase pleasure and avoid pain. From this, a formal theory of consumer behavior arose, portraying the consumer as a utility-maximizer who carefully assesses the benefits and costs of alternative actions. This theory allowed economists to better understand how changes in economic variables such as prices and income levels affect individual decisions and market outcomes. Not all economists accepted this new approach, however. Some rejected utilitarianism as an accurate depiction of human behavior. Others argued that because science demands measurement and utility is not measurable, utility theory didn't pass muster as a scientific approach to consumer behavior.

In 1893, German economist and mathematician Andreas Voigt offered the first strong response to critics who argued that utility was not measurable. Drawing on recent work in mathematics, he distinguished between "cardinal" and "ordinal" utility, introducing these terms into economic discourse. Cardinal utility suggests that utility can be expressed in units, allowing the relative satisfaction provided by two products to be expressed as a ratio; for example, a person can receive twice the utility from an apple that she does from an orange. Jevons, Walras, and Edgeworth had used this conception of utility in their work. Ordinal utility, in contrast, says you can only determine whether one product provides the consumer with greater or less utility than another, not the degree of this difference. This means that you don't have to worry about whether utility is measurable when working with a utility function to describe consumer preferences and derive demand curves.

Voigt's distinction between cardinal and ordinal utility remained largely unknown for many years. Italian economist Vilfredo Pareto is typically credited as the first to work out a consumer theory grounded in ordinal utility in 1900, and Voigt's cardinal-ordinal distinction would only re-emerge when John Hicks and R. G. D. Allen made their seminal contribution to the theory of consumer behavior in the 1930s.

SEE ALSO The Invention of Calculus (c. 1665), Utilitarianism (1789), The Marginal Revolution (1871), Jevons's *Theory of Political Economy* (1871), Walras's *Elements of Pure Economics* (1874), Edgeworth's *Mathematical Psychics* (1881), Indifference Curves (1906), The Hicks–Allen Consumer Theory (1934)

Pommes et Oranges (1899) by Paul Cezanne (1839–1906). *Ordinal utility theory allows economists to rank a consumer's preferences for apples and oranges without needing to know the degree to which she prefers one item over the other.*

Tugan-Baranovsky and the Trade Cycle

Mikhail I. Tugan-Baranovsky (1865–1919)

During the 1800s, Say's Law had a powerful grip on economic thinking. Believing that there can never be an economy-wide excess of supply over demand, economists lacked a well-developed theory to explain the business cycle—the upward and downward oscillations of the economy. Economists typically attributed these cycles to external shocks, such as banking crises, changes in demands for a country's exports, or technological innovation. Though French historian and economist Jean Charles Léonard de Sismondi first observed the existence of these cycles in 1819, it wasn't until the late 1890s that Russian economist Mikhail Tugan-Baranovsky explained why these fluctuations will occur even without such shocks.

Tugan-Baranovsky located the origins of the business cycle within the economy itself—specifically, in business investments and the concentration of financial capital among a small group of capitalists. When the economy is humming along, profits rise. Capitalists use their earnings to purchase physical capital and borrow to finance even further expansion after depleting their funds. This drives up interest rates but, more importantly, results in an over-supply of capital goods, such as machinery, used to create other products. The return received on these investments thus drops. Businesses react by decreasing their investment and borrowing, and by reducing the demand for capital goods. This ultimately leads to an economic downturn. How does the economy put itself back on an upward path? Tugan-Baranovsky assumed that the downturn would not greatly affect savings behavior. As individuals continued to save their money, the supply of loanable funds increases until interest rates fall sufficiently to encourage new business investment, which stimulates economic growth.

Tugan-Baranovsky's theory suggested that business cycles are inherent in capitalism. Not only did it reveal the error of Say's Law, it also posed a challenge to Marx's theory of crisis. Instead of heading for destruction, capitalism contained self-correcting forces that kept it on a cyclical path of ups and downs. Tugan-Baranovsky's analysis would inspire future business-cycle research by Wesley Clair Mitchell, Nikolai Kondratiev, and Ragnar Frisch, who sought to measure these cycles and deepen our understanding of why they persist.

SEE ALSO Say's Law (1803), The Theory of Crisis (1867), Mitchell's *Business Cycles* (1913), Kondratiev Waves (1925), Mathematical Dynamics (1933), The Tinbergen Model (1936), The Multiplier–Accelerator Model (1939), Real Business Cycle Models (1982)

This illustration, featured on a vintage postcard, shows the Staten Island Savings Bank in New York. Mikhail Tugan-Baranovsky believed that fluctuations in business borrowing were an important driver of business cycles.

The Benefit Principle of Taxation

Knut Wicksell (1851–1926), Erik Lindahl (1891–1960)

Government officials have pondered the best way to finance government services since ancient times. One approach involves distributing the tax burden based on one's ability to pay, which John Stuart Mill described as "an equality of sacrifice." Adam Smith suggested, though, that an individual's tax payment should reflect the benefits he receives from government goods and services. But this "benefit principle" of taxation creates an incentive for people to lie about the benefits they receive to reduce their tax burden. Given this, how should government expenditures and the taxes to finance them be determined?

In 1896, Swedish economist Knut Wicksell offered an answer in his book *Finanztheoretische Untersuchungen (Studies in the Theory of Public Finance)* by suggesting all tax-expenditure proposals be put to a vote. Each voter will support a proposal only if her expected benefit is at least as great as her tax cost. This means that any government action for which total benefits exceed total costs to society will garner unanimous approval if the tax burden is distributed according to the benefit principle. Thus, only spending proposals that garner unanimous approval should be implemented. Moreover, Wicksell contended, if the distribution of income in society is just, then the distribution of the tax burden will be as well. In 1919, another Swedish economist, Erik Lindahl, demonstrated that this outcome would also be efficient if each individual paid a tax equal to the marginal benefit she received from governmental goods and services.

As Wicksell realized, achieving unanimous consent is impossible. He thus recommended that a supermajority be required to pass tax-expenditure policies, reasoning that this would approximate the ideals of the benefit principle and minimize the possibility of a slim majority of voters forcing others to pay for services that don't benefit them. Basing an entire tax system on the benefit principle remains unfeasible, but toll roads, and hunting and fishing license fees, are just two examples of its basic principles in action, as the revenues are typically used to finance services provided to those paying these fees.

SEE ALSO Rent and the Theory of Surplus (1662), Smith's *Wealth of Nations* (1776), Mill's *Principles of Political Economy* (1848), The Single Tax (1879), Public Choice Analysis (1962), Optimal Taxation (1971)

This 1902 picture shows a toll gate for a road in the Catskill Mountains in New York. Toll roads are often considered an example of the benefit principle in action.

Unemployment

John A. Hobson (1858–1940)

Severe unemployment had been a problem at numerous points during the nineteenth century and formed the backdrop for many economic writings. But it was not until the 1880s that economists began to treat it as a fact of economic life, a problem that could become severe during depressions and that caused serious difficulties for the working class. British writer John A. Hobson brought this new view into focus in his book, *The Problem of the Unemployed*, in 1896.

Hobson's work on unemployment is perhaps best known for the definition that he gave to the term: "all forms of involuntary leisure suffered by the working classes." By describing an unemployed worker as someone who was willing but unable to work rather than someone who voluntarily chose not to work, he shifted the conversation about unemployment from concerns over personal moral shortcomings, such as laziness, to social-economic causes.

Hobson located the cause of unemployment in underconsumption. Foreshadowing ideas later associated with John Maynard Keynes, he argued that economic downturns resulted from a deficiency of aggregate demand caused by oversaving. While saving might be good for the individual, too much saving could result in underconsumption in the economy as a whole. To remedy this, Hobson advocated a program of income redistribution that would boost consumption and employment by taking money away from wealthy savers and giving it to the lower classes to spend, alleviating unemployment by preventing it from happening in the first place.

Due to the grip of Say's Law, which suggested that overproduction and underconsumption couldn't exist in a market, economists of the period deemed Hobson's views on underconsumption heretical. But Hobson was not deterred. As part of a group known as the "New Liberals," who believed that laissez-faire principles had failed to provide economic stability and widespread prosperity, he continued to hammer away at classical economics and its approach to economic policy in a series of widely read writings into the 1930s. He pushed for the implementation of a "living wage" and condemned financial speculation on imperialist colonial ventures, money that he felt could have been better spent dealing with unemployment and underconsumption problems at home.

SEE ALSO Say's Law (1803), Underconsumption (1804), Luxemburg's *Accumulation of Capital* (1913), The Oxford Approach to Welfare (1914), Keynes's *General Theory* (1936)

An engraving from the 1880s, portraying tickets for a soup kitchen being distributed to unemployed workers in London.

The Real Rate of Interest

Irving Fisher (1867–1947)

Irving Fisher, a professor of mathematics and then of economics at Yale University, was perhaps the most influential American economist of the early twentieth century. Known for his contributions to monetary economics, he expressed the quantity theory of money in mathematical terms, describing the direct relationship between the money supply and the price level with this formula: $MV = PT$, where M is the money supply, V denotes velocity (the speed at which money circulates), P is the price level, and T represents the volume of transactions, or output, in the economy.

More significant, though, was his distinction between the real and nominal rates of interest and how they affect savings and investment decisions. The nominal interest rate is the rate at which money is lent in the marketplace. But in his book *Appreciation and Interest* (1896), Fisher argued that the nominal rate isn't the one that actually matters to borrowers, savers, and lenders. What does is the *real* rate of interest, which is the nominal rate less the rate of inflation. If the nominal interest rate on a loan is 6 percent and the rate of inflation is 3 percent, then the real return to the lender is only 3 percent. Inflation erodes half the purchasing power of this payment, and because that inflation will push up the borrower's income, the real cost of the interest payments also falls by half. Furthermore, *real* interest rates, like prices, are governed by supply and demand; people's preference for present versus future consumption affects the supply of loanable funds, while the productivity of investing impacts demand.

Fisher's insight resolved a good deal of the confusion about the role of interest rates in the economy. Even a very low nominal interest rate may not be sufficient to encourage investment when business prospects are poor, since borrowers are weighing the real rate of interest against their expected returns on an investment they are financing by the borrowing. Since the Great Recession, real interest rates have been near zero, and even negative, thanks to the Federal Reserve's efforts to stimulate investment and economic growth by making funds more cheaply available.

SEE ALSO The Quantity Theory of Money (1568), Thornton's *Paper Credit* (1802), The Abstinence Theory of Interest (1836), Mill's *Principles of Political Economy* (1848), Böhm-Bawerk's *Capital and Interest* (1884), Marshall's *Principles of Economics* (1890), Wicksell's Cumulative Process (1898)

A portrait of Irving Fisher (1927), whose work on interest rates shed light on how individuals and businesses make saving and investment decisions.

Wicksell's Cumulative Process

Knut Wicksell (1851–1926)

Since the 1500s, economic thinkers have used the quantity theory of money to understand the relationship between the money supply, price level, and output in the economy. In the early nineteenth century, Henry Thornton suggested that interest rates affect the extent to which prices will rise following a change in the money supply. In 1898, Swedish economist Knut Wicksell's model of the "cumulative process" solidified this link.

Wicksell theorized that there exists a "natural" interest rate that aligns consumer savings decisions with producer investment decisions. This natural rate of interest reflects the long-term average productivity of business investment and can only be estimated. If banks set the market interest rate equal to this natural rate, no inflation will result. But if the market interest rate falls below this threshold, businesses, seeing the opportunity to profit by borrowing funds at rates below their natural rate of return, will turn to banks for credit to finance new investment. This new investment increases the demand for resources in the economy, pushing up prices. This "cumulative process," as Wicksell called it, of prices spiraling upward can continue indefinitely as long as the market rate of interest remains below the natural rate and banks have an unlimited supply of credit.

Persistent inflation, then, can be traced to the effects of credit on the money supply when market interest rates fall below their natural levels. Requirements in some countries that banks maintain a share of customers' savings deposits as reserves help to limit the inflationary spirals that concerned Wicksell. These "reserve requirements" eventually lead banks to limit credit by curtailing their lending, which pushes market rates of interest upward. Observation of this dynamic led Wicksell to a theory of the business cycle, detailing how divergences between the market and natural rates of interest drive economic fluctuations through their impact on incentives for saving and borrowing. Estimating the natural rate of interest is of great concern to monetary policymakers as they seek to drive interest rates toward their natural levels to keep inflation under control.

SEE ALSO The Quantity Theory of Money (1568), Thornton's *Paper Credit* (1802), The Bullionist Controversy (1810), Tugan-Baranovsky and the Trade Cycle (1894), Mitchell's *Business Cycles* (1913), Kondratiev Waves (1925), Mathematical Dynamics (1933), The Tinbergen Model (1936), The Multiplier–Accelerator Model (1939), Real Business Cycle Models (1982)

In the early twentieth century, banks kept their required reserves in vaults similar to the one featured here, which was used for safeguarding depositor valuables.

Veblen's *Theory of the Leisure Class*

Thorstein Veblen (1857–1929)

American economist Thorstein Veblen was one of the most eminent critics of the marginalist approach to economic analysis. In a series of books and articles, he outlined an evolutionary approach to studying economic affairs, one grounded in the importance of the institutions, including laws, habits and customs, and technology, that govern economic activity. Veblen's insights laid some of the foundations for institutional economics, an approach that would play a prominent role in American economic thought during the first third of the twentieth century.

Veblen's most influential contribution came via his satirical book *The Theory of the Leisure Class*, published in 1899, which wedded sociology to economic analysis. Taking aim at the marginalists' portrayal of producers and consumers as rational utility maximizers, Veblen argued that the drive for social status motivated human behavior. At the most basic level, society was divided into a "leisure class," consisting of business people, lawyers, and other professionals, and a working class, the latter of which, through its labor, generated the wealth of the former. The working class's productivity allowed the upper class to devote its energies to the "conspicuous consumption" of leisure activities and goods that would reinforce its members' social status, including sports such as tennis and horse racing, religion, social activities including theater and opera, and fine clothing. As Veblen put it, "Conspicuous consumption of valuable goods is a means of reputability to the gentleman of leisure." Members of the lower classes, meanwhile, engage in "status emulation," imitating the consumption patterns of the upper classes, where possible, to convey the image of higher social status.

Veblen used this theory as the basis for his critique of capitalism. Where Karl Marx had praised capitalism for its productivity, Veblen dismissed its productive and acquisitive activity as socially wasteful, diverting resources from the production of more practical goods. Echoes of Veblen's critique can be found in contemporary discussions of rampant consumerism, and modern behavioral economics reflects an effort to construct a theory of human behavior that captures some of the broader forces observed by Veblen.

SEE ALSO Hesiod's *Work and Days* (c. 700 BCE), Productive and Unproductive Labor (1776), Marx's *Das Kapital* (1867), The Marginal Revolution (1871), Institutional Economics (1919), Behavioral Economics (1979)

An illustration (1905) by Albert Levering shows members of Veblen's leisure class attending a ball.

Clark's *Distribution of Wealth*

John Bates Clark (1847–1938)

At the end of the nineteenth century, American economists began to make the contributions that gave them international prominence. Among the first to do so was Columbia University professor John Bates Clark, who began his career as an opponent of capitalism but eventually became one of its most staunch defenders. His 1899 book, *The Distribution of Wealth*, provided a highly influential theoretical argument for the virtues of the competitive market process.

Clark outlined a theory of income distribution that explained how wages, profits from production, and rent from land are determined in a competitive system. Using the mathematical tools of the marginalists, Clark demonstrated that, under competition, the return to labor, capital, and land will equal the value of the additional output produced by the last unit of that input employed. This additional output is known as that input's marginal product. For example, a laborer's wage is given by the value of the output sacrificed if the business employed one less worker, while the return to the capitalist on an investment would be equal to the value of the additional output directly attributable to that investment. If all production inputs are paid according to their marginal product, these payments will exhaust the value of the output.

Clark used this theory to provide an ethical defense of the competitive capitalist system. The owners of production inputs should receive a return equal to the value they produce; any other distribution, he argued, would be unfair. Critics argued that Clark's theory was little more than an apology for the high profits earned by capitalists during a period of growing economic inequality. However, it also worked as an effective argument against socialism at a time when socialist ideas were gaining in popularity, since it countered Karl Marx's view that production generates a surplus that the capitalist can steal from labor. The marginal productivity theory remains central to economists' understanding of how the prices of production inputs are determined in capitalist economies. Later extensions of Clark's theory have clarified the ways in which such prices may deviate from this when the market isn't as highly competitive as Clark assumed.

SEE ALSO Thünen's *Isolated State* (1826), The Wages Fund Controversy (1866), The Labor Theory of Value and the Theory of Exploitation (1867), The Marginal Revolution (1871), *The Economics of Imperfect Competition* (1933)

Two women prepare materials at a shoe factory in Massachusetts, 1895. John Bates Clark's marginal productivity theory explains why, in a perfectly competitive market, workers' wages are determined by the value of the output they produce.

The Economics Tripos at Cambridge

Alfred Marshall (1842–1924)

As the science of political economy evolved during the nineteenth century, it began appearing in university curricula, eventually becoming the subject of study for full-blown degree programs. While the University of London offered the first undergraduate economics degree program in 1901, with several other universities following suit over the next few years, the Economics Tripos, created at Cambridge University in 1903, proved to be the most influential and helped to solidify Cambridge as the center of the economics universe in the first part of the twentieth century.

"Tripos" is the term used by Cambridge to denote a program of study leading to a bachelor's degree in a particular discipline or set of disciplines. Though students could study economics at Cambridge as part of the "moral sciences," Alfred Marshall, the professor of political economy, wanted an independent degree program in the discipline to provide "systematic training in its basic principles for future academics, businessmen and public administrators." His goal was not so much practical as to train students in a particular method of reasoning—economic reasoning. Students enrolled in the original Economics Tripos were steeped in economic analysis, but they also studied subjects such as political theory, international law, and economic history. This breadth forms a stark contrast to today's mathematics- and statistics-laden economics curricula.

The Economics Tripos was revised several times over the next few decades to further emphasize theoretical economics at the expense of politics and law. Its students had the benefit of being taught by several of the world's leading economists, including Joan Robinson, A. C. Pigou, and John Maynard Keynes. Though student demand for a specialized economics degree didn't begin to swell until the 1950s, Marshall's vision for the training of students skilled in economic reasoning was widely copied, paving the way for the development of economics as an academic discipline and for its eventual integration into the halls of policymaking, business, and finance.

SEE ALSO The German Historical School (1843), The Professionalization of Economics (1885), Marshall's *Principles of Economics* (1890)

King's College, University of Cambridge (1890–1900). King's College has been home to famous economists including John Maynard Keynes, A. C. Pigou, Richard Kahn, Nicholas Kaldor, and Richard Stone.

Pareto Optimality and Efficiency

Vilfredo Pareto (1848–1923)

Italian economist Vilfredo Pareto, who succeeded Léon Walras as a professor at the University of Lausanne in 1893, did more than any other economist to extend Walras's theoretical system and to emphasize the importance of general equilibrium analysis at the turn of the century. Pareto's training as a mathematician and engineer helped shape his approach to economics, which combined mathematics with a strong interest in empirical verification. He displayed these twin interests prominently in his *Manual of Political Economy*, published in 1906.

Pareto's conception of efficiency—now typically referred to as "Pareto optimality"—is his most influential contribution. F. Y. Edgeworth had provided a primitive conception of efficiency in 1881 that was related to situations in which each individual's utility is maximized, given the utility levels of others. In his *Manual*, Pareto extended this notion to an economy that involved production and exchange. He defined the optimum—or, in his words, society's "maximum ophelimity" (an economic term that Pareto himself invented)—as occurring when it isn't possible to identify a small change from that position which will make every individual either better off or worse off. In other words, a situation is Pareto-efficient if there is no move from that position that will make someone better off without making at least one other person worse off. If it is possible to improve the welfare of at least one person without reducing that of anyone else, the outcome is deemed inefficient.

This conception of efficiency neatly avoids the ethical problem of comparing those who gain utility with those who lose utility, since no change can be deemed an improvement if someone is made worse off. Though it is widely used for assessing efficiency in welfare economics, its practicality is very limited. Because most economic changes involve both winners and losers, they can't pass the Pareto test. As such, the Pareto criterion effectively reinforces the status quo. Economists have responded by developing other methods, such as the Kaldor–Hicks criterion, to judge whether outcomes are efficient, as well as social-welfare functions that allow economists to simultaneously consider different fairness issues.

SEE ALSO Consumer Surplus (1844), Edgeworth's *Mathematical Psychics* (1881), The Bergson Social Welfare Function (1938), The Kaldor–Hicks Efficiency Criterion (1939), The Fundamental Theorems of Welfare Economics (1943), The Theory of Second Best (1956)

Vilfredo Pareto's concept of "maximum ophelimity" became a cornerstone for evaluating whether economic outcomes are efficient.

Indifference Curves

Francis Ysidro Edgeworth (1845–1926), Vilfredo Pareto (1848–1923)

The ordinal conception of utility, which says that consumers can rank the bundles of goods available for purchase from most to least preferred, paved the way for the introduction of a new graphical tool, the indifference curve. A bundle of goods that a consumer prefers more provides greater utility than one that she prefers less, but a consumer is indifferent among various bundles when they each provide an identical level of utility. On a graph, the indifference curve represents this set of bundles. F. Y. Edgeworth formulated the original mathematical derivation and graphical illustration of these curves in his *Mathematical Psychics* (1881), but Italian economist and sociologist Vilfredo Pareto's *Manual of Political Economy* (1906) laid out these curves in the form familiar to anyone studying economics today.

Edgeworth saw indifference curves as a useful theoretical construct for analyzing the effects of changes in prices and income levels, but Pareto believed that it was possible to construct indifference curves empirically, using observed individual behavior instead of an ad-hoc assumption about the nature of utility. This meant that a map of indifference curves, each reflecting the set of bundles that provide a particular level of utility, could represent real-life consumer preferences and show how consumers judge each potential bundle as superior, inferior, or equivalent to others based on the satisfaction that it generates. For Pareto, this indifference map provides "a photograph of consumer tastes." The intersection of these tastes with the constraints faced by the consumer determines the bundle of goods and services she actually chooses, and this allows the economist to trace the effects on consumer choices caused by changes in those constraints.

Indifference curves became an important element of ordinal utility analysis and revealed preference theory, which suggests that an individual's preferences can be revealed by the consumption choices she makes in different circumstances. This eventually supplanted the cardinal approach that characterized traditional utilitarian analysis and assumed utility is measurable. Though it later became more fashionable and useful to express these relationships mathematically, indifference curves remain a standard device for illustrating to students the consumer choice process and the underpinnings of the demand curve.

SEE ALSO Edgeworth's *Mathematical Psychics* (1881), Ordinal Utility (1893), Income and Substitution Effects (1915), The Hicks–Allen Consumer Theory (1934), Revealed Preference Theory (1938)

Vilfredo Pareto believed that empirical observations could help create indifference curves that mapped the real-life preferences of consumers, such as this young child considering the various goods featured in a holiday window display.

Pigou's *Wealth and Welfare*

Arthur Cecil Pigou (1877–1959)

Adam Smith's concern with increasing national wealth, as measured by the value of society's output, has remained a focus in economics since *Wealth of Nations* was published in 1776. Utilitarian thinking, though, suggested that there are factors to consider besides wealth. Economists grew increasingly concerned with how to measure "welfare" and how it is affected by changing circumstances. In the twentieth century, this concern gave rise to the field of "welfare economics," the basic outlines of which were originally provided by Cambridge economist Arthur Cecil Pigou in his 1912 treatise, *Wealth and Welfare*.

Pigou was concerned that the market system too often failed to maximize welfare when left to its own devices. Though he was unable to devise a method for measuring welfare that went beyond national wealth, he cited the emergence of monopolies, unemployment, pollution, and the insufficient production of certain important goods and services such as lighthouses and scientific research as examples of market outcomes that could prevent a nation from maximizing its output. For Pigou, the significance of these problems suggested that the government could intervene in the marketplace to increase economic welfare.

Pigou was by no means the first to identify the potential shortcomings of a market system and laissez-faire. For more than a century, economists had chipped away at Smith's conception of the invisible hand, which suggested that the pursuit of their self-interest by producers and consumers would be in society's best interests. However, Pigou situated these concerns within the marginalist framework of cost–benefit analysis handed down by his teacher, Alfred Marshall. This allowed him to demonstrate more formally where private and social interests diverged and why market outcomes can fail to maximize welfare. He also used these tools to show how various forms of government intervention, from public provision of roads to the taxation or regulation of pollution, could remedy these market failures. In the 1930s, economists including Abram Bergson and Paul Samuelson began to develop social-welfare theories that captured broader conceptions of welfare, including society-wide utility or welfare functions that can give greater weight to particular outcomes, such as the well-being of the poor.

SEE ALSO Smith's *Wealth of Nations* (1776), The Invisible Hand (1776), Marshall's *Principles of Economics* (1890), External Economies and Diseconomies (1912), The Bergson Social Welfare Function (1938), Arrow's Impossibility Theorem (1951), Public Goods (1954), Externalities and Market Failure (1958), *Collective Choice and Social Welfare* (1970)

"Five Cent a Spot" by Jacob Riis (1849–1914) captures lodgers living in a crowded tenement in New York City, depicting conditions that called into question whether a market system would operate in society's best interests.

External Economies and Diseconomies

Arthur Cecil Pigou (1877–1959)

Economic activity involves individuals making decisions within a larger social context, and the effects of these choices often spill over onto others. The production of steel, for example, may generate pollution, which harms the environment or the health of those living near the factory. Education provides benefits to society as a whole by increasing worker productivity. A market system sometimes doesn't force individuals to account for those "external" benefits and costs when they make decisions, resulting in inefficient outcomes where there are too many activities with negative spillover effects and too few with positive effects.

Alfred Marshall first developed a theory of external economies (positive spillovers) and external diseconomies (negative spillovers) in his *Principles of Economics* (1890). He observed that the expansion of an industry may change production costs for all producers. For example, the invention of cost-saving machinery or the development of transportation networks, such as railroads, may not be worthwhile when an industry is small but yet repay themselves handsomely on a larger scale. But it was Marshall's pupil, A. C. Pigou, who applied this theory more broadly in *Wealth and Welfare* (1912). These "externalities," as they came to be called, represent failures of the "invisible hand" to generate outcomes that maximize societal wealth. For Pigou, the government should correct these shortcomings if it can do so effectively. The best strategy, he argued, would be to use taxes to reduce activities with negative externalities and to offer subsidies for activities with positive externalities. These measures came to be known as Pigovian taxes and subsidies.

Though later challenged by Ronald Coase, who argued that Pigou had underestimated the difficulties of computing the appropriate tax and subsidy rates, Pigou's theory of externalities remains central to modern economic analysis and policy. Today, governments utilize Pigovian taxes and subsidies to address a wide range of externalities, including carbon taxes to combat pollution and subsidies for higher education. In fact, William Nordhaus won the 2018 Nobel Prize in economics partly due to his estimates of the benefits associated with carbon taxes.

SEE ALSO The Invisible Hand (1776), Marshall's *Principles of Economics* (1890), Veblen's *Theory of the Leisure Class* (1899), Pigou's *Wealth and Welfare* (1912), Resources for the Future and Environmental Economics (1952), Externalities and Market Failure (1958), The Coase Theorem (1960), Emissions Trading (1966)

This painting of the Bethlehem Steel Works (1881) by American artist Joseph Pennell shows the plant emitting air pollution, an example of an external diseconomy.

Mitchell's *Business Cycles*

Wesley Clair Mitchell (1874–1948)

During the first half of the twentieth century, economists turned their attention to the causes of the business cycle, the tendency for the economy to oscillate between expansion and contraction. American economist Wesley Clair Mitchell, a student of Thorstein Veblen, distinguished himself with his novel approach to the subject during that period.

Rather than constructing a theory of the cycle and searching for evidence that would support or refute it, Mitchell began with economic data. He believed that business cycles affect the entire economy and are highly complex, defying any single causal explanation. Understanding these boom–bust cycles thus required gathering and analyzing massive amounts of data on variables such as prices, profits, and employment. Mitchell and his many students occupied themselves with this statistical work, which began with the preparation of his 1913 book, *Business Cycles*, and continued until his death in 1948. He drew his data from business periodicals and government records and, because Mitchell worked in an era before the advent of computers, he analyzed the figures by compiling them into tables and graphs to assess changes over time. This inductive approach—letting a theory emerge from the data—was typical of the institutional economists of the period. Mitchell's appointment, in 1920, as the first director of the National Bureau of Economic Research advanced his research further, as he steered much of the Bureau's effort to this project.

Through his work, Mitchell moved empirical studies of the business cycle to the front burner of economic research and captured the interest of politicians and business leaders who wanted to understand the causes of economic cycles and to forecast future economic activity. Mitchell was never able to construct a general theory of business cycles from his analysis, but his 1913 book set the tone for the next three decades of business-cycle research. Though Cowles Commission economists later disparaged his statistical methods because they didn't rely on an underlying economic theory to guide the data-analysis process, the attention he brought to business cycles laid the groundwork for the Keynesian and real business cycle theories that came to dominate economics later in the twentieth century.

SEE ALSO Tugan-Baranovsky and the Trade Cycle (1894), Veblen's *Theory of the Leisure Class* (1899), Institutional Economics (1919), The National Bureau of Economic Research (1920), Kondratiev Waves (1925), The Cowles Commission (1932), Mathematical Dynamics (1933), Keynes's *General Theory* (1936), The Tinbergen Model (1936), The Multiplier–Accelerator Model (1939), Real Business Cycle Models (1982)

Employees work in the Division of Vital Statistics, a division of the U.S. Census Bureau (1909). Wesley Clair Mitchell used data from the Census Bureau and other sources to chart and analyze business cycles.

The Federal Reserve System

The first recognized central bank, the Swedish Riksbank, was founded in 1668, and the Bank of England, the most prominent central bank of that era, was established in 1694. These early banks were tasked with financing their government's debt and managing the nation's supply of money and credit. Today, these functions remain at the heart of modern central banking.

Central banking in the U.S. has a rocky history. Alexander Hamilton, the country's first Secretary of the Treasury, met considerable resistance when he tried to establish a central bank in the late 1700s. Though he ultimately prevailed, the charter of the First Bank of the United States wasn't renewed in 1811. Over the next century, efforts to reestablish a central bank ebbed and flowed as different currencies issued by state banks proliferated. Financial panics became common as depositors, fearing bank failures, rushed to withdraw their funds. Though many recognized the need for monetary stability, they also found centralized control over the nation's money supply unacceptable. The Panic of 1907, which saw the stock market fall by nearly fifty percent, finally persuaded policymakers to take decisive action.

The Federal Reserve Act of 1913 established the Federal Reserve System. Comprised of twelve regional banks, it supports the U.S. banking system by lending money to private banks when they can't secure needed funds from other sources. By the 1920s, the Fed, as it is known, solidified its role as a monetary policymaker when it purchased government securities (debt instruments issued by the U.S. Treasury), signaling its willingness to influence the money supply and credit markets. The Great Depression became the first major test of the Fed's power to handle an economic crisis. Though it didn't prevent banking collapses, it received the power to regulate the banking system and monitor its health in the Depression's aftermath. Later, Milton Friedman and Anna Schwartz would argue that the Fed could have prevented the Depression if it hadn't contracted the money supply. The Fed has continued to manage the nation's money stock since then, and, when faced with the Great Recession, helped stave off a banking crisis by propping up troubled banks.

SEE ALSO Thornton's *Paper Credit* (1802), The Great Depression (1929), *A Monetary History of the United States* (1963), The Great Recession (2007)

A contemporary photo of the Marriner S. Eccles Building, home to the Board of Governors of the United States Federal Reserve System, located in Washington, D.C. The building was completed in 1937.

Luxemburg's *Accumulation of Capital*

Rosa Luxemburg (1871–1919)

Karl Marx's *Das Kapital*, like other great treatises in the history of economics, contained gaps, errors, and contradictions with which later generations of thinkers have grappled. Polish-born German economist Rosa Luxemburg questioned how capitalists would find a market for their products as the living conditions of the working class worsened and unemployment continued to increase. If the working class couldn't afford to purchase goods, not only would business profits fall, but it would also be impossible to accumulate the capital needed to finance labor-saving machinery. This machinery is key to Marx's theory of crisis because it would lead to increasing unemployment and create the conditions that would ultimately inspire the proletariat to revolt against the business class.

Luxemburg offered a resolution for this contradiction in her book *Accumulation of Capital* (1913) by linking Marx's analysis of capitalism with an explanation for imperialism. Underconsumption at home, she argued, spurred the expansion of colonial empires to non-capitalist regions, which offered markets for the country's products. As underconsumption increased on the home front, competition among countries to expand their colonial empires would intensify. In the process, these non-capitalist areas are drawn into the orbit of capitalism—sometimes peacefully, and other times at the point of the sword. But at some point the ability of these colonies to feed the capitalist machine, too, will weaken. At this point, the capitalist system will begin to break down, ushering in the crisis that Marx had predicted.

Luxemburg's underconsumptionist theory of capitalism put her within a tradition that included T. R. Malthus, J. A. Hobson, and, not long thereafter, John Maynard Keynes. The coercive and militaristic nature of colonial capitalism made her a staunch anti-war activist, as well as an agitator for a socialist revolution in Germany. Her involvement with these revolutionaries led to her execution at the hands of the German government in 1919. Though some details of *Accumulation of Capital* were criticized by Marxists and non-Marxists alike, it has been widely hailed as one of the most important contributions to the Marxist literature since *Das Kapital*.

SEE ALSO Underconsumption (1804), Marx's *Das Kapital* (1867), Unemployment (1896), Keynes's *General Theory* (1936)

Rosa Luxemburg addresses a crowd gathered for the Seventh Congress of the socialist organization Second International, 1907.

The Oxford Approach to Welfare

John A. Hobson (1858–1940)

Because he believed underconsumption by the wealthy reduced production and employment, and also because he rejected several tenets of the marginal revolution, English economist J. A. Hobson called himself an "economic heretic." In fact, his major work on welfare economics, *Work and Wealth*, was a reaction against A. C. Pigou's *Wealth and Welfare*, which represented the marginalist methods of cost–benefit analysis that he opposed. Hobson particularly objected to equating wealth with material goods, believing that it would narrow the focus of economic analysis to the production of such items. In response, Hobson designed an approach to economic welfare that went beyond this focus, developing what came to be known as the Oxford approach.

Hobson disagreed with Alfred Marshall's conception of economics as a science unconcerned with the political, social, and ethical impacts of a market-based economy geared to growing national wealth. He advocated for an "organic" conception of welfare, prioritizing the well-being of society as a whole over individual desires. Society should offer its members the ability to have "the good life," which allows health, justice, freedom, and creativity to flourish. Rejecting the marginalist notion that economic welfare was measurable, he called for assessing outcomes based on the "aggregate effect upon the life and character of the agent," especially the human cost of labor. He supported access to education for all and the more equal redistribution of wealth.

The Oxford approach conceptualized by Hobson and others, including John Ruskin, Arnold Toynbee, and R. H. Tawney, stood apart from the Cambridge view of welfare that dominated British economics and linked welfare to the value of goods produced. Even so, the Oxford approach had an impact in Britain; its basic principles guided the design of the British welfare state in the early 1900s, which included higher taxes on the wealthy and national unemployment insurance. Many American institutionalists eagerly seized on Hobson's work, making it required reading in their courses. Contemporary pushes for greater redistribution of wealth, living minimum wages, and climate protection at the expense of economic growth show that the concerns raised by these Oxford thinkers remain with us today.

SEE ALSO Underconsumption (1804), The Dismal Science (1849), The Marginal Revolution (1871), Marshall's *Principles of Economics* (1890), Pigou's *Wealth and Welfare* (1912), Institutional Economics (1919)

A nineteenth-century photo of the University of Oxford, for which the Oxford approach was named.

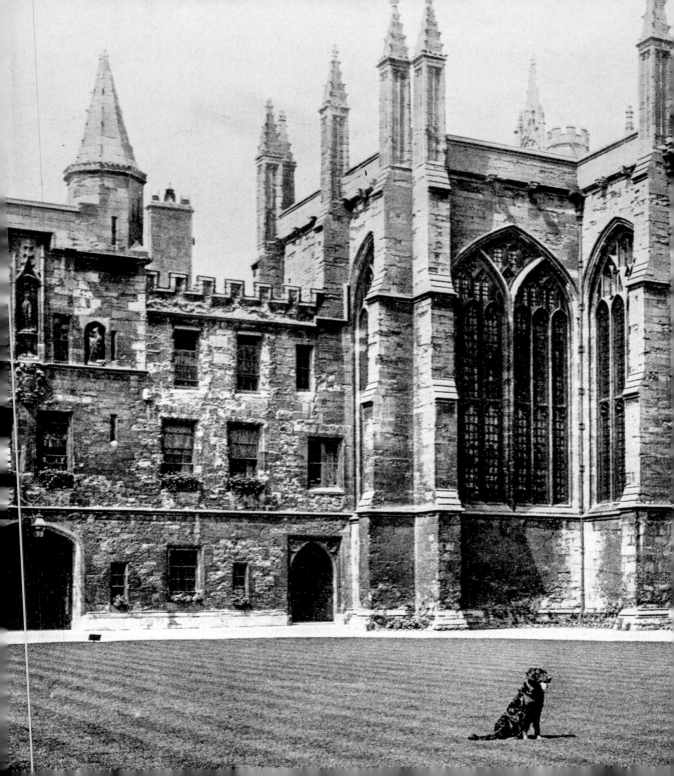

Income and Substitution Effects

Evgeny "Eugen" Evgenievich Slutsky (1880–1948)

In 1915, Russian economist, mathematician, and statistician Eugen Slutsky published an article in the Italian economics journal *Giornale delgi Economisti*, advancing the insights on utility and demand that Vilfredo Pareto had outlined in the same journal more than two decades earlier. Though Slutsky's article went unnoticed for some twenty years, J. R. Hicks and R. G. D. Allen "rediscovered" his contributions while working on their own influential theories on consumer demand.

Slutsky demonstrated that the overall impact of a change in price can be broken down into *income* and *substitution effects*. Let's consider the impact of a ten-percent increase in the price of orange juice. People will now buy less juice and more of other beverages like milk, even if their incomes rise commensurately, simply because juice prices are now relatively higher. This is the substitution effect. Because higher-priced juice also eats up more of people's income, they have less money available for other goods; thus, the amount of juice demanded will fall still further. This is the income effect.

Slutsky showed that the total effect of a price change is the sum of these two effects, creating what is now called the "Slutsky equation." Today, it remains central to modern demand theory. Apart from providing greater insight into the law of demand, the ability to identify the substitution effect allows economists to measure losses in efficiency caused by taxes and tariffs, which distort the choices of consumers.

Slutsky also distinguished between "relatively indispensable goods," the consumption of which rises with income, and "relatively dispensable goods," the consumption of which falls with income. The former are now better known as "normal goods" and the latter as "inferior goods." While most products fall into the first category, the demand for some items, such as boxed macaroni and cheese or generic-branded food, decreases as income rises. If the income effect associated with an inferior good were large enough, the demand for the good could even rise with its price. Economists call these "Giffen goods," after Scottish economist Robert Giffen (1837–1910), but generally believe that they don't exist, as they contradict the law of demand.

SEE ALSO The Law of Demand (1820), Indifference Curves (1906), The Hicks–Allen Consumer Theory (1934), Revealed Preference Theory (1938)

Coffee and tea are examples of substitutes. An increase in the price of one product will increase the demand for products that are substitutes for it.

Institutional Economics

John R. Commons (1862–1945), Wesley Clair Mitchell (1874–1948), Walton H. Hamilton (1881–1958), John Maurice Clark (1884–1963)

Institutional economics represented the first distinctively American school of economic thinking. It came of age in 1919 when economist Walton Hamilton published a manifesto for an "institutional approach" to economics, one that examined how institutions, such as law and social norms, molded human behavior. Institutionalism's most notable early supporters included Hamilton, John Maurice Clark (the son of John Bates Clark), and Wesley Clair Mitchell. Their work rejected the existence of a "homo economicus" who continually calculates benefits and costs, and emphasized how law, custom, and technology can influence economic outcomes.

Unlike the marginalists, who analyzed the economy from a static point of view, institutional economists saw the economy as an evolving organism, where those holding economic power have disproportionate control over the distribution of income and wealth. Citizens and business interests create pressures for legal and social changes that affect economic activity, while technological advances such as industrialization alter the economy's basic structure. Institutional economists borrowed insights from other disciplines, including psychology, sociology, and law, to better understand the economy, and they adopted more "scientific," data-driven methods to study economic questions. They were also concerned with the "problem of control," which meant developing policies to deal with economic problems that resulted from the market system and the growth of corporate power. For example, Commons studied the role of labor unions in curbing the power that business had over the working classes, while Clark probed the challenges of controlling monopolies. The institutionalists' investigative approach contrasted starkly with the abstract, mathematical theorizing favored by the marginalists.

The institutional approach soon occupied a prominent place in economics. Its followers found their way to Washington, D.C., where they helped develop labor and social welfare policies, including the New Deal. Institutionalism fell out of favor following World War II with the rise of Keynesianism, and the increasing preference for mathematical methods of theorizing.

SEE ALSO The Marginal Revolution (1871), Wicksell's Cumulative Process (1898), Veblen's *Theory of the Leisure Class* (1899), Clark's *Distribution of Wealth* (1899), Mitchell's *Business Cycles* (1913), *Legal Foundations of Capitalism* (1924), Logical Positivism (1938), The Keynesian Revolution (1947)

Because laws, including their interpretation by the U.S. Supreme Court, often significantly affect how markets work, institutional economists considered the study of legal systems an important part of economic analysis.

The National Bureau of Economic Research

Wesley Clair Mitchell (1874–1948)

Economics was primarily a theoretical science until well after World War II. Economists to this point had developed theories based on logical—and eventually mathematical— deductions from a set of basic assumptions, though they anchored a good share of their analysis in events that they observed around them. Alfred Marshall, for example, described having "visited the poorest quarters of several cities . . . looking at the faces of the poorest people", as an inspiration for becoming an economist. Nonetheless, economics was anything but a science based on the collection and analysis of data.

This began to change with the founding, in 1920, of the National Bureau of Economic Research (NBER) under the direction of Columbia University economist Wesley Clair Mitchell. Like others involved in the Bureau's founding, Mitchell believed that sound theory and policy could only be developed from a firm quantitative footing. This required scholars to engage extensively with economic data, using statistical techniques. Mitchell paid particular attention to business cycles, and much of the NBER's early efforts were devoted to increasing our understanding of the forces driving the economy's ups and downs. By bringing together a group of similarly interested economists, the NBER expanded the amount of empirical analysis conducted on the subject and made this work more efficient.

The work of NBER economists in the early years went well beyond business cycles. Studies of the determinants of national income, the distribution of income, and price movements figured prominently in the Bureau's output. The NBER also modeled how to undertake sophisticated quantitative analysis, facilitating the expansion of this approach within the economics profession. Business cycle analysis remains a core activity of the NBER today; its Business Cycle Dating Committee is a go-to source for identifying the start and end dates of recessions in the United States. With affiliated researchers now numbering in the hundreds at universities across the U.S., and spanning virtually every corner of economic analysis, the Bureau remains a major force in economics research.

SEE ALSO Mitchell's *Business Cycles* (1913), The Econometric Society (1930), The Cowles Commission (1932), Mathematical Dynamics (1933), National Income Accounting (1934), The Tinbergen Model (1936), The Consumer Price Index (1946), *A Monetary History of the United States* (1963)

Wesley Clair Mitchell (right) delivers an address at the tenth anniversary of the Social Science Research building's dedication at the University of Chicago, 1939.

The Socialist Calculation Debate

Ludwig von Mises (1881–1973), Fred M. Taylor (1855–1932), Oskar Lange (1904–1965), Abba Lerner (1903–1982), Friedrich A. Hayek (1899–1992)

The growth of industrial capitalism in the late nineteenth and early twentieth centuries brought with it the rise of Marxism and renewed interest in socialism. But with this interest came questions about how to operate a socialist economy. Could the performance of a socialist economy, in which the public or the government owns the means of production, equal or exceed that of capitalism? Though Marx and Engels had been largely silent on these matters, those sympathetic to socialism essentially took it for granted that centralized economic planning offered a superior alternative.

In 1920, Austrian economist Ludwig von Mises launched a full-on attack against socialism's possibilities. He argued that, with government ownership of the means of production, prices couldn't guide the allocation of capital to its most valued uses. As a result, socialist production would be inefficient. Undeterred by Mises's critique, defenders of socialism, including economists Fred Taylor, Abba Lerner, and Oskar Lange, contended that market prices are unnecessary for allocation, suggesting instead that planners could use a mathematical model of the economy, akin to that laid out by Léon Walras, to determine prices. Lange, in particular, argued that the government could play the part of the Walrasian auctioneer, adjusting prices until a stable and efficient equilibrium was achieved. Linear programming, a mathematical method for solving complex optimization problems developed in part to assist Soviet economic planning, is an example of Lange's insight in action.

In writings published during the 1930s and 1940s, F. A. Hayek made the case that government planners couldn't possibly possess all the information about the demands for, quality of, and availability of goods that is conveyed by the pricing system. Resources would inevitably be misallocated, and, as such, socialism could never hope to replicate the efficiency of capitalism. This argument, though, was not sufficient to deter some socialists. While the poor performance of socialist economies, such as the Soviet Union, would seem to put history on the side of the critics of socialism, advances in computation continue to suggest, for some, that efficient socialist planning is very much within the realm of possibility.

SEE ALSO *The Communist Manifesto* (1848), Marx's *Das Kapital* (1867), The Austrian School (1871), Walras's *Elements of Pure Economics* (1874), Pareto Optimality and Efficiency (1906), Hayek's *Road to Serfdom* (1944), Hayek's "Use of Knowledge in Society" (1945), Linear Programming (1947), Computation: The Orcutt Regression Analyzer and the Phillips Machine (1948)

A crowd of socialists gathers for a May Day demonstration at Union Square in New York City, 1912. May Day, also known today as International Workers' Day, is a public holiday in many countries around the world.

Knight's *Risk, Uncertainty, and Profit*

Frank H. Knight (1885–1972)

Frank Hyneman Knight was a founder of what has become known as the Chicago School of Economics, both loved and reviled for its faith in competitive markets and suspicion of government intervention in the economy. His 1921 book, *Risk, Uncertainty, and Profit*, remains a classic of modern economics for exploring the sources of profit within a competitive market. Though risk had for centuries been noted as a factor that justified the ability to reap profits and helped determine how much profit can be made, Knight provided an in-depth explanation for this relationship.

Knight found a contradiction between the assumptions underpinning perfectly competitive markets and the ability to turn a profit. The assumption of perfect knowledge, in which buyers and sellers have perfect information about the present and the future, is especially problematic. With perfect knowledge, it's impossible for firms to turn a profit, because prices will equal the costs of production. Even if an opportunity to make a profit arises, new sellers will immediately enter the market, driving prices back down to a level that just covers production costs. Profits, then, result only when there is a departure from perfect competition, such as when knowledge is imperfect.

To explain the possible effects of imperfect knowledge, Knight distinguished between risk and uncertainty. Risk is calculable because it's based on the known probability of an event occurring, allowing producers to account for it when calculating the best way to maximize their profits. For example, farmers might purchase drought insurance to cover the risk of drought-induced losses, which transfers the risk to the insurance company. Uncertainty, on the other hand, is unknowable. For example, there was no way in the 1990s to predict that in just a few years people would be willing to pay $4 for coffee-flavored drinks and that the coffeehouse industry would explode. Profits, then, are the return to diving into this world of uncertainty and, in essence, stumbling onto success. In fact, Knight's distinction between risk and uncertainty established a role for the entrepreneur within the economy as a figure who commits resources to production in the face of uncertainty while accepting the liability for failure.

SEE ALSO Bernoulli on Expected Utility (1738), Turgot's *Reflections* (1766), The Austrian School (1871), The Chicago School (1946), The Permanent Income Hypothesis (1957), The Economics of Information (1961), Public Choice Analysis (1962)

Thomas Edison uses a dictation machine, 1914. Knight believed that profits were the reward to entrepreneurs, such as Edison, for innovating in the market in the face of uncertainty.

Legal Foundations of Capitalism

John R. Commons (1862–1945)

John R. Commons was an American economist and social reformer who belonged to the school of institutional economics. His two significant works in economic theory, *Legal Foundations of Capitalism* (1924) and *Institutional Economics* (1931), attempted to broaden economic analysis beyond the individualism of the classical and marginalist approaches. At the heart of Commons's framework was an emphasis on "collective action," which described how society shapes the actions of individuals and changes economic and social conditions through law, custom, and other institutions.

For Commons, it was impossible to understand the forces that govern economic activity without considering the legal system that underlies them. His *Legal Foundations of Capitalism* attempts to explain the interaction between legal and economic forces. Industrial capitalism of the early 1900s was characterized by the growth of big business, low wages, and difficult and unsafe working conditions. Commons argued that these conditions didn't simply result from individual calculations of profit and utility, technological advances, and economies of scale; changes in the legal structure also played an essential role. Courts at this time redefined and modified existing laws governing property, pricing practices, trade unions, and the valuation of corporate assets. These changes altered the terms for the transactions that take place between buyers and sellers, investors and business managers, and employers and employees. In turn, production, prices, the distribution of income and wealth, and the path of economic growth were transformed just as dramatically.

Commons believed that these changes tilted the playing field in favor of big business, validating pricing practices that harmed consumers and reducing the power of labor unions to defend worker interests. As a frequent adviser to state and federal governments, he drafted numerous important pieces of progressive legislation on industrial relations, workplace-safety regulation, public-utility regulation, and unemployment insurance. The lessons here for Commons, though, went beyond policy. He believed that both sound economic analysis and continued economic progress require careful attention to the legal system.

SEE ALSO The Marginal Revolution (1871), Jevons's *Theory of Political Economy* (1871), Marshall's *Principles of Economics* (1890), Antitrust Laws (1890), Veblen's *Theory of the Leisure Class* (1899), Institutional Economics (1919), The Economic Analysis of Law (1973)

Unionized workers at Woolworth's, striking for a forty-hour work week, pose for a group photo, 1937. For John R. Commons, labor unions were an example of the "collective action" that can impact economic conditions.

Kondratiev Waves

Nikolai Kondratiev (1892–1938)

Researchers studying the business cycle seek to capture the causes and patterns of short-term fluctuations in the economy, typically over periods lasting seven to eleven years. In 1925, however, Soviet economist Nikolai Kondratiev used nineteenth-century data to argue that economic activity is governed by much longer cycles, or long waves, that last 50 to 60 years and contain shorter business cycles. Austrian economist Joseph Schumpeter, one of the leading proponents of Kondratiev's ideas, christened these cycles "Kondratiev waves."

Kondratiev, a student of business cycle analysis pioneer Mikhail Tugan-Baranovsky, devoted much of the 1920s to studying economic cycles before his career—and eventually his life—was cut short by Joseph Stalin's regime. By examining 150 years' worth of data on retail and wholesale prices, interest rates, and the production of goods such as coal, lead, and pig iron in the United States, England, Germany, and France, he determined that long waves could be broken down into three phases: expansion, stagnation, and decline. Each phase lasted a fairly consistent length of time across the historical cycles. Kondratiev suggested that, over the preceding 150 years, cycles had been sparked by the Industrial Revolution, the invention of steam power and railway expansion, and developments in steel, electricity, and engineering. Some economists think that the twentieth century witnessed two more long cycles triggered by the arrival of the automobile and mass production, and by advances in computing and telecommunications.

Kondratiev's writings were quickly translated into other languages. They were controversial but attracted significant support among leading business cycle analysts. The Econometric Society held his work in such high regard that it elected him to its first group of Fellows in 1933. Kondratiev believed that understanding long waves and their causes could help forecast future economic performance, but whether his findings reflected real economic forces or resulted from a statistical anomaly remains unclear. Today, mainstream economists reject long-wave theory because they don't see sufficient evidence for the existence of these waves or their ability to predict future economic activity. However, the theory remains popular among some heterodox economists who believe that these waves show capitalism's long-term instability.

SEE ALSO Tugan-Baranovsky and the Trade Cycle (1894), Mitchell's *Business Cycles* (1913), The Econometric Society (1930), Mathematical Dynamics (1933), Creative Destruction (1942)

Railroad workers sit on the engine car of a train, 1918. Nikolai Kondratiev believed that the expansion of railway transportation and innovations in steel production launched a long wave around 1850.

The Cobb–Douglas Function

Charles W. Cobb (1875–1949), Paul H. Douglas (1892–1976)

The Cobb–Douglas function is widely used to model both the production process and consumer utility. Though originally proposed by Swedish economist Knut Wicksell, it took its name from mathematician and economist Charles Cobb and economist (and eventual U.S. Senator) Paul Douglas. In their 1928 paper, "A Theory of Production," they demonstrated the function's usefulness for econometric analysis.

The Cobb–Douglas function originated in Douglas's analysis of U.S. manufacturing data. He discovered that there was a stable relationship between labor and capital inputs used in production and the resulting level of output. After he consulted with Cobb, they decided to measure the contribution of labor and capital to the production process. First, they adopted Wicksell's production function and expressed it in this form: $P = bL^kC^{1-k}$. P indicates quantity of output, L and C denote labor and capital inputs, respectively, and b and k are constant terms, with k and $(1-k)$ measuring the relationship between input levels and outputs. They then used statistical analysis and data on output, labor, and capital to estimate b and k. The results indicated that their production function fit the data very well, generating accurate predictions of manufacturing output.

Economists quickly realized that this function had applications beyond manufacturing. Douglas himself used it to estimate the relationship between wages and worker productivity, and economists soon began to model consumer utility in the same fashion by combining the Cobb–Douglas function with the consumer's budget constraint to derive demand functions for different goods. The coefficients in these demand functions, which show the relationship between the quantities consumed on the one hand and prices, incomes, and consumer tastes and preferences on the other, can be estimated with economic data, showing how demand responds to changes in factors such as prices and incomes.

Though the Cobb–Douglas form has some technical limitations that need not concern us here, it generates accurate estimates in areas as wide-ranging as productivity studies, the analysis of economic growth, and the demand for everything from labor to child care to automobiles. Because of this, it remains an essential part of the economist's theoretical and empirical toolkit.

SEE ALSO Elasticity (1890), The Benefit Principle of Taxation (1896), Wicksell's Cumulative Process (1898), The Econometric Society (1930)

Paul Douglas (right) and Harvard economist Alvin Hansen (left) review charts before Senate hearings on unemployment in 1938.

The Hotelling Model of Locational Choice

Harold Hotelling (1895–1973)

Though useful in many ways, Cournot and Bertrand's analysis of competition in oligopolies, or markets with few sellers, couldn't account for this common situation: when sellers offer an identical good at different prices, consumers don't all purchase from the seller offering the lowest price. In 1929, Stanford University economist Harold Hotelling explained this phenomenon and introduced the economic analysis of locational choice.

The starting point for Hotelling's work was the depiction of the market as an extended region. Rather than congregating around a point, sellers disperse across this area: for example, along a "Main Street." Each consumer will purchase from the seller offering the lowest net price, accounting for the costs of traveling to and from the seller's location. Consumers living near to seller A, then, will only purchase from seller B if B's price is low enough to offset the higher transportation costs. Seeking to maximize profit, sellers adjust prices with this in mind, potentially leading to an equilibrium in which each seller offers the same good at a different price.

When firms can adjust their locations, Hotelling showed that each firm can increase its profits by moving toward the other firm, attracting customers who may not have patronized it before. As firms continue to adjust their locations to boost profits, both firms will ultimately locate next to each other, at the center of Main Street. Sometimes known as the "Principle of Minimum Differentiation" or "Hotelling's Law," this idea explains why you see certain types of businesses, such as fast-food restaurants, located in close proximity to each other. Hotelling's insight also forms the foundation of modern location theory, which examines why specific economic activities are located in particular places. Its implications, though, go beyond business practices. Hotelling's theory inspired Anthony Downs's work on the median voter theorem, which says that the outcome selected under a majority voting system will be that preferred by the individual whose preferences are in the middle of the political spectrum.

SEE ALSO Thünen's *Isolated State* (1826), Cournot's *Researches* (1838), The Bertrand Model (1883), The Median Voter Theorem (1948), The Rational Voter Model and the Paradox of Voting (1957)

According to the Hotelling model of locational choice, fast-food restaurants will locate in proximity to one another to maximize their profits.

The Great Depression

As the most severe economic downturn since the Industrial Revolution, the Great Depression lived up to its name. It began in the United States with the stock-market crash of October 29, 1929, now known as "Black Tuesday."

The tremendous boom in the stock market during the Roaring Twenties, fueled by rapid economic growth and surging consumer and business confidence, masked an unhealthy economy. By 1929, wages and productivity were declining, while unemployment and consumer debt levels crept upwards. When panicked investors, fearing a major market reversal, started to sell off stocks in droves, the market went into a tailspin. Widespread layoffs soon followed; at the height of the depression in 1933 more than 15 million Americans were unemployed. People made runs on banks, withdrawing their funds because they feared for the safety of their deposits. Despite efforts by the Federal Reserve to prop up some banks, these panics caused nearly half the nation's banks to fail. Worse still were the human costs. Families lost their homes and farms, and hunger was a constant presence for many. "Use it up, wear it out, make do, or do without" became the motto for many households.

When Franklin D. Roosevelt became president in 1932, he launched the New Deal, a collection of economic policies that provided the first large-scale example of a government jump-starting the economy. Jobs programs and massive public-works projects tackled unemployment, and legislation such as the Glass-Steagall Act and the Securities Exchange Act provided banking and financial regulations that helped stabilize markets. These policies were overseen by new federal agencies, including the PWA (Public Works Administration), FDIC (Federal Deposit Insurance Corporation), and SSA (Social Security Administration). Some of these "alphabet soup agencies" still operate today.

The Depression lasted until the start of World War II in 1939, when the latter's enormous demands for output and manpower alleviated one set of economic problems while introducing another. The Depression's length and severity provided many important lessons, showing the need to regulate financial markets, the importance of the Federal Reserve as a lender of last resort, and the ability of deficit spending to spur economic recovery.

SEE ALSO The Industrial Revolution (1760), The Federal Reserve System (1913), World War II (1939), *A Monetary History of the United States* (1963), The Great Recession (2007)

Men line up for a free meal at a Depression-era soup kitchen, 1936.

The Econometric Society

Irving Fisher (1867–1947), Ragnar Frisch (1895–1973), Charles F. Roos (1901–1958)

1930

Though the marginal revolution presented mathematics as a powerful tool for economic analysis, economists who used sophisticated mathematical and statistical methods prior to World War II formed a distinct, if growing, minority. By 1930, the idea of a scholarly society dedicated to advancing work that integrated economic theory, mathematics, and statistics, which Norwegian economist Ragnar Frisch called "econometrics," began to gain traction. Soon, the Econometric Society was born.

The Econometric Society was the brainchild of Frisch, Irving Fisher, and Charles Roos, who polled like-minded economists on their interest in an organization that would promote this type of analysis, hold regular conferences, and create a network of scholars interested in this work. After receiving a warm response, they held an organizational meeting in Cleveland, Ohio, in December 1930, immediately after the meetings of the American Economic Association, the American Statistical Association, and the American Association for the Advancement of Science, also happening in Cleveland at that time. Though most economics professional societies in this period were organized along national lines, the Econometric Society actively recruited scholars from around the world. European economists were well represented in the initial 173 members, and economists from Algeria, China, and Japan were also counted among their numbers. The Society's first annual meeting was held in Lausanne, Switzerland, in September 1931.

The goals of the Society, as laid out by Fisher, Frisch, and Roos, were "the advancement of economic theory in its relation to statistics and mathematics" and to promote studies that used these methods to study real-world economic problems. In doing so, economics could provide "a constructive and rigorous way of thinking similar to that which has come to dominate in the natural sciences." With the financial support of American financier Alfred Cowles III, the Society in 1933 started a new journal, *Econometrica*, to disseminate this work. In the ensuing decades, the Econometric Society, along with the Cowles Commission, a research institute dedicated to advancing econometric analysis, helped transform economics into a mathematical and quantitative science. Now one of the world's largest societies of economists, the Econometric Society continues to promote research that relies on rigorous mathematical and quantitative methods.

SEE ALSO The Marginal Revolution (1871), The Real Rate of Interest (1896), The Cowles Commission (1932), Mathematical Dynamics (1933)

A bird's-eye view (1931) of Lausanne, Switzerland, where the Econometric Society held its first annual meeting.

The Multiplier

Richard Kahn (1905–1989)

The Great Depression raised the question of whether government investment in public works, such as the construction of roads, dams, and schools, could increase employment and income. No one had devised a mechanism to estimate the magnitude of these gains until Cambridge University economist Richard Kahn came up with the concept of the "multiplier," which measures how a dollar of additional spending affects national output and income.

In a 1931 article called "The Relation of Home Investment to Unemployment," Kahn posed a practical problem: If a road-building project employs an additional worker, and that worker uses his income to purchase goods and services from other sectors, how many more workers will be employed economy-wide? Kahn's answer involved determining the share of his income that the worker spends on these purchases. He formulated a multiplier that depends on the marginal propensity to consume, or the percentage of an income increase that consumers spend rather than save, finding that the greater the marginal propensity to consume, the greater is the boost to overall employment that results from hiring that additional worker.

While Kahn focused on the employment effects of public investment, his work helped his Cambridge colleague John Maynard Keynes make the case that deficit spending can lift an economy out of a recession. When government spending increases, production also increases, raising incomes for those involved in this production. This fuels additional consumer spending, boosting aggregate demand, output, and income even further and eventually putting the economy on an upward trajectory again.

Economists continue to dispute the magnitude of the multiplier. Some even suggest that it is close to zero, meaning that every dollar of additional government spending causes nearly a dollar of private output to disappear. Even so, policymakers often invoke Kahn's multiplier to argue that increases in government spending or tax cuts can boost economic activity. Indeed, this motivated the U.S. government's response to the Great Recession; its massive fiscal stimulus package included everything from the "cash for clunkers" program (to encourage new car purchases) to financing for massive public-works projects, the benefits of which spread across the economy.

SEE ALSO The Great Depression (1929), The Circular Flow Diagram (1933), Keynes's *General Theory* (1936), The Multiplier–Accelerator Model (1939), The Keynesian Revolution (1947), The Great Recession (2007)

Workers compact concrete used to build the Boulder Dam (later renamed the Hoover Dam), located on the border of Arizona and Nevada, 1934. Kahn's multiplier suggested that each dollar spent on a public works project like this would boost national output by more than one dollar.

Scarcity and Choice

Lionel Charles Robbins (1898–1984)

The definition of *economics* has evolved significantly over time, reflecting changes in how economists and others have conceptualized the subject. The Ancient Greeks defined it as the art of household management. Adam Smith considered political economy "a branch of the science of a statesman or legislator" targeted at increasing a nation's wealth. In 1890, Alfred Marshall shifted the subject's focus to people, changing the name of the subject to "economics" and defining it as "a study of mankind in the ordinary business of life." For Marshall, economics examines "that part of individual and social action which is most closely connected with the attainment and with the use of the material requisites of wellbeing."

By the early 1930s, none of these definitions adequately captured what economists were doing and how they were doing it. The marginal revolution had changed the approach to many economic questions by portraying consumers and producers as rational calculators of benefits and costs concerned with deciding how best to allocate their resources. This led Lionel Robbins, then a young professor at the London School of Economics, to suggest an alternative definition. In his *Essay on the Nature and Significance of Economic Science* (1932), Robbins described economics as "the science which studies human behaviour as a relationship between ends and scarce means which have alternative uses," an idea that dates back to the Ancient Greek poet Hesiod, who highlighted scarcity as the fundamental economic problem.

Today, Robbins's definition of economics as the study of choices made under conditions of scarcity is central to the discipline's identity, but it took two decades for it to gain widespread acceptance. Some rejected it because it didn't rule out subjects, such as politics, that lie outside the discipline's traditional boundaries. Indeed, Robbins opened the door to the study of any situation that involves making choices, expanding economics into areas including law, politics, marriage and divorce, and even religion. This movement is sometimes called "economics imperialism," suggesting that economists are trying to "take over" other social sciences. While that hasn't happened, economic analysis does inform inquiry in these areas, thanks to Robbins's definition.

SEE ALSO Hesiod's *Work and Days* (c. 700 BCE), Xenophon's *Oeconomicus* (c. 370 BCE), Smith's *Wealth of Nations* (1776), Marshall's *Principles of Economics* (1890), Logical Positivism (1938), "The Methodology of Positive Economics" (1953), The Economics of Discrimination (1957), Public Choice Analysis (1962), The Economic Analysis of Law (1973)

Lionel Robbins defined economics as the study of choices made under the conditions of scarcity, such as this shopper's decision about how much of her budget to spend on fruits and vegetables each week.

The Cowles Commission

Alfred Cowles (1891–1984)

The business and economic forecasting tools used around the beginning of the Great Depression often failed to provide accurate predictions of the stock market's movements. Dissatisfied with these existing methods, American investment adviser Alfred Cowles III embarked on a search for economists with strong quantitative backgrounds to improve them. After receiving a suggestion that he approach members of the Econometric Society about his interests, Cowles contacted two of its founders, Irving Fisher and Charles Roos. In the ensuing months, they sketched plans for the Cowles Commission, a new research organization overseen by the Econometric Society and funded by Cowles.

Much of the Cowles Commission's earliest research centered on the quantitative analysis of financial markets. The Commission also sponsored a series of conferences that gave leading mathematical economists and econometricians from around the world an informal setting to discuss their work. When the Commission moved from the more isolated Colorado Springs to the University of Chicago in 1939, its research program expanded to include mathematical economic theory along with econometric analysis.

The Commission's move to Chicago brought some members of the University's economics faculty into its fold and helped attract new talent and financial backing. The Cowles Commission expanded its operations under the guidance of Jacob Marschak, known as the "father of econometrics," who was appointed as Cowles research director in 1943, and of Tjalling Koopmans, his eventual successor. Its research played a key role in the development of general equilibrium theory, macroeconomic forecasting models, and new mathematical and statistical techniques. The Commission's research staff during the 1940s and 1950s included future Nobel Laureates Trygve Haavelmo, Koopmans, Lawrence Klein, Leonid Hurwicz, Kenneth Arrow, Gérard Debreu, Franco Modigliani, Harry Markowitz, and James Tobin. In 1955, the Cowles enterprise moved to Yale University, where it continues to exist as the Cowles Foundation for Research in Economics and to devote itself to "foster[ing] the development and application of rigorous logical, mathematical, and statistical methods of analysis."

SEE ALSO The Econometric Society (1930), Haavelmo's "Probability Approach" (1944), Linear Programming (1947), The Theory of Portfolio Selection (1952), Proving the Existence of a General Equilibrium (1954), Large-Scale Macroeconometric Models (1955), The Modigliani–Miller Theorem (1958), Debreu's *The Theory of Value* (1959), The Theory of Auctions (1961)

Alfred Cowles (pictured at his desk) meets with, from left to right, Herbert E. Jones, Harold T. Davis, Gerhard Tintner, and Dickson H. Leavens in Colorado Springs, 1937. Jones, Davis, Tintner, and Leavens were important contributors to the Cowles Commission's work in its formative years.

The Modern Corporation and Private Property

Adolf A. Berle (1895–1971), Gardiner C. Means (1896–1988)

In early twentieth-century America, the rise of big business in sectors such as heavy manufacturing, oil, railroads, and even retail challenged existing theories of competitive markets, which assumed small, profit-maximizing firms that can't control prices. In *The Modern Corporation and Private Property* (1932), lawyer Adolf Berle and economist Gardiner Means examined how the corporation's structure threatens its shareholders and even the foundations of democracy.

Joint-stock companies, which sell shares of ownership stock that can be bought and sold by investors, are a forerunner of the modern corporation. Issuing these shares, often to scores of people, provided companies with financing for massive expansion. Berle and Means described how corporate law separated ownership from control by facilitating the development of these joint-stock companies. Shareholders are typically far removed from a corporation's day-to-day operations, while managers make the primary decisions about what gets produced, how production is organized, and how prices are established. This becomes a problem when the interests of managers and board members, whose compensation often isn't tied to the firm's profits, diverge from those of the shareholders, whose holdings grow more valuable if profits grow. Because shareholders are uninvolved with the corporation's daily operations, they often can't monitor whether managers are truly operating in the shareholders' interests—a problem that worsens as the corporation's size and the number of shareholders increase.

For Berle and Means, this separation of ownership from control concentrates economic power in the hands of the select few who control large corporations. Eventually, the influence of self-serving corporate managers would rival political power within the U.S., a problem that Berle and Means felt could only be addressed by granting shareholders greater power. Later developments in agency theory suggested that owners can structure contracts to avoid these conflicts of interest, but the issues raised by Berle and Means still play out in today's debates over measures for regulating corporate governance and restricting the influence of corporate insiders.

SEE ALSO Antitrust Laws (1890), Institutional Economics (1919), *Legal Foundations of Capitalism* (1924), The Great Depression (1929), Agency Theory (1973), The New Institutional Economics (1997)

Adolf A. Berle in 1965. Though most well known for his work on the modern corporation, he spent many years in government service, including a stint as the U.S. ambassador to Brazil.

The Circular Flow Diagram

Frank H. Knight (1885–1972), Paul A. Samuelson (1915–2009)

For every student of introductory economics, the circular flow diagram, which depicts how income and products flow through the economy, has become a familiar sight. In the 1750s, Richard Cantillon provided an intuitive description of these movements when discussing the amount of money that needs to circulate in an economy to sustain its operations, and François Quesnay's *Tableau Économique* provided an early diagram of them not long thereafter. Though economists continued to discuss the flow of resources between sectors of the economy, nearly two centuries would pass before the first circular flow diagram appeared in University of Chicago economist Frank Knight's pamphlet, *The Economic Organization* (1933).

Called the "wheel of wealth" by Knight, his version of the diagram illustrated how businesses and households exchange productive inputs, such as labor and the use of property, for consumer goods. It also tracked the corresponding exchange of money. For Knight, this wheel of wealth didn't merely represent the movements of goods and income; it also showed how marketplace interactions between individuals and businesses determine both how society is organized and the interdependence between production and consumption in a market economy.

Knight's pupil, Paul Samuelson, devised the circular flow diagram as we know it today, using the image of a hydraulic machine to show money, inputs, and goods being pumped, like water, throughout the economy. In its simplest version, Samuelson's illustration showed the building blocks of national accounting: productive inputs flow from the public to firms in return for income, while consumer goods and services flow from firms to the public in exchange for payment. A more complicated version depicted investment being "pumped into" the system and savings "leaking from" it, illustrating both the multiplier, which translates a dollar of additional expenditure into output worth more than the original expenditure, and the basic Keynesian proposition that the economy is in equilibrium when savings are equal to investment. Recent depictions of the circular flow have added more details to the system, featuring banking and government sectors as areas of injection and leakage. The diagram remains an indispensable tool for illustrating how resources flow through a complex economic system.

SEE ALSO Cantillon's *Essay on the Nature of Trade* (1755), The *Tableau Économique* (1758), Knight's *Risk, Uncertainty, and Profit* (1921), The Multiplier (1931), National Income Accounting (1934), Keynes's *General Theory* (1936), Samuelson's *Economics* (1948)

Main image: *Paul Samuelson used an image of a water pump to show how investment flows into the economy and boosts national income.* **Inset:** *An example of a simple circular flow diagram.*

Goods and services

Consumer expenditure

Wages, rent, dividends

Households

Factors for production

Firms

Émigré Economists

The rise of Hitler and the Nazi party in Germany, along with similar fascist and anti-Semitic movements across Northern and Eastern Europe, closed off academic employment opportunities to many economists of Jewish ancestry or with suspect political affiliations. More than 3,000 scholars were dismissed from positions in German-speaking countries between 1933 and 1939, including more than 250 economists. With dim employment prospects and even life-threatening conditions at home, these economists migrated, sometimes at great personal risk, to more hospitable countries— particularly England and the United States. The landing points for these émigrés included the London School of Economics and Harvard University. In New York City, the "University in Exile," later the Graduate Faculty of Political and Social Science at the New School for Social Research, became home to the largest collection of émigré scholars in the U.S.

Though the rise of the Soviet Union and other totalitarian regimes in the late 1910s and the 1920s led to a similarly large exodus, it was the group of émigré economists from the 1930s who went on to make numerous groundbreaking contributions to the subject. These included some of the most talented economists of Europe at the time, as well as several children who went on to become leading minds in the field. Future Nobel Prize winners Simon Kuznets, Wassily Leontief, Franco Modigliani, Leonid Hurwicz, Tjalling Koopmans, Trygve Haavelmo, and Robert Aumann, as well as Cowles Commission research director Jacob Marschak, were among their ranks. By the end of World War II in 1945, half the articles appearing in the *American Economic Review* were authored by foreign-born economists who held academic positions at American institutions. While a handful of the émigrés returned to their home countries following the war, most remained in the U.S. and Britain. This migration helped shift the locus of economic thought from Europe to America in the postwar period and also brought to the U.S. a significant cadre of economists who were well-versed in mathematical and quantitative techniques and would reshape the very character of economic analysis.

SEE ALSO The Cowles Commission (1932), World War II (1939), The "Nobel Prize" in Economics (1969)

Franco Modigliani (1918–2003) takes a phone call in a photo created on the same day that he learned he had won the 1985 Nobel Prize in economics. He fled fascist Italy in 1938 and emigrated to the United States, where he received his PhD at the New School.

The Theory of Monopolistic Competition

Edward H. Chamberlin (1899–1967)

By the 1930s, a gap in Marshallian economic thinking had emerged. Alfred Marshall and his protégés had proposed theories describing perfect competition, on the one hand, in which large numbers of sellers offered identical products for sale, and its antithesis, a monopoly, where one firm dominates the market. The theory of "monopolistic competition" helped fill the gulf between these two extremes. In 1933, Harvard's Edward Chamberlin and Cambridge University's Joan Robinson, working independently of each other, published works that explain why the markets for, say, blue jeans or beer work differently than those for wheat and corn. Chamberlin's book, *The Theory of Monopolistic Competition*, gave this new set of ideas its name.

Marshall's analysis of the market assumed that a large number of firms sell identical products and that competition is based solely on the price of this good. Believing that this was unrealistic, Chamberlin pointed out that most markets begin as an oligopoly, a market with a small number of sellers where the actions of each firm depend on those of others. As more sellers enter the market, firms go to increasingly great lengths to differentiate their products from those produced by their competitors. Firms can distinguish their goods by changing the details of the product, such as the ingredients in beer or the detailing of blue jeans, or through advertising, which allows sellers to associate a particular image with their product. By highlighting why its product is unique, each firm in the market maintains some degree of monopoly power and will retain many of its customers if it increases its prices. But as there are other sellers offering a similar product, each firm also has to contend with competition.

The major lesson from Chamberlin's book was that there are a host of situations that fall between monopoly and perfect competition. If economists wanted their theories to accurately reflect reality, they needed to consider these scenarios in their work. Members of the Chicago school would question the need for this theory, suggesting that the model of perfect competition provided a close-enough approximation for most markets. Nonetheless, monopolistic competition remains a centerpiece of market-structure analysis.

SEE ALSO Cournot's *Researches* (1838), The Bertrand Model (1883), Marshall's *Principles of Economics* (1890), *The Economics of Imperfect Competition* (1933), The Chicago School (1946), The New Keynesian Economics (1977), The New Trade Theory (1979)

An advertisement for carbonated water, 1931. Advertising is one tool that firms can use to differentiate their products.

1790 – 1931

To-day, as for the past one hundred and forty years, where quality is the sole criterion, the Soda Water is Schweppes.

The Heckscher–Ohlin Model

Eli Heckscher (1879–1952), Bertil Ohlin (1899–1979)

David Ricardo's theory of comparative advantage, which suggested that countries should specialize in the production of goods that they can create at the lowest opportunity cost, formed the foundation of the classical theory of international trade for more than a century. Despite its staying power, it had a major limitation. Ricardo explained that comparative advantage arises due to differences in production capabilities across countries. It couldn't, however, explain why trade occurred between countries with identical production capabilities. Swedish economist Eli Heckscher and his student, Bertil Ohlin, solved this problem by explaining that comparative advantage results from the availability of production inputs in one country relative to another. After Heckscher provided the original insight in 1919, Ohlin expanded it into a general equilibrium framework in his 1933 book, *Interregional and International Trade*. This theory became known as the Heckscher–Ohlin model.

To create goods, producers need various types of labor, capital, materials, and land. The availability of these inputs can differ greatly from country to country. Countries with a plentiful amount of one resource will have a cost advantage in producing goods which use that resource heavily. For example, countries with abundant sources of oil, such as those in the Middle East, or skilled labor, such as the U.S., will tend to specialize in the production of oil- or skilled-labor–intensive goods; they will export those goods in exchange for goods produced with inputs in relatively scarce supply at home.

The Heckscher–Ohlin model earned Ohlin a share of the 1977 Nobel Prize (Heckscher was by that time deceased) and provided the cornerstone for theories that explore how international trade leads to economic development and growth. That said, research by economists Max Corden and Peter Neary in the early 1980s found that the specialization of the Heckscher–Ohlin model can be destructive. As a country's revenue increases following the discovery of natural-resource deposits, its currency appreciates, making its other exports less competitive and potentially devastating those industries. This phenomenon is known as the "Dutch Disease," because it describes the decline in Dutch manufacturing following the discovery of natural gas off its coastline in 1959.

SEE ALSO The Balance-of-Trade Controversy (1621), The Division of Labor (1776), Classical Political Economy (c. 1790), The Theory of Comparative Advantage (1817), Walras's *Elements of Pure Economics* (1874), The Stolper–Samuelson Theorem (1941), The Factor-Price Equalization Theorem (1948), The New Trade Theory (1979)

In this illustration from the 1930s, a New Orleans–based receiving station handles new shipments of bananas. The Heckscher–Ohlin model posits that countries such as Ecuador and Costa Rica specialize in banana production because their plentiful amounts of labor and favorable climate allow them to grow bananas at a low cost.

Unloading Bananas,
New Orleans, La.—60

The Economics of Imperfect Competition

Joan Robinson (1903–1983)

Economics, like most academic disciplines, has traditionally been dominated by men. Writers such as Jane Marcet and Harriet Martineau popularized economic ideas, but apart from Mary Paley Marshall, the wife and sometimes coauthor of Alfred Marshall and the first female lecturer in economics at Cambridge, women were not among those making cutting-edge contributions to the field, as until the twentieth century they were typically excluded from the educational opportunities that would facilitate these contributions. Cambridge University professor Joan Robinson made her mark as the first woman to significantly alter the course of economic analysis with *The Economics of Imperfect Competition* (1933).

Like Edward Chamberlin, who developed his theory of monopolistic competition at the same time, Robinson believed that economists had erred in focusing on perfect competition. She offered her book as a "box of tools" to broaden their analysis to markets where imperfect competition existed. Rather than ground her analysis in product differentiation, as Chamberlin had done, Robinson took a more general approach that focused on sellers producing goods that serve as imperfect substitutes for those made by other firms. To illustrate the interplay of monopolistic and competitive processes in these markets, she introduced the downward-sloping marginal-revenue curve, which tracks the additional revenue received from the sale of another unit of a good. While a wheat farmer can sell every bushel he can grow at the going market price, a dish-soap producer has to lower its price to attract more customers and increase sales. As a result, the additional revenue from selling an additional unit of the product is less than the price of the good, which affects the imperfectly competitive firm's production decisions.

Robinson also drew conclusions for economic welfare from her analysis, paying special attention to the production inefficiencies and exploitation of labor that can arise under imperfect competition. She coined the term "monopsony" to describe markets where there are only a small number of buyers but many sellers, and described how "monopsony power" can be a particular problem in labor markets with few employers and many prospective workers by giving employers significant power over wages.

SEE ALSO Cournout's *Researches* (1838), The Labor Theory of Value and the Theory of Exploitation (1867), Marshall's *Principles of Economics* (1890), Clark's *Distribution of Wealth* (1899), Pigou's *Wealth and Welfare* (1912), *The Theory of Monopolistic Competition* (1933), Keynes's *General Theory* (1936)

Joan Robinson, pictured here in the 1920s, authored a groundbreaking analysis of imperfect competition.

Mathematical Dynamics

Ragnar Frisch (1895–1973)

When the first Nobel Prize in economics was awarded in 1969, the Prize Committee recognized two pioneers in mathematical economics and econometrics, Ragnar Frisch of Norway and Jan Tinbergen of the Netherlands. Frisch gave up a position in his family's precious-metals business to pursue a degree in economics, eventually earning a PhD in mathematical statistics in 1926. He devoted his career at the University of Oslo to advancing the mathematical basis of economics. He was a founding member of the Econometric Society, having coined the term "econometrics," and, as the first editor of its journal, *Econometrica*, provided a professional venue for economists to spread these quantitative methods.

In "Propagation Problems and Impulse Problems in Dynamic Economics," his classic 1933 paper on the business cycle, Frisch presented a method for modeling the ups and downs of the economy and introduced the terms "macro" economics, describing the study of the aggregate economy, and "micro" economics, the study of individual consumers, firms, and markets, into the lexicon. Frisch suggested that the economy's pendulum-like movements are the product of recurrent "impulses," or external shocks to the economy, such as technological innovations. The shocks are then transmitted through the economy by propagation mechanisms, which he described as laws of motion intrinsic to the economy. Frisch was able to simulate these processes with his model, generating realistic cycles. He called it a "rocking-horse" model because the motion caused by the initial impulse would eventually die out, just as a rocking horse in motion will eventually stop moving.

Frisch's theoretical analysis of the business cycle signaled a sharp turn away from the more empirical approach of Wesley Mitchell and the NBER. Instead of collecting and analyzing data, his approach suggested that economists model how an economy generates business cycles. By wedding sophisticated mathematical analysis to econometric techniques, Frisch developed a model that provided reasonably realistic simulations of these cycles, demonstrating how such methods could deepen our understanding of important economic problems. When combined with the lessons soon to emerge from Keynes's *General Theory*, Frisch's work ushered in a new era of macroeconomic analysis.

SEE ALSO Tugan-Baranovsky and the Trade Cycle (1894), Mitchell's *Business Cycles* (1913), The National Bureau of Economic Research (1920), The Econometric Society (1930), Keynes's *General Theory* (1936), The Tinbergen Model (1936), Hicks's *Value and Capital* (1939), The Multiplier–Accelerator Model (1939), *Foundations of Economic Analysis* (1947), Real Business Cycle Models (1982)

Children sit atop rocking horses in this photo from the early 1900s. Ragnar Frisch created a "rocking-horse" model of business cycles to explain how shocks to the economy would eventually dissipate.

The Stackelberg Model

Heinrich von Stackelberg (1905–1946)

The models of monopolistic competition that emerged in 1933 from Edward Chamberlin and Joan Robinson addressed one set of departures from perfect competition: markets with a large number of sellers that offer different versions of the same product. But this left unexamined a whole range of situations, including markets that may not be very competitive because they're dominated by few sellers. German economist Heinrich von Stackelberg helped fill this gap in our understanding in his 1934 book, *Market Structure and Equilibrium*, by providing one of many new models that examined these situations.

The Stackelberg model describes a duopoly, or a market with two sellers, where additional firms are unable to enter the market. One seller, by virtue of its size, dominates the market and is the acknowledged leader of the industry. The smaller firm bases its decisions on the leader's actions. Stackelberg, like Cournot, assumed that firms compete based on quantity produced, with the good's price determined by the forces of supply and demand. Under these conditions, the decision-making process for these two firms becomes a game of strategy. The leader knows with certainty that the follower will choose its output based on the leader's output choice. The leader will use this knowledge to set the level of production that maximizes its profits given the anticipated behavior of the follower. The follower's best option for maximizing profits is then to produce as the leader expects it to—it can do no better than this. The resulting equilibrium, Stackelberg demonstrated, finds the leader maintaining its dominant position.

The insights of game theory have extended Stackelberg's work to many contexts, including markets with multiple followers and leaders, dynamic environments in which the "game" between firms plays out over time, instances where one firm has more information than another, and situations where followers can make credible threats against the leader. Though no real-world situation fits the Stackelberg model perfectly, it explains how General Motors dominated the U.S. auto industry during the 1960s and Microsoft did the same for the software market in more recent years.

SEE ALSO Cournot's *Researches* (1838), The Bertrand Model (1883), Game Theory Enters Economics (1944), Non-Cooperative Games and the Nash Equilibrium (1950)

Parked cars sit along the Allegheny River in Pittsburgh, Pennsylvania, 1938. The mid-twentieth-century U.S. automobile industry is often considered an illustration of the Stackelberg model at work, with General Motors playing the leader's role.

National Income Accounting

Simon Kuznets (1901–1985), James E. Meade (1907–1995), Richard N. Stone (1913–1991)

Though economic growth has been a major subject of analysis since the eighteenth century, economists didn't develop methods to measure national income until the twentieth century. Initial attempts, often made for taxation purposes, were incomplete because the individuals who made them lacked the data and the manpower needed for accurate accounting. This began to change as nations grappled with the economic challenges of reconstruction after World War I, the Great Depression, and the looming possibility of another global conflict. The Great Depression led the U.S. Senate in 1933 to call for estimates of national income since 1929. Simon Kuznets, later the 1971 Nobel Laureate in economics, was tasked with preparing these estimates, as he had already assembled such data for the NBER during the 1920s. Kuznets and the researchers working with him delivered these estimates a year later.

The process of measuring national income was complicated, as there was no agreed-upon definition of "national income." To address this, Kuznets and his team prepared two sets of estimates, one measuring the value of all goods and services produced (based on market prices) and the other measuring incomes received. However, one major item that they omitted was the value of household labor, from house cleaning to child care provided by a stay-at-home parent—an omission against which Kuznets strenuously objected but that persists in today's measures of national income and output.

Kuznets's method had another major drawback: it lacked basis in economic theory. British economists and future Nobel Laureates James Meade and Richard Stone resolved this problem during the 1940s. Building on John Hicks's statement of gross national product as the sum of consumption, investment, and government expenditures ($Y = C + I + G$), Meade and Stone used double-entry accounting to create detailed national records of production and expenditure. Because the figures in their columns had to balance, this form of accounting ensured more reliable results and reflected the Keynesian proposition that aggregate demand should equal aggregate supply in a given year. This work led to the development of today's standardized system of national accounting, which can be used to compare national incomes across countries.

SEE ALSO The National Bureau of Economic Research (1920), The Great Depression (1929), The Circular Flow Diagram (1933), Hicks's *Value and Capital* (1939), Development Economics (1954)

Two sisters wash dishes from an early-morning breakfast, 1937. Official definitions of national income, such as GDP, do not count the value of cleaning, child-rearing, and other forms of household labor.

The Hicks–Allen Consumer Theory

John R. Hicks (1904–1989), R. G. D. Allen (1906–1983)

Alfred Marshall used the concept of cardinal utility, which implies that utility is measurable, to underpin his influential theory of demand. Though utility can't be measured, Marshall's theory dominated economic thinking well into the twentieth century. The ordinal approach to utility, which avoids the measurability issue by stating consumer preferences in terms of which options are better or worse, had been around since the late 1800s, but it didn't become the basis for a new approach to consumer behavior until British economists J. R. Hicks and R. G. D. Allen constructed their theory of demand in 1934.

Marshall's demand theory, which was grounded in marginal utility analysis, suffered from several pitfalls. It failed to account for complementarity between goods—that the satisfaction received from one good, such as gin, may depend on the amounts of other goods, such as tonic water, consumed. It also couldn't fully explain why demand curves slope downward. Drawing on earlier work by F. Y. Edgeworth and Vilfredo Pareto, Hicks and Allen turned Marshall's theory on its head by creating a framework based on indifference curves and the marginal rate of substitution, the rate at which consumers are willing to trade off one good for another.

Using this approach, they showed that demand curves could be derived from indifference curves and budget constraints, which show the bundles of goods that a consumer can afford to purchase with her income. When prices change, the bundles of goods that a consumer can afford to purchase also change, affecting her purchasing habits. Hicks and Allen demonstrated that the effects of a price change can be broken down into two components, a *substitution effect* and an *income effect*, a result previously discovered by Eugen Slutsky but virtually unknown until this point, and outlined the conditions under which goods can be considered complements or substitutes for one another. The Hicks–Allen theory can explain why higher-income workers may work less when wages rise, while lower-income workers work more, as well as why direct-income transfers to the poor are more likely to improve their well-being than goods subsidies, such as food stamps.

SEE ALSO Utilitarianism (1789), Jevons's *Theory of Political Economy* (1871), Edgeworth's *Mathematical Psychics* (1881), Marshall's *Principles of Economics* (1890), Ordinal Utility (1893), Indifference Curves (1906), Income and Substitution Effects (1915), Revealed Preference Theory (1938).

A woman shops at an American supermarket, 1948. The Hicks–Allen consumer theory provides insight into why shoppers choose particular bundles of goods and why these choices might change.

Keynes's *General Theory*

John Maynard Keynes (1883–1946)

If there is a modern work in economics that has been as influential as Adam Smith's *Wealth of Nations*, it is John Maynard Keynes's 1936 book, *The General Theory of Employment, Interest and Money*. *The General Theory* is at once a product of the Great Depression, a stunning rebuke to the still-dominant classical approach to macroeconomics, and a compilation of work from the intellectual community of Cambridge economists in the late interwar period.

Classical economics had its grounding in Say's Law, which claimed that wages and prices would adjust to economic shocks and quickly remedy unemployment. The Great Depression made it very difficult to sustain this claim. At the heart of Keynes's approach was aggregate demand—the sum of consumption, investment, and government spending (written as $C + I + G$). He argued that aggregate demand, not prices, determines output and employment. Unemployment results from insufficient aggregate demand—and, as seen with the Great Depression, this insufficiency could persist for long periods of time. Keynes suggested that the government could play a role in stimulating the economy, in stark contrast to the classical view that government intervention was either not necessary or likely to do more harm than good. He showed that debt-financed government spending and tax cuts could boost aggregate demand and thus output and employment. By the same token, the government could help calm an overheated economy by raising taxes or reducing spending.

Though it had detractors, *The General Theory* was praised for offering a fresh approach to macroeconomic theory and policy, and the basic aggregate demand–aggregate supply model found in economics textbooks descends from the innovations found in this book. By the late 1950s, Keynes's ideas had transformed economic thinking and were becoming a staple of economic policymaking. Though the Arab oil embargo and recession of the 1970s seemed to have discredited key elements of Keynes's theories, the Great Recession once again brought his insights firmly into focus by illustrating how government policy can boost an economy during a recession.

SEE ALSO Smith's *Wealth of Nations* (1776), Classical Political Economy (c. 1790), Say's Law (1803), The Great Depression (1929), The Multiplier (1931), The Keynesian Revolution (1947), The Phillips Curve (1958), The Natural Rate of Unemployment (1967), The New Classical Macroeconomics (1972), The Policy Ineffectiveness Proposition (1975), The New Keynesian Economics (1977), The Great Recession (2007)

John Maynard Keynes lounging, in a photo from a scrapbook found in Monk's House, in the home of writer Virginia Woolf (1882–1941, c. 1939). Keynes and Woolf were members of the Bloomsbury Group, a circle of twentieth-century British writers, artists, and intellectuals.

Liquidity Preference and the Liquidity Trap

John Maynard Keynes (1883–1946)

In *The General Theory* (1936), Keynes showed how expectations and uncertainty play a major role in economic activity by influencing both investment by producers and the behavior of consumers. On the consumer side, uncertainty about future income can cause people to postpone spending, particularly on big-ticket items, and shy away from investing in financial assets if they believe that the short-term risk of losing money is too great. Instead, they will choose to hold on to their money until they are sufficiently optimistic to resume their typical savings and investment patterns. As Keynes observed, holding money in this way allows consumers to maintain its value over time and satisfies consumer preferences for liquidity—ready access to their assets—in uncertain times. This desire for increased liquidity can worsen an economic downturn, since money hoarded by consumers can't be spent or used to finance business investment, and, by further slowing the economy, ultimately *reduces* savings—a phenomenon known as the "paradox of thrift."

This preference for liquidity can push the economy into a "liquidity trap." As real interest rates approach zero, as can happen during a recession, people will increasingly prefer to save their cash. Banks will likewise prefer to hold this cash rather than lend it out. The central bank can try to stimulate the economy by increasing the money supply, but this won't encourage spending or reduce the interest rate to a level that would induce additional investment. Monetary policy becomes an ineffective tool for fighting the recession, leaving only fiscal policy, in the form of increases in debt-financed government spending, as a means to push the economy out of the liquidity trap and the recession.

Though the concept of the liquidity trap is widely taught, the lack of any empirical evidence of its occurrence caused it to fall into disrepute until the combination of real interest rates of roughly zero, the hesitancy of businesses to invest and banks to lend, and the ineffectiveness of expansionary monetary policy during the Japanese depression of the 1990s, known as the Lost Decade, and the Great Recession suggested that liquidity traps may exist after all.

SEE ALSO The Real Rate of Interest (1896), The Federal Reserve System (1913), Keynes's *General Theory* (1936), The Phillips Curve (1958), The Rational Expectations Hypothesis (1961), The Natural Rate of Unemployment (1967), The New Classical Macroeconomics (1972), The Policy Ineffectiveness Proposition (1975), The Great Recession (2007)

When facing uncertainty about their future income, consumers will shy away from purchasing big-ticket items, such as refrigerators and other expensive household appliances.

The Tinbergen Model

Jan Tinbergen (1903–1994)

In 1936, Dutch economist Jan Tinbergen built the first econometric model of an entire economy—that of the Netherlands. Tinbergen was trained as a physicist but came to economics because he thought it more useful for solving social problems, such as unemployment. His model of the Dutch economy reflected both of these influences. He wanted his model to have empirical relevance. It had to be at once realistic, simple enough to be manageable, and grounded in sophisticated economic theory. The result was a set of equations describing an economy with the relationships between variables estimated using economic data, now known as a "macroeconometric" model.

Tinbergen had been analyzing business cycles at the Central Bureau for Statistics in the Netherlands since the late 1920s. Though he started with Ragnar Frisch's dynamic model of the business cycle, he went beyond Frisch, with whom he later shared the 1969 Nobel Prize. Where Frisch's model used only three equations and variables, Tinbergen employed twenty-four equations and thirty-one economic variables, which helped him capture more of the actual economy's complexity. While Frisch had employed what he considered plausible guesses for the coefficients in his equations, Tinbergen estimated many of them using statistical techniques. He showed that his model not only generated economic cycles consistent with data on the Dutch economy, but also estimated the effects of government spending and tax policies designed to stabilize business cycles. Three years later, Tinbergen published a much larger model of the U.S. economy for a project commissioned by the League of Nations.

Tinbergen's work demonstrated the potential for macroeconometric models to inform both economic theory and policymaking. His model revealed points at which existing theories might be deficient and led Tinbergen to conclude that achieving multiple policy targets—for example, both low inflation and greater exports—requires the simultaneous use of multiple policy instruments. Thus, if a government entity has only one policy tool at its disposal, it can't effectively pursue all its goals. Today's more sophisticated macroeconometric models evolved from Tinbergen's and are widely used in economic forecasting by governments and central banks around the globe.

SEE ALSO Tugan-Baranovsky and the Trade Cycle (1894), Wicksell's Cumulative Process (1898), Mathematical Dynamics (1933), Keynes's *General Theory* (1936), Large-Scale Macroeconometric Models (1955)

Jan Tinbergen at his office, 1960.

The IS–LM Model

Alvin Hansen (1887–1975), John R. Hicks (1904–1989)

John Maynard Keynes's *General Theory* initially puzzled economists, both because it portrayed the economy very differently from his predecessors and because it wasn't entirely clear how the pieces of his system fit together. To cut through the mystery, some economists converted his analysis into mathematical form. John Hicks's work stands out not only for developing a mathematical model to capture Keynes's ideas but also for translating that model into the IS–LM diagram, assisted by the later work of Harvard economist and leading American Keynes apostle Alvin Hansen.

The IS–LM model analyzes how aggregate demand affects the economy via the relationship between output and interest rates. It captures the central variables in Keynes's system: investment (I), savings (S), liquidity preference (L), and the money supply (M). The IS curve shows combinations of output and interest rates that produce an equilibrium where savings equals investment and thus aggregate demand is equal to aggregate supply. It slopes downward because investment rises as interest rates fall. The LM curve shows combinations of output and interest rates that lead to equilibrium in the money market. It slopes upward because interest rates must increase with output to maintain money-market equilibrium.

Hicks used this diagram to demonstrate that Keynes hadn't overthrown classical economics, but showed when its predictions didn't hold true. An increase in government spending boosts aggregate demand. If the LM curve indicates that the demand for money is very sensitive to the interest rate, this results in an increase in output, as Keynes predicted. But if the LM curve suggests that money demand isn't at all sensitive to the interest rate, this increased spending just leads to higher interest rates, as the classical approach suggested. In the common case where money demand is moderately sensitive to the interest rate, a government spending increase will boost both output and interest rates.

The IS–LM model's ability to capture the effects of virtually any change in economic conditions quickly made it the standard tool for illustrating the workings of the macroeconomy and the potential effects of macroeconomic policy until the recession of the 1970s, which called the Keynesian approach into question.

SEE ALSO Classical Political Economy (c. 1790), Keynes's *General Theory* (1936), Hicks's *Value and Capital* (1939), The Keynesian Revolution (1947), Large-Scale Macroeconometric Models (1955), The Permanent Income Hypothesis (1957), The Phillips Curve (1958), The New Classical Macroeconomics (1972), The Policy Ineffectiveness Proposition (1975)

Main image: *This 1935 cartoon pokes fun at the Roosevelt administration's propensity to create costly new government agencies and relief programs during the Great Depression. The IS–LM model can be used to illustrate how increased government spending can stimulate the economy.* **Inset:** *This graph shows the IS curve shifting to the right, which captures the effects of an increase in government spending on output and interest rates.*

OH, COULDN'T YOU JUST DRIFT ON LIKE THIS FOREVER?
ER--NOT AT A MILLION BUCKS AN HOUR!
PAYING
SPENDING
i
LM
i2
i1
IS2
IS1
Y1
Y2
Y

Coase's "Nature of the Firm"

Ronald H. Coase (1910–2013)

Firms that use labor, materials, and machinery to produce goods and services have been fundamental features of economic analysis since Adam Smith's *Wealth of Nations*. Yet, until the 1930s, the firm was something of a "black box"—assumed to exist, but without much attention to how it organizes production. Why, for example, would a producer choose to make some inputs and purchase others in the marketplace?

British economist Ronald Coase answered this question in a 1937 article, "The Nature of the Firm." For Coase, the scope of a firm's operations comes down to a cost–benefit calculation. Firms will choose to organize transactions—exchanges of goods and services—internally or through the marketplace, based on which option is less costly. Economists typically assumed market transactions are costless; but, as Coase pointed out, firms wouldn't exist under these conditions: all production would be done by a network of independent contractors with each person making a contribution to the production process and then sending it on to the next contractor. In reality, purchasing inputs through the market exposes the buyer to transaction costs. Searching for appropriate suppliers can take time; it may be difficult to negotiate contracts or adjust orders; and suppliers may fail to deliver on time. Producers can eliminate some transaction costs by producing the goods themselves. A firm that makes its own inputs can simply increase production if it needs more. If it needs parts in a different color, the manager simply orders the workers to paint them a different color. While hiring a manager to monitor workers involves some costs, it may be cheaper than purchasing the inputs through the market.

Coase's article attracted little attention until the 1970s, when Oliver Williamson (b. 1932) used it as a springboard to study the inner workings of the firm. This work has spawned an enormous literature examining not only the organization of production but, at the hands of economists such as Oliver Hart (b. 1948), the design of contracts that can overcome some problems related to transaction costs. These contributions eventually helped earn Coase (1991), Williamson (2009), and Hart (2016) the Nobel Prize.

SEE ALSO Institutional Economics (1919), *Legal Foundations of Capitalism* (1924), The Coase Theorem (1960), Agency Theory (1973), The New Institutional Economics (1997)

Coase's theory of the firm explains why some beer companies choose to manufacture their own bottles and cans, such as the cans seen in this display at the Coors Brewery in Colorado.

1938

Logical Positivism

Terence W. Hutchison (1912–2007)

Economic methodology concerns itself with an important question: What are the principles that should underlie economic reasoning? Since the nineteenth century, economists have debated whether they should engage in abstract theorizing or develop theories based on current and historical evidence. In 1932, Lionel Robbins portrayed economic science as a set of deductions that come from analyzing individual choices under conditions of scarcity. Terence Hutchison offered a counterpoint and attempted to redirect modern economic methodology with his 1938 book, *On the Significance and Basic Postulates of Economic Theory.*

Hutchison, who studied economics at Cambridge, disagreed profoundly with Robbins's increasingly popular emphasis on pure theory and his belief that economics could be a purely deductive science. Instead, Hutchison advocated for methods with a more evidence-based scientific footing. His book introduced logical positivism—the idea that ultimate knowledge can be found only through empirical verification—into economics. Hutchison described pure theory, where conclusions follow logically from assumptions, as more akin to philosophy than to science. It tells us something about the relationships between the variables in question under the assumed conditions, but it doesn't inform us whether that theory has real-world applications. Hutchison argued that a theory has value only if it generates hypotheses that can be tested against relevant data. For economics to make progress as a science, it needed to prioritize the search for empirically testable hypotheses and move away from theories that are little more than tautologies derived from assumptions and that say nothing about the real world.

Though Hutchison's book hardly convinced economists to put aside pure theory, it sparked spirited debate. The history of economics in the postwar period reveals an ongoing tension between these competing views. Though economists have increasingly constructed models that lend themselves to empirical testing, many economists insist that theories which don't lend themselves well to such tests, such as game-theoretic models, can still provide useful insights into a wide variety of economic circumstances.

SEE ALSO The Positive-Normative Distinction (1836), Walras's *Elements of Pure Economics* (1874), Knight's *Risk, Uncertainty, and Profit* (1921), Scarcity and Choice (1932), Game Theory Enters Economics (1944), "The Methodology of Positive Economics" (1953), Economics Becomes Applied (1970), Natural Experiments (1990)

A chart on employment in non-agricultural occupations during the Great Depression, created by the U.S. Bureau of Labor Statistics in 1938. Logical positivism emphasizes developing theories that can be tested against the relevant data in order to ensure the theories' real-world applicability.

EMPLOYMENT LOST IN DEPRESSION
IN NON-AGRICULTURAL OCCUPATIONS

43,435

MILLIONS OF MAN YEARS

40

30

20

10

0

MILLIONS OF MAN YEARS

40

30

20

10

0

1929 1930 1931 1932 1933 1934 1935 1936 1937 1938   TOTAL LOSS
1930-38

U.S. BUREAU OF LABOR STATISTICS

The Bergson Social Welfare Function

Abram Bergson (1914–2003)

When Vilfredo Pareto introduced the concept of optimality in 1906, he provided a useful tool for evaluating economic welfare, suggesting that a situation is optimal, or efficient, if it isn't possible for a change from that position to make one person better off without making someone else worse off. However, its application lacked a key element: a definition of "welfare." In 1938, Abram Burk (later, Bergson), then a Harvard graduate student, offered the concept of a social-welfare function as a solution to this ambiguity in "A Reformulation of Certain Aspects of Welfare Economics."

Bergson formulated social welfare as a mathematical function that incorporates the factors on which the analyst believes social welfare depends. A social-welfare function can represent the well-being of society as a function of its members' utilities or the aggregate consumption levels of various goods (and "bads," harmful things such as pollution). It can even weigh the conditions of some groups (such as the poor) more heavily. The analyst can then use the function to rank which outcomes are more or less desirable.

While this might seem like a vague way to resolve the ambiguity about welfare, its non-specificity is precisely the point. The major virtue of Bergson's formulation is its generality: it allows you to define social welfare any way you want and analyze the effects of any potential policy or economic change with this definition in mind. You can use a single metric to tackle both efficiency (for example, getting the most output out of society's resources) and income-distribution concerns. You can evaluate the impact of an income-tax increase or tariffs on imports based on different value judgments or ethical criteria.

Bergson's insight became a centerpiece of welfare economics when his friend Paul Samuelson further developed it in *Foundations of Economic Analysis* (1947), formulating the Bergson–Samuelson social-welfare functions. Other types of welfare functions were later developed, incorporating concepts such as fairness, income equality, freedom, and individual responsibility. Social-welfare functions are commonly used to assess the consequences of many policies, including those related to taxes, income redistribution, the environment, and health care.

SEE ALSO Consumer Surplus (1844), Pareto Optimality and Efficiency (1906), Pigou's *Wealth and Welfare* (1912), The Kaldor–Hicks Efficiency Criterion (1939), *Foundations of Economic Analysis* (1947), Arrow's Impossibility Theorem (1951), The Theory of Second Best (1956), Cost–Benefit Analysis (1958), *Collective Choice and Social Welfare* (1970), Optimal Taxation (1971)

A U.S. government employee runs a machine that signs Social Security checks, 1939. The Bergson social welfare function offers economists a tool to evaluate the relative merits of policies such as social security and national health insurance.

Revealed Preference Theory

Paul A. Samuelson (1915–2009)

Paul Samuelson, the 1970 recipient of the Nobel Prize in economics, emerges as a central figure in the history of economics. Samuelson was trained at Harvard, where he also spent the first few years of his academic career. In 1940, he moved to the Massachusetts Institute of Technology (MIT). His presence helped transform its economics division into one of the world's preeminent departments by the late 1950s.

The theory of revealed preference, outlined in his 1938 article "A Note on the Pure Theory of Consumer's Behaviour," was Samuelson's first pathbreaking contribution. Because utility and indifference curves are unobservable and the assumption that consumers maximize utility may not accurately reflect their thinking, utility-based theories formed a weak foundation for analyzing consumer behavior. Samuelson offered a replacement for utility-based approaches by conjecturing that the consumption choices which individuals make under different circumstances can uncover their preferences. His theory finds its basis in the "weak axiom of revealed preference," which simply assumes that consumer behavior is consistent. If, given her income and any particular set of prices, an individual chooses bundle of goods A over bundle of goods B, she won't choose bundle B over bundle A under the same conditions. You can thus learn all of the consumer's preferences by observing how the consumer responds to changes in the prices of goods and income levels.

Using revealed preference theory, Samuelson derived demand curves that capture the inverse relationship between a good's price and the quantity people demand, as well as the dependence of the demand for one good on the prices of related goods. Because the results didn't depend on unobservable phenomena, they could be empirically tested. Hendrik Houthakker (1924–2008) later showed that Samuelson's approach is consistent with ordinal utility theory and that indifference curves could be derived from these preferences. This meant that economists could use ordinal utility or revealed preference methods interchangeably, depending on which is most convenient. Samuelson's work gave economists confidence that it has solid empirical underpinnings.

SEE ALSO Utilitarianism (1789), Jevons's *Theory of Political Economy* (1871), Edgeworth's *Mathematical Psychics* (1881), Ordinal Utility (1893), Indifference Curves (1906), Income and Substitution Effects (1915), The Hicks-Allen Consumer Theory (1934), *Foundations of Economic Analysis* (1947), Samuelson's *Economics* (1948), The Solow–Swan Growth Model (1956)

The cover of a Sears, Roebuck and Company catalog from 1899. Paul Samuelson proposed that a consumer's preferences among the many goods available to her can be determined by observing consumer choices under different circumstances, such as changes in price and incomes.

SEARS, ROEBUCK AND CO.

INCORPORATED.

CHEAPEST SUPPLY HOUSE

ON EARTH

OUR TRADE REACHES AROUND

THE WORLD

AUTHORIZED AND
INCORPORATED UNDER
THE LAWS OF ILLINOIS
WITH A CAPITAL AND SURPLUS
OF **$700,000.00**
PAID IN FULL.

REFERENCES
BY SPECIAL PERMISSION
METROPOLITAN NAT'L BANK, CH'GO
CORN EXCHANGE NAT'L BANK, "
GERMAN EXCHANGE BANK, N. Y.

CONSUMERS GUIDE

THIS BOOK

TELLS JUST WHAT YOUR STOREKEEPER AT HOME PAYS FOR EVERYTHING HE BUYS — AND WILL PREVENT HIM FROM OVERCHARGING YOU ON ANYTHING YOU BUY FROM HIM

78 TO 96 FULTON
73 TO 87 DESPLAINES
AND 13 TO 31 WAYMAN STREETS,

CHICAGO, ILL., U.S.A.

CATALOGUE No. 108

Hicks's *Value and Capital*

John R. Hicks (1904–1989)

Léon Walras made a splash in the 1870s with general equilibrium theory by portraying the economy as a vast, interconnected set of markets through a lengthy system of mathematical equations. Work on this subject then fell dormant. Some eminent economists, such as Vilfredo Pareto and Sweden's Gustav Cassel (1866–1945), expanded Walras's work, but few economists outside Continental Europe came across it, and most general equilibrium analysis was extremely abstract. It had yet to prove its usefulness for studying concrete economic problems.

This began to change when John R. Hicks, then a professor at the University of Manchester, published *Value and Capital* in 1939. Hicks demonstrated that all of economics, from consumer and producer behavior to capital theory to macroeconomic analysis, could be united under the umbrella of general equilibrium. In doing so, he accomplished for modern economics what Adam Smith had done in *Wealth of Nations*, combining an extensive array of ideas from writers including Walras, Alfred Marshall, Pareto, Eugen Slutsky, and John Maynard Keynes with new insights to create a more general system of analysis. Hicks's general equilibrium approach transformed the way that economists studied dynamic processes, such as the business cycle. His framework allowed them to trace the effects of external shocks to the economy by observing the behavior of consumers and producers. Changes in prices, output levels, and employment showed the effects of these shocks as they worked their way through the economic system over time.

Most importantly, Hicks translated general equilibrium theory into English, using words and some diagrams, and relegating the mathematics to appendices, as Marshall had done to explain complex theories in his *Principles of Economics*. This gave *Value and Capital* a level of accessibility that extended its reach beyond the small group of economists who could understand Walras's and Pareto's mathematics. The book gained a wide audience within the discipline and encouraged economists to add general equilibrium methods to their analytical tool kit.

SEE ALSO Smith's *Wealth of Nations* (1776), Walras's *Elements of Pure Economics* (1874), Marshall's *Principles of Economics* (1890), Pareto Optimality and Efficiency (1906), Income and Substitution Effects (1915), Mathematical Dynamics (1933), The Hicks–Allen Consumer Theory (1934), Keynes's *General Theory* (1936), The Tinbergen Model (1936), The Harrod–Domar Growth Model (1939), The Keynesian Revolution (1947), *Foundations of Economic Analysis* (1947)

John Hicks and his wife Ursula Hicks, a prominent public-finance economist. This photo was taken soon after Hicks learned that he had won the 1972 Nobel Prize.

The Harrod–Domar Growth Model

Roy F. Harrod (1900–1978), Evsey Domar (1914–1997)

When John Maynard Keynes wrote *The General Theory* (1936), he provided a road map for reaching full employment without explaining how it could be maintained over time. Because he focused on dealing with short-run fluctuations rather than detailing the conditions needed to sustain long-term growth, it fell to others to develop a growth model that was consistent with Keynes's basic macroeconomic insights, particularly the importance of savings and investment for economic stability.

British economist Roy Harrod in 1939 and the U.S.'s Evsey Domar in 1946 independently worked out the first Keynesian growth model. The Harrod–Domar model suggests that economic growth depends on two factors: the level of savings and the capital-output ratio, the latter of which shows the rate at which capital is converted into output. Higher savings facilitates more investment, and a low capital-output ratio means that the economy gets more output from a limited amount of capital. Harrod defined the economy's "warranted rate of growth" as the growth that takes place if all savings is invested; this can be found by dividing the savings rate by the capital-output ratio. For instance, if people save 20 percent of their income and the capital-output ratio is 5, the economy can grow by 4 percent. Harrod defined the economy's "natural rate of growth" as the growth rate of the labor force. The interaction of these two growth factors shows why economies won't simply continue growing. If the savings rate is too low, making the warranted rate of growth less than the natural one, progressively increasing unemployment results. If, on the other hand, the warranted rate exceeds the natural rate, labor shortages will constrict output, leading to inflation. The economy will only experience steady growth if the two rates are identical.

The Harrod–Domar model has important implications for policies that promote growth in developing nations. The higher the savings rate, and the more productive a nation's capital stock, the greater the possibilities for economic growth. Less-developed nations often have low savings rates owing to poverty, and vastly inferior physical capital, problems that must be reversed to stimulate growth.

SEE ALSO Keynes's *General Theory* (1936), Development Economics (1954), The Solow–Swan Growth Model (1956), Endogenous Growth Theory (1986)

A couple stops by the window of a local bank to examine an advertisement for an interest-bearing savings account. In the Harrod–Domar growth model, the savings rate is an important determinant of a nation's economic growth.

BANKERS TRUST COMPANY
REGO PARK OFFICE

NKING HOURS
MON. TO FRI. 9:00 A.M - 3:00 P.M.
MON. EVENINGS 5:00 P.M - 8:00 P.M.

RSONAL LOANS
9:00 A.M - 5:00 P.M

BANKERS TRUST
SAVINGS ACCOUNTS

3% ANNUAL
INTEREST

EARNED FROM DAY OF DEPOSIT

COMPOUNDED AND PAID QUARTERLY

World War II

Economists proved their mettle as policy advisers during the Great Depression, but during World War II their influence exploded. Working in Washington, D.C., London, or their home universities, economists had their fingers in wartime planning, especially in the U.S. and Great Britain, and economic science took as much out of this work as economists put into it.

American and British economists, including John Maynard Keynes and John Kenneth Galbraith, as well as future Nobel Laureates such as Paul Samuelson, Milton Friedman, James Meade, and Simon Kuznets, contributed to the war effort in many ways. Some turned their attention to economic planning. They devised policies to regulate wages and goods prices, finance the war effort, and allocate labor and materials to ramp up production of military hardware while ensuring a steady supply of consumer goods. The last of these was particularly challenging: a significant share of the male labor force was engaged in military service, which drew women into the factories in larger numbers, and the military's enormous need for supplies and equipment meant that supplies of goods on the home front were sometimes rationed. Others advanced the war effort in ways that, on the face of it, had little to do with economics. They applied their mathematical and statistical skills to areas as diverse as munitions testing, the development of radar systems, and weather research for flight planning.

Economists had to bring more than their existing knowledge to the table. They developed new ideas and tools, including statistical sampling techniques (developed to test the quality of batches of munitions), to meet the pressing and unique needs of the war. At times, these fresh developments resulted from economists' interactions with mathematicians, statisticians, and scientists from other fields. Many of these made their way into economic analysis in the postwar period. Their successes during the war and with postwar economic planning, both at home and through international efforts such as the Marshall Plan for revitalizing European economies and the Bretton Woods Plan for restructuring the international monetary system, solidified the place of economists as key government-policy advisers.

SEE ALSO The Great Depression (1929), Émigré Economists (1933), Hayek's *Road to Serfdom* (1944), Game Theory Enters Economics (1944), The Bretton Woods Agreement (1944), The Council of Economic Advisers (1946), RAND and the Cold War (1948)

Above: *A ration coupon issued by the Office of Price Administration for meat, fats, fish, and cheese issued during World War II.* **Main image:** *Wartime economic planning involved rationing to meet the increased demand for goods needed by both military and civilian consumers. Posters presented rationing as a patriotic activity.*

RATIONING SAFEGUARDS YOUR SHARE

The Multiplier–Accelerator Model

Alvin Hansen (1887–1975), Paul A. Samuelson (1915–2009)

In 1939, Paul Samuelson formulated the modern theory of the business cycle by integrating Richard Kahn's multiplier and the acceleration principle, devised in the early 1900s by Albert Aftalion and John Maurice Clark. The result is known as the multiplier–accelerator model. The multiplier process, which Keynes made a central feature of his analysis in *The General Theory* (1936), shows how a one-dollar increase in spending by consumers, the government, or through business investment increases output and incomes in the economy by more than one dollar. Significant boosts in spending, then, would have even more significant effects on GDP. However, the basic multiplier assumed that the economy had enough capital to generate the output needed to meet this growing demand. If the economy is already operating at capacity, new investment—sometimes called "derived investment"—will be needed to increase production. This effect of increased consumption on investment is known as the acceleration principle. Like the initial investment, this derived investment also has multiplier effects, stimulating demand and income even further. For Samuelson, neither the multiplier effect nor the accelerator principle alone can fully explain the effects of new investment; they must be paired together.

Samuelson attributed this insight to his mentor at Harvard, Alvin Hansen. Samuelson's model gave Keynesian economics a dynamic element and explained short-term economic fluctuations. Because investment decisions are based on previous economic activity, growth can eventually lead to overinvestment as the multiplier's effects begin to dissipate. When businesses then pull back on investment, the multiplier effect pushes the economy downward until corresponding underinvestment propels economic activity upward again. These cycles may become increasingly severe, or dampen over time, depending on the strength of the accelerator mechanism.

Because the multiplier–accelerator model showed how business cycles could emerge naturally from the interaction of two basic economic forces, economists began incorporating it into other macroeconomic and growth models being developed in the postwar period.

SEE ALSO Tugan-Baranovsky and the Trade Cycle (1894), Wicksell's Cumulative Process (1898), The Multiplier (1931), Mathematical Dynamics (1933), Keynes's *General Theory* (1936), The Harrod–Domar Growth Model (1939), The Keynesian Revolution (1947), The New Classical Macroeconomics (1972), Real Business Cycle Models (1982)

This illustration portrays a busy day on Wall Street, a hub for the financing of business investment in the U.S. New business investment to satisfy greater consumer demand for goods "accelerates" the multiplier effects of this increased consumer demand, generating even stronger economic growth.

The Kaldor–Hicks Efficiency Criterion

John R. Hicks (1904–1989), Nicholas Kaldor (1908–1986)

The concept of Pareto optimality, describing a position from which no change can make someone better off without making someone else worse off, provided a precise definition of efficiency that fit well with the new mathematical approaches to economics. In practice, however, it suffered from a serious problem: virtually no proposed economic policy could meet the Pareto criterion's condition for a welfare improvement—that at least one person is made better off and no one is made worse off. Any policy change inevitably benefits some and imposes costs on others. This meant that the Pareto criterion couldn't provide much guidance for policymaking.

John Hicks and Nicholas Kaldor offered a way around this problem, one that retained some of the advantages of Pareto's approach. In 1939, they proposed the use of a "compensation test" to evaluate efficiency. A change would be labeled an improvement if those who gain from the change could, hypothetically, fully compensate the losers for all their losses and still be better off themselves. If no such change were possible, the existing situation would be deemed efficient. The Kaldor–Hicks criterion is weaker than the Pareto criterion, since it doesn't require individuals to pay this "hypothetical" compensation and thus allows changes that result in gains to some and losses to others. In short, the Kaldor–Hicks criterion judges a change to be efficiency-enhancing if the overall benefits exceed the costs and efficiency-diminishing if the costs outweigh the benefits.

Unlike Abram Bergson's social-welfare function, the Kaldor–Hicks criterion only measures efficiency and isn't concerned with how the gains from these changes are distributed. Some see this failure to consider distribution, along with the fact that the hypothetical compensation isn't actually paid, to be significant shortcomings. Nonetheless, the criterion's practicality has made it very influential. Many economists use it to assess the efficiency of taxes, business regulations, international trade policies, and laws, and the U.S. government requires the use of cost–benefit analysis, which employs the Kaldor–Hicks criterion, to evaluate any new proposed regulation.

SEE ALSO Consumer Surplus (1844), Pareto Optimality and Efficiency (1906), The Bergson Social Welfare Function (1938), Cost–Benefit Analysis (1958)

The Kaldor–Hicks criterion suggests that a change enhances efficiency if the benefits exceed the costs. But as this New Deal cartoon illustrates, making accurate projections of these benefits and costs is often not easy.

The Stolper–Samuelson Theorem

Wolfgang F. Stolper (1912–2002), Paul A. Samuelson (1915–2009)

In the 1930s, Eli Heckscher and Bertil Ohlin developed a model of international trade that located each country's comparative advantage in the availability of production inputs in one country relative to another. One of the most important results stimulated by their analysis is the Stolper–Samuelson theorem, developed in a 1941 article, "Protection and Real Wages." In their article, Wolfgang Stolper and Paul Samuelson considered a world with two goods and two factors of production. The theorem tells us that when the relative price of one of these goods increases, the price of the factor used more intensively in that good's production will rise, while the price of the factor used less intensively will fall.

Agriculture illustrates the intuition and implications of this theorem. Imposing a tariff on agricultural products, which increases their prices, will increase real wages for agricultural workers and decrease the real return to capital. By the same token, a move to free trade in agriculture, which involves eliminating tariffs, would reduce wages and increase the return to capital. The explanation for these different effects on input prices is the factor-intensity of production. Agricultural production is labor-intensive. Since labor is used more intensively, a change in the price of the agricultural product has a disproportionate effect on the return to labor, meaning that the return to capital will move in the opposite direction.

The Stolper–Samuelson theorem suggests that trade policy can significantly affect the distribution of income. Though the theorem is applicable only to a world with two goods and two factors of production, a more general version suggests that at least one factor of production will experience a decrease in real income if a country moves toward free trade. The losers are likely to be the factors that play the most vital role in the production of the imported goods. For example, the theorem predicts that increased purchases of labor-intensive products from China will hurt domestic wages in these sectors, and there is some evidence to support this. That said, policies, including educational subsidies, that allow workers to develop new skills offer a buffer against these changes.

SEE ALSO The Balance-of-Trade Controversy (1621), The Equalization of Returns (1662), The Theory of Comparative Advantage (1817), The Heckscher–Ohlin Model (1933), The Factor-Price Equalization Theorem (1948), The New Trade Theory (1979)

A postcard showing workers harvesting oranges by hand in California. Because orange cultivation is labor-intensive, the Stolper–Samuelson theorem predicts that a tariff on imported oranges will increase the wages of domestic workers in this industry.

Input–Output Analysis

Wassily Leontief (1906–1999)

Léon Walras's theory of general equilibrium lacked the ability to measure how a change in one sector affected the others. Harvard economist and Russian émigré Wassily Leontief filled the gap with his 1941 book, *The Structure of the American Economy, 1919–1929*, which featured input–output tables for the U.S. economy.

Leontief drew inspiration from François Quesnay's *Tableau Économique*. Like their ancestor, his tables focused on production, tracking how the outputs in each sector of the economy are used as inputs in others. An input–output table for an economy with five industries would have five rows and five columns, with each cell showing how many units of one industry's output (e.g., tires) are required to produce one unit of another industry's output (e.g., cars). Leontief compared the table to a cooking recipe, showing how much of each ingredient is needed to make a loaf of bread. With this table, you could trace how, for example, an increase in the consumption of cars affects the use of inputs in the automobile industry and its impact on other industries that supply inputs to automobile production. You could then forecast the economy-wide production demands that accompany an increase in automobile consumption.

Input–output models proved useful for policy analysis and planning, and this work earned Leontief the 1973 Nobel Prize. Limited data on the details of industrial production and doing complex computations with early handheld calculators made the process painfully slow. By the end of World War II, the U.S. Bureau of Labor Statistics had developed a 400-sector (versus Leontief's forty-four) input–output table to analyze postwar employment in the U.S., and early computers were available to manage the calculations. The Organisation for Economic Co-operation and Development (OECD) and World Bank have used this analysis in constructing economic development programs and to study issues including the effects of international trade and the environmental impacts of production.

SEE ALSO The *Tableau Économique* (1758), Walras's *Elements of Pure Economics* (1874), Émigré Economists (1933), Computation: The Orcutt Regression Analyzer and the Phillips Machine (1948)

A page showing a table comparing the ingredients needed for different varieties of bread. Like a recipe that shows how much of each ingredient is needed to make a single loaf, an input–output table shows the amount of each input required to produce a unit of each of the goods produced in an economy.

FLOUR.	YEAST AND FOOD.	HEATS, TIMES, AND SYSTEMS.	INFORMATION AND SUGGESTIONS ON THE QUALITY.
Half English pats. and supers. Vienna flour is less used for fancy bread than formerly.	10oz., and sugar 5oz.	Straight dough, 3½ hours start to finish, 3 quarts milk, 3 quarts water, 6oz. salt, 12oz. margarine, liquor 80°, cut back 1¼ hours, after making, ordinary bread oven, baked half hour.	Nice long roll or stick or yard loaf for flour and oven ; rather over-fermented ; nicely short to eat. Keep covered and moist or else wash with scalded flour when drawing.
140lb.	1¼lb., and malt extract 4oz.	Straight dough with skimmed milk, 1½lb. lard, 1¾lb. salt.	Quantities used by a prize-winner. The entries at the shows in Vienna and milk are usually very few.
14 bushels of bread from ⅓ Minn. pats., ⅓ town households, ⅓ town whites.	Four quarts patent yeast in ferment, and 20lb. fruit. In sponge 8oz. distillers'.	Ferment with 6 gallons water and half quartern tin full of flour, with yeast and fruit for 8 hours, sponge with three pails (12 gallons), ready in 2 hours, dough with double quantity of liquor as in sponge, 7lb. salt, rise 2 hours.	Loaf from this gained third prize in fancy bread at London Exhibition.
280lb. best British pats.	3lb. (Overproof prevents rolls breaking out nicely.)	Straight dough, 12 gallons water at 120°, 3 gallons milk, 4lb. lard, 3½lb. salt, in trough 2 hours, baked at 500°.	Excellent commercial loaf, good as need be in all points. Carefully made. Carbonate of soda and borax hides or checks sourness in milk.
140lb. (In a collection of fancy bread recently received from practically every large town on the Continent of Europe, Antwerp was the best.)	1¾lb. (The glazed crust is due to the moisture in conjuncture with heat, making dextrin.)	Sponged at 2.30 a.m., doughed at 3.30, cut over 4 a.m., scaled 4.30, in oven 5.30 a.m., baked 45 minutes, lard 4lb., milk 18 quarts, with water, salt 2½lb.	Good bread, worth 85 marks out of 100. Very fully proved, rather too loose, wants keeping back more by labour for exhibition quality. Milk should add to nutrition, sweetness, and moistness, the important ingredients being the milk, sugar, fat, and albuminoids.

Creative Destruction

Joseph A. Schumpeter (1883–1950)

From Karl Marx to J. A. Hobson, many critics of industrial capitalism noticed that industrialization had left scars, lowering wages and sometimes bringing rampant unemployment. Their recommended remedies ranged from government regulation and social-welfare programs to the replacement of the entire capitalist system with some form of socialism. Marx most famously had predicted that these scars both were inherent in capitalism and would only worsen over time. Capitalism was unsustainable, and workers eventually would revolt against their capitalist oppressors.

In his 1942 book, *Capitalism, Socialism, and Democracy*, Harvard economist Joseph Schumpeter, a student of Eugen von Böhm-Bawerk who emigrated to the U.S. in 1932, interpreted this destructive dynamic in a very different, and somewhat more positive, way. For him, capitalism is an evolutionary process. He described an "industrial mutilation that incessantly revolutionizes the economic structure from within, incessantly destroying the old one, incessantly creating a new one," whether that came from new modes of transportation, new consumer goods, or the growth of industrial conglomerates that upset the existing economic order. Schumpeter labeled this process "creative destruction," calling it "the essential fact about capitalism."

Innovation, for Schumpeter, is the source of change in capitalism, but it destroys old methods of production and habits of consumption. New technology displaces workers, and some goods and even entire industries disappear. The driving force behind this disruptive dynamic is the entrepreneur, who exploits opportunities for innovation and, in doing so, continues to push the economy upwards. Capitalism's demise comes not through violent revolution, as Marx suggested, but because the spark of entrepreneurship is gradually extinguished by growing bureaucracies. A desire for the equality, security, and regulation that is more consistent with socialism would replace capitalist attitudes.

The parallels to Marx's theory of crisis aren't accidental—Schumpeter developed his theory based on a close reading of Marx's work. While his message was more optimistic than Marx's, he highlights an important lesson: economic growth comes with cost and pains, whether that be the hand-loom weavers cast aside by the power loom, modern-day auto workers displaced by robots, or social-media websites revolutionizing the way we live our lives.

SEE ALSO Ibn Khaldun's *Al-Muqaddimah* (1377), The Machinery Question (1817), Marx's *Das Kapital* (1867), Böhm-Bawerk's *Capital and Interest* (1884), Unemployment (1896), Kondratiev Waves (1925), Endogenous Growth Theory (1986)

The forces of creative destruction have been powerful in the world of transportation, where new modes of transport, such as the commercial airplane, have supplanted more established ones, such as railroads.

The Fundamental Theorems of Welfare Economics

1943

Vilfredo Pareto (1848–1923), Maurice Allais (1911–2010), Kenneth J. Arrow (1921–2017), Gérard Debreu (1921–2004)

The idea that competition in the marketplace can direct resources to their best uses is a major theme of *The Wealth of Nations*. Since its publication in 1776, economists have devoted their time and energy to exploring competitive market outcomes and the conclusions for economic welfare that we can draw from them. Two of these conclusions are embodied in the fundamental theorems of welfare economics.

The first of these theorems originated with Vilfredo Pareto in 1906 and states that a competitive market economy yields a Pareto optimal equilibrium, meaning that it is impossible to make at least one person better off without making someone else worse off. The second fundamental theorem asserts that it is possible to achieve any Pareto optimal equilibrium under perfect competition with appropriate income redistribution. French economist and 1988 Nobel Laureate Maurice Allais provided the mathematical proofs for these theorems in his 1943 book, *A La Recherche d'une Discipline Économique*, with Kenneth Arrow and Gérard Debreu refining this work in the 1950s.

Why are these theorems "fundamental"? Some see the first fundamental theorem as a proof of Adam Smith's "invisible hand" working its magic. This view is something of a stretch, but the theorem does tell us that perfectly competitive markets generate efficient outcomes. It also establishes a benchmark against which to measure the performance of real-world markets and provides some justification for promoting competition. The second fundamental theorem tells us that society can address its distributional goals without sacrificing efficiency. It can choose among the many possible Pareto optimal outcomes simply by—as one popular textbook puts it—"appropriately redistributing wealth and then letting the market work."

Despite the fact that real-world markets don't satisfy the perfectly competitive conditions that these theorems assume, they offer what many economists believe to be a powerful argument for using competitive markets to allocate resources in society.

SEE ALSO Smith's *Wealth of Nations* (1776), The Competitive Process (1776), The Invisible Hand (1776), Pareto Optimality and Efficiency (1906), The Bergson Social Welfare Function (1938), Public Goods (1954), The Theory of Second Best (1956), The Tiebout Model (1956), Externalities and Market Failure (1958), Debreu's *The Theory of Value* (1959), The Economics of Information (1961)

Maurice Allais, shown here in 1992, distinguished himself through his rigorous mathematical analysis of the efficiency of markets.

Hayek's *Road to Serfdom*

Friedrich A. Hayek (1899–1992)

Though economics became an increasingly specialized academic discipline during the beginning of the twentieth century, economists sometimes wrote for general audiences. Friedrich Hayek authored one of the most widely read of these works, *The Road to Serfdom* (1944). The book hit the shelves during a time when intellectuals and laypeople alike began to find socialism attractive. The success of wartime planning, when government controls over production and prices across the economy had a strong socialist flavor, suggested that scientific expertise could improve economic performance. The claims of economic growth made by socialist planners in the Soviet Union while the West was in the throes of the Great Depression further reinforced this.

Hayek had emigrated from his native Austria to England and the London School of Economics in 1931. In *The Road to Serfdom*, he warned that Hitler's fascist National Socialism, then the scourge of most of the Western world, and the Soviet Union's socialist regime, which became increasingly attractive to intellectuals in the West, were two sides of the same coin. Both were antithetical to democracy; they replaced control by the many with control by the few, leading the government to restrict economic and personal liberty. A move to socialist centralized planning, he argued, would bring a gradual decline into totalitarianism. This didn't mean that there is no role for government, of course, but its chief aim should be to create an environment in which economic and personal liberty can flourish. Government can accomplish this by establishing a legal system that will support the success of a market-based economy and providing goods and services that markets can't adequately supply.

Condensed versions of *The Road to Serfdom* found their way into popular outlets such as *Reader's Digest*, exposing millions to Hayek's message. It soon galvanized opposition to policies ranging from price regulations to the nationalization of industries. Hayek's defense of capitalism still attracts attention, as concerns about what some consider the ever-expanding scope of government action continue to trouble many today. In fact, the recently published "definitive edition" of the book has sold more than 400,000 copies since its publication in 2007.

SEE ALSO *The Communist Manifesto* (1848), Émigré Economists (1933), World War II (1939), Hayek's "Use of Knowledge in Society" (1945), Supply-Side Economics (1974)

Shoppers in the Soviet Union wait in a long line at a bakery, 1931. Friedrich Hayek warned his readers of the dangers of the centrally planned socialist system, such as that used by the Soviet Union to organize its economy.

Game Theory Enters Economics

Oskar Morgenstern (1902–1977), John von Neumann (1903–1957)

Until the twentieth century, economic theory rested on competitive underpinnings, assuming agents make decisions without reference to what their rivals are doing. In reality, many economic interactions don't take place between isolated individuals who do nothing more than react to market prices. They involve significant interdependence, with each agent reacting to and trying to influence the actions of its rivals. Game theory offers a set of tools for modeling these strategic actions.

John von Neumann, a Hungarian-born mathematician who helped develop modern computing and was a key participant in the Manhattan Project, pioneered game theory by formulating the mathematical tools to model strategic decision-making in a wide range of contexts. Von Neumann's "The Theory of Parlor Games" (1928) was inspired by games such as chess and poker. While it laid the foundation for game theory, Princeton University economist Oskar Morgenstern interested von Neumann in its application to economic problems. Their 1944 book, *The Theory of Games and Economic Behavior*, took this analysis in a new direction by showing how theories about strategic interactions could be applied to economics.

Von Neumann and Morgenstern's book attracted the attention of defense strategists and mathematicians, including future Nobel Prize recipients John Nash, Richard Selten, and Robert Aumann. One of the book's most important contributions wedded utility theory and Bernoulli's analysis of risk to develop the theory of expected utility, which became the basis for the analysis of economic decision-making under conditions of uncertainty. Despite the several enthusiastic reviews of the book in leading economics journals, economists took up game theory very slowly because of their discomfort with the mathematics and belief that it had at best limited applicability beyond the realm of military strategy. Many also perceived the book as an attack on John Hicks and Paul Samuelson's work on general equilibrium theory, which emphasized competitive markets and had begun to dominate the profession. It was only in the 1970s that economists began to see the tools of game theory as useful methods to examine economic problems ranging from the behavior of cartels, such as OPEC, to building voting coalitions in legislative bodies.

SEE ALSO Bernoulli on Expected Utility (1738), The Bertrand Model (1883), Hicks's *Value and Capital* (1939), *Foundations of Economic Analysis* (1947), RAND and the Cold War (1948), Non-Cooperative Games and Nash Equilibrium (1950), The Prisoner's Dilemma (1950), The Shapley Value (1953), Mechanism Design (1972), The Experimental Turn (1986)

John von Neumann was inspired by parlor games, especially poker, in which players use strategy to help them win a hand.

Haavelmo's "Probability Approach"

Trygve Haavelmo (1911–1999)

Trygve Haavelmo's "The Probability Approach" (1944) has distinguished itself as the founding work in modern econometrics by providing a blueprint for improving empirical analysis and the conclusions drawn from it. Haavelmo, a Norwegian, was a student of Ragnar Frisch in Oslo but came to the U.S. shortly before the start of World War II. He had planned to continue his studies in statistics and economics for a year before returning to Norway. As it happened, he didn't return to Norway for nearly a decade, and it was during this time in the U.S. that he wrote "The Probability Approach."

At the heart of Haavelmo's contribution was a basic question: How do we judge the relationship of economic models to reality? Economists working during this time saw the equations in their models as depictions of the natural laws that govern economic activity, so what remained for empirical work was to measure the coefficients of an equation's variables. Haavelmo believed this approach was misguided. These models are abstractions from the real world, and the model and the real world will never exactly correspond to each other. Because there isn't an exact relationship between, for example, the demand for automobiles and the prices and consumer incomes which influence that demand, it becomes essential to assess the probability that your statistical estimates accurately represent the relationships between these variables. Only then can we know what confidence we can place in estimates of, say, the effects of new tariffs on domestic employment levels or of changes in income-tax rates on consumer spending.

For Haavelmo, a theory is essentially a statistical hypothesis, and econometrics is a method of hypothesis testing. The probability approach allowed economists to test their theories using statistical methods. Only then would they see how the theories corresponded to data and compared to others purporting to explain the same phenomena. The adoption of the probability approach was key to the efforts to make economic analysis more scientific. Haavelmo's work, for which he was recognized with the 1989 Nobel Prize, permanently altered not only the practice of econometrics but also the way that economists view their theories.

SEE ALSO The Cowles Commission (1932), Mathematical Dynamics (1933), Logical Positivism (1938), "The Methodology of Positive Economics" (1953), Large-Scale Macroeconometric Models (1955), Economics Becomes Applied (1970), Natural Experiments (1990)

Depictions of the normal distribution, also known as the Gaussian distribution or bell curve, which is commonly used in econometric analysis.

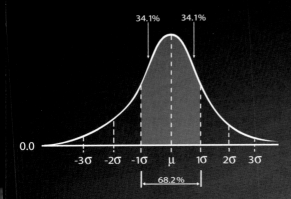

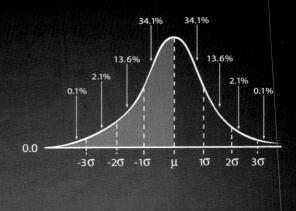

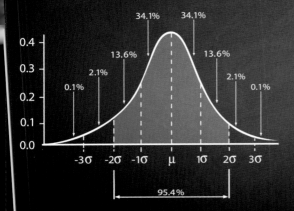

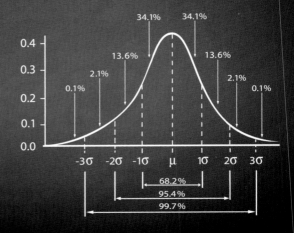

Hayek's "Use of Knowledge in Society"

Friedrich A. Hayek (1899–1992)

The socialist calculation debate of the 1920s and 1930s cast doubt on the idea that central planning could improve on or even replicate the performance of a competitive market economy. But the successes of centralized economic planning in the U.S. and Great Britain during World War II, when governments controlled prices and production to support the war effort and the needs of the citizens, gave new life to this notion. To counter this tide of opinion, London School of Economics economist F. A. Hayek, the intellectual leader of the laissez-faire–oriented Austrian school during this period, wrote "The Use of Knowledge in Society" in 1945.

Hayek explained that an immense amount of information about costs, prices, and the quality and availability of goods is necessary to make an economic system function properly. Models developed by economists masked this fact by assuming perfect information, that everyone knows everything about everything.

In reality, information is spread across millions of individuals and is constantly changing, requiring producers and consumers to continually adapt, said Hayek. All of these moving parts make it impossible for a centralized planning board to possess the knowledge needed to respond appropriately to the circumstances of a specific moment. A well-functioning economy, Hayek argued, requires *decentralized* decision-making, specifically through a market pricing system. Only decentralization would "ensure that the knowledge of the particular circumstances of time and place will be promptly used." Though the market doesn't guarantee that all this information is used to maximize economic growth, it does so more effectively than a centralized planner.

Though Hayek's article targeted socialism, it kick-started the development of the economics of information, which studies the effects of information problems on individual behavior and market outcomes, in the second half of the twentieth century. Slightly further afield, Hayek's basic thesis that localized knowledge is often superior to centralized knowledge also helped inspire Jimmy Wales to create Wikipedia.

SEE ALSO Laissez-Faire (1695), The Invisible Hand (1776), *The Communist Manifesto* (1848), Marx's *Das Kapital* (1867), The Austrian School (1871), Pareto Optimality and Efficiency (1906), The Socialist Calculation Debate (1920), World War II (1939), Hayek's *Road to Serfdom* (1944), The Economics of Information (1961), The Market for "Lemons" (1970), Signaling (1973), Supply-Side Economics (1974), Screening—or Pooling and Separating Equilibria (1976)

Managers at General Motors update a control board to track materials needed for wartime production during World War II.

The Council of Economic Advisers

When tasked with providing economic advice to U.S. presidents during the Great Depression and World War II, American economists did so on an ad-hoc basis, as with the "Brain Trust" of advisers that surrounded President Franklin Roosevelt during that period. Economic advisers often created proposals on the fly, even during these serious economic emergencies. When it became clear that economists had played an important role in dealing with these crises, a desire for a more formalized, permanent role for them within the government's executive branch emerged. Congress fulfilled this wish by establishing the Council of Economic Advisers as part of the Employment Act of 1946.

Congress charged the three-member Council with developing economic policies that would minimize economic fluctuations and promote employment, production, and low inflation "under free competitive enterprise." The Council evaluates existing government policies and programs and provides advice on policy options facing the president. It also assists with the preparation of the annual "Economic Report of the President," which provides data and insights into the state of the American economy. The president appoints the Council's members, selecting individuals who "as a result of [their] training, experience, and attainments, [are] exceptionally qualified to analyze and interpret economic developments, to appraise programs and activities of the Government." The Council is typically composed of senior academic economists on leave from their universities. Harry Truman, who was president when the Council was established, relied very little on the Council's advice, but the influence of this uniquely American body grew under Presidents Eisenhower and Kennedy. The Council cemented its place as an important input into the economic policymaking process when Kennedy took its advice and implemented tax cuts that brought the economy out of a recession.

Because the president appoints Council members, the Council's history reflects how economic wisdom has evolved and political winds have shifted. Staunch Keynesians dominated the Council during the 1960s and early 1970s, while those favoring more limited government intervention held sway during the Reagan and Bush presidencies. The Council, then, is not merely a repository of economic wisdom, but a source of contrasting visions of deficit spending, monetary policy, and the appropriate role for government in the economy.

SEE ALSO The Great Depression (1929), World War II (1939), The Keynesian Revolution (1947)

Members of the Council of Economic Advisers work with cabinet members and White House staff to compile President Truman's midyear economic report, 1949.

The Chicago School

Frank H. Knight (1885–1972), George J. Stigler (1911–1991), Milton Friedman (1912–2006), Gary S. Becker (1930–2014)

No economics department in the postwar period has been as influential as that at the University of Chicago, or gained as much notoriety for its distinctive free-market approach to economic policy and willingness to push the boundaries of economics into every nook and cranny of life. The Chicago school's approach dates back to the 1920s, with Frank Knight's arrival at Chicago, but the pivotal moment came when Milton Friedman joined the Chicago economics faculty in 1946 and became its public and professional face.

The Chicago school rejected general equilibrium analysis, theories of imperfect competition, and Keynesian macroeconomics, all of which dominated economic thinking at mid-century. It preferred the simple price theory of Alfred Marshall, grounded in the partial equilibrium analysis of supply and demand in competitive markets, and described the money supply as the most important influence on macroeconomic performance. Through the work of Nobel Laureates George Stigler and Gary Becker, Chicago also expanded the boundaries of economics to cover topics such as information, law, politics, and family life. On policy, Chicago defined itself by opposing many forms of government intervention in the marketplace, including regulations on pricing and production methods, based on a belief that most markets are competitive and thus efficient.

The "Chicago" approach, particularly to macroeconomics, has evolved significantly. Milton Friedman's monetarism, which warned against the inflation that resulted from an increasing money supply, has now given way to theories grounded in rational expectations and general equilibrium analysis. Nonetheless, by assembling top scholars who shared an approach to economic analysis and worked in a more conservative political climate that favored their policy recommendations, the Chicago school achieved unrivaled influence. Thirteen members of its faculty have been awarded the Nobel Prize, and economists around the world have adopted many elements of its approach. Though born as a heretical movement, the Chicago approach is now squarely a part of the mainstream of economic thinking.

SEE ALSO Marshall's *Principles of Economics* (1890), Knight's *Risk, Uncertainty, and Profit* (1921), Keynes's *General Theory* (1936), "The Methodology of Positive Economics" (1953), The Economics of Discrimination (1957), The Permanent Income Hypothesis (1957), Human Capital Analysis (1958), The Economics of Information (1961), The Natural Rate of Unemployment (1967), The Economics of Crime and Punishment (1968), The New Classical Macroeconomics (1972), The Economic Analysis of Law (1973)

The economics department at the University of Chicago housed in the Social Sciences Research building (right), shown facing the Harper Quadrangle in this photo.

The Consumer Price Index

It was clear that severe price inflation could greatly harm consumers, even in the centuries before economists and statisticians developed effective methods for measuring inflation in the late 1800s. During World War I, when inflation was severe and wages didn't seem to keep pace with increased production in war-related fields, many countries, including the United States, began strengthening the quality of their measures. In the United States, the consumer price index (CPI) captures the change over time in the prices of a particular bundle of goods consumed by the average individual, from food to housing to transportation. Its origins lie in the Tariff Act of 1890, when Congress asked the Bureau of Labor (later the Bureau of Labor Statistics, BLS) to assess the Act's impact on industrial production. The BLS's creation of a "Cost of Living Index" during World War I laid the groundwork for the modern-day CPI, the name it was given in 1946.

The evolution of the CPI reflects its political, economic, and data-gathering purposes. The earliest indices captured a narrow range of goods, numbering in the dozens, whereas more recent indices consider hundreds of prices. The weights given to various items in the consumer budget were biased early on by measuring only the expenditure patterns of white families, who typically had higher incomes and different purchasing habits than African-American and Latino families. As a measure of inflation, the CPI helps us understand the state of the economy and how it has changed, but because it is used to adjust wages and government transfer payments such as Social Security, it also affects the economic conditions that it captures. This has caused controversy. Wage adjustments in collective bargaining agreements, for example, are typically tied to the CPI. This became a point of contention during World War II, when the prices of many goods increased significantly, but the CPI did not, in part because some goods measured in the CPI, such as appliances and automobiles, were simply unavailable. Today, the BLS continues to modify its methods and issues several versions of the CPI to capture different aspects of price changes.

SEE ALSO Index Numbers (1863), The National Bureau of Economic Research (1920), National Income Accounting (1934)

Employees at the U.S. Bureau of Labor Statistics draw charts by hand, 1962. A line graph tracking changes in the CPI hangs on the back wall.

The Keynesian Revolution

Alvin Hansen (1887–1975), John R. Hicks (1904–1989),
Lawrence R. Klein (1920–2013)

1947

Keynes's *General Theory* ushered in a new era in macroeconomic analysis. By explaining how the economy could fall into prolonged recession and the government could use deficit spending and tax cuts to stimulate economic growth, it set off a "revolution" in economic analysis and policymaking. Economists began fleshing out and, at times, modifying Keynes's system. J. R. Hicks translated his concepts into mathematical form, while Alvin Hansen earned the nickname the "American Keynes" for his earnest and enthusiastic promotion of Keynesian thinking. Lawrence Klein even called his PhD dissertation *The Keynesian Revolution*; published in 1947, it systematized the previous decade of work derived from *The General Theory*.

In some ways, calling Keynes's ideas revolutionary is overblown. Like Adam Smith's *Wealth of Nations*, *The General Theory* wove together many ideas that were already circulating. There was also no immediate *en masse* movement within the economics profession toward Keynes's views when the book was published. Paul Samuelson reports that the younger generation enthusiastically embraced Keynes's ideas, but many of their senior colleagues remained wedded to traditional thinking and harshly criticized Keynes's theory. Although Keynesian policies had helped combat the Great Depression, Keynesians were even lumped in with communists and other subversives during the McCarthy era in the U.S.

Nonetheless, macroeconomic analysis from the 1940s through the mid-1970s took its inspiration from the basic Keynesian model. Nobel Prizes went to Samuelson, Klein, Richard Stone, James Tobin, Franco Modigliani, and Edmund Phelps for developing insights based on Keynes's work. On the policy front, governments successfully adopted Keynesian insights, as with the Kennedy administration's tax cuts, one of the two key stimulus tools recommended by Keynes, which helped to lift the economy out of a recession. The effectiveness of the economic stimulus programs in the U.S. and Europe during the Great Recession has brought renewed attention to Keynesian thinking.

SEE ALSO The Great Depression (1929), The Multiplier (1931), Keynes's *General Theory* (1936), The IS–LM Model (1937), Hicks's *Value and Capital* (1939), The Multiplier–Accelerator Model (1939), Samuelson's *Economics* (1948), Large-Scale Macroeconometric Models (1955), The Phillips Curve (1958), The Natural Rate of Unemployment (1967), The New Classical Macroeconomics (1972), The New Keynesian Economics (1977)

Keynesian economic thinking helped inspire many infrastructure projects, such as the construction of the U.S. interstate highway system. President Dwight D. Eisenhower (1890–1969) signed the Federal-Aid Highway Act of 1956 in the hope that the program would create jobs and reduce unemployment.

Foundations of Economic Analysis

Paul A. Samuelson (1915–2009)

Though some economists had been using mathematics to explore economic questions since the early 1800s, most writing on the subject was of a non-mathematical nature until the mid-twentieth century. Paul Samuelson was at the forefront of the move to make economics a mathematical science with *Foundations of Economic Analysis* (1947), a book derived from his 1941 Harvard PhD thesis. The book contends that virtually all economic analysis can be unified under a common mathematical structure. Most important, this structure would allow scholars to derive "operationally meaningful theorems," hypotheses about the world that are potentially refutable by the data.

Samuelson's approach rested on two principles. First, equilibria—where economic forces, such as supply and demand, are in balance—are the outcome of individual optimization problems—the maximization of profits or utility, or minimization of costs. Second, such equilibria must be stable (or persistent) so long as there are no other changes in the system. Stable equilibria allow you to use comparative statics, the comparison of one equilibrium situation to another, to assess how economic outcomes are affected over time by a policy change or other shock to the system. Samuelson's analysis of production, consumer behavior, income distribution, international trade, business cycles, and welfare economics demonstrated how many existing theories could be brought under this unifying framework. He extended these fields in new directions, particularly through his exploration of dynamic considerations.

Foundations was an immediate hit with economists. For a profession transitioning from verbal to mathematical methods of reasoning, it showcased how scholars could fruitfully apply sophisticated mathematical tools to economic problems at a time when Alfred Marshall's *Principles*—which presented concepts using words and graphs and relegated mathematics to brief appendices—remained the first choice for teaching economic theory. It's fair to say that Samuelson's *Foundations*, by inducing economists to make mathematics the engine of their analysis and providing the tools for this, influenced many of the most important advances in economic analysis that emerged over the next quarter-century.

SEE ALSO Pythagoras and Ordering Society (c. 530 BCE), The Invention of Calculus (c. 1665), Walras's *Elements of Pure Economics* (1874), Marshall's *Principles of Economics* (1890), Mathematical Dynamics (1933), The Bergson Social Welfare Function (1938), Linear Programming (1947)

Paul Samuelson in an MIT classroom. Samuelson's Foundations *played a major role in transforming economics into a mathematical science, evidence related to which appears on the chalkboard behind him.*

Linear Programming

Leonid V. Kantorovich (1912–1986), George B. Dantzig (1914–2005), Tjalling C. Koopmans (1910–1985)

World War II yielded numerous advances in economics, from game theory to statistical methods, but linear programming provided an important tool for both economists and businesses. Independently developed by L. V. Kantorovich in Russia and Tjalling Koopmans and George Dantzig in the U.S., linear programming provided a method for solving highly complex optimization problems. Optimization problems deal with how best to achieve a particular goal. For example, if a company has 1,000 packages to deliver every day and eight delivery trucks, what is the most cost-effective way to get the deliveries to their destinations? Linear programming allows you to assume that the relationships between the variables in the problem are linear—that the delivery trucks can drive in a straight line from one destination to the next. Unlike the standard calculus-based maximization techniques, which typically involve non-linear relationships, linear programming techniques can produce numerical computations.

Kantorovich, Koopmans, and Dantzig developed their techniques beginning in the late 1930s to plan the wartime production, transportation, and procurement of goods, but it was Dantzig, inspired by Harvard economist Wassily Leontief's input–output analysis, who expanded its application when he developed an algorithm known as the "simplex method" in 1947. It became the standard method for solving linear-programming problems. The RAND-sponsored publication of *Linear Programming and Economic Analysis* (1958) by Robert Dorfman, Paul Samuelson, and Robert Solow outlined the range of applications in economics, from transportation to welfare economics.

One of the earliest practical applications was the so-called "diet problem," which examines the least costly way to provide a diet that satisfies a variety of nutritional requirements, given the amounts of nutrients in different foods. Though originally developed to devise a low-cost way of meeting the dietary needs of U.S. soldiers, it informs present-day policy decisions about how best to fund an adequate diet for social-welfare recipients. Linear programming has also become an indispensable business tool. It can solve problems involving the organization of personnel within a company, optimal production techniques, transportation logistics, and marketing.

SEE ALSO The Invention of Calculus (c. 1665), The Cowles Commission (1932), World War II (1939), Input–Output Analysis (1941), RAND and the Cold War (1948), The Theory of Portfolio Selection (1952)

This 1943 photo shows the contents of a K-ration, which include canned corned beef, biscuits, and chewing gum. Linear programming would later be used to determine the contents of a soldier's combat rations.

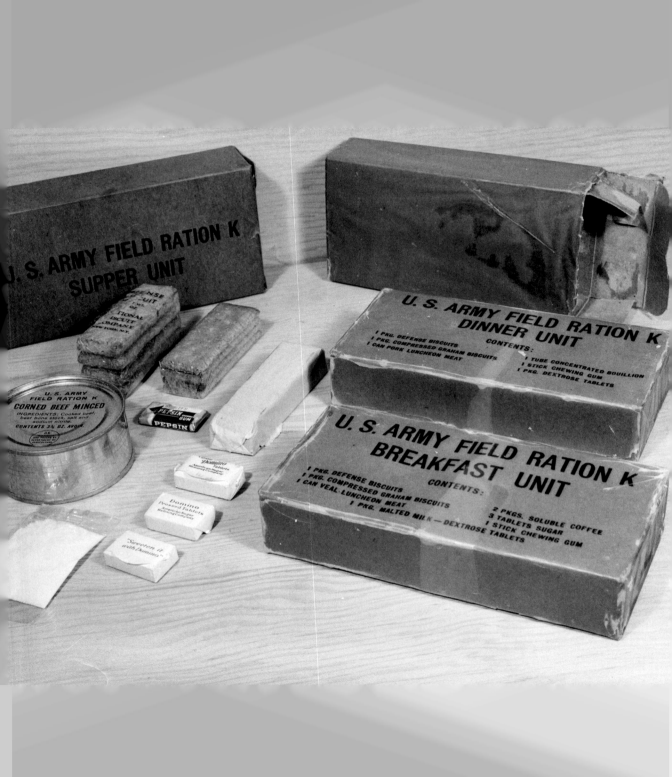

Samuelson's *Economics*

Paul A. Samuelson (1915–2009)

Economics instruction in the late 1940s was still dominated by Alfred Marshall's *Principles of Economics*, published more than a half-century earlier. This began to change in 1948, when Paul Samuelson released his introductory textbook, *Economics*. Samuelson, then in his early thirties and a professor at MIT, wrote the book to help modernize that school's economics curriculum. Despite his relative youth, he emerged as the obvious choice to spearhead this effort, as he had already made many important contributions to economics scholarship, placing him head and shoulders above his more senior colleagues.

Samuelson's textbook did far more than serve as the basis for the economics course taught to engineering students at MIT: it soon shaped the economics education of millions of students around the world, and did so for decades to come. It was one of the first to introduce Keynesian ideas from Britain to American undergraduate students, explaining the forces that cause national income to fluctuate and the use of government policy tools to address these changes. It featured the circular flow diagram, which illustrates how resources move through the economy, and showed how both macro- and microeconomic analysis could offer insight into important policy questions, ranging from unemployment to business regulation. The book also broke ground with its pedagogical approach. Samuelson combined theoretical rigor with historical detail: each chapter featured real and fictional illustrations and case studies to which students could relate. Its engaging writing style surprised many, given the highly mathematical nature of Samuelson's scholarly works.

The book's Keynesian approach to macroeconomic analysis and policymaking, along with Samuelson's willingness to admit that government regulation of the marketplace may be consistent with (and may improve) free enterprise, generated a firestorm of controversy. Prominent MIT alumni demanded that administrators ask Samuelson to eliminate these "radical" ideas from the text or at least devote more attention to other schools of economic thinking. But the university stood behind Samuelson, and the book went on to dominate the introductory-textbook market for several decades. *Economics*, the 19th edition of which remains in use today, has been translated into twenty languages and sold millions of copies.

SEE ALSO *Conversations on Political Economy* (1816), *Illustrations of Political Economy* (1832), Mill's *Principles of Political Economy* (1848), Marshall's *Principles of Economics* (1890), The Circular Flow Diagram (1933), Keynes's *General Theory* (1936), The Keynesian Revolution (1947), *Foundations of Economic Analysis* (1947)

Stacks of Paul Samuelson's classic textbook Economics.

The Factor-Price Equalization Theorem

Paul A. Samuelson (1915–2009)

Opponents of free trade often argue that it benefits countries that have lower labor costs and disadvantages countries where workers earn high wages. High wages at home make it difficult for companies to produce goods that can compete with imports from low-wage countries, leading to unemployment. As far back as the 1500s, this argument was used to justify trade barriers and policies that kept domestic wages low. Building on the insights of Eli Heckscher and Bertil Ohlin, Paul Samuelson proved that this argument doesn't hold in a competitive market in a 1948 article, "International Trade and the Equalisation of Factor Prices." According to his factor-price equalization theorem, free trade will cause the prices of production inputs, such as labor and capital, to equalize across countries.

Samuelson's finding applies a principle that has been a staple of economic thinking since William Petty's writings from the 1660s: rates of return to production inputs will equalize across their different uses. There are limits on the ability of factors of production to move from low-wage to high-wage countries. At first glance, these limitations would seem to prevent the prices of production factors, such as labor and materials, from equalizing, but Samuelson showed that this was not the case. For example, if wages in Europe are lower than those in the U.S., then Europe can sell cheaper goods, increasing world demand for their goods and lowering the demand for America's. This, in turn, increases the demand for labor in Europe and decreases it in America. Wages in Europe are driven up and wages in America are pushed down until, in equilibrium, the wage rates are identical.

This theorem plays an essential role in the theory of international trade. Though it rests on somewhat restrictive assumptions, such as strong competition and countries having identical production technology, empirical evidence has shown that factor prices tend to converge. For example, wage increases for Japanese auto workers since the 1980s and wage decreases in the U.S. have narrowed the cost advantages for Japanese automakers producing cars in Japan, which has encouraged them to build production facilities in the U.S. and elsewhere.

SEE ALSO Mercantile Policies (1539), The Balance-of-Trade Controversy (1621), The Equalization of Returns (1662), Turgot's *Reflections* (1766), Clark's *Distribution of Wealth* (1899), The Heckscher–Ohlin Model (1933), The Stolper–Samuelson Theorem (1941), The New Trade Theory (1979)

This Nepalese woman is harvesting millet in a field. The factor-price equalization theorem suggests that free trade will tend to equalize the wages of agricultural workers across countries.

The Median Voter Theorem

Duncan Black (1908–1991), Anthony Downs (b. 1930)

When Harold Hotelling developed his model of locational choice, he noted that the positions of political candidates tend to converge, just as the locations of sellers who offer similar products move toward the center of a "main street." In his 1948 article, "On the Rationale of Group Decision Making," Scottish economist Duncan Black provided an explanation for Hotelling's observation, which became known as the median voter theorem.

Black focused his attention on committees that make decisions by majority vote. He discovered that if a committee is considering different decisions on a single issue and its members do not prefer both extremes to the middle position, the committee will make the decision preferred by the median voter. For example, suppose that a committee needs to choose how many tanks to provide for the army. Bob prefers 10 tanks, Susan prefers 20 tanks, and Fred prefers 30 tanks. Black showed that Susan's preferences will win out; when offered the choice between 20 and 10 tanks or 20 and 30 tanks, a majority of voters would choose the 20-tank option in both voting contests.

Anthony Downs expanded Black's analysis to political elections in a representative democracy, showing that the candidate who can capture the median voter will win an election in a majority voting system. If the spectrum of voters runs fairly evenly from liberal to conservative, then a moderate candidate will capture a majority. If the election is taking place in a conservative district, then the median voter will be quite conservative and that district will elect a candidate with similar views. The median voter theorem has important implications for political behavior. Candidates will tend to position themselves to capture the median voter, and authors of legislation or ballot initiatives will typically tailor the language of their proposals to do the same. The median voter theorem became a centerpiece public choice theory, the economic analysis of the political process, which emerged during the 1960s and 1970s as some economists began to question whether the political process could produce results that are in society's best interests.

SEE ALSO The Hotelling Model of Locational Choice (1929), Arrow's Impossibility Theorem (1951), The Rational Voter Model and the Paradox of Voting (1957), Public Choice Analysis (1962)

Campaign buttons for a variety of U.S. presidential candidates. Anthony Downs concluded that candidates running for office in a democracy will fare the best if they appeal to the median voter and will therefore tailor their campaigns to do so.

RAND and the Cold War

The Cold War, like World War II, brought economists into contact with mathematicians, natural scientists, and others, leading to new developments in economic analysis. Among the several institutions that facilitated these collaborations, the RAND Corporation stands out for the breadth of its influence and the number of eminent economists in its ranks, particularly during the 1950s.

RAND, short for Research ANd Development, was originally created by the Douglas Aircraft Company to conduct research for the U.S. Air Force. It became an independent nonprofit corporation in 1948, and though its core mission involved planning and developing strategies for deterring nuclear war, its domain quickly expanded. RAND researchers contributed to the space program, computing, game theory, linear programming, and artificial intelligence, as well as economics. Working with the Cowles Commission, its researchers studied topics such as transportation, health care, defense economics, the economics of technological change, and government budgeting processes. Nobel Laureates Kenneth Arrow, John Nash, Leonid Hurwicz, Richard Markowitz, Lloyd Shapley, Herbert Simon, and Robert Solow were just some of the leading economists who had affiliations with RAND. Two of the most influential pieces of research to emerge from RAND's economics group were Arrow's book *Social Choice and Individual Values* (1951), which gave us Arrow's impossibility theorem, and Charles J. Hitch and Roland N. McKean's book, *The Economics of Defense in the Nuclear Age* (1960), which became the basis for the Kennedy administration's Cold War planning.

More importantly, RAND was a hot spot for cutting-edge mathematical techniques, exposing economists to game theory, linear programming, and operations research at a time when very few in the field could work with or even understand these methods. What unites these tools is the theory of rational choice, the logical pursuit of self-interest given a set of constraints. RAND's researchers refined and pushed this theory to new limits. If economics is, as many now describe it, "the science of rational choice," this evolution gained momentum thanks to RAND's influence on economics research.

SEE ALSO The Cowles Commission (1932), Game Theory Enters Economics (1944), Linear Programming (1947), Non-Cooperative Games and Nash Equilibrium (1950), Arrow's Impossibility Theorem (1951), The Theory of Portfolio Selection (1952), The Shapley Value (1953), Bounded Rationality (1955), The Solow–Swan Growth Model (1956), Mechanism Design (1972)

RAND economist and researcher Nancy Nimitz flips through the pages of a Soviet newspaper, 1958.

Computation: The Orcutt Regression Analyzer and the Phillips Machine

A. W. Phillips (1914–1975), Walter Newlyn (1915–2002), Guy H. Orcutt (1917–2006)

Efforts to make economics more of an empirical science hinged on three crucial factors: the availability of the needed data, the development of mathematical and statistical techniques to study that data, and access to computational tools that could employ them. It was the last of these that took the longest to arrive. The introduction of mechanical calculating machines, first produced for sale in the mid-1800s, could accurately handle large addition, subtraction, multiplication, and division problems, but the genesis of electronic computing in the 1940s and 1950s finally made complex calculations feasible.

Wassily Leontief used one of the earliest electro-mechanical computers, the Harvard Mark II, for input–output analysis in the mid-1940s. The Mark II was much faster than its predecessors and could perform many advanced computations, including those involving square roots and logarithms. In his 1944 University of Michigan PhD thesis, Guy Orcutt designed a machine that he called a "regression analyzer," which could compute correlations and regression coefficients in systems involving several variables. He introduced his working version, which had box-like components that fit on a desktop, in his 1948 article (which included photographs), "A New Regression Analyser."

The most unusual of these early computing devices was the Monetary National Income Analogue Computer (MONIAC), often referred to as the "Phillips machine." Invented by Bill Phillips (of Phillips curve fame) and Walter Newlyn in 1949, this machine was essentially a circular flow device, pumping water through tanks (representing sectors of the economy) and pipes to model income and expenditure flows. As a self-contained Keynesian system that classified economic activity in terms of consumption, investment, government spending, and trade, it allowed its users to simulate economic changes—all by adjusting valves that determined water flows.

Though these devices went the way of the horse and buggy with the evolution of modern computing, they illustrated the research and pedagogical power of computational methods. Economists could now make calculations in minutes that would previously have taken hours and even days, as well as provide more precise economic forecasts.

SEE ALSO The Econometric Society (1930), The Circular Flow Diagram (1933), Keynes's *General Theory* (1936), Input–Output Analysis (1941), The Keynesian Revolution (1947), The Phillips Curve (1958), Economics Becomes Applied (1970), The Personal Computer (1981)

This Phillips Machine, restored in 1993, shows the system of water tanks and pipes that Phillips used to illustrate the flow of money through the economy.

Non-Cooperative Games and Nash Equilibrium

John Forbes Nash, Jr. (1928–2015)

The pioneering work of John von Neumann and Oskar Morgenstern gave birth to the field of game theory, which analyzes situations of strategic interaction among agents, but it was John Nash's work in the early 1950s that gave the subject broad application. Nash was a Princeton-educated mathematician and completed his PhD thesis at age 20. The thesis distinguished non-cooperative games from cooperative ones and conceptualized the equilibrium that bears his name.

Von Neumann and Morgenstern focused on cooperative games, in which individuals can make binding agreements and form coalitions. The purchase of an automobile and the passing of legislation are two examples. Nash turned his attention to non-cooperative games, where players act independently of one another and binding contracts are not possible. Examples of non-cooperative games include poker, sporting contests, and, in economics, the Cournot duopoly model, the prisoner's dilemma, and the free-rider problem.

Still more important, Nash characterized an equilibrium for a non-cooperative game. In this "Nash equilibrium," as it came to be called, each player in the game is playing her optimal strategy given the strategies pursued by others. Thus, no player can improve her situation by altering her strategy; everyone is doing the best they can, given what the other players are doing. A game may have multiple Nash equilibria, or it may have none. Economists and other social scientists use the concept of the Nash equilibrium to predict the outcomes of various strategic interactions.

Non-cooperative game theory provides neat explanations for why countries sometimes violate arms-control or pollution-reduction treaties, where detection of violations and enforcement of penalties are difficult. It also explains why fisheries and mineral resource deposits are often overexploited and helps us to understand companies' pricing and marketing practices. Though these situations appear to be worlds removed from rock-paper-scissors, tic-tac-toe, chess, and the like, the contributions by Nash and other game-theory pioneers showed us that the same underlying forces govern behavior in these very divergent scenarios.

SEE ALSO Cournot's *Researches* (1838), The Bertrand Model (1883), The Hotelling Model of Locational Choice (1929), The Stackelberg Model (1934), Game Theory Enters Economics (1944), The Prisoner's Dilemma (1950), The Free-Rider Problem (1965), Screening—or Pooling and Separating Equilibria (1976)

John Nash expanded the study of game theory to non-cooperative games, such as chess. In non-cooperative games, players act independently and can't form binding agreements with each other.

The Prisoner's Dilemma

Merrill Flood (1908–1991), Melvin Dresher (1911–1992)

The prisoner's dilemma reveals how individuals making rational decisions in pursuit of their self-interest can generate outcomes that make them all worse off. This famous thought experiment came from Merrill Flood and Melvin Dresher, mathematicians working at the RAND Corporation in 1950, during the early years of the Cold War. Princeton mathematician Albert Tucker, whose students included Nobel Laureates John Nash and Lloyd Shapley, subsequently named and explained the problem in terms of prisoner confessions.

Consider two people who are accused of a crime and jailed without a way to communicate with each other. If they both remain silent, each receives a five-year prison sentence. If one confesses and the other remains silent, the confessor gets a two-year prison sentence while the other spends twenty years in prison. If both parties confess, each gets a prison term of ten years. Clearly, these individuals would be best off if they both keep silent, yet it is in each agent's self-interest to confess. If Cindy confesses, Sam gets twenty years in prison if he remains silent and ten years in prison if he confesses. If Cindy remains silent, Sam gets two years in prison if he confesses and five years if he remains silent. Cindy faces the same incentives. No matter what the other party chooses, each agent receives a shorter sentence by confessing. What is rational for the group, then, isn't rational for each individual when there isn't something that enforces cooperation, such as knowing that your criminal gang may harm your family if you confess.

Cartel behavior, where producers collude to increase prices, illustrates the prisoner's dilemma at work in markets. When cartels collude and agree to restrict output and thus increase prices, they can maintain these agreements only if cartel members don't cheat by increasing output levels. But the incentive to cheat is powerful, causing agreements to eventually break down. This same logic explains why political parties often fail to cooperate on legislation, why countries continue to build and maintain nuclear arsenals rather than disarming, and even swiping strategies on dating apps.

SEE ALSO Game Theory Enters Economics (1944), RAND and the Cold War (1948), Non-Cooperative Games and Nash Equilibrium (1950), The Shapley Value (1953), The Experimental Turn (1986), Governance of the Commons (1990)

The prisoner's dilemma explains why groups of criminals often confess to their crimes even though it would appear better for them to remain silent.

Arrow's Impossibility Theorem

Kenneth J. Arrow (1921–2017)

Social-welfare functions, as originally developed by Abram Bergson, are theoretical tools used to aggregate individual preferences and then rank alternative states of the world. But how might we arrive at such rankings in reality? One answer is to use voting as a means to translate individual preferences into a social choice. Kenneth Arrow examined the feasibility of such procedures in his Columbia University PhD thesis, subsequently published as *Social Choice and Individual Values* (1951).

Arrow argued that any social-choice process should satisfy a basic set of criteria. These include transitivity (if A is preferred to B and B is preferred to C, then A is also preferred to C), "non-dictatorship" (one person's preferences are not allowed to dominate those of everyone else), the "Pareto principle" (if everyone prefers option A to option B, then A should be chosen), and "independence of irrelevant alternatives" (if everyone prefers A to B, a change in C does not affect society's preference for A over B). Arrow then proceeded to prove that there is *no* voting process that will simultaneously satisfy these assumptions and provide a unique ranking of the various alternatives—a result known as Arrow's impossibility theorem. You can derive a unique ranking only if you relax one of these assumptions: for example, you could allow one person to be a "dictator" so that her preferences determine the outcome.

Some argue that Arrow's impossibility theorem shows that the idea of a social-welfare function isn't tenable, because it is impossible to aggregate individual preferences into social preferences without violating one of its assumptions. Others see it as evidence that rational collective decisions in a democratic society are impossible. Both of these interpretations, as well as whether it is reasonable to insist that a choice process satisfy all of Arrow's assumptions, are controversial. The field of social-choice analysis, which sprang from Arrow's work, devotes much attention to these questions, focusing particularly on which type of voting system—a simple majority, plurality (winner-take-all) voting, or other ranking methods—is most likely to generate outcomes consistent with voter preferences in a given electoral context.

SEE ALSO The Bergson Social Welfare Function (1938), Hicks's *Value and Capital* (1939), The Fundamental Theorems of Welfare Economics (1943), The Median Voter Theorem (1948), Proving the Existence of a General Equilibrium (1954), The Rational Voter Model and the Paradox of Voting (1957), *Collective Choice and Social Welfare* (1970)

Women count votes that have been cast at a polling location in Worcester, Massachusetts. Arrow's impossibility theorem questions the extent to which we can draw conclusions about society's preferences from the voting process.

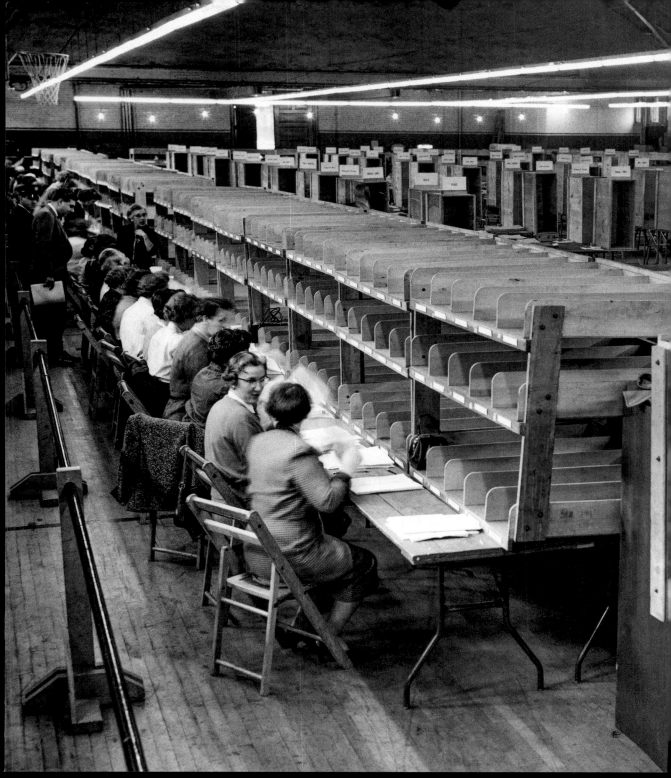

Resources for the Future and Environmental Economics

Allen V. Kneese (1930–2001), John V. Krutilla (1922–2003)

Environmental and natural-resource issues have concerned economic thinkers at least as far back as the nineteenth century, when John Stuart Mill argued that preservation of the natural environment can't be left to the market. However, the application of economic methods to environmental issues began in earnest during the early 1950s. The most important institutional springboard for environmental economics research came from the 1952 founding of Resources for the Future (RFF), the first think tank devoted to environmental issues, and the work of the two most influential economists associated with it, Allen Kneese and John V. Krutilla. The publication of Rachel Carson's *Silent Spring* (1962) and concerns about the effects of large-scale air and water pollution put environmental problems on the front burner in the 1960s, leading to a tremendous surge in environmental economics research.

Many early environmental economists at RFF and in the academic world saw economics as a tool that could help preserve natural resources and reduce environmental damage. What distinguished economists from others working on environmental issues, though, was their evaluation of pollution reduction in terms of its benefits and opportunity costs. This led to the very controversial realization that, beyond some point, the benefits of further pollution reduction would be outweighed by the costs. For environmentalists who considered nature as something too valuable to have a price, assessing environmental impacts in this way was disgraceful.

Economists' advice was ignored early on, but in recent decades they have had significant influence on environmental-policy debates. Several nations have adopted carbon taxes, long advocated by economists as superior to pollution regulations, and economists assisted in the development of emissions trading systems. Economists have also made great strides in modeling the economic and environmental impacts of climate change, and Yale economist William Nordhaus received the 2018 Nobel Prize for his work on this subject and the benefits of using carbon taxes to combat it.

SEE ALSO Classical Political Economy (c. 1790), Opportunity Cost (1889), External Economies and Diseconomies (1912), The Kaldor–Hicks Efficiency Criterion (1939), The Common Pool Problem (1954), Externalities and Market Failure (1958), Cost–Benefit Analysis (1958), Emissions Trading (1966), Economics Becomes Applied (1970)

Opened bags of pesticides used for aerial application in Fresno, California, 1972.

The Theory of Portfolio Selection

Harry M. Markowitz (b. 1927)

In 1952, Harry Markowitz, a graduate student and Cowles Commission member at the University of Chicago, wrote "Portfolio Selection," an article that marks the birth of financial economics and earned its author the Nobel Prize. At the time, most investors believed that you could eliminate risk from your financial portfolio without reducing its return by diversifying your assets—mixing stocks and bonds, and making sure that your stock portfolio included a variety of companies from different sectors of the economy. Markowitz demonstrated mathematically, though, that it is generally only possible to *reduce* risk through diversification without impacting your return.

As Markowitz observed in his article and 1959 book of the same title, investors have to choose between higher returns and lower risk. This makes portfolio selection an optimal-allocation problem that can be solved with economic analysis. Markowitz argued that a rational investor will maximize the portfolio's expected return while minimizing its variance. The investor's optimal portfolio will thus depend on her attitude toward risk—and, because people's aversion to risk varies, portfolio composition will also vary among investors.

Markowitz also argued that it is not the risk associated with a particular stock, bond, or other financial instrument that matters to the investor, but its contribution to the overall risk of the portfolio. The rational investor won't look at how the risk and return of a given security compares with those of others, but instead will examine how its return varies with changing market conditions as compared with other items in the portfolio.

Markowitz's work provided investors with rules for constructing an optimal portfolio, depending on their desired returns and tolerance for risk. In 1958, his Cowles Commission colleague, James Tobin, used portfolio theory to explain the demand for money, the holding of which reduces overall portfolio risk. These insights later provided the basis for other important contributions in financial economics, including the capital asset pricing model. Markowitz's prescriptions for the rational investor have become indispensable for financial managers, who pair modern portfolio theory with sophisticated computer models to structure portfolios that match their clients' preferences.

SEE ALSO The Cowles Commission (1932), The Capital Asset Pricing Model (1962), The Efficient Markets Hypothesis (1965), The Black–Scholes Model (1973)

Stockholders and brokers in Brooklyn, New York, watch the board showing changes in stock prices, 1958. Harry Markowitz's theory of portfolio selection explained how risk tolerance and the desire for higher returns factor into the creation of an optimal investment portfolio.

The Shapley Value

Lloyd S. Shapley (1923–2016)

Mathematician and Nobel Prize–winning economist Lloyd Shapley is considered by some to be the greatest game theorist who ever lived. Shapley was first exposed to game theory at RAND, and, after his graduate studies in mathematics at Princeton, he returned in 1954, remaining there until he accepted a position at UCLA in 1981. The most significant of his contributions is the Shapley value.

In cooperative game theory, which studies interactions among coalitions (or groups) of players, the Shapley value shows the expected payoff required to persuade a player to collaborate with others. The Shapley value equals the player's expected marginal contribution to a randomly chosen coalition within the game and embodies the idea that each coalition member should receive a payoff equivalent to his marginal contribution. As such, it captures economists' emphasis on marginal benefits and costs and reflects social norms of fairness.

Suppose that three neighboring towns need an airplane runway, but each town requires one of a different length. Flowerville needs $1/3$ mile, Newtown requires $2/3$ mile, and Oldtown 1 mile. Each $1/3$ mile of runway costs 10 million dollars. They can each build their own runway, or they can cooperate and build a single runway long enough to accommodate everyone's needs. Because each town needs the first $1/3$ mile, they split this cost equally. The second $1/3$ mile is needed only by Newtown and Oldtown, so they share that cost. The final $1/3$ mile is needed by just Oldtown, so it bears the entire cost. The Shapley value says that Flowerville should contribute 3.3 million dollars, Newtown 8.3 million, and Oldtown 18.3 million. The towns pay far less than had they built their own runways, and each town's share of the cost reflects its addition to the project's cost.

Cooperative games have many possible outcomes, depending on the interactions of the players and the coalitions they form. The Shapley value doesn't predict what happens, but rather suggests a fair resolution. Economists have used it to calculate airport landing fees, determine the risk of a financial portfolio, and even divide the assets in a bankruptcy according to the rules in the Jewish Talmud.

SEE ALSO Game Theory Enters Economics (1944), Non-Cooperative Games and Nash Equilibrium (1950), The Theory of Portfolio Selection (1952)

In addition to recommending how the cost of building airport runways should be split, the Shapley value can be applied to help airports decide how much to charge airlines to land their planes.

"The Methodology of Positive Economics"

Milton Friedman (1912–2006)

Milton Friedman's essay "The Methodology of Positive Economics" (1953) is one of the most influential writings on economic methodology published during the twentieth century. Friedman received his training in statistics and economics, and his influences included Arthur Burns (1904–1987), Wesley Clair Mitchell, and Simon Kuznets, all economists affiliated with the National Bureau of Economic Research (NBER). Friedman's research program and his approach to economics reflected the NBER's preference for empirical, policy-relevant research over abstract theorizing, and his essay on positive economics melds his dual interests in economic theory and empirical analysis.

Friedman's position can be summarized simply: it is the ability of an economic theory to *predict well*, not the realism of its assumptions or its ability to describe real-life behavior, that ultimately matters. A good theory, Friedman contended, will almost always be unrealistic, because generating predictive power requires stripping away all but the most important elements of the phenomena being studied. Most markets don't satisfy the extreme assumptions of perfect competition, and consumers may not actually calculate the marginal benefits and costs of their purchases. But if these theories predict outcomes accurately, Friedman said, they are useful theories. It's enough to say that markets operate "as if" these assumptions are true.

Friedman's position challenged institutionalism, which criticized both classical economics and mathematical modes of theorizing for their lack of realism, and newer approaches to economic inquiry, such as general equilibrium analysis, that didn't lend themselves well to empirical testing. His argument stimulated a good deal of controversy and led Paul Samuelson to counter that the chief purpose of economic theory is to describe and explain real-world phenomena. In time, however, Friedman's approach to evaluating theories became something of a mantra for many economists, particularly as the development of empirical techniques and computing power made the testing of theories a more prominent part of economics research.

SEE ALSO Classical Political Economy (c. 1790), Walras's *Elements of Pure Economics* (1874), Mitchell's *Business Cycles* (1913), Institutional Economics (1919), The National Bureau of Economic Research (1920), Scarcity and Choice (1932), National Income Accounting (1934), Logical Positivism (1938), Hicks's *Value and Capital* (1939), The Chicago School (1946), *Foundations of Economic Analysis* (1947)

Milton Friedman, pictured here, shaped economic methodology by asserting that economists need only be concerned about a theory's predictive power, not whether its assumptions are realistic.

Proving the Existence of a General Equilibrium

Lionel W. McKenzie (1919–2010), Kenneth J. Arrow (1921–2017), Gérard Debreu (1921–2004)

When León Walras developed a mathematical theory of general equilibrium in the 1870s, he masterfully captured the interdependence between the many variables that make up the economic system. A change in, say, the demand for steel sets off a chain reaction of adjustments that are felt in input and output markets across the economy until, eventually, the system settles down to a new equilibrium where demand and supply are equal in all markets. What Walras hadn't done, however, was to prove that a general equilibrium—a simultaneous and consistent equilibrium in all markets—exists. Would a perfectly competitive system of markets actually arrive at such an equilibrium position?

In the early 1950s, Kenneth Arrow and Gérard Debreu, and Lionel McKenzie, simultaneously developed the first existence proofs. Debreu and McKenzie were then at the Cowles Commission, whose economists had taken a strong interest in general equilibrium analysis, and Arrow had recently departed Cowles for Stanford. Though the three originally worked independently, Arrow and Debreu joined forces when they learned of each other's work. The proofs developed by Arrow and Debreu, and by McKenzie, were published in *Econometrica* in 1954.

Because no real-world economy comes close to matching the frictionless world described by Walras, Arrow–Debreu, and McKenzie, the existence of a general equilibrium may seem like an irrelevant, abstract flight of fancy. But economists' conceptions of how the real economy operates are often informed by the lessons of their model. A proof of this equilibrium's existence provides a basis for analyzing how markets operate when the model's highly restrictive assumptions are loosened. Economists' confidence in the rigor of these proofs, which helped earn Nobel Prizes for Arrow and Debreu, and their growing comfort with increasingly advanced mathematics, encouraged them to make extensive use of general equilibrium modeling, which remains at the core of much of contemporary economic thinking.

SEE ALSO Walras's *Elements of Pure Economics* (1874), The Econometric Society (1930), The Cowles Commission (1932), The Fundamental Theorems of Welfare Economics (1943), Non-Cooperative Games and Nash Equilibrium (1950), Arrow's Impossibility Theorem (1951), Debreu's *The Theory of Value* (1959)

Kenneth Arrow (pictured here in a 1972 photo) and Gérard Debreu published their proof showing the existence of a general equilibrium in the July 1954 issue of Econometrica.

Public Goods

Paul A. Samuelson (1915–2009)

In *Wealth of Nations*, Adam Smith assigned to the government the role of providing "certain public works" that the marketplace can't effectively supply. Though Smith's idea of "public works" appeared in economic writings during the next two centuries, economists didn't develop a theory to explain this market failure until the mid-1950s. In "The Pure Theory of Public Expenditure" (1954), the shortest classic journal article in the history of economics at just three pages, Paul Samuelson described the conditions necessary to provide public goods, such as national defense, roads, and police protection, in a way that maximizes social welfare.

Samuelson noted that the problem with public goods, or items intended for collective consumption, is that many individuals use them simultaneously. Unlike a private good, such as an apple, which can only be eaten by one person, all citizens benefit from national defense jointly, and no one citizen's consumption of it detracts from its consumption by others. To provide the efficient amount of a *private* good, suppliers only need to produce goods up to the point at which marginal benefit to each consumer equals the marginal cost of producing the good. However, in the case of *public* goods, suppliers must produce until the *sum* of the marginal benefits across all individuals equals the marginal cost.

These conditions make it difficult for the market to provide efficient amounts of public goods. People have no incentive to accurately reveal their preferences, since they can benefit from public goods whether they have paid for them or not, a scenario that economist Mancur Olson later called the free-rider problem. Because it is difficult, if not impossible, to charge a price to those who benefit from public goods, the private sector won't supply them—or the supply will fall well short of the efficient amount. Thus, Samuelson concluded, the government needs to step in, using its authority to levy taxes, fees, and tolls to finance the provision of these goods. Whether the government can actually provide public goods in the efficient amounts is another question, one to which public-choice analysis offered a resounding negative answer in the 1960s.

SEE ALSO Smith's *Wealth of Nations* (1776), *La Scienza della Finanze* (1883), The Benefit Principle of Taxation (1896), Pigou's *Wealth and Welfare* (1912), *Foundations of Economic Analysis* (1947), Public Choice Analysis (1962), The Free-Rider Problem (1965), Mechanism Design (1972), Supply-Side Economics (1974), The Experimental Turn (1986).

Firefighting services are an example of public goods, from which all citizens benefit jointly.

Development Economics

Simon Kuznets (1901–1985), W. Arthur Lewis (1915–1991)

Until the 1950s, the analysis of economic growth focused on already-developed economies and had less to say about the development process itself. Nobel Laureates W. Arthur Lewis, then of the University of Manchester, and Johns Hopkins's Simon Kuznets shifted this focus by pioneering the field of development economics.

Lewis's 1954 article, "Economic Development with Unlimited Supplies of Labor," located the roots of economic development in the "dual economies" that exist within a country during its early stages of development. One is a large subsistence economy that revolves around peasant agriculture and has little capital, and the other is a capital-driven economy of industry and commerce. This capitalist sector lures workers from the subsistence economy, and the abundance of workers allows firms to offer low wages. These low labor costs lead to large profits; with the reinvestment of these profits, the capitalist sector grows. As the surplus of labor diminishes, the economy reaches a "turning point": wages rise, the associated cost advantage disappears, and the rapid productivity growth comes to an end.

As a country becomes industrialized, its income distribution changes. Kuznets contended that income inequality is likely to increase in the early stages of economic development before ultimately decreasing, depicting the relationship between inequality and per-capita income as an inverted "U" that would later be called the Kuznets curve. This occurs because development simultaneously increases profits for firms in the capitalist sector and creates new investment opportunities. Meanwhile, wages remain largely stagnant until the demand for labor has grown sufficiently, due to these opportunities, to put upward pressure on wages and allow the country to establish taxpayer-funded welfare programs that address inequality.

Lewis and Kuznets's work justified measures to promote industrialization during the 1950s and 1960s. The Kuznets curve, however, has attracted controversy. While it fits the pattern of development in parts of Western Europe, Latin America, and China, increasing inequality in some *developed* economies seems to contradict the Kuznets curve's prediction. The "environmental Kuznets curve," which suggests that environmental degradation will increase in the early stages of development but then begin to steadily diminish, too, has been the subject of debate.

SEE ALSO National Income Accounting (1934), The Harrod–Domar Growth Model (1939), The Solow–Swan Growth Model (1956), Endogenous Growth Theory (1986)

China's recent economic growth has been fueled in part by plentiful supplies of cheap labor, but economists now debate whether China is reaching a Lewis turning point as these supplies begin to dry up.

The Common Pool Problem

H. Scott Gordon (b. 1924)

In the nineteenth century, economists including John Stuart Mill, William Stanley Jevons, and Henry Sidgwick observed that a market system could promote the overexploitation of natural resources. Jevons, for example, suggested that Britain was in danger of running out of coal after noticing how ravenously British industry and shipping consumed it. Still, the subject received little attention until the 1950s, when concerns about pollution and the overuse of natural resources led policymakers to prioritize environmental and natural-resource conservation. Canadian economist H. Scott Gordon provided a launching point for this interest with his classic analysis of fisheries management.

In his 1954 article, "The Economic Theory of a Common Property Resource: The Fishery," Gordon noted that biologists tended to treat fisheries as an inexhaustible resource, a view that he thought both erroneous and dangerous because it ignored the problem of overexploitation. Though every fisherman would benefit from the long-term health of the fishing stock and would wish to limit their yearly catch to support this, they can't rely on other fishermen to exercise the same restraint. As a result, each fisherman will attempt to catch as many fish as possible, depleting the fishery.

The root of this "common pool" problem lies in the absence of private-property rights, which makes it difficult to exclude people from using a resource. As Gordon put it, "everybody's property is nobody's property." If a single agent owned the fishery and had the power to stop people from using it, that agent, whether an individual or the government, would have an incentive to limit the catch to avoid overfishing. (And, in the case of a private owner, this limitation would also increase long-term profit.)

Gordon's work offered policymakers a new approach for tackling concerns about overexploitation. His insights also provided the foundation for Garrett Hardin's article "The Tragedy of the Commons," which applied the common pool problem to issues ranging from overpopulation to the growth of government spending. In 2009, Elinor Ostrom was awarded the Nobel Prize for her research on governance mechanisms, which deal with the common pool problems that Gordon described.

SEE ALSO Mill's *Principles of Political Economy* (1848), Jevons's *Theory of Political Economy* (1871), External Economies and Diseconomies (1912), Resources for the Future and Environmental Economics (1952), Externalities and Market Failure (1958), The Coase Theorem (1960), Emissions Trading (1966), Governance of the Commons (1990)

Lobster traps are stacked on a dock in Maine. To address the common pool problem described by H. Scott Gordon, many American states and Canadian provinces regulate where lobster fishermen can place their traps and how many can be used.

Bounded Rationality

Herbert A. Simon (1916–2001)

Herbert Simon became known as one of the twentieth century's most influential scholars for his analysis of individual and group decision-making and contributions to fields including economics, artificial intelligence, political science, psychology, and computer science. Though Simon studied political science at the University of Chicago, he wanted to become a "mathematical social scientist." He spent time with the economists at the Cowles Commission in the years between the completion of his graduate studies and his move to Carnegie Mellon University in 1949, which greatly enhanced his exposure to economics and its advanced mathematical methods.

Simon soon became interested in the limits of rational decision-making. For Simon, the idea that individuals could evaluate a wide array of possible alternatives, account for all the probabilities and contingencies associated with them, and then select the best option was completely unrealistic. His 1955 article, "A Behavioral Model of Rational Choice," and a series of subsequent writings argued that limits on available information, the computational capacity of the human mind, and the timeframe for making decisions posed the biggest obstacles to the type of rational decision-making that economic agents were assumed to employ. Instead, individuals create simplified models of the real world—shortcuts, or rules of thumb—to inform their decisions. This "bounded rationality," Simon suggested, leads to "satisficing" behavior, where agents settle for an acceptable solution that meets or exceeds certain criteria, rather than maximizing in the sense suggested by rational choice theory. For example, if one brand of jam meets a shopper's standards, she may purchase that jam every month rather than exploring the numerous options on the shelves. Managers, meanwhile, may shoot for meeting just the basic profit expectations of the company's owners to maintain a more pleasant work environment.

Simon's work on decision theory and the analysis of organizations earned him the 1978 Nobel Prize and eventually set off an explosion of research in organization theory and behavioral economics. This work has shed new light on how owners can structure contracts with managers to prioritize profit maximization and the various ways in which individual decision-making departs from the predictions of rational choice theory.

SEE ALSO *Homo Economicus* (1836), Jevons's *Theory of Political Economy* (1871), The Cowles Commission (1932), *The Modern Corporation and Private Property* (1932), RAND and the Cold War (1948), The Efficient Markets Hypothesis (1965), Behavioral Economics (1979), The Experimental Turn (1986)

This medical illustration shows the different lobes of the brain—including the frontal lobe, which plays an important role in decision-making. For Herbert Simon, limits on the brain's decision-making capacity cast doubt on how rational it is possible for real-life economic agents to truly be.

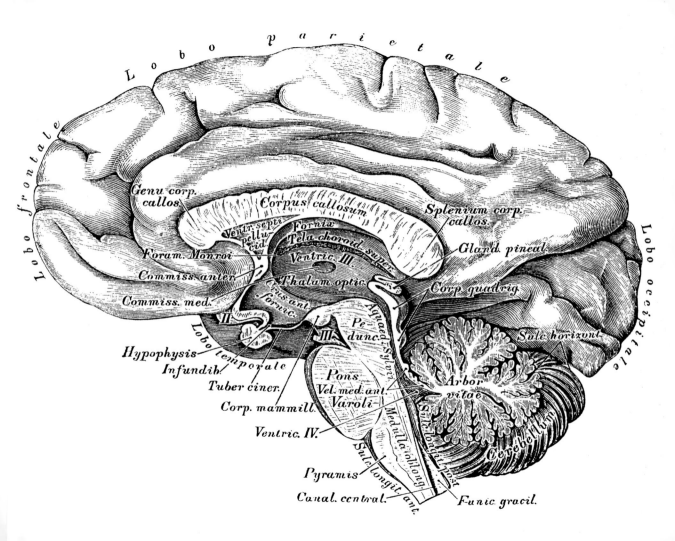

Large-Scale Macroeconometric Models

Lawrence R. Klein (1920–2013), Arthur S. Goldberger (1930–2009)

One of the most important policy-related advances in modern economics was the development of large-scale macroeconometric models. These models can be used to forecast the economy's path and to assess the potential effects of major economic policies, such as changes in the money supply, government spending, or the tax system. The seeds of this work lie in Jan Tinbergen's models of the Dutch and American economies in the late 1930s, which showed that it was possible to construct dynamic models to accomplish these tasks. The researchers at the Cowles Commission advanced this work by building larger, improved models of the national economy, but University of Michigan economist Lawrence Klein and his doctoral student, Arthur Goldberger, set macroeconometric modeling on its modern path with the construction of the Klein–Goldberger model of the U.S. economy in 1955.

The Klein–Goldberger model, which was inspired by the IS–LM model, provided the first large-scale representation of an economy that was firmly grounded in Keynesian macroeconomic theory. It was also the first model used to make economic forecasts, the initial one being for 1953. This model consisted of twenty equations, using detailed demand functions for consumption, investment, government spending, labor, and imports. Klein and Goldberger used the latest econometric techniques developed at Cowles to estimate its parameters—showing, for example, how a change in wages affects consumption.

The model's success spawned many imitators over the next two decades. Increasingly sophisticated models, utilizing hundreds of equations that captured detailed relationships between variables across the economic system, were developed by many public and private entities during the 1960s and 1970s. Some of these even became commercial successes, as governments and businesses became customers of economic forecasting services. The Klein–Goldberger model and the legion of later models that it inspired became important tools for macroeconomic policymaking in countries around the world. They also reinforced the dominance of Keynesian thinking among both economists and policymakers. Though eventually eclipsed by dynamic stochastic general equilibrium (DSGE) models, these large-scale macroeconometric models remain a part of the forecasting tool kits of many governments and central banks.

SEE ALSO The Cowles Commission (1932), Keynes's *General Theory* (1936), Liquidity Preference and the Liquidity Trap (1936), The Tinbergen Model (1936), The IS–LM Model (1937), Haavelmo's "Probability Approach" (1944), The Keynesian Revolution (1947), *Foundations of Economic Analysis* (1947), The Lucas Critique (1976), Dynamic Stochastic General Equilibrium Models (2003)

Lawrence Klein pioneered the construction of econometric models that captured the complex workings of a country's economy and significantly enhanced economists' forecasting capabilities.

The Theory of Second Best

Richard G. Lipsey (1928–), Kelvin Lancaster (1924–1999)

Economists extol the virtues of competitive markets because they tend to produce efficient outcomes. But what if it isn't possible to satisfy the dictates of efficiency in all sectors of the economy? One natural solution to this problem entails pursuing efficiency in as many markets as possible to get us as close as we can to an overall efficient outcome. But as Richard Lipsey and Kelvin Lancaster of the London School of Economics demonstrated in their 1956 article "The Generalized Theory of Second Best," it can be difficult to figure out the "second-best" solution.

Lipsey and Lancaster's theory of second-best contends that if there exists an inefficiency in one part of the system, the pursuit of efficiency in other areas typically will make matters worse. Consider an economy with several monopolists, each of whom is a polluter. Both monopoly and pollution generate inefficiencies: monopoly because it produces too little output relative to what a society wants, and pollution because its costs are not borne by those emitting it. Eliminating the monopolies and replacing them with competitive markets will reduce the monopolistic inefficiency. But because competitive markets produce more output than monopolies, this change will lead to more pollution. And using government regulation to reduce the pollution introduces the inefficiencies associated with government bureaucracies. In short, it may just be better to live with the monopolists and their pollution.

Lipsey and Lancaster's result showed that the economist's piecemeal approach to identifying and correcting individual sources of inefficiency is often misguided. However, no simple solution exists. The economist or policy-maker might not have the information required to identify and implement the "second-best" solution—such as knowing the optimal amount of pollution and how best to achieve it.

The theory of second-best has been particularly important for examining the efficiency of tax policy, trade policy, and price regulations on monopolies, where distortions are common. While the theory seems to offer good reason to be pessimistic, it has also encouraged economists to be more judicious with their policy recommendations.

SEE ALSO Smith's *Wealth of Nations* (1776), The Competitive Process (1776), The Invisible Hand (1776), Pareto Optimality and Efficiency (1906), The Bergson Social Welfare Function (1938), The Kaldor–Hicks Efficiency Criterion (1939), The Fundamental Theorems of Welfare Economics (1943), Public Goods (1954)

The Point Arena Lighthouse, one of the first lighthouses built in California. Public goods, such as lighthouses, typically will not be provided in efficient amounts through the market. According to the theory of second best, however, having the government build more lighthouses might create another problem: distortions caused by the taxes needed to finance them.

The Tiebout Model

Charles Tiebout (1924–1968)

Paul Samuelson and Richard Musgrave's work on public goods in the early 1950s suggested that there is no way to efficiently provide these goods and services through the market. Just a few years later, Northwestern University's Charles Tiebout, who had been Musgrave's PhD student at the University of Michigan, reached a different conclusion. His 1956 article "A Pure Theory of Local Expenditures" argued that while Samuelson and Musgrave's conclusion may hold for public goods supplied by the federal government, market-like forces play a prominent role in determining the provision of public goods, such as schools, parks, and police and fire protection, at the local level.

You can think of local communities, Tiebout explained, as suppliers of tax-funded public-goods packages, and these packages often differ significantly across communities. Because people are highly mobile, they will "vote with their feet," choosing to live in the community with the package that best satisfies their particular preferences for public goods and willingness to pay for them. Some may be happy to pay a tax premium for an area with better schools, a community with a premier municipal golf course, or one with good public-safety services. Still others may want very low taxes and only minimal services. According to Tiebout, choosing where to live is no different than choosing where to shop. Though people, as Samuelson noted, have an incentive to disguise their preferences for national public goods, such as defense, the process of choosing a place to settle forces them to reveal their preferences for local public goods. People will sort themselves across different communities based on the bundles of services they offer, leading to an efficient provision of public goods at the local level.

Though all but ignored until the late 1960s, the Tiebout model has become an important tool for economists interested in studying local-government public policy. It offers insights into school financing, school choice, competition between municipalities offering big tax breaks to attract businesses, and zoning regulations that affect neighborhood quality and housing prices.

SEE ALSO Pigou's *Wealth and Welfare* (1912), The Fundamental Theorems of Welfare Economics (1943), Public Goods (1954), Externalities and Market Failure (1958)

This vintage postcard shows visitors enjoying a pool and water slide in Midland Beach, Staten Island. Charles Tiebout contended that individuals will "vote with their feet," moving to towns with the public goods—such as recreational facilities—that appeal to them.

The Solow–Swan Growth Model

Robert M. Solow (b. 1924), Trevor Swan (1918–1989)

Until the mid-1950s, the Harrod–Domar model dominated the study of economic growth. Though it offered much more insight into the growth process than earlier theories, it had one major shortcoming: it failed to account for the fact that improved machinery and production methods could increase the output that resulted from a given expenditure on labor or capital. In 1956, Robert Solow and Trevor Swan independently developed an alternative theory that would revolutionize our understanding of the forces that drive economic growth, pinpointing technological progress as the key.

Unlike Harrod and Domar, Solow grounded his work in general equilibrium analysis, bringing it into line with the most recent developments in economic theory. He also allowed the capital–output ratio in the economy to vary, as one would expect it to in the long run. This enabled him to demonstrate that the economy is likely to achieve stable growth in the long run, in contrast to the Harrod–Domar model's suggestion that growth is precarious. Solow also stood conventional thinking on its head by showing that the savings rate has no impact on the long-run rate of economic growth. An increase in savings and investment will boost output, making the country richer, but it won't make the economy grow faster. In a follow-up article, Solow provided evidence that technological progress spurs long-term growth and, in fact, it is the only source of growth in per-capita incomes.

The Solow–Swan model launched growth theory as a distinct field of research and became the basis for the next thirty years of growth economics. It has helped us understand China's rapid economic growth in recent years, as it adopted technology from other countries and experienced a huge boost in productivity as a result. The model also tells us why the continued growth of wealthier countries relies on ongoing innovations that advance worker productivity. Solow, who earned the 1987 Nobel Prize for his work, and other scholars extended the model to analyze issues such as population growth and technological growth, and conducted empirical studies to assess its claims. In doing so, they laid the foundation for "growth accounting," which measures the contributions of labor, capital, and productivity to economic growth.

SEE ALSO Walras's *Elements of Pure Economics* (1874), Keynes's *General Theory* (1936), Hicks's *Value and Capital* (1939), The Harrod–Domar Growth Model (1939), Development Economics (1954), Endogenous Growth Theory (1986)

Automated manipulators used for welding undergo tests before being shipped to a car manufacturer. Robert Solow determined that technological progress, such as developments in automated production, can drive economic growth.

The Economics of Discrimination

Gary S. Becker (1930–2014)

In the second half of the twentieth century, economics expanded its boundaries, applying the assumption that people are rational, utility-maximizing creatures to all aspects of human behavior. The individual sparking this transformation was University of Chicago economist Gary Becker, who used economic reasoning to study subjects as diverse as discrimination, altruistic behavior, marriage and divorce, addiction, and criminal activity. Though these topics seem far removed from the study of markets, inflation, and unemployment, this analysis is a direct extension of Lionel Robbins's definition of economics as the study of choice under conditions of scarcity.

In *The Economics of Discrimination*, a 1957 book based on his PhD thesis, Becker focused his attention on choice in the labor market and suggested that people may have a "taste for discrimination." Just as those with a taste for pizza are willing to pay to indulge it, some people are willing to pay a price to avoid associating with certain groups of people or will only associate with those groups if the price is low enough. For example, a white employer who doesn't want to be associated with African Americans will prefer to hire a less-efficient white employee rather than a more-efficient black employee, accepting lower profits in the process, or hire her only if the wage is low enough to offset his distaste for working with a black employee.

Becker's analysis was largely ignored for a decade following its publication in 1957. In fact, it went so far beyond the boundaries of traditional economic thinking that it was unclear whether it was an acceptable economics PhD thesis, and the University of Chicago Press was initially reluctant to publish the book. But as the Civil Rights movement in the United States gained force, so too did the efforts of economists and sociologists to shed light on the causes and effects of discrimination. This research suggested that anti-discrimination legislation may be helpful, but promoting greater competition in labor markets and enhancing educational opportunities for groups subject to discrimination may be even more effective in the long run.

SEE ALSO Scarcity and Choice (1932), The Chicago School (1946), The Economics of Crime and Punishment (1968), Economics Becomes Applied (1970)

A large crowd gathers in front of the Lincoln Memorial in Washington, D.C., for the March on Washington for Jobs and Freedom, held on August 28, 1963. Gary Becker's research shed new light on the consequences of discrimination and remedies for it, including legislation barring employment discrimination on the basis of race.

The Permanent Income Hypothesis

Milton Friedman (1912–2006)

Keynesian economics assumed that the share of income that people devote to consumption, or the marginal propensity to consume (MPC), is stable over time, but this seemed to conflict with the empirical evidence. Young people, who are financing college and purchasing homes, tend to spend a much larger fraction of their income than people approaching retirement, who are busily saving to build their nest eggs. The evidence also suggested that the propensity to consume varies inversely with income over the business cycle.

Milton Friedman laid out a new theory of consumption that addressed this discrepancy in his 1957 book *A Theory of the Consumption Function*. His "permanent income hypothesis" came to be the widely accepted explanation for consumption and saving patterns over an individual's life. Friedman argued that changes in consumption result from changes in "permanent income," a person's expected long-term average income. People will smooth consumption over their lifetimes. Rather than consuming less early and late in life, when income is lower, they will borrow early to finance large expenditures in low-income years and save in high-income years to fund consumption in old age. The permanent income hypothesis also suggests that people will spread the effects of temporary income changes on consumption over time, saving a significant share of a salary bonus or drawing on savings to maintain some of their normal consumption habits when they're laid off.

What does Friedman's theory mean for Keynesian policies? If individuals spend a smaller share of their incomes during a recession (as consumption smoothing predicts), government stimulus programs will be much less effective than expected. Indeed, Friedman concluded that fiscal policy was unlikely to help stabilize the economy. The evidence for the permanent income hypothesis, though, is mixed. Some studies suggest that temporary income increases, such as tax refunds, generate significant increases in spending, while other findings are more consistent with Friedman's hypothesis. Even so, Friedman's idea that consumers take a long-run view when allocating their income has become the standard depiction of how individuals spend and save.

SEE ALSO Keynes's *General Theory* (1936), The Keynesian Revolution (1947), The Modigliani–Miller Theorem (1958)

Milton Friedman's permanent income hypothesis explains why young people, such as the first-time homeowners pictured here, often borrow against future earnings to finance expensive purchases.

The Rational Voter Model and the Paradox of Voting

Anthony Downs (b. 1930)

Voting procedures have intrigued some of history's leading minds, including philosopher Nicolas de Condorcet and mathematician Charles Dodgson (better known as Lewis Carroll, of *Alice in Wonderland* fame). One early attempt to apply economic theory to the voting process came from Anthony Downs, who, in 1957, published *An Economic Theory of Democracy*, which was derived from his Stanford University PhD thesis.

Downs described the voter as a rational actor. At the polls, the rational individual will vote in her self-interest, rather than some larger civic interest, just as she does with her dollars at the grocery store. When deciding among political candidates or how to vote on a referendum, she will compare her expected utility from each available option and cast her ballot for the outcome that maximizes it.

However, Downs discovered a paradox here: for the self-interested individual, voting is an irrational act. Because it takes time to register to vote and to go to the polls, voting is costly. But as Downs noted, the benefits of voting are minuscule, given the low probability that a single vote will influence an election's outcome. Because there is virtually no expected benefit, it isn't worthwhile to incur any costs to vote. This paradox remains unresolved, though some scholars have suggested that the utility gained from doing one's civic duty or expressing support for a candidate may persuade people to incur these costs.

What Downs's rational voter theory does explain is the behavior of parties and candidates during election cycles. Voters often have little incentive to be fully informed on the candidates and issues for the same reasons that voting is irrational. Given this, it is often rational for candidates and parties to be ambiguous about their positions. This allows them to avoid offending people whose votes they might need and to sway the electorate through sloganeering. The idea that voters and other political agents are rational decision-makers has replaced the traditional view that these agents act in the public interest. The old adage that "people vote their pocketbooks" and the evidence supporting this suggests that Downs's model has considerable practical relevance.

SEE ALSO *Homo Economicus* (1836), *La Scienza della Finanze* (1883), The Benefit Principle of Taxation (1896), The Hotelling Model of Locational Choice (1929), The Median Voter Theorem (1948), Arrow's Impossibility Theorem (1951), The Economics of Information (1961), Public Choice Analysis (1962)

Voters in Barpeta, India hold out their identification cards while waiting in line at a polling station in 2018. Casting a ballot in an election imposes many costs, such as long waits and the effort it can take to first secure a voter ID.

Human Capital Analysis

Jacob Mincer (1922–2006), Theodore W. Schultz (1902–1998), Gary S. Becker (1930–2014)

Adam Smith noted in 1776 that "the acquired and useful abilities of all the inhabitants or members of the society"—what economists now call a person's "human capital"— play an important role in determining society's productive potential. Yet economists paid scant attention to the relationship between education and worker productivity until the mid-twentieth century.

Columbia University graduate student Jacob Mincer provided the first systematic exploration of how human capital affects labor-market outcomes in his 1958 article "Investment in Human Capital and Personal Income Distribution." Mincer examined U.S. Census data on income, education, and job categories to determine the influence of education and training on wages. He found that each additional year of schooling increased a worker's wages by 5 to 10 percent. These findings made it clear that, as Theodore Schultz emphasized in 1961, skills and knowledge are a form of capital.

Schultz and Gary Becker soon developed a theory to explain *why* an individual would choose to invest in education and training, suggesting that individuals weigh the costs of that education (including foregone earnings) against the potentially higher earnings over their working lives. This research explains why training for skills that are easily transferable from one company to another, such as accounting, is provided in the education sector while training for other more firm-specific skills is provided by employers. (The answer: employers don't want to spend money teaching workers, only to lose them to another firm offering slightly higher pay.) Finally, human capital research has suggested policies that could benefit overall economic performance, including increased support for education and the prevention of brain drain in less developed economies.

Human capital analysis, which helped earn Schultz and Becker the Nobel Prize, transformed labor economics, inspiring labor economists to shift their focus from labor unions and collective bargaining to analyzing the underpinnings of the labor market. The relevance of this work is front-and-center in today's news, which is full of stories featuring data on the returns to a college education, the burden of student debt, and families deciding, as human-capital theory suggests, whether the gains from higher education are really worth the costs.

SEE ALSO Development Economics (1954), The Economics of Discrimination (1957), The Economics of Crime and Punishment (1968), Economics Becomes Applied (1970), Endogenous Growth Theory (1986)

Obtaining higher education is one way for individuals to build their human capital.

Externalities and Market Failure

Francis M. Bator (1925–2018)

The first fundamental theorem of welfare economics tells us that equilibrium in a competitive market is efficient; but what continued to vex economists were scenarios where efficiency wasn't attainable. Why did complications such as external economies and diseconomies lead to less than optimal outcomes in the marketplace? Paul Samuelson made important headway on this question in his analysis of public goods, but it was another MIT economist, Francis Bator, who provided a more comprehensive explanation in his 1958 article "The Anatomy of Market Failure."

For Bator, market failures occur when a market can't "sustain 'desirable' activities or to estop 'undesirable' activities," where desirability corresponds to an activity's effect on social welfare. To achieve efficiency, the prices of all activities that affect social welfare must reflect their true benefits and costs to society. The problem is that certain economic interactions aren't naturally part of the price system, and thus market valuations don't take them into account. Bator called these interactions "externalities" because their benefits and costs are external to the process by which market prices are determined. Pollution is a classic example. Factory owners may pay little or no attention to the human and environmental costs associated with their emissions because there is no established price for using clean air or water.

Bator explained that externalities, whether negative ones like pollution, or positive ones such as scientific discoveries, emerge from the absence of property rights over certain resources. Without property rights, the air can be used for free, and the benefits of a new invention, which will be quickly copied by others, can't be fully captured by the inventor. As a result, there will be too much pollution and too little effort devoted to scientific discovery. There are instances where property rights can be assigned to ward off these problems, such as the use of patents to give an inventor ownership of her discovery. But in many situations, assigning rights is problematic. For example, it is difficult to create private rights over air, lakes, and rivers. This has led economists to recommend tax, subsidy, or regulatory solutions to efficiently resolve these issues.

SEE ALSO Pigou's *Wealth and Welfare* (1912), External Economies and Diseconomies (1912), The Fundamental Theorems of Welfare Economics (1943), Public Goods (1954), The Common Pool Problem (1954), The Tiebout Model (1956), The Coase Theorem (1960), Emissions Trading (1966)

Waste from a paper mill pollutes the Nashua River in Massachusetts, an example of a negative externality.

Cost–Benefit Analysis

Roland N. McKean (1917–1993), Otto Eckstein (1927–1984), John V. Krutilla (1922–2003)

Cost–benefit analysis dates back to the nineteenth century with Jules Dupuit and the French engineering tradition, but it wasn't commonly used as a policy tool until more than a century later. The U.S. Flood Control Act of 1936, which established that the government should participate in flood-control efforts "if the benefits to whomsoever they accrue are in excess of the estimated costs," facilitated its modern emergence. In the late 1950s, economists began to develop advanced methods to evaluate these costs and benefits when examining water-resource development and conservation projects.

Economists Otto Eckstein (Harvard), John V. Krutilla (Resources for the Future), and Roland McKean (RAND) spearheaded this effort in two 1958 books that integrated the practical concerns of policymakers with welfare economics to study water-resource issues. They emphasized the importance of measuring opportunity costs, discounting future benefits and costs, predicting a project's economic impact, and considering its effects on income distribution. By the mid-1970s, the use of cost–benefit analysis to evaluate policies, projects, and regulations had spread around the globe and to international economic development agencies such as the World Bank.

Cost–benefit analysis remains controversial in certain quarters, because some balk at the idea of measuring certain benefits and costs in monetary terms. Estimated values of a human life, which are used regularly to assess policies that impact the risk of death, such as workplace safety regulations, are particularly contentious. The U.S. government currently uses a value of approximately 9 million dollars based on an extrapolation of the average person's willingness to take small additional risks of death in turn for greater financial rewards, such as the higher wage that comes with a more dangerous occupation. To measure the value of environmental attributes, economists use "hedonic prices," which use market measures to value non-market goods. For example, the value of a beautiful mountain view can be found by examining the difference between property values with and without the view. Though these methods don't capture *all* benefits and costs, they can estimate the value of items whose worth to individuals and society is difficult to assess.

SEE ALSO The French Engineering Tradition (1830), Consumer Surplus (1844), Opportunity Cost (1889), Pigou's *Wealth and Welfare* (1912), The Multiplier (1931), Keynes's *General Theory* (1936), The Kaldor–Hicks Efficiency Criterion (1939), RAND and the Cold War (1948), Resources for the Future and Environmental Economics (1952)

The Kinzua Dam in Pennsylvania was one of many projects commissioned as part of the U.S. Flood Control Act of 1936. The dam created a reservoir that was originally designed to control flooding from the Allegheny River but also serves as a recreational area and a generator of hydroelectric power.

The Modigliani–Miller Theorem

Franco Modigliani (1918–2003), Merton H. Miller (1923–2000)

Some of the most important findings in economics are "irrelevance" results, which show that changes in important variables, or the choice made among multiple options, has no effect on an ultimate outcome. One of the most central of these results is the Modigliani–Miller theorem, developed in a 1958 article, "The Cost of Capital, Corporation Finance, and the Theory of Investment," by future Nobel Prize recipients Franco Modigliani and Merton Miller. This theorem moved finance away from the fuzzy "rule-of-thumb" thinking in vogue at the time toward more rigorous analysis.

The Modigliani–Miller theorem, as popularly understood in the field of finance, says that a firm's financial structure and decisions don't affect its value. It's irrelevant whether a company finances its operations through borrowing or by issuing additional shares of its stock, even if it chooses the more expensive option. This upended the traditional view that debt financing is superior to equity financing because of its lower cost and that there is an optimal financing structure unique to each firm's situation. But this isn't what the theorem actually demonstrates: rather, it shows *the conditions under which* these financial decisions don't affect the firm's value. They are very restrictive: the transaction costs for buying and selling financial instruments must be zero; the tax system treats all options identically; and both firms and investors have the same access to credit markets and the same information. In other words, markets must work perfectly.

It's tempting to dismiss the Modigliani–Miller theorem as hopelessly unrealistic, but it has become a cornerstone of corporate finance for two reasons: First, it shows that it is a company's business strategy, not its financing decisions, that determines its value. Second, it highlights how factors such as tax codes (including the deductibility of interest on debt), bankruptcy costs, and information asymmetries may affect the optimal financing decision at any given time by encouraging firms to favor one type of financing over another. Indeed, the research into why the Modigliani–Miller theorem often fails to hold in the real world has spawned a much more scientific approach to corporations' financing decisions, highlighting the major relevance of irrelevance results.

SEE ALSO *The Modern Corporation and Private Property* (1932), The Coase Theorem (1960), The Capital Asset Pricing Model (1962), The Efficient Markets Hypothesis (1965), Agency Theory (1973), The Black–Scholes Model (1973)

A stock certificate for the Greyhound Corporation, 1936. The Modigliani–Miller theorem states that a firm's decision to finance its operations by issuing additional shares of stock rather than by issuing bonds will not impact its value.

V3966

NUMBER

NU0000

SHARES

INCORPORATED UNDER THE LAWS

OF THE STATE OF DELAWARE

THE GREYHOUND CORPORATION

THIS CERTIFICATE IS TRANSFERABLE IN THE CITY OF NEW YORK OR IN CHICAGO

This Certifies that

is the owner of

shares of Common Stock of The Greyhound Corporation, fully paid and non-assessable, without par value and transferable in person or by duly authorized attorney, upon surrender of this certificate properly endorsed. The designations, preferences and rights of the various classes of stock or series thereof and the qualifications, limitations and restrictions of such rights are set forth in full in the Certificate of Incorporation, as amended, of said corporation (a copy of which is on file with the transfer agent) the pertinent paragraphs of which are set forth in full on the back hereof. This certificate is not valid unless countersigned by the transfer agent and registered by the registrar.

Witness the seal of the corporation and the facsimile signatures of its duly authorized officers.

Dated

SPECIMEN

SPECIMEN

R. E. Maxwell
SECRETARY

C. R. Wickman
PRESIDENT

REGISTERED:
CITY BANK FARMERS TRUST COMPANY,
(NEW YORK)
REGISTRAR

AUTHORIZED OFFICER

COUNTERSIGNED
BANKERS TRUST COMPANY,
(NEW YORK)
TRANSFER AGENT

ASSISTANT SECRETARY

COLUMBIAN BANK NOTE COMPANY

The Phillips Curve

A. W. Phillips (1914–1975)

Inflation and unemployment are two of the most vexing problems of macroeconomic policy. Bill Phillips, a New Zealand–born economist, provided a large step forward in our understanding of their relationship with his 1958 study of wages and unemployment in Great Britain. Drawing on nearly a century of data, Phillips discovered that unemployment and wage inflation tend to move inversely—that high inflation rates are associated with low unemployment rates, and vice-versa. The diagram illustrating this inverse relationship became known as the Phillips curve.

Though the original Phillips curve was strictly an empirical observation, Canadian economist Richard Lipsey provided a theoretical explanation for this relationship using demand-and-supply analysis in 1960. Paul Samuelson and Robert Solow found a similar relationship using U.S. data during that same year. Unlike Phillips, who focused on changes in wages, they examined data on the relationship between unemployment and price inflation and observed an inverse relationship between these two factors as well. Almost immediately, the Phillips curve became associated with the relationship that unemployment had with changes in good prices, rather than wages.

Many economists used the Phillips curve as evidence of a trade-off between unemployment and inflation, one that presents policymakers with a menu of inflation–unemployment combinations from which to choose. It is possible to have high inflation and low unemployment, low inflation and high unemployment, or moderate amounts of each—but not low amounts of both. Economists made empirical studies that would allow them to pin down this trade-off more precisely. These findings allowed economists, at last, to employ large-scale Keynesian macroeconometric models to forecast price level changes and provided government officials with the hope that they could use fiscal and monetary policy to maintain specific unemployment and inflation targets. However, when the Arab oil embargo and a severe recession in the early 1970s brought stagflation (high rates of both inflation and unemployment), they started rethinking the trade-off between unemployment and inflation and the effectiveness of the policies it inspired.

SEE ALSO Unemployment (1896), Keynes's *General Theory* (1936), Large-Scale Macroeconometric Models (1955), The Natural Rate of Unemployment (1967), The New Classical Macroeconomics (1972), OPEC and the Arab Oil Embargo (1973), The Policy Ineffectiveness Proposition (1975)

A chalkboard drawing of the Phillips curve, which shows an inverse relationship between unemployment and inflation rates.

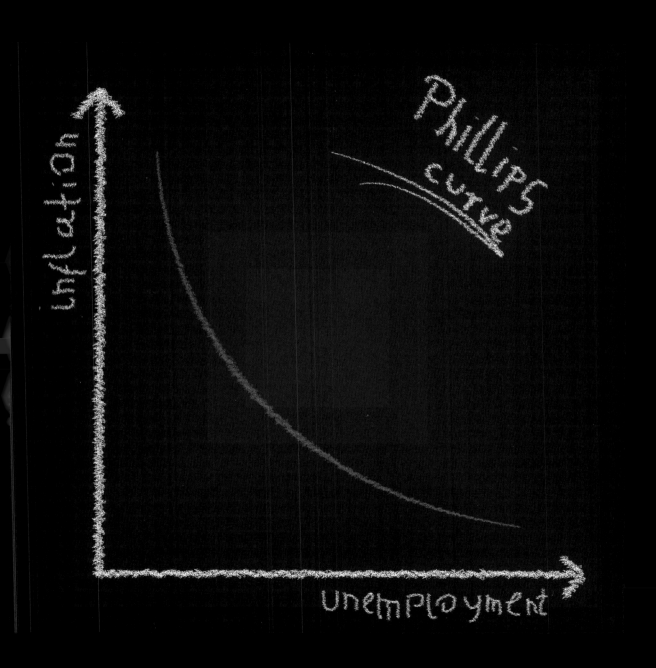

Galbraith's *The Affluent Society*

John Kenneth Galbraith (1908–2006)

In 1958, Harvard economist John Kenneth Galbraith published *The Affluent Society*, a book that challenged the link between affluence and well-being. Galbraith, in the tradition of John Ruskin and J. A. Hobson, argued that though the American economy was affluent in terms of its gross national product, its wealth didn't correspond with the country's provision of public services, infrastructure, and a social safety net.

Galbraith blamed consumer culture. Advertising conditioned people to want better consumer goods: "more elegant automobiles, more exotic food, more erotic clothing, more elaborate entertainment—indeed, the entire modern range of sensuous, edifying and lethal desires." By devoting society's resources to satisfying these demands, consumers sacrificed important forms of public spending on education, infrastructure, health care, environmental protection, and support for culture and the arts. It was only by reorienting societal attitudes and using the government's power to tax consumption, Galbraith argued, that America could slow this consumerist tide, alleviate poverty, and provide more socially beneficial goods and services.

Galbraith also believed that existing economic theories, being derived from the work of eighteenth- and nineteenth-century classical economists, failed to capture the realities of modern society. They came from an age when widespread poverty was a fact of life and ways to improve the condition of the impoverished masses were a major concern. Now that the United States enjoyed a higher standard of living and production had shifted beyond creating basic necessities, such theories no longer had much relevance. He called for a new way of organizing the economy, one that abandoned the sanctity of markets, recognized the important role of labor unions in offsetting the influence of big business, and relied on regulation and public ownership of businesses based on society's needs.

Galbraith's engaging writing style won him a broad audience, including President John F. Kennedy, for whom he had served as economics tutor at Harvard in the 1930s. Though *The Affluent Society* did little to stymie consumerism, his views on the merits of business regulation appealed to Democratic policymakers, and his work on the problems facing developing countries extended his influence around the globe.

SEE ALSO Smith's *Wealth of Nations* (1776), Classical Political Economy (c. 1790), The Dismal Science (1849), Antitrust Laws (1890), The Oxford Approach to Welfare (1914), Institutional Economics (1919), *The Theory of Monopolistic Competition* (1933)

An American family watches television in this photo from the late 1950s. Postwar prosperity allowed many households in the United States to enjoy a higher standard of living.

Debreu's *The Theory of Value*

Gérard Debreu (1921–2004)

Though Kenneth Arrow and Gérard Debreu had proved the existence of equilibrium in a competitive economy in 1954, Debreu continued to delve deeper into this subject in the following years. His work culminated with his publication of *The Theory of Value* in 1959. Debreu was a French mathematician educated in the influential Bourbakist tradition, which was dedicated to making mathematics more abstract and rigorous. As he was finishing his studies in the mid-1940s, he came across the work of French economist and 1988 Nobel Laureate Maurice Allais. It introduced him to Walrasian general equilibrium analysis and sparked his interest in economics.

The Theory of Value grew out of nearly a decade's work at the Cowles Commission, where Debreu worked as a research associate. The book offered, in the words of economist Lawrence Blume, "a statement of method that has profoundly changed the way economics is practised." Debreu applied the axiomatic approach of Bourbakist mathematics full on to economics, describing the theory of general equilibrium using a set of axioms, or basic propositions, that could be used to derive theorems. Debreu also developed an existence proof that was much more general than those of Arrow–Debreu and Lionel McKenzie, isolating the assumptions necessary for the analysis of general equilibrium and demonstrating that the results applied to a much wider variety of circumstances than had previous proofs.

Debreu relied heavily on abstract mathematical techniques, such as set theory and topology, instead of calculus, which he considered less precise. Economists, including Arrow, had viewed general equilibrium analysis as formulated by Léon Walras, John Hicks, and Paul Samuelson as an abstract representation of reality that could say useful things about the world. Debreu rejected such an approach, pushing it away from any pretension to realism and into the realm of pure mathematics. Though very few economists circa 1960 could understand and work with the mathematical tools that Debreu employed in his research, these tools gave economics "greater logical solidity," accelerated the development of modern economic theory, and eventually became indispensable for anyone wishing to do advanced work in the field.

SEE ALSO The Invention of Calculus (c. 1665), Walras's *Elements of Pure Economics* (1874), The Cowles Commission (1932), Proving the Existence of a General Equilibrium (1954)

Gérard Debreu, shown here in this 1977 photo, applied complex and abstract mathematical tools to general equilibrium analysis.

The Coase Theorem

Ronald H. Coase (1910–2013)

British economist and 1991 Nobel Laureate Ronald Coase formulated one of the most famous theorems in economics in his classic article "The Problem of Social Cost" (1960). The Coase Theorem tells us that, in a world without transaction costs, such as those associated with gathering information and negotiating contracts, it is possible for a market with externalities to achieve efficiency without governmental intervention.

Coase noted in an earlier article on the Federal Communications Commission that radio stations, left to their own devices, will congregate on the same parts of the broadcast spectrum, where the signal is strongest. This leads to signal interference. The traditional solution to this problem was to have the government allocate space on the frequency spectrum to separate broadcasters. Coase argued that, absent transaction costs, this regulation was not only unnecessary but also unlikely to allocate the spectrum efficiently, putting each frequency in the hands of the station that valued it most. If the government simply gave each station property rights over a frequency and allowed these frequencies to be exchanged like other goods, Coase said, the interference and inefficiency problems would both be resolved, as each frequency would end up in the hands of those who valued it most highly, regardless of how the frequencies were initially assigned.

Coase's insight partly inspired the recent decisions to auction off slices of the frequency spectrum and to establish emissions-trading schemes to combat pollution. The Coase theorem also has important implications for law: it tells us that judges' decisions are irrelevant, for legal rights will ultimately end up in the hands of those who are willing to pay the most for them.

The existence of transaction costs, which as Coase noted are often significant, limits the direct application of the Coase theorem to the real world. But as Coase emphasized, government regulation is also costly, and policymakers need to pay close attention to the benefits and costs of their remedies. Nonetheless, some have used the Coase theorem as a justification for minimizing government interference in the economy beyond defining property rights.

SEE ALSO External Economies and Diseconomies (1912), Coase's "Nature of the Firm" (1937), The Chicago School (1946), The Common Pool Problem (1954), Externalities and Market Failure (1958), The Modigliani–Miller Theorem (1958), Emissions Trading (1966), The Economic Analysis of Law (1973)

Ronald Coase's studies on the allocation of radio frequencies led him to observe that it is possible for markets with externalities to achieve efficiency without government intervention.

Cliometrics: The New Economic History

Douglass C. North (1920–2015), Robert W. Fogel (1926–2013)

1961

Economic history, the analysis of the economic conditions and events of the past, emerged as a distinct field of study in the late 1800s thanks to the German Historical School. While anyone who has taken a history course would recognize their approach to the subject, the birth of cliometrics transformed how economists analyzed economic history. Named after Clio, the Ancient Greek muse of history, cliometrics describes the application of economic theory and econometric methods to study historical events.

American economists and 1993 Nobel Laureates Douglass North and Robert Fogel jump-started the development of cliometrics with their studies of American agriculture and transportation. Their work illustrated the novel insights that economic methods could provide. North's 1961 book, *The Economic Growth of the United States, 1790–1860*, amassed empirical evidence showing that regional specialization in production, particularly in the cotton-plantation system, helped spur economic growth. Fogel's 1962 article, "A Quantitative Approach to the Study of Railroads in American Economic Growth," showed that railroads—typically thought of as an important technological advance—contributed much less to economic growth in the late nineteenth century than traditional, non-quantitative methods of economic history had suggested; an old-style system of canals and barges would have worked nearly as well. Cliometricians have since used economic models and empirical techniques to explain events including the rise and decline of industries, the evolution of legal rules affecting various sectors of the economy, and even the operations of the Catholic Church during the medieval period.

This work hasn't been without controversy. Fogel's book *Time on the Cross*, written with Stanley Engerman, generated intense criticism for suggesting that slavery in the United States was both profitable and efficient and may even have provided some economic benefits to African-Americans. Economists have also been accused of ignoring traditional historical methods and relying too much on the aspects of past events that can be captured within their models and quantitative techniques. Nonetheless, these "new" methods have dominated the study of economic history and have led to a re-evaluation of traditional explanations for events throughout human history.

SEE ALSO The German Historical School (1843), World War II (1939), The New Institutional Economics (1997)

This painting by German artist Gerhard von Kügelgen shows Clio, the Greek muse of history and the inspiration for the term cliometrics.

The Economics of Information

George J. Stigler (1911–1991)

The rational agent relies on information—about prices, the quality of goods, and alternative versions of a product—to make decisions about what to consume or produce. But people in everyday life often don't have all the information relevant to their decision-making, even when there are entire industries, such as advertising, to provide details about products and prices. If information is valuable, and more information results in better choices, why don't agents gather everything they need to know to help them make decisions?

University of Chicago economist and 1982 Nobel Laureate George Stigler provided the initial answer to this question in his 1961 article, "The Economics of Information." He framed information as a commodity. Like any other good, information is costly, particularly when one considers the time and effort needed to search for it. The rational consumer, Stigler argued, will search for additional information only if the expected benefits of additional searching, such as the savings from discovering a lower price or information about a good's quality, outweigh the expected costs of the search effort. Advertising serves as one vehicle for reducing such costs; it lets consumers know who is selling a good and, in many cases, how much they're charging. Traditionally, it has been seen as a socially wasteful expenditure whose sole purpose is to lure consumers and may merit governmental restriction. Here, advertising facilitates efficiency. So too does the Internet, which provides a very important source of low-cost (though not always accurate) information.

Using this framework, Stigler developed the idea of "rational ignorance." As he put it, "Ignorance is like subzero weather: by a sufficient expenditure its effects upon people can be kept within tolerable or even comfortable bounds, but it would be wholly uneconomic entirely to eliminate all its effects." There are many times in a person's life when the search for additional information isn't worth the effort beyond a specific point. For example, people typically don't learn about the ingredients of everything in their shopping cart. Instead, they often rely on brands and stores they can trust to provide them with the combination of price and quality that they desire.

SEE ALSO *The Theory of Monopolistic Competition* (1933), The Rational Voter Model and the Paradox of Voting (1957), The Market for "Lemons" (1970), Regulatory Capture (1971), Signaling (1973), Screening—or Pooling and Separating Equilibria (1976)

An advertisement from 1961 shows the wide range of home appliances that shoppers could purchase from Sears. Advertisements such as this can lower the cost of acquiring information.

In rear, Glen Nordstrom (left) and Charles Peters, of the Sears Service Center in Phoenix, are typical of Sears' 8,500 servicemen.

How |Sears| restores your faith in <u>service</u> on home appliances

Getting service on appliances is one of the consumer's biggest headaches today. Read how Sears, Roebuck and Co. gives <u>efficient</u> service on the Sears appliances you buy.

A‍LL the modern work-savers make life a dream. *Just as long as they stay on the job.*

But maybe you've sometimes lost faith in this brave new mechanical world. When your TV set went on the blink again, just after it was fixed. Or your freezer failed, and you couldn't get service for days. Or you needed spare parts for the washer, and found them out of stock.

Such frustrating things do happen. Whether your home appliances are a torture or a blessing depends on *service.*

That's why Sears has taken steps to give you the kind of complete, dependable service you have every right to expect. Here are the three ways Sears does it.

First, through merciless testing in the famous Sears laboratory. Thoroughly *proved* appliances are less likely to break down in the first place.

Second, by always keeping replacement parts on hand for the Sears appliances or mechanical items you buy—during their reasonable life expectancy.

Third, by providing *1,700 Sears service units* across the country. Prompt and efficient service by a Sears repair specialist is available, at reasonable cost, in every town that has a Sears retail store or catalog sales office.

All this costs Sears a packet of money, but it pays dividends—by making people like you loyal customers.

The Theory of Auctions

William Vickrey (1914–1996)

The use of auctions to sell goods and services goes back to the ancient world, where the Greek historian Herodotus describes auctions used to pair women with husbands. Since auctions are about establishing prices to allocate resources, they are a natural subject of study for economists. Yet economists only began examining them seriously in the 1960s. Columbia University economist William Vickrey provided a launching point with his 1961 article, "Counterspeculation, Auctions, and Competitive Sealed Tenders."

At first glance, auctions seem ideal for allocating goods efficiently since they are sold to those who value them the most. But efficiency also requires that goods be priced according to their social-opportunity cost—their value to society in their best alternative use. The traditional English auction may not accomplish this, due to asymmetric information: sellers don't know a bidder's true valuation of the item being auctioned. Vickrey showed that the sealed-bid or "Vickrey" auction can circumvent this issue.

In a Vickrey auction, used by stamp collectors since the late 1800s, bidders submit sealed bids for an item. The winner is the individual submitting the highest bid, but she pays the price submitted by the second-highest bidder. Vickrey demonstrated that each bidder will offer an amount exactly equal to their maximum willingness to pay. Overbidding may cause the winner to pay more than the good was worth to her, while underbidding runs the risk of losing to someone who values the good less. Since the winner actually pays an item's social-opportunity cost, which is the next-highest bidder's valuation, the Vickrey auction allocates goods efficiently.

The English auction, used by barking auctioneers and eBay, remains the most common way to auction goods, and sealed-bid auctions, which governments use to hand out contracts, seldom rely on the second-price method despite its benefits. Vickrey auctions also come with caveats. They incentivize people to game the system, whether by submitting bids using multiple identities, or colluding with other players to keep bids low. Even so, Vickrey revealed how auctions can be designed to accomplish a particular goal, which helped earn him a share of the 1999 Nobel Prize.

SEE ALSO Game Theory Enters Economics (1944), Non-Cooperative Games and Nash Equilibrium (1950), Mechanism Design (1972), The Experimental Turn (1986)

A London-based auction house sells off artwork (1961) using an English auction, where the winner is the bidder who offers the highest price.

The Rational Expectations Hypothesis

John F. Muth (1930–2005)

Producers and sellers operate in an environment that is constantly changing and filled with uncertainty. Their expectations about the future inform how they determine output levels and prices, how many workers they should hire, and whether they should invest in new plants and equipment. Expectations likewise inform how consumer purchasing and saving habits respond to changing circumstances. In this sense, economic outcomes result in part from the expectations of economic agents, and, given this, economists need to account for these expectations when they construct forecasts and model economic phenomena.

It was not until the twentieth century that economists such as John Maynard Keynes stressed that expectations are important determinants of macroeconomic performance. Most economists in the early postwar era assumed that agents form their expectations adaptively, meaning that they based their expectations of the future on their experiences in the recent past. But in 1961, American economist John F. Muth suggested that these existing theories fell short on two fronts. First, if expectations are informed predictions, they should be based on more than observations about the past. Second, these theories were inconsistent with how economists model the world.

If agents are rational, as economic models assume, then expectations should be formed rationally, based on *all* available information. Muth believed that the agents within an economic model should behave as if they know the model itself and form expectations consistent with the predictions of the model. Thus, the actual economic outcomes that result won't differ systematically from what agents expect them to be. Though some forecasts may prove incorrect, those errors are purely random and won't occur persistently.

Muth's rational-expectations hypothesis became part of a larger effort to put macroeconomic analysis on firmer microeconomic foundations, grounding aggregate economic behavior in the maximizing behavior of rational individuals. It was a key ingredient in both the new classical and new Keynesian approaches that transformed macroeconomic thinking in the 1970s and 1980s. The rational-expectations hypothesis also reshaped how economists approached macroeconomic policymaking, suggesting that many economic policies will be ineffective because people will anticipate their effects and adjust their behavior accordingly.

SEE ALSO Keynes's *General Theory* (1936), The Natural Rate of Unemployment (1967), The New Classical Macroeconomics (1972), The Policy Ineffectiveness Proposition (1975), The Lucas Critique (1976), The New Keynesian Economics (1977), Real Business Cycle Models (1982)

A newspaper reader reads about updates about the market as he sits outside the New York Stock Exchange building. John Muth argued that individuals use all available information to make decisions rather than relying solely on observations about the recent past, as macroeconomists had traditionally assumed.

The Capital Asset Pricing Model

John Lintner (1916–1983), Jack L. Treynor (1930–2016), William F. Sharpe (b. 1934)

Investors hope to minimize the overall level of risk of their portfolios, but they also recognize that doing so might lead to lower returns. How should investors address this trade-off between risk and return when they balance their portfolios? Prior to the 1960s, there was no answer to this question. The capital asset pricing model (CAPM), developed by Jack Treynor in a 1962 paper and later refined by William Sharpe and John Lintner, changed all that.

The CAPM begins by recognizing that there are two different types of risk: Systematic risk is endemic to the stock market; it results from swings in the market caused by changes in interest rates, the possibility of recession, or dramatic political events that alter consumer confidence or business prospects. Specific risk is associated with a particular company's stock and doesn't depend on such larger movements. It can come from questions about a company's leadership or the possibility that a new product will flop. While a diversified portfolio only protects against specific risk, the CAPM offers a way to measure systematic risk and the return that a portfolio would need to produce to make it a worthwhile investment.

The CAPM builds on the idea that the expected return on a stock will be equal to a risk-free return, such as that on a government bond, plus a premium that accounts for the stock's risk. The key element of the CAPM is a stock's volatility compared to the market average. The riskier a stock is, the larger should be its return. Using data on a stock's volatility, average market returns, and the risk-free rate of return, an investor can determine whether that stock's price is consistent with its expected return and thus whether the stock is overpriced or priced at a bargain level.

The CAPM revolutionized finance through its ability to account for an investment's risk, and it spawned many innovations, including the Black–Scholes model of options pricing. Though the empirical evidence for its accuracy is mixed, it is easy to compute, making it a go-to tool for mutual fund managers and financial advisers.

SEE ALSO The Theory of Portfolio Selection (1952), The Efficient Markets Hypothesis (1965), The Black–Scholes Model (1973)

The CAPM gives investors a method to measure systematic risk of their portfolio by examining the volatility and the average return of their stock holdings.

Public Choice Analysis

James M. Buchanan (1919–2013), Gordon Tullock (1922–2014)

Economics underwent a major transformation when economists extended its domain into topics generally associated with other social sciences, such as law and sociology. The pioneering work in public-choice analysis came from Duncan Black and William Riker in the 1940s and 1950s, but American economists James Buchanan and Gordon Tullock played the central roles with their 1962 book, *The Calculus of Consent*, and their efforts to establish a scholarly community of like-minded researchers and to train graduate students in public-choice analysis.

Traditional political analysis at the time posited that political agents, from voters to legislators and government bureaucrats, act in the public interest. Buchanan and Tullock argued that people are primarily motivated by self-interest, just as they are in the marketplace. Individuals vote for the candidate who will prioritize their concerns. Legislators support bills that will give them the best chances of reelection. Bureaucrats aim to maximize their budgets and thus spheres of influence. These self-interested actions can lead to policies that create inefficiency in the market and run contrary to the public interest.

Buchanan and Tullock believed that economists had for decades taken the wrong approach to analyzing policy. Elegant and widely accepted theories of regulation, taxation, and macroeconomic stabilization policy showed how government intervention could correct market imperfections by assuming that government agents could effectively carry out the prescribed policies. In contrast, public-choice theory suggests that "government failure," the inability of government to efficiently carry out the tasks entrusted to it, is every bit as real as market failure. Though originally seen as something of a libertarian fringe movement, public-choice analysis has led economists of all stripes to adopt a more nuanced view of government action. It has encouraged them to explore methods for minimizing the conflict between public interest and self-interest, whether through alternative voting procedures, cost–benefit tests on new regulations, or the simple recognition that government intervention may be worse than the original market inefficiency.

SEE ALSO Laissez-Faire (1695), *La Scienza della Finanze* (1883), The Benefit Principle of Taxation (1896), Scarcity and Choice (1932), The Median Voter Theorem (1948), Public Goods (1954), The Tiebout Model (1956), The Rational Voter Model and the Paradox of Voting (1957), Externalities and Market Failure (1958), The Free-Rider Problem (1965), Rent Seeking (1967), Supply-Side Economics (1974)

Clerks discuss the stacks of bills that have been introduced to the U.S. Congress during its 71st session, 1929. Public choice analysis posits that legislators act in their self-interest rather than in the public interest, whether they are drafting bills or finalizing a government budget.

A Monetary History of the United States

Milton Friedman (1912–2006), Anna J. Schwartz (1915–2012)

By the early 1960s, Keynesian economics had a strong hold on leading U.S. economists. Within the small tribe of critics, though, one figure stood out. In a 1956 article, Milton Friedman attempted to rehabilitate the status of the quantity theory of money, which attributed changes in the price level to variations in the money supply. For Friedman, this theory suggested that monetary policy, rather than the government spending and taxation adjustments of Keynesian fiscal policy, could manage the economy most effectively. This view became known as "monetarism." Recognizing that theory alone wouldn't persuade most economists, he searched for data to support his claims. Friedman turned to Anna Schwartz, whose long affiliation with the NBER had made her a leading authority on monetary data and history. Together they wrote A *Monetary History of the United States, 1876–1960* (1963).

A *Monetary History* is a monumental work, some seventeen years in the making, and one of the most important economics books of the last century. In its pages, Friedman and Schwartz observed that, since the Civil War, the money supply in the United States had fluctuated significantly prior to the peaks and troughs of the country's economy, suggesting that these fluctuations played a major role in its business cycles. Friedman and Schwartz's most famous claim concerned the Great Depression. Unlike Keynesians, who saw underinvestment and the lack of confidence in banks as its main causes, Friedman and Schwartz argued that by tightening the money supply, the Fed had failed to provide the banking system with the money needed to prevent widespread bank failures. An expansionary policy that pumped money into the banking system would have reduced consumer panic and stemmed bank runs. Its contractionary monetary policy had instead worsened the Depression's severity and duration.

This conclusion remains controversial. Many economists believe that bank failures resulted from the economic contraction, and that Friedman and Schwartz's explanation ignores larger global forces in play at the time. However, the Fed may have taken note of their lessons during the Great Recession, pursuing quantitative easing, which entailed massive increases in the money supply to prop up the failing financial system.

SEE ALSO The Quantity Theory of Money (1568), The Velocity of Money (1668), The Federal Reserve System (1913), The National Bureau of Economic Research (1920), The Great Depression (1929), Keynes's *General Theory* (1936), The Great Recession (2007), Cryptocurrency (2009)

A crowd of customers gathers at the American Union Bank in New York City to withdraw their deposits during one of many bank runs that occurred in 1932.

The Free-Rider Problem

Mancur Olson, Jr. (1932–1998)

There is a fireworks display for the Fourth of July, organized and funded by our local government, happening near my house as I type this essay. Given the popularity of events like these, why doesn't a private company host them and charge admission? The answer lies in what economists call the free-rider problem. As Mancur Olson observed in his 1965 book, *The Logic of Collective Action*, free riding makes it difficult for both the market and government to operate efficiently.

There are two characteristics that differentiate a public good like fireworks from, say, bow ties. First, there is no rivalry in the consumption, meaning that one person's enjoyment of them doesn't affect another's ability to benefit from them. If I'm wearing one of my bow ties, you can't wear it simultaneously. Consumption of a public good is also non-excludable. Once the fireworks show exists, no one can be excluded from its benefits, even if you didn't pay any taxes to support it. With a good like the bow tie, you have to purchase it from the seller to enjoy it. Because of these two features, individuals don't have any incentive to help finance public goods. If the provision of these goods were left to the market, they would be underproduced and perhaps not provided at all.

Olson pointed out that the magnitude of the free-rider problem grows as the size of the group that would benefit from the good increases. In the political sphere, this explains why special-interest lobbying groups, such as labor unions, can exert political pressure more effectively than larger, more diffuse groups. People often blame "big money" lobbying for the failure to pass broadly popular gun-control legislation or to restructure corporate tax breaks, but Olson's analysis tells us that this blame is misplaced. The free-rider problem makes organizing and fundraising difficult for larger groups, allowing the narrower, more concentrated interests to carry the day. This casts doubt on the government's ability to respond efficiently to larger social needs, suggesting that the tyranny of the minority may be more problematic than the tyranny of the majority.

SEE ALSO The Benefit Principle of Taxation (1896), Public Goods (1954), Public Choice Analysis (1962), Mechanism Design (1972), The Experimental Turn (1986)

Both national defense and ticker-tape parades are examples of public goods that would be underprovided if their provision were left to the market. Once a public good is provided, no one can be excluded from its benefits, leaving individuals with little incentive to voluntarily contribute to its financing.

The Efficient Markets Hypothesis

Paul A. Samuelson (1915–2009), Eugene F. Fama (b. 1939)

The efficient markets hypothesis (EMH), developed independently by American economists Eugene Fama and Paul Samuelson in 1965, revolutionized the field of finance. Its message can be summed up very simply: market prices reflect all available information. Rational agents acting in competitive markets instantaneously process and act on all available information related to an investment's value. If positive information about a company becomes available, investors will instantly purchase its stock, triggering an immediate price increase that reflects the additional value contained in this information. Because of this, stocks are always traded at their true value, making it impossible to gain an above-average return from trades based on that information. In fact, some proponents of the EMH see insider trading as a way to move information into the market more quickly, rather than as an unfair advantage.

By depicting asset price changes as random and unpredictable, the EMH tells us that a sophisticated financial analyst can do no better in the market than a blindfolded monkey throwing darts at a page of stock listings. It is pointless to search for stocks that are undervalued, and today's stock prices have no bearing on tomorrow's. In short, there is no "beating the market"; the only way to earn higher-than-average returns is to make riskier investments. Because the prices of assets, whether tulips in the 1600s or houses in the early 2000s, always accurately reflect their value, the EMH also suggests that speculative bubbles don't exist.

The EMH became the basis for key developments in economics and finance, including the Black–Scholes model of options pricing and the creation of index funds (mutual funds that track a major stock index, such as the S&P 500 or the Dow Jones Industrial Average). But the EMH is not without its critics. The empirical evidence for its validity is decidedly mixed. Behavioral economics research has called the rationality of investors into question, especially given their herd mentality and the outsized confidence of some in their own investing capabilities. Some blame the EMH for the Great Recession by leading investors to believe that tremendously overvalued financial instruments reflected their true value.

SEE ALSO Tulipmania (1636), John Law and Paper Money (1705), The Theory of Portfolio Selection (1952), The Capital Asset Pricing Model (1962), The Black–Scholes Model (1973), The Great Recession (2007)

A woman updates the stock prices on a board used by American stockbrokers at their London-based office. According to the EMH, these new prices reflect all available information about the market at this given moment.

Emissions Trading

John H. Dales (1920–2007), Thomas D. Crocker (b. 1936)

Emissions-trading programs, now commonly called "cap and trade" policies, have been one of the greatest successes of environmental economics. From an economic perspective, pollution creates market inefficiencies because prices don't capture the costs of the harm caused by pollution. Economists have often recommended pollution taxes as a solution to that problem. In 1966, American economist Thomas Crocker suggested that the market could resolve pollution problems if polluters were given the rights to emit a particular amount of pollutant and could trade those rights. Two years later, Canadian economist John H. Dales further developed this insight in his book, *Pollution, Property and Prices*.

   With emissions trading, a government can set a target for overall emissions, create permits allowing companies to release a specific quantity of pollution based on that target, and hand out or auction off those rights. Firms with more permits than needed can sell them to firms that require more, allowing the market to determine their prices, as it does with most goods and services. Firms that can reduce or eliminate pollution cheaply will sell off their permits to firms for whom such costs are higher, typically because they use older production methods or machinery. Emissions trading offers a way around the most vexing problem with pollution taxes: determining the tax rate that will achieve the desired level of pollution reduction. And because they avoid the information problems and bureaucracy needed to levy taxes or enforce pollution regulations, they can be more cost-effective.

   In the 1980s, the U.S. Environmental Protection Agency put the first emissions-trading scheme in place to reduce the levels of lead in gasoline. Emissions-trading programs for most greenhouse gases, including carbon dioxide and sulfur oxide, are now widely used in the United States and Europe and are gaining momentum in Asia and Africa. The global markets for carbon are now valued at more than $175 billion annually. Though critics charge that emissions trading wrongly puts a price on the environment and allows wealthy firms and countries to buy their way out of reducing pollution, their success has made them an increasingly important tool for reducing climate change.

SEE ALSO External Economies and Diseconomies (1912), Resources for the Future and Environmental Economics (1952), The Common Pool Problem (1954), Externalities and Market Failure (1958), The Coase Theorem (1960)

A coal-burning power plant emits fumes into the air, 1973. Emissions trading has helped reduce the release of carbon and other greenhouse gases.

Rent Seeking

Gordon Tullock (1922–2014), Anne O. Krueger (b. 1934)

When the United States government announces plans for building a new fighter jet, airplane manufacturers roll out intense and expensive lobbying efforts to compete for the contract. Why don't they simply submit their best bid and leave it at that? The answer is that the winner of the contract is given the extremely valuable position of operating as a monopoly and will perhaps make billions of dollars in profits. When the benefits of winning are so lucrative, it makes sense that the manufacturers would be eager to spend large sums of money in pursuit of this prize. The same process also plays out for smaller contracts, such as a license to operate a restaurant at an airport or a contract from the local government to repave a highway.

While this may appear relatively harmless, and at worst a bit unsavory, public-choice analysis pioneer Gordon Tullock explained that it is socially wasteful in his 1967 article, "The Welfare Costs of Tariffs, Monopolies, and Theft." This lobbying involves the expenditure of resources solely to transfer income from others to oneself. No new goods and services or wealth are created in the process. If every member of society devoted their working hours to such an endeavor, nothing of value would ever be produced. Economist Anne Krueger, then at the University of Minnesota, called such activities "rent seeking," in a 1974 article that provided a formal model of the rent-seeking process and estimated the magnitude of these rents in India and Turkey.

Rent seeking isn't limited to attempts to secure a government contract. Companies regularly lobby for regulations that will reduce competition in their industry. Senior-citizen groups lobby for increases in Social Security payments, which diverts funds from other uses, and French farmers lobby vigorously to maintain European Union agricultural subsidies. Rent seeking can also exacerbate income inequality, as those with the most money to spend on these activities can further redistribute income and wealth in their favor. Diverting resources from productive activities slows economic growth and, in the most extreme cases, can put a brake on economic development.

SEE ALSO *La Scienza della Finanze* (1883), Public Choice Analysis (1962), The Free-Rider Problem (1965), Economics Becomes Applied (1970), Regulatory Capture (1971)

Bidding for a contract to build a fighter jet for the military can lead to rent seeking, as manufacturers have an incentive to spend large sums of money to secure the contract.

The Natural Rate of Unemployment

Milton Friedman (1912–2006), Edmund S. Phelps (b. 1933)

In the late 1950s and early 1960s, the discovery of a potential trade-off between inflation and unemployment sparked a host of studies that tried to pin down its precise nature. Some of these studies began to cast doubt on the inverse relationship between inflation and unemployment depicted in the Phillips curve. The problem, as first suggested by Nobel Laureates Edmund Phelps and Milton Friedman in 1967, was the curve's theoretical grounding. It assumed that wage contracts reflect *existing* rather than *expected* inflation rates. If workers demand wage increases based on expected inflation, the relationship changes.

As the Phillips curve suggests, increases in government spending or the money supply will initially reduce unemployment and increase inflation. But workers, expecting inflation to be higher going forward, demand higher wages. Firms respond by reducing hiring, restoring unemployment to its initial level. In effect, this stimulus shifts the Phillips curve upward: any particular unemployment rate is now associated with a higher inflation rate. This means that there is no long-run trade-off between inflation and unemployment. Moreover, if the government tries to keep unemployment below a certain level, which Friedman labeled the "natural rate of unemployment," the inflation will continue to rise. Keynesian policies to manage aggregate demand may reduce unemployment below this level in the short term, but it will eventually rebound to the natural rate and accelerate inflation. This very scenario occurred in the 1970s when the United States entered a recession and experienced stagflation.

Friedman and Phelps's idea that there is an unemployment rate consistent with a stable rate of inflation became widely accepted, though it is now referred to as the "non-accelerating inflation rate of unemployment" (NAIRU) rather than the "natural" rate. Central banks rely on the NAIRU to help them control the money supply so as to minimize unemployment without triggering inflation. Until recently, it was believed that the NAIRU for the U.S. was around 5 percent. But as unemployment has fallen to historically low levels over the last several years without triggering inflation, economists and central bankers are unsure what it really is, making monetary policy just that much more challenging.

SEE ALSO Unemployment (1896), Keynes's *General Theory* (1936), The Phillips Curve (1958), The New Classical Macroeconomics (1972), OPEC and the Arab Oil Embargo (1973), The Policy Ineffectiveness Proposition (1975)

Demonstrators gather in New York City to protest against high food prices during the stagflation of the 1970s.

The Economics of Crime and Punishment

Gary S. Becker (1930–2014)

The study of crime typically fell under the sociologist's purview rather than the economist's until Gary Becker sketched out how an economic approach to criminology might work in "Crime and Punishment" (1968). The inspiration for this article came from Becker's decision to park illegally when running late for a university meeting, one he made after quickly calculating its benefits and costs.

When Becker was writing, criminals were often portrayed as victims of larger social circumstances; many thought criminal behavior arose from factors such as mental illness and social oppression. Becker, on the other hand, saw most criminals as rational people; like everyone else, they make choices in the face of specific constraints. The decision to violate the law involves weighing benefits and costs. A criminal compares the expected gain from a crime, whether that be the value of stolen goods or the utility gained from inflicting violence, against the expected punishment if caught. She would also consider the likelihood of being caught in the first place and then convicted.

Becker's framework explains why many people exceed the speed limit while relatively few people commit armed robberies. It describes how punishments are simply prices of criminal activity. The amount of criminal activity that occurs will respond predictably to changes in a punishment's severity and to policies that increase economic opportunities in noncriminal sectors.

Becker further argued that, from an economic-efficiency perspective, the optimal amount of crime isn't zero. The expense of devoting additional resources to crime prevention will eventually outweigh the benefits of reduced crime. This has implications for penal systems. Levying fines is a far less costly process than incarceration; a steep fine may be a better option for deterring certain types of crime. Similarly, social programs and increased educational opportunities may provide a less costly deterrent. Becker's work helped create a wide-ranging research program in the economic analysis of law, and the U.S. Sentencing Commission has used the economic approach to crime in developing sentencing guidelines for federal courts.

SEE ALSO Scarcity and Choice (1932), The Economics of Discrimination (1957), Human Capital Analysis (1958), The Coase Theorem (1960), Economics Becomes Applied (1970), The Economic Analysis of Law (1973)

According to Gary Becker, the rational criminal weighs the expected cost of a crime, including the potential punishment such as imprisonment and penal labor, against its expected benefit.

The "Nobel Prize" in Economics

In 1895, Alfred Nobel, the inventor of dynamite, bequeathed his fortune to establish the prizes that bear his name. He wanted these awards to honor achievements in five subjects: chemistry, physics, literature, medicine, and the promotion of peace. Economics was not on the list. The prize in economics, officially known as the Sveriges Riksbank Prize in Economic Sciences in Memory of Alfred Nobel, was not created until 1969, when the Swedish central bank celebrated its 300th anniversary by providing the necessary funding. Though the Nobel Foundation agreed to the bank's proposal, members of the Nobel family disapproved on the grounds that Alfred Nobel hadn't intended such a prize to exist; his great-great nephew believed that it would run counter to his belief that businessmen prioritized profits over societal well-being. These objections account for the unusual name given to the economics prize.

Given that other prominent subjects, such as mathematics, were left out in the cold by Nobel's will, you can certainly argue that economics was an unusual choice for a "new" prize. However, the creation of the economics Nobel has enhanced the profession's prestige, enshrining its scientific status alongside fields such as chemistry and physics. As it happened, the initial awards were given to Ragnar Frisch, Jan Tinbergen, Paul Samuelson, Simon Kuznets, John R. Hicks, and Kenneth Arrow, all of whom helped shape economics into a mathematical and quantitative discipline.

As of 2019, eighty-one individuals have received the economics prize. Roughly two-thirds of the winners have been Americans, reflecting how the center of economics shifted from Europe to the United States after World War II, facilitated in part by the emigration of many prominent European economists fleeing Nazi persecution during the 1930s and the growth of American research universities. Even more remarkable is the fact that twenty-nine of these Nobelists have been associated with the University of Chicago as students or faculty members. The prize has also been given to a few non-economists who have made important contributions, including mathematicians, political scientists, and a psychologist. One of these political scientists, Elinor Ostrom, is the sole woman to receive the prize.

SEE ALSO The Chicago School (1946), Behavioral Economics (1979), Governance of the Commons (1990)

The winners of the 1969 Nobel Prizes pose for a group photo, including Jan Tinbergen (right), who shared the first prize in economics with Ragnar Frisch. The other winners included, from left to right, Murray Gell-Mann (physics), Derek Barton (chemistry), Prof. Odd Hassel (chemistry), Max Delbrück (medicine), Alfred Hershey (medicine), and Salvador Luria (medicine).

Economics Becomes Applied

Despite the advances in econometrics during the twentieth century, theoretical analysis—and general equilibrium analysis in particular—was considered far more important than doing the empirical work that provided evidence for a theory's explanatory power. The theory itself, meanwhile, often seemed to bear little correspondence to economic reality or to touch on the day-to-day problems that affect people's lives. The tide began to turn in the 1970s, however, as applications of the economist's theoretical and empirical tools to everything from family life to the determinants of unemployment among black youth gained increasing attention and prestige.

Several factors led to this change. With the basic contours of economic theory—including the theories of rational choice and market structures—in place, the search for new ways to apply that theory and test it against real-world data became the logical next step. The greater availability of large data sets, advances in computing power, and the development of software that could handle advanced statistical analysis made it easier to conduct more rigorous and detailed empirical work. With the huge expansion of economics faculties and the "publish or perish" mentality that took over universities, applied economics became a surer route to a successful career.

While the math behind their theories was more advanced than ever, economists' interest in applying economic theory to subjects as diverse as health, urban life, the environment, and inequality showed that economic theory could provide insights for real-world problem-solving. Papers offering empirical analysis to support the theory or relying on empirical analysis alone became increasingly prominent. General equilibrium models were wedded to data to simulate the effects of changes in the tax system, the money supply, and international trade policies. Experimental economics, which tests economic theories using human subjects in the laboratory, gained legitimacy as a rigorous and informative approach. Its connection to many economic and social issues gave this applied research tremendous policy relevance and increased the demand for economists in government agencies, think tanks, and policy organizations.

SEE ALSO Computation: The Orcutt Regression Analyzer and the Phillips Machine (1948), Resources for the Future and Environmental Economics (1952), Public Choice Analysis (1962), The Economic Analysis of Law (1973), The Personal Computer (1981), The Experimental Turn (1986), Natural Experiments (1990)

This photo of a computer room from the 1970s shows an example of the technology that allowed applied economics to gain a stronger foothold in the field.

The Market for "Lemons"

George Akerlof (b. 1940)

George Stigler's 1961 analysis of the economics of information unleashed numerous investigations into the effects of imperfect information, scenarios in which buyers and sellers don't have all the information necessary to make fully informed choices. A young American economist named George Akerlof focused on situations in which the goods in a market vary in quality and the information that buyers and sellers have about their quality isn't identical, or symmetric. His 1970 article, "The Market for 'Lemons,'" demonstrated that the presence of low-quality goods in the market can drive out high-quality ones.

Akerlof illustrated the effects of asymmetric information using the market for used automobiles. Some cars are "lemons," containing serious defects, while others are in excellent condition. Unlike sellers, prospective buyers can't be certain about the quality of any given used car and so can't discern its true value. As a result, buyers won't be willing to pay the premium commanded by high-quality used cars. Because buyers are unwilling to pay this premium, the owners of those cars will pull them from the market, leaving only lemons and cars of middling quality. Buyers, again, will adjust their willingness to pay downward to this decrease in average quality, leading sellers of average-quality cars to remove them from sale. In the end, only lemons remain. This is an example of adverse selection: a situation where asymmetric information disadvantages one party and causes prices to adjust to compensate for this lack of information. Adverse selection can even cause the market for certain products to disappear altogether, as some suggest happened to various financial assets during the Great Recession.

Akerlof's theory, which earned him a share of the 2001 Nobel Prize in economics, has many applications. Markets for employment, insurance, and credit experience these problems, as businesses can't truly be certain of a worker's productivity, a person's propensity to engage in risky behavior, or one's likelihood to repay a loan. Quality guarantees, licensing requirements, and services that provide reports on vehicle history can help mitigate some adverse selection effects, however, and firms have also developed methods for screening potential business partners and customers to circumvent these information problems.

SEE ALSO Gresham's Law (1558), The Economics of Information (1961), Signaling (1973), Screening—or Pooling and Separating Equilibria (1976)

Used cars are parked in a lot outside a dealership specializing in secondhand vehicles, 1970s. George Akerlof explored how asymmetric information about product quality can impact the market for used cars.

Collective Choice and Social Welfare

Amartya Sen (b. 1933)

Arrow's impossibility theorem pessimistically suggested that there is no way to combine the preferences of the members of society and arrive at a sound conclusion about what society prefers. It spawned a host of studies that have tried to show that there exist democratic choice processes which allow us to compare societal welfare levels under different scenarios. The most important contribution to this literature came from Indian economist and 1998 Nobel Laureate Amartya Sen, whose 1970 monograph, *Collective Choice and Social Welfare*, drew on economics, mathematics, and philosophy to revolutionize social-choice analysis.

Sen's analysis was highly technical. It at once reinforced Arrow's conclusions and showed that economists *can* make social-welfare assessments if some of Arrow's restrictive assumptions, such as those related to the possibility of comparing individual utilities, are relaxed. Perhaps the most controversial aspect of Sen's analysis is his "liberal paradox," which states that individual liberty and Pareto efficiency are incompatible. Voting processes can't simultaneously respect individual freedom while also yielding efficient outcomes—a result that he illustrated using a debate over whether to ban D. H. Lawrence's titillating novel *Lady Chatterley's Lover* (1929).

Sen also turned back the clock on welfare analysis, calling to mind the roots of economics in moral philosophy, by incorporating ethics into welfare analysis. He emphasized that distributive justice must play a role alongside efficiency in assessing economic outcomes, and that broader measures of a society's well-being are necessary to properly account for social welfare. In 1990, this led to the creation of the Human Development Index, which uses data on life expectancy, education, and per-capita income to measure a country's development. This work is consistent with the other major thrust of Sen's research, in the field of development economics, where his efforts to explain the causes and effects of famine and proposals for preventing and limiting its severity provided important new insights into the forces underlying starvation and poverty. In both his welfare analysis and his work on economic development, Sen's attention to society's most disadvantaged people has helped bring distributional issues to the foreground of economic analysis.

SEE ALSO The Bergson Social Welfare Function (1938), Arrow's Impossibility Theorem (1951), The Atkinson Inequality Index (1970)

Amartya Sen's work has focused on issues of social choice and economic welfare, including methods to measure economic well-being and the integration of ethics and economics.

The Atkinson Inequality Index

Anthony B. Atkinson (1944–2017)

Economics has never been entirely silent on issues of income distribution, but economists have shied away from evaluating distributional outcomes and have focused instead on assessing efficiency. Few had tried integrating measures of inequality into social welfare functions, which would allow economists to judge whether some income-distribution scenarios are more desirable than others.

British economist Anthony Atkinson took an important step toward filling this void in his 1970 article, "On the Measurement of Inequality." He proposed a method, now known as the Atkinson index, to rank different possible income distributions within a country. Previous estimates of inequality either tended to measure the variance of incomes from the mean, or relied on the Gini coefficient, which compares a country's actual distribution of income to one of complete equality. The Atkinson index reduces each possible distributive outcome to a single number between 0 and 1 which indicates the share of its total income society is willing to give up, maintaining a constant level of social welfare, for all incomes to be equal. If the index equals 0.20, for example, society would be willing to give up 20 percent of its income to achieve complete equality.

Atkinson connected the distribution of income to views of social welfare by introducing a parameter reflecting inequality aversion. A society that is more averse to inequality will experience greater welfare gains when lower-income groups see their incomes rise. This suggests that a redistribution of income from the rich to the poor can improve welfare. A society less averse to inequality, meanwhile, benefits more from higher *average* incomes than from efforts to redistribute it.

Numerous other measures of inequality have been developed since—and sometimes based on—Atkinson's index, but it remains one of the most widely used tools due to its ability to identify which end of the income distribution is contributing the most to inequality. The Atkinson Index's ability to train our focus on the lower end of the income distribution makes it especially relevant to current policy debates, where issues including wage stagnation, access to health care, and mortality rates among the poor have attracted increased attention.

SEE ALSO The Positive–Normative Distinction (1836), Index Numbers (1863), The Bergson Social Welfare Function (1938), *Collective Choice and Social Welfare* (1970)

Shanties crowd the shores of the Martin Peña Canal in Puerto Rico while modern buildings can be seen in the distance, 1973. The Atkinson index shows the extent to which redistributions of income from rich to poor can affect society's welfare.

Regulatory Capture

George J. Stigler (1911–1991)

Those who support government regulation of business typically believe that it protects consumers or the larger public interest. However, in his 1971 article, "The Theory of Economic Regulation," George Stigler came to the opposite conclusion. Using basic demand-and-supply analysis, he suggested that regulators may actually be doing the bidding of the businesses because regulatory bodies are vulnerable to "capture" by special interests.

The government has the power to confer benefits on particular individuals or groups, and Stigler saw the voting and legislative processes as markets in which agents compete for those benefits. The demand for regulation reflects the desire of industries to limit competition by deterring entry into the market. Occupational licensing is a classic example: it increases the costs of entry into a profession, keeping its ranks smaller and wages higher. On the supply side, legislators deliver the regulations if these industries can offer sufficient votes and campaign contributions to attract legislative support.

If this regulation, by limiting competition and thus artificially inflating prices, benefits a particular industry at the public's expense, how does it pass muster in a democratic society? Stigler answered by pointing out that the benefits of business regulations are tightly concentrated while the costs are diffused. The beneficiaries thus have a powerful incentive to support regulatory legislation, while individual citizens, each of whom bears only a small share of its cost, have less motivation to mobilize against it—if they even know it is being considered in the first place.

The theory of regulatory capture has been expanded to account for special interests using their influence to control the agendas of regulatory agencies. The controversies that arise when industry insiders are appointed to (to name just a few examples) agencies that oversee financial markets, the pharmaceutical industry, or workplace safety illustrate the issues at stake. Greater transparency is often seen as a key to minimizing regulatory capture, but for others the only solution is to decrease reliance on regulation, based on the belief that it may do more harm than good.

SEE ALSO The Demand–Supply Model (1890), The Economics of Information (1961), Public Choice Analysis (1962), Rent Seeking (1967)

A lab worker tests car exhaust emissions for the Environmental Protection Agency (EPA), 1977. Government-run agencies, such as the EPA, can be susceptible to regulatory capture.

Flexible Exchange Rates:
The End of Bretton Woods

Since the end of World War II, the Bretton Woods Agreement had maintained a system of fixed exchange rates that valued world currencies against the U.S. dollar. By the 1960s, the combination of large U.S. trade deficits and high spending on foreign aid and the military, due to the Vietnam War and efforts to counter Soviet influence, led to a glut of dollars around the world. This quantity far exceeded the amount that the U.S. could redeem from its existing gold stocks at the fixed price of $35 per ounce, specified by the agreement. Significant inflation, caused in part by the need to finance the war and President Lyndon Johnson's Great Society programs, further eroded the dollar's value and international confidence in it.

As the faith in the dollar declined, more nations looked to convert their dollars into gold, stretching the limits of already shrinking U.S. gold reserves. The increasingly weak dollar also harmed American exports. These issues led President Richard Nixon to suspend the dollar's convertibility to gold in 1971. Though a new effort, known as the Smithsonian Agreement, attempted to reestablish a system of fixed exchange rates, this proved unworkable, and in 1973 the Bretton Woods system was abandoned in favor of floating rates, where market forces determine relative currency values.

Some economists had been championing a move to flexible exchange rates. With increased economic interdependence due to the expansion of international trade, economic conditions in one country had an increasing impact on conditions elsewhere, making it difficult to maintain fixed exchange rates. Because the success of a fixed-rate system requires countries to pursue macroeconomic policies which maintain those rates, it can impede a country's ability to manage pressing domestic problems. The demise of the Bretton Woods system gave countries increased flexibility to manage their economic affairs and led to the globalization and deregulation of the world's financial system. This brought with it both benefits and costs. Private financing could now move quickly across the globe, generating great prosperity when funds flow in but significant instability when signs of economic downturn lead investors to withdraw their money.

SEE ALSO The Gold Standard (1717), The Bullionist Controversy (1810), The Bretton Woods Agreement (1944), OPEC and the Arab Oil Embargo (1973)

On August 15, 1971, President Richard Nixon announced that the United States would suspend the convertibility of dollars into gold, part of a series of economic policy changes colloquially known as the "Nixon shock."

Optimal Taxation

Frank Ramsey (1903–1930), James A. Mirrlees (1936–2018)

How do you structure a tax system so that it maximizes societal welfare and provides enough revenue for the government's needs? To what extent does the pursuit of greater equality through the tax system impact economic efficiency? Questions such as these had long perplexed economists, but in his 1971 article, "An Exploration in the Theory of Optimum Income Taxation," Oxford professor and 1996 Nobel Laureate James Mirrlees offered a way to figure out some answers.

Optimal tax theory examines how to design taxes that both maximize a particular social welfare function, allowing economists to take equity considerations into account, and satisfy a specified revenue constraint. In 1927, British economist Frank Ramsey demonstrated that the optimal commodity tax is one that is levied most heavily on goods with the most inelastic demands. Mirrlees took up where Ramsey left off and drew inspiration from other work on the effects of asymmetric information. Consider a government that wishes to tax high-income people and redistribute those funds to low-income people. Though it can observe income, it can't determine the ability and effort that went into earning that money. The government is faced with a trade-off between equity and efficiency. Taxing the highest earners at a very high marginal rate reduces their incentive to be productive, reducing output in the economy. The challenge becomes designing a tax system that simultaneously achieves certain equity goals but doesn't discourage effort among high earners. Surprisingly, Mirrlees found that the optimal income tax is a flat-rate tax of around twenty percent.

Mirrlees's findings have been challenged, largely because of the complexity of determining optimal tax rates in the real world. His model, nonetheless, still provides the basic framework through which economists analyze income taxes. In the policy realm, the theory has prompted some countries, including the U.S. and Great Britain, to move away from high marginal tax rates on the wealthy. This, of course, hasn't been without controversy, and the current popularity of proposals to dramatically increase tax rates on high-income individuals may indicate a greater preference for equality (at the expense of inefficiency) in some circles.

SEE ALSO Rent and the Theory of Surplus (1662), The Benefit Principle of Taxation (1896), The Bergson Social Welfare Function (1938), The Market for "Lemons" (1970), Signaling (1973), Supply-Side Economics (1974), Screening—or Pooling and Separating Equilibria (1976)

Optimal tax theory shows that the most efficient taxes are those levied on goods with inelastic demand, such as cigarettes. Ironically, these taxes tend to be quite popular, as they are widely believed to discourage "vices" such as smoking.

The New Classical Macroeconomics

Robert E. Lucas (b. 1937)

In 1971, U.S. president Richard Nixon famously proclaimed that "we are all Keynesians now." Of course, not all economists *were* Keynesians at this time. In a series of articles published in 1972 and 1973, American economist Robert Lucas challenged the Keynesian approach that had dominated macroeconomics for some three decades. He believed that existing macroeconomic theories hadn't been constructed upon proper microeconomic foundations. His efforts to remedy this shortcoming led to the creation of new classical macroeconomics.

Lucas criticized Keynesian theories for assuming that agents have adaptive expectations, forming their beliefs of the future based solely on the present and the past. For Lucas, as for John Muth a decade earlier, this approach was inconsistent with the generally accepted view in microeconomics that agents behave rationally and have rational expectations informed by all available information.

According to Lucas, Keynesian macroeconomic models were also inconsistent with Walrasian general equilibrium theory, which informs us that markets clear almost instantaneously, with prices adjusting to equalize supply and demand. Keynesians said that unemployment resulted because employers failed to cut wages when aggregate demand fell, creating involuntary unemployment. But rational employers would certainly do so, as it would increase their profits. Any worker who would not accept this lower wage could easily be replaced. In the general-equilibrium world of microeconomics, persistent involuntary unemployment isn't possible, since wages will quickly adjust to clear labor markets. To make macroeconomic models and microeconomic analysis consistent, Lucas insisted that macro models must be put on a Walrasian footing.

By wedding rational expectations and general equilibrium analysis, Lucas turned Keynesian economics on its head. If markets clear immediately and consumers and producers are rational, it's impossible for monetary policy to permanently reduce unemployment or affect other "real" variables, such as output and consumption—a concept known as monetary neutrality. Lucas's new classical macroeconomics transformed macroeconomics.

SEE ALSO Keynes's *General Theory* (1936), The Phillips Curve (1958), The Rational Expectations Hypothesis (1961), The Policy Ineffectiveness Proposition (1975), The Lucas Critique (1976), Real Business Cycle Models (1982), Dynamic Stochastic General Equilibrium Models (2003)

Applicants for unemployment benefits wait in lines at the Baltimore Welfare Office. Robert Lucas's attempt to construct macroeconomics on microeconomic foundations suggested that it is not possible for monetary policy to achieve permanent reductions in unemployment.

Mechanism Design

Leonid Hurwicz (1917–2008), Eric S. Maskin (b. 1950), Roger Myerson (b. 1951)

Game theory tells us that private information leads individuals to act in ways that inefficiently allocate resources. For example, how does the government ensure that cell phone frequencies are auctioned to those who value them most highly when only the prospective buyers know how much these frequencies are worth to them? How can governments design highway construction contracts to ensure that highways are built at the lowest cost? Mechanism design theory provides answers to these questions.

While game theory gives solutions to specific games, mechanism design theory reverses the process, designing a game that generates a particular outcome. In 1960, Leonid Hurwicz pioneered this approach after being inspired by debates about whether a socialist economy could be designed to generate productivity and efficiency levels comparable to capitalism. Hurwicz's 1972 article, "On Informationally Decentralized Systems," and subsequent work on decision-making under asymmetric information by fellow 2007 Nobel Laureates Eric Maskin and Roger Myerson in the late 1970s, laid the foundation for this new approach.

Mechanism design functions as a form of economic engineering that considers how a system's design facilitates efficiency. Maskin illustrates this process with the example of a parent who wants to divide a cake fairly between two children without leaving either unhappy, but who does not know their preferences. One mechanism for accomplishing this is to allow one child to cut the cake and the other to have first choice among the pieces. Mechanisms like this one provide agents with incentives to reveal private information. In this case, the parent knows that neither child wants to end up with the smaller piece. The first child will cut the cake in half, ensuring her happiness, and the other gets first choice among the two equal-sized pieces, ensuring his happiness—and a fair outcome.

Mechanism design has often been used in auction theory, but fruitful real-world applications have also appeared in international development projects, voting procedures, charitable giving, and matching medical students with residency programs. One interesting example is the kidney exchange, pioneered by economist Alvin Roth and others. Someone who needs a new kidney may have a willing donor who isn't a good biological match. By facilitating chained donations, kidney exchanges offer a mechanism that provides transplants for many more people in need of one.

SEE ALSO The Socialist Calculation Debate (1920), Game Theory Enters Economics (1944), Non-Cooperative Games and Nash Equilibrium (1950), The Theory of Auctions (1961), The Free-Rider Problem (1965), The Experimental Turn (1986)

Surgeons perform a kidney transplant. Kidney exchanges have offered a mechanism that allows more patients in need of transplants to be matched with compatible donors.

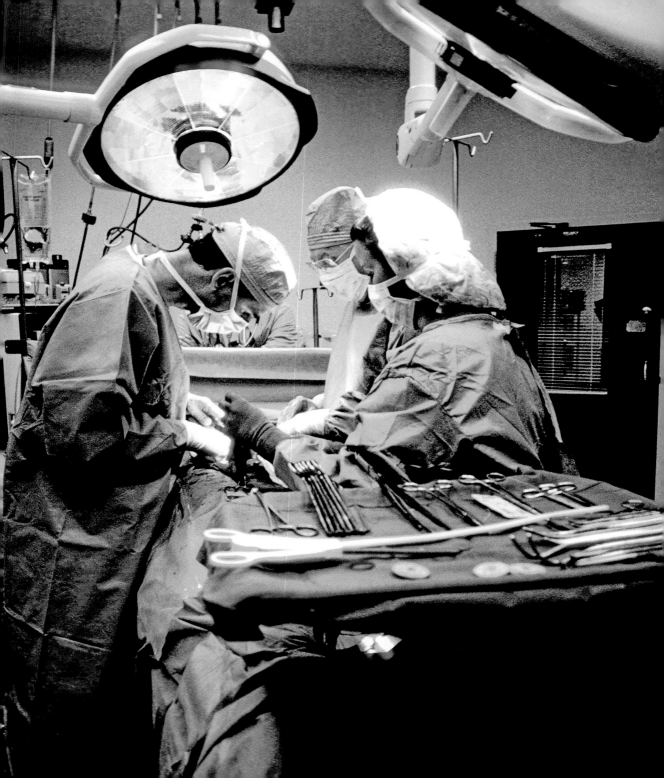

The Economic Analysis of Law

Richard A. Posner (b. 1939)

The contemporary law-school student will come across economic analysis at many points during her legal education. This would have been almost unthinkable a half century ago, when the application of economics to law was confined largely to antitrust law and certain aspects of government regulation. The notion that you could apply economics to other areas of law, such as property, contract, tort, and criminal law, began to crystallize during the 1960s through the work of economists Ronald Coase and Gary Becker, as well as Yale law professor Guido Calabresi. But it was University of Chicago law professor (and former federal judge) Richard Posner who showed how dramatically economic reasoning can impact our understanding of legal issues.

Posner's 1973 treatise, *Economic Analysis of Law*, used three basic principles to assess virtually every area of law. First, he assumed that individuals approach law-related matters rationally. A rational agent will breach a contract or commit a crime only if the expected benefits of doing so exceed the expected costs. Second, legal rules have the same function as prices, meaning that increasing the cost of illegal behaviors will reduce their occurrence. Finally, legal rules can be assessed based both on traditional notions of justice and their ability to produce economically efficient outcomes. Where traditional legal thinking might wish to discourage most agents from breaching their contract, economics suggests that breach should be encouraged if doing so moves resources to more valuable uses.

Posner's treatise, and the economic approach to law generally, generated enormous controversy within the legal community. Even economists resisted it, at least initially. Some believed that the rational-agent model didn't accurately describe the decision to obey or disregard legal rules. Still more suspect was the idea that economic efficiency, rather than the application of traditional notions of justice, should be the goal of legal decision-making. In the end, however, this approach to law won over many converts. In fact, its influence extends even to judicial decisions; with more judges being trained in the application of economic principles to the law, the use of economic reasoning in judicial opinions has increased significantly.

SEE ALSO Scarcity and Choice (1932), The Coase Theorem (1960), The Economics of Crime and Punishment (1968), Economics Becomes Applied (1970)

Former federal appellate judge Richard Posner speaking at Harvard University.

Agency Theory

Stephen A. Ross (1944–2017), James A. Mirrlees (1936–2018), Joseph E. Stiglitz (b. 1943), Oliver Hart (b. 1948), Bengt Holmström (b. 1949)

The principal–agent problem arises when one individual, the agent, makes decisions on behalf of another, the principal. The principal and the agent may have different interests, and because the principal can't observe or perfectly monitor the agent's actions, the agent's behavior may lead to results that conflict with her goals. The principal–agent dynamic occurs between employer and employee, voters and legislators, and athletes and their financial managers, to cite just a few examples. In 1973, Stephen Ross of the University of Pennsylvania first modeled the agency problem, and James Mirrlees and Joseph Stiglitz developed some of the earliest incentive mechanisms to resolve these conflicts of interest in the mid-1970s.

Agency theory seeks to answer a basic question: How do you overcome the principal–agent problem? The answer typically hinges on designing a contract between the two parties that aligns their incentives. A well-designed contract, which specifies how the agent is compensated, should maximize the expected utility of the principal, while taking account of the fact that the agent will then act to maximize her utility given the terms of the contract. This requires providing the agent with incentives to pursue the principal's interests. In situations where contracting isn't possible, as between voters and their elected representatives, aligning incentives can be much more difficult.

MIT economist Bengt Holmström applied agency theory to employee and executive compensation, showing how performance pay, when workers earn money on a piecework basis or when a manager's compensation is linked tightly to the firm's profits, can align the interests of the principal and agent. Agency theory has important implications for economic development, as agencies such as the International Monetary Fund cannot easily ensure that governments are putting development funds to their intended uses. It also forms the basis for the economic analysis of a wide range of contracting practices. For example, Harvard's Oliver Hart has explained why writing incomplete contracts rather than specifying all relevant terms in detail may enable individuals and businesses to better respond to changing circumstances. Hart and Holmström's work on agency theory and its implications for contracting earned them the 2016 Nobel Prize.

SEE ALSO *The Modern Corporation and Private Property* (1932), The Economics of Information (1961), The Market for "Lemons" (1970), Signaling (1973), Screening—or Pooling and Separating Equilibria (1976)

Typists work at their desks in an office in Munich, Germany, 1973. Principal–agent problems can arise between employees and their managers, who can't perfectly monitor each individual worker's behavior.

The Black–Scholes Model

Fischer Black (1938–1995), Myron S. Scholes (b. 1941), Robert C. Merton (b. 1944)

Financial assets, such as stocks and bonds, are risky because their values can change in a heartbeat. Some investors seek out higher-risk assets, while others prefer to avoid significant risk. To allocate this risk properly, financial markets require precise risk-assessment methods so that investors can accurately value these assets. One of the most widely used tools is the Black–Scholes model of option pricing, developed by Fischer Black, Robert Merton, and Myron Scholes at MIT in the early 1970s. An option is the right, but not the obligation, to purchase or sell a security at a particular price (the "strike" price), on or before a specified date. As such, the option is traded at a discounted price compared to a share of stock. Options belong to a class of securities known as "derivatives" because their value is derived from the value of another security—in this case, the price of a share of a company's stock. They are essentially speculative instruments, allowing investors to profit from changes in the underlying asset's value without owning the asset itself.

Before the development of the Black–Scholes model, few investors traded options because they seemed too risky. Options become worthless if the stock price moves in the wrong direction, whereas a share of stock only becomes worthless if the company goes out of business. The Black–Scholes model helps investors manage this risk by estimating an option's value using data on a stock's current price, its volatility, the risk-free interest rate, the strike price, and the time until the option expires. In a nutshell, the model evaluates whether the stock's market price will deviate from the strike price, and by how much, on a specified date.

As investors gained confidence that the Black–Scholes model could accurately measure the value of options and other derivatives, derivative markets expanded dramatically. Scholes and Merton shared the 1997 Nobel Prize for their work. (Black was deceased by then, and thus ineligible for the Prize.) Though developed as a response to market volatility, the growing use of options exacerbated the effects of shocks to financial markets, contributing to the Great Recession.

SEE ALSO The Theory of Portfolio Selection (1952), The Capital Asset Pricing Model (1962), The Efficient Markets Hypothesis (1965), The Great Recession (2007)

Traders on the trading floor in the New York Stock Exchange, c. 1970s. The Black–Scholes model provides a tool for investors to manage the risk associated with trading options.

Signaling

Michael Spence (b. 1943)

In addition to illustrating the problems of asymmetric information in the marketplace, George Akerlof's analysis of the used-car market raised the possibility of creating mechanisms that provide or elicit accurate and verifiable information. In a 1973 paper, Michael Spence outlined one such device for overcoming information problems in the job market: signaling.

Spence presents an employer's decision to hire a new employee as an investment made under uncertainty. The prospective employee knows how productive and qualified she is, but the employer can't be certain of this without actually employing the worker. The employer is willing to offer high wages to high-productivity workers but only lower wages to low-productivity workers. High-productivity job seekers want to provide prospective employers with a signal of their productivity level to receive the higher wage. Education is one vehicle for doing this. How? Spence assumed that the costs of signals such as education are negatively correlated with productivity; a more productive person can acquire a given level of education at a lower cost (in terms of effort, time, and money) than a less productive person. High-productivity people thus will acquire more education than low-productivity people. If experience reveals to employers that workers with more education are more effective and productive, then examining a job seeker's education level becomes an effective way to judge these qualities, turning education into a prerequisite for a high-wage job.

This theory of signaling suggests that education may not actually enhance productivity, as the human capital model predicts. The value of education comes from its ability to *signal* productivity and a person's willingness to incur costs to provide that signal. Spence's article and subsequent book on economic signaling inspired a large body of research in this area and earned him a share of the 2001 Nobel Prize. The theory's implications, though, go well beyond education. A business may delay negotiating a contract with a supplier to signal bargaining power and induce more favorable terms. Product warranties can also be explained seen as a signal of quality, with longer and more comprehensive warranties suggesting that a good is higher-grade.

SEE ALSO Human Capital Analysis (1958), The Economics of Information (1961), The Market for "Lemons" (1970), Screening—or Pooling and Separating Equilibria (1976)

Job-fair attendees meet prospective employers, 1965. To help distinguish between high-quality and low-quality workers, employers sometimes rely on signals, such as an attainment of a college degree, to evaluate job candidates.

OPEC and the Arab Oil Embargo

In October 1973, the Organization of Petroleum Exporting Countries (OPEC) imposed an embargo on oil exports to the United States and several of its allies. OPEC, whose twelve member nations, including Saudi Arabia, Iran, and Iraq, are concentrated in the Middle East, used the embargo to target the United States and the Netherlands for supporting Israel in the Yom Kippur War. The Arab states also hoped that this "oil weapon" would provide leverage in peace negotiations. The embargo's effects were immediate; oil prices shot up fourfold.

In the United States, which then was heavily dependent on foreign oil, the shock was felt throughout the economy. Consumers paid higher gasoline prices, and producers faced skyrocketing costs. The government imposed price controls, but this only led to gas shortages and rationing. Ballooning oil prices caused inflation to spike. Labor unions responded by negotiating significant wage increases with employers, which generated a wage–price spiral that compounded inflation's effects. Plus, the U.S. economy was already slipping into a recession due to increasing international competition faced by U.S. manufacturing, the collapse of the Bretton Woods Agreement, and a stock market crash. This collision of events brought stagflation, the simultaneous existence of high inflation and high unemployment. For the unemployed and workers whose wages didn't keep up with inflation, the period was particularly painful.

This stagflation was both inconsistent with the Phillips curve and seemingly immune to Keynesian fiscal policy. Any government stimulus designed to increase demand and reduce unemployment would worsen the severe inflation, while measures to slow down inflation, such as tax increases, would exacerbate unemployment. Faced with evidence that Keynesian tax and spending policies were ineffective, countries began to turn toward monetary policy measures, and economists explored alternative theories, particularly rational expectations models, to explain macroeconomic performance.

The embargo was lifted in March 1974 when Israel withdrew its troops from the west side of the Suez Canal, but OPEC maintained oil prices well above their pre-embargo levels. Its actions pushed the United States to promote greater energy independence by putting into place measures to support domestic oil production, promote energy conservation, and establish strategic petroleum reserves.

SEE ALSO Keynes's *General Theory* (1936), The Keynesian Revolution (1947), The Phillips Curve (1958), The Natural Rate of Unemployment (1967), Flexible Exchange Rates: The End of Bretton Woods (1971), The New Classical Macroeconomics (1972)

Gasoline shortages caused by the Arab Oil Embargo caused gas stations throughout the United States to close.

CLOSED
DUE TO
GASOLINE
SHORTAGE
OPEN 7 AM
CLOSED SUNDAY

Supply-Side Economics

Robert Mundell (b. 1932), Arthur Laffer (b. 1940)

After World War II, the desire to create a more just society and provide a reasonable standard of living for all led to the birth of the modern welfare state. Though their particulars vary across countries, welfare states, such as the U.S., Great Britain, and Sweden, share many features, including social insurance, health-care provision, and income redistribution programs. Paying for these initiatives, though, requires high marginal income tax rates. In the 1950s–1970s, they exceeded 70 percent for the highest U.S. earners. It seems intuitive that these high tax rates would generate more tax revenue, but supply-side economics, an approach closely associated with Canadian economist Robert Mundell and American economist Arthur Laffer, reached the opposite conclusion.

During a dinner in 1974, Laffer persuaded Donald Rumsfeld (b. 1932) and Dick Cheney (b. 1941), then advisers to President Richard Nixon, that higher taxes reduce revenue. Writing on a napkin, he explained, "If you tax a product, less results," and "We've been taxing work, output, and income. . . . The consequences are obvious!" He illustrated this with what became known as the Laffer curve, which shows that tax revenues will increase with tax rates when these rates are relatively low, but fall when they exceed a certain level (Mundell has suggested 25 percent). This occurs because higher tax rates reduce the incentive to work and encourage individuals to shelter income from taxes. Led by Laffer and Mundell, whose writings and policy advice helped to spread their message, supply-side economists advocated for lower marginal tax rates to inspire people to earn more income and stimulate greater economic growth. This growth, in turn, would generate additional tax revenue that more than compensates for the lower tax rates.

Supply-side economics soon expanded to emphasize the growth-promoting benefits of deregulation. In the 1980s, it became the basis for economic policy during the administrations of Ronald Reagan (1911–2004) and Margaret Thatcher (1925–2013). Despite steep tax cuts, the promised revenue growth didn't materialize. Tax increases during later administrations dramatically increased government revenues, casting further doubt on the supply-siders' anti-tax credo. Though economists today dismiss supply-side economics, it retains strong support among conservative politicians and businesspeople.

SEE ALSO The Single Tax (1879), Fabian Socialism (1884), The Benefit Principle of Taxation (1896), The Oxford Approach to Welfare (1914), Hayek's *Road to Serfdom* (1944), Public Goods (1954), Public Choice Analysis (1962), Optimal Taxation (1971)

Arthur Laffer re-created the diagram that he sketched for Dick Cheney and Donald Rumsfeld on a cloth napkin for this reproduction that he gave to journalist Jude Wanniski (1936–2005), who was credited with coining the term supply-side economics.

If you tax a product less results
" " subsidize " " more "
We've been taxing work, output and income
and subsidizing non-work, leisure and unemployment.
The consequences are obvious!

$$\frac{dTR}{dt} < 0$$

Prohibitive
Range

Normal Range
$$\frac{dTR}{dt} > 0$$

To Don Rumsfeld.
at our Two Continents
Rendezvous
9/13/74

Arthur B. Laffer

The Policy Ineffectiveness Proposition

Neil Wallace (b. 1939), Thomas Sargent (b. 1943), Robert Barro (b. 1944)

For Keynesian economists, monetary and fiscal policy serve as powerful tools for counteracting recessions. The "new classical" approach to macroeconomics, though, suggested that this view was completely wrongheaded. Thomas Sargent and Neil Wallace introduced the policy ineffectiveness proposition in a 1975 paper, "'Rational' Expectations, the Optimal Monetary Instrument, and the Optimal Money Supply Rule." They argued that anticipated policy moves have no real effects, and that the effects of unanticipated policies are only transitory.

Suppose the Fed announces that it will be expanding the money supply to reduce unemployment. Rational agents know that an increase in the money supply will push up prices; to keep their "real" wages constant, workers will demand correspondingly higher wages without supplying more labor. Producers, also anticipating that their costs will increase, have no incentive to increase output or hire more workers. This might suggest that the Fed should simply avoid announcing its intentions, so as to trick the public. Even then, Sargent and Wallace suggested that prospects here aren't much better. If people have rational expectations, then they can't be fooled time and again. Though firms may initially respond by increasing labor demand and output, and workers by supplying more labor, they will soon realize their mistake, returning output and employment to their former levels. Robert Barro later showed that the policy ineffectiveness proposition applies to other recession-fighting fiscal policies using his Ricardian equivalence theorem. For example, if the government attempts to use debt-financed spending increases to boost the economy, rational individuals, anticipating that higher taxes will be necessary to pay off the debt, will respond by saving more, offsetting the government's stimulus.

Empirical evidence has shown that markets don't adjust as quickly as the policy ineffectiveness proposition predicts. This means that monetary and fiscal policies can have beneficial effects in the short run, even though their long-run effects may be negligible.

SEE ALSO Keynes's *General Theory* (1936), The IS–LM Model (1937), The Phillips Curve (1958), The Rational Expectations Hypothesis (1961), The Natural Rate of Unemployment (1967), The New Classical Macroeconomics (1972), The Lucas Critique (1976)

The policy ineffectiveness proposition says that anticipated changes in monetary policy, such as the printing of more money, will not have any significant long-term effects on output and employment.

Screening—or Pooling and Separating Equilibria

Michael Rothschild (b. 1942), Joseph E. Stiglitz (b. 1943)

In debates over health-care reform in the U.S., insurance coverage for pre-existing conditions and mandatory participation in an insurance plan are issues that loom large, especially since consumers insist on the former and insurance companies on the latter. A 1976 article by Michael Rothschild and Joseph Stiglitz, "Equilibrium in Competitive Insurance Markets," explains why and how these two concerns are connected.

Insurance companies have two groups of consumers, high-risk and low-risk, but they can't determine which consumers fall into which group. High-risk consumers have no incentive to disclose this information, creating the potential for moral hazard—a situation where a person has an incentive to engage in more risky behavior because she doesn't bear its cost. Rothschild and Stiglitz showed that, as a result, there is no equilibrium price that covers these high-risk and low-risk consumers in a single market. Any price high enough to account for the costs of covering high-risk individuals would be more than what low-risk individuals would be willing to pay. The only possible equilibrium is one that separates the market into low-risk and high-risk groups, with the members of the former group paying lower premiums than those in the latter group.

These "separating equilibria" provide a screening mechanism that uninformed agents can use to differentiate customers. This explains why insurance companies charge high premiums for coverage with low deductibles and offer partial coverage with much higher deductibles at low premiums. This pricing structure effectively sorts frequent users of health-care services, such as those with pre-existing conditions, into the high-premium plans while allowing very healthy individuals to choose insurance that meets their more limited needs at low cost. The theory has also been applied to credit markets, where lenders use differences in credit records to compile a menu of interest-rate terms for consumers. In labor markets, commission- or other performance-based compensation packages induce low-productivity employees to self-select out of the hiring pool. The importance of this work contributed to Stiglitz's receipt of the 2001 Nobel Prize, which he shared with George Akerlof and Michael Spence "for their analyses of markets with asymmetric information."

SEE ALSO The Economics of Information (1961), The Market for "Lemons" (1970), Signaling (1973)

A brochure advertising the benefits of Medicare, one of the national health insurance programs in the United States. Programs like Medicare provide affordable coverage for individuals who have been screened as "high-risk" or frequent users of health care—particularly the elderly.

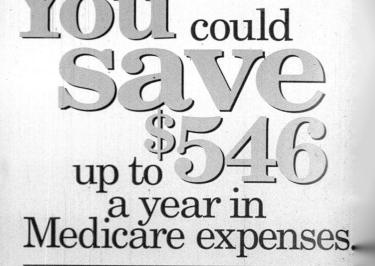

You could save up to $546 a year in Medicare expenses.

Follow these three steps to find out how.

1. Learn about cost savings programs in this brochure

2. Answer three important questions on page 2

3. Call **1-800-MEDICARE** (1-800-633-4227)

Medicare &You

The knowledge to make good decisions

The Lucas Critique

Robert E. Lucas (b. 1937)

The large-scale macroeconometric models developed during the 1950s and 1960s represented a triumph of economic expertise. Their hundreds of equations gave economists great confidence that these models could provide accurate economic forecasts and generate reasonable predictions about economic policy. But, as with other aspects of Keynesian macroeconomics, the new classical approach offered a stiff challenge in the mid-1970s with Robert Lucas's assault on Keynesian macroeconomic modeling practices.

In his 1976 article, "Econometric Policy Evaluation: A Critique," Lucas argued that though Keynesian models could accurately forecast outcomes under a given policy regime, they did a poor job of predicting what happens when policy changes. The culprit, according to Lucas, was the use of historical data to estimate key variables. Lucas believed economic agents form expectations rationally, adjusting decision rules to changing circumstances. By looking backward, historical data fail to capture these decision-making processes. When expectations change, the models' equations change, making them worthless for forecasting and policy analysis.

Consider the effects of a one-percent increase in the price level on unemployment. If monetary policy has been consistently generating one-percent inflation, output and employment won't change, because rational agents expect this increase to occur again and again. But if this one-percent increase were unanticipated, unemployment would change, falling if inflation had been zero or rising if it had been above one percent. In short, there is a different Phillips curve for each monetary rule; an econometric model that relies on data from one scenario won't accurately predict outcomes for another.

How, then, are economists supposed to make forecasts or analyze policy? Lucas's answer was to formulate models with parameters that aren't sensitive to changes in economic policy. Because this has proved to be difficult in practice, economists have moved away from large-scale Keynesian macroeconometric models, relying more heavily on dynamic stochastic general equilibrium models, which assume that individual preferences are stable and thus are considered immune to the Lucas critique.

SEE ALSO Keynes's *General Theory* (1936), The Keynesian Revolution (1947), Large-Scale Macroeconometric Models (1955), The Phillips Curve (1958), The New Classical Macroeconomics (1972), Dynamic Stochastic General Equilibrium Models (2003)

Robert Lucas's critique of Keynesian macroeconometric modeling pointed out the pitfalls of relying on historical data to estimate how key economic variables respond to changes in economic policy.

The New Keynesian Economics

Edmund Phelps (b. 1933), Stanley Fischer (b. 1943), John Taylor (b. 1946)

By the late 1970s, new classical macroeconomics had supplanted the Keynesian approach as the dominant paradigm in macroeconomics, particularly in the United States. But work by Stanley Fischer, Edmund Phelps, and John Taylor in 1977 inspired a rehabilitation of Keynesian thinking. This line of analysis, labeled "new Keynesian," was built on the foundations of the new classical approach while also incorporating several fundamental aspects of Keynesian economics.

Like the new classical approach, and in contrast to traditional Keynesianism, the new Keynesian models are built on microeconomic foundations. They assume people form expectations rationally, using all available information, and are optimizing agents. Unlike the new classical models, their new Keynesian counterparts depart from the Walrasian universe of perfect competition by allowing wages and prices to be "sticky," meaning that they don't adjust instantaneously to changing conditions. Wage and price stickiness results from factors such as long-term contracts, which can legally prevent price adjustment, and monopolistic competition, which may make it most profitable for firms to maintain prices even in changing conditions.

This stickiness means the economy may fall short of full employment, in keeping with traditional Keynesian thinking. When demand is slack, increased unemployment will result unless wages decrease sufficiently to induce employers to maintain existing workforce levels. For new Keynesians, the concept of involuntary unemployment and the Phillips curve, which describes the trade-off between inflation and unemployment, have relevance. Wage and price stickiness allows—and justifies—the use of monetary and fiscal policy to influence output and employment in the short run during a downturn, in contrast to the policy-ineffectiveness argument of the new classical economists. However, both schools maintain that these policies may not have significant long-run output and employment effects. Though some macroeconomists continue to hew to the new classical line, assuming that markets adjust quickly and efficiently, the current consensus runs in the direction of the new Keynesians.

SEE ALSO *The Theory of Monopolistic Competition* (1933), Keynes's *General Theory* (1936), The Keynesian Revolution (1947), The Phillips Curve (1958), The New Classical Macroeconomics (1972), Real Business Cycle Models (1982), Dynamic Stochastic General Equilibrium Models (2003)

Workers in West Virginia wait in line to pick up their pay, 1938. New Keynesian economists emphasize the role that sticky wages play in causing involuntary unemployment, a major problem during economic downturns such as the Great Depression.

The New Trade Theory

Paul Krugman (b. 1953)

The Heckscher–Ohlin model dominated international trade theory until the emergence of the "new trade theory," spearheaded by 2008 Nobel Laureate Paul Krugman, in the early 1980s. Empirical studies had revealed several problems with the Heckscher–Ohlin model over the years. For example, it couldn't explain why two countries with similar technological capabilities and similar resources, especially developed countries, would trade with each other (and trade identical products, no less). It also had no insight into why the U.S., a capital-rich country, exports many of its labor-intensive products.

Krugman, now well known as a columnist for the *New York Times* but then a young economics professor at Yale University, suggested two additional factors that determine trade patterns: the consumer's desire for a wide variety of goods, and the presence of increasing returns to scale in production. The Heckscher–Ohlin approach assumed a perfectly competitive marketplace with identical products and constant returns to scale. Krugman thought this wrongheaded and based his model on markets exhibiting monopolistic competition. Because consumers prefer diversity, different countries have an incentive to specialize in the production of different versions of the same basic product. The economies of scale arising from this specialization generate large cost advantages, particularly if there is strong demand for the good both at home and abroad.

To see Krugman's theory in action, look no farther than the market for automobiles, where the United States, Germany, and Japan export cars to, and import cars from, each other. Consumers view different brands very differently, and the ability of each country to specialize in the production of a different type of car allows them to benefit from trade with each other even though they have very similar technological capacities and labor pools. Krugman utilized this same framework to offer a theory of why the production of certain goods tends to be concentrated in particular geographic locations, which helped explain the increasing concentration of people in major urban centers over the last century and launched a field known as the new economic geography.

SEE ALSO Mercantile Policies (1539), The Balance-of-Trade Controversy (1621), Smith's *Wealth of Nations* (1776), The Division of Labor (1776), The Theory of Comparative Advantage (1817), *The Theory of Monopolistic Competition* (1933), The Heckscher–Ohlin Model (1933), The Stolper–Samuelson Theorem (1941), The Factor-Price Equalization Theorem (1948)

Signs hang outside the shops of luxury watchmakers along Bahnhofstrasse, one of the main streets in downtown Zurich, Switzerland. Paul Krugman's new trade theory explains why Switzerland specializes in the production of upscale watches and imports middle-of-the-market watches from other countries, such as Japan.

Behavioral Economics

Daniel Kahneman (b. 1934), Amos Tversky (1937–1996), Richard H. Thaler (b. 1945)

Since the mid-twentieth century, rational choice models have formed the backbone of economics. While there have been challenges to the rational-choice approach, including Herbert Simon's concept of bounded rationality, the major push to revisit the economist's conception of human behavior owes much to the research of psychologists Daniel Kahneman and Amos Tversky and economists such as Richard Thaler.

In the late 1970s, Kahneman and Tversky conducted experiments which suggested that people don't always make decisions rationally, particularly when risk is involved. Their results, presented in a 1979 paper, "Prospect Theory: The Analysis of Decision Under Risk," showed that people dislike losses more than they value an equivalent gain, a phenomenon known as loss aversion. Thaler later presented evidence that people tend to demand more money to give up an item that they already own than they would pay to acquire it in the first place, a finding he named the "endowment effect." People also treat a given amount of money differently depending on its origins, which explains why many people are willing to spend more when using a credit card than when using cash.

These discoveries cast doubt on whether bedrock economic theories, ranging from the efficient markets hypothesis to the Coase theorem, could explain economic outcomes. They were originally viewed as anomalies; but, as the experimental evidence mounted, it became clear that these decision-making quirks were regular features of human behavior. People behave irrationally, but in predictable ways. As a result, economists can construct models that account for this irrational behavior (the extent of which is still debated) and generate testable predictions.

Kahneman and Thaler received the Nobel Prize for formulating this behavioral approach to economics. (Tversky was deceased by then and ineligible.) It has influenced fields including finance, law and economics, and game theory. "Nudge theory," which posits that subtle policy changes can induce people to make better choices, is also an important outgrowth of this research and explains why laws that automatically enroll people in organ-donation programs and retirement savings plans, unless they choose to opt out, have greatly increased participation.

SEE ALSO World War II (1939), RAND and the Cold War (1948), Bounded Rationality (1955), The Coase Theorem (1960), The Efficient Markets Hypothesis (1965), The Economic Analysis of Law (1973)

Daniel Kahneman (left) receives the 2002 Nobel Prize in economics for his work in behavioral economics from King Carl Gustav of Sweden (right).

The Personal Computer

Few inventions have transformed our daily lives as much as the personal computer (PC). PCs program the robots that now produce many of the goods we consume, help artists and engineers design products, and allow us to gather in seconds information that previously would have taken days and even weeks to acquire. Their power has at once dramatically increased productivity and transformed the ways in which we use our time. The first mass-marketed PC, a desktop box with a small monitor, was introduced by IBM in 1981. Though its capacity and power were limited—it couldn't even hold or operate today's basic word-processing software packages—its revolutionary potential was apparent. PC capabilities increased at a rapid clip, expanding their applications to massive projects, complex computations, and sophisticated graphical imaging. Computing, which had previously been the province of specialists working on mainframe computers the size of refrigerators, was now available to all.

The personal computer altered the course of modern economics as well. Before the PC, economists had to conduct their econometric and computational analysis on mainframe computers. This was expensive, as time on the mainframe often had to be purchased. Because these mainframe computers handled everything from university records to professors' regressions, computing centers carefully rationed access to hardware and software.

With the PC, professors now had their own increasingly powerful machines, often both in their offices and at home. The rapid pace of hardware and software development made it increasingly easy to work with large data sets and perform sophisticated computations. The quantity and quality of research increased dramatically. Greater computing speed meant that economists could run dozens of regressions and simulations in a day. Journal editors began demanding more sensitivity analysis to assess the extent to which small changes in the model or the data would affect the results. The PC also transformed experimental economics, allowing a move from cumbersome pen-and-paper methods to laboratories where subjects could have instantaneous interaction with each other via networked computers. As the price of PCs continued to fall, experimental economics labs became commonplace rather than the exclusive province of a few well-funded research centers.

SEE ALSO The Econometric Society (1930), Haavelmo's "Probability Approach" (1944), Computation: The Orcutt Regression Analyzer and the Phillips Machine (1948), Economics Becomes Applied (1970), Dynamic Stochastic General Equilibrium Models (2003), Cryptocurrency (2009)

The IBM Personal Computer, shown here on display at the Musée Bolo in Lausanne, Switzerland, could run basic econometric software.

Real Business Cycle Models

Finn E. Kydland (b. 1943), Edward C. Prescott (b. 1940)

1982

The new classical macroeconomics had to contend with the challenge of providing an explanation for business cycles. Traditional theories portrayed these cycles as consequences of aggregate demand fluctuations combined with sticky wages and prices. For a school of thought claiming that prices adjust quickly to clear markets, this account posed a problem. Robert Lucas had suggested that business cycles originated in unanticipated monetary shocks, but empirical studies offered little support. In 1982, Finn Kydland and Edward Prescott proposed that technology shocks resulting from new inventions and other productivity-related innovations cause business cycles.

Kydland and Prescott suggested that, because the rate of technological advance varies over time, it is also responsible for short-run fluctuations. The "propagation mechanism" that spreads the effects of an advance over time is the "time to build," as it can take years for the productivity-increasing effects of new technology to manifest themselves. "Half-finished ships and factories," as they note, "are not part of the productive capital stock." Business cycles, then, can be viewed as efficient responses to shocks caused by "real" forces—hence the term "real business cycles." Since cycles are efficient responses to these shocks, there is no need for counter-cyclical policy to offset their effects.

To test their theory, Kydland and Prescott turned to simulations. They found that the introduction of technology shocks (short-run variations in technology growth) into their model allowed them to simulate a business cycle that corresponded with the actual business cycles in the United States between 1950 and 1975. The results were far from perfect, but they were promising enough to attract many imitators. The most recent real business cycle models, developed in response to the Great Recession, give greater weight to the possibility that imperfections in financial markets may worsen the effects of these real shocks, something unaccounted for in earlier models.

SEE ALSO Walras's *Elements of Pure Economics* (1874), Kondratiev Waves (1925), Mathematical Dynamics (1933), The Solow–Swan Growth Model (1956), The Rational Expectations Hypothesis (1961), The New Classical Macroeconomics (1972), The New Keynesian Economics (1977), Dynamic Stochastic General Equilibrium Models (2003)

A visualization of the traffic on the National Science Foundation Network (NSFNET), which provided a foundation for the Internet. Purple denotes areas with no traffic, and white denotes areas with 100 billion bytes of traffic. The rise of the Internet, which has led to the emergence of new industries and allowed workers to become more productive, is an important recent example of a technology shock.

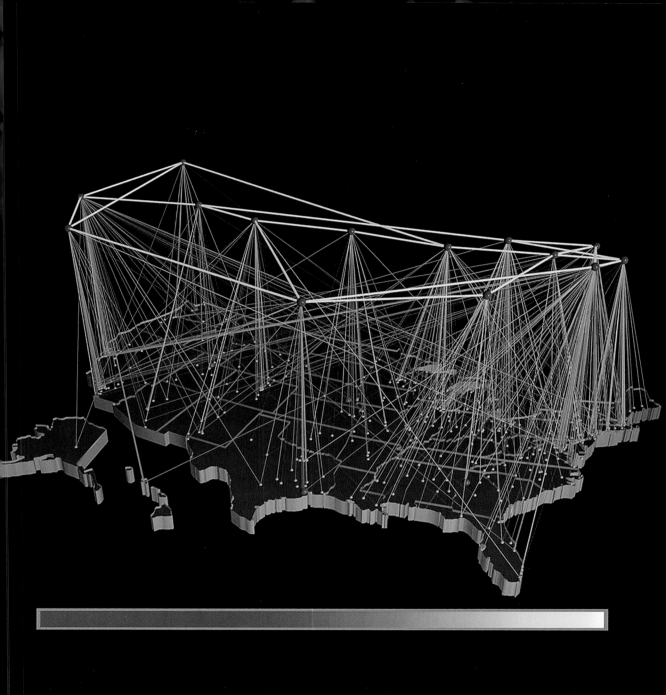

The Experimental Turn

Vernon L. Smith (b. 1927), Charles Plott (b. 1938)

Twentieth-century economists adopted mathematical tools and developed econometric techniques in an attempt to make economic analysis more "scientific," but they still lacked the most important element of scientific investigation: the laboratory experiment. Though a few isolated efforts to run bargaining and auction experiments occurred during the 1950s and 1960s, it was only in the 1970s that a small handful of economists, including Charles Plott and Vernon Smith, who received the 2002 Nobel Prize for his pioneering work, began applying experimental methods to economic analysis in earnest. The focus of their experiments went to the heart of economic thinking: Could they validate the predictions of the rational-choice model and other basic economic principles in the laboratory?

Acceptance of experimental economics came slowly. The laboratory environment was considered too artificial to yield valid insights, especially since most test subjects were college students. With time, however, experimental economics began to thrive. The Economic Science Association, which created a network of experimental economists and raised the profile of these new methods, was established in 1986. Computerization dramatically reduced the costs of experiments, and methods for conducting experiments became standardized. Today, running experiments is no longer a specialist subject, and many professors even use them as teaching tools. Economists use experimental methods to examine behavior and outcomes in many contexts, assessing how people respond to opportunities for strategic behavior, subsidies and regulations, and even their preferences for income redistribution.

The findings emerging from the lab have reinforced some aspects of economic thinking and challenged others, particularly the assumption that agents consistently make rational choices. In fact, the results of experimental research are largely responsible for launching the field of behavioral economics. They have also informed the auction methods used to allocate frequency spectrum licenses to cellular data providers and landing slots at airports, as well as the design of stock markets in countries such as Australia and New Zealand.

SEE ALSO Game Theory Enters Economics (1944), Non-Cooperative Games and Nash Equilibrium (1950), The Prisoner's Dilemma (1950), The Theory of Auctions (1961), Economics Becomes Applied (1970), Mechanism Design (1972), Behavioral Economics (1979), Natural Experiments (1990)

The earliest economics experiments utilized pencil and paper, but most experiments today take place in computer laboratories such as this one.

Endogenous Growth Theory

Paul Romer (b. 1955)

Some countries' economies consistently grow much more rapidly than others, which leads to enormous differences in national income across countries. The Solow–Swan model of economic growth, which had dominated growth theory since the 1950s, predicted the opposite, suggesting that diminishing returns to technology will slow the rate of growth in rich countries relative to that in poor ones. The root of this discrepancy comes from Solow's assumption that technology is determined by exogenous shocks, or forces that exist outside the system. But as American economist Paul Romer pointed out in "Increasing Returns and Long-Run Growth" (1986), technological progress is strongly conditioned by endogenous forces, those that operate within an economy itself.

Building on insights from Joseph Schumpeter's theory of creative destruction, Romer argued that innovation and human capital, which consists of society's cumulative knowledge, are actually the key drivers of growth, determining both technological progress and labor productivity. An environment that encourages individuals to acquire human capital and fosters innovation by promoting the discovery of new knowledge or the development of new products is likely to stimulate stronger and more consistent economic growth. For example, when more scientists are searching for cancer cures or working to develop better rocket engines, more discoveries are typically made. Economic forces, whether in the form of corporations looking to make a profit or the availability of tax-funded government research grants, provide essential spurs for this innovation, and the economic growth that results continues to feed the innovation machine.

Savings are crucial to this process as a source of financing for both business investment and education funding. Endogenous growth theory also points to the important role played by public policy in promoting or retarding growth. It suggests that China's one-child policy, for example, may have harmed both its economic growth and that of other nations because a smaller population generates fewer new ideas. Perhaps most importantly, it highlights how funding for research and development, the protection of intellectual property rights, and the tax breaks for things like education and R&D expenses affect the incentives for individuals to innovate and create the new knowledge that promotes economic growth.

SEE ALSO The Harrod–Domar Growth Model (1939), Creative Destruction (1942), Development Economics (1954), The Solow–Swan Growth Model (1956), Human Capital Analysis (1958), The New Keynesian Economics (1977)

A laboratory technician tests blood for the presence of HIV antibodies in 1985. Innovation resulting from scientific research can stimulate economic growth, which in turn facilitates even more innovation.

Governance of the Commons

Elinor Ostrom (1933–2012)

The "tragedy of the commons," a term coined by ecologist Garrett Hardin, describes how common pool resources—those that anyone can freely access—will be overexploited. Research by 2009 Nobel Laureate Elinor Ostrom challenged this long-standing view. Drawing on an extensive array of field studies, her 1990 book, *Governing the Commons*, showed that small communities often develop methods to manage common-property resources in efficient and ecologically sustainable ways.

Earlier research made it clear that communities have an incentive to avoid overexploitation, but choices that are rational for the group are sometimes not rational for the individuals within it. To mitigate the incentives that motivate individuals to act against the group's interest, some communities have developed rules to govern use of common resources and methods of enforcing regulations. Ostrom found examples of these communities around the world, with rules governing grazing, cultivation, and water use dating back hundreds of years. Democratic decision-making plays a particularly important role in this process; methods of governing the commons tend to work best when all parties with a stake in the issue have an equal say. Laboratory experiments conducted by Ostrom and her colleagues tested how communication methods, trust-building, and the process of rule creation can all affect the ability to create agreements about shared resources.

Ostrom's research suggested that typical measures for protecting common property resources, such as taxation, regulation, and privatization, aren't necessary to resolve common pool problems. In fact, they might even be harmful. Collective governance of the commons is more likely to succeed when trust exists between members of the community. Communities are likely to see rules imposed by outsiders or even powerful insiders as less legitimate and thus are more likely to violate them. Ostrom's approach has had a profound effect on development studies, which brings together researchers from a variety of academic backgrounds, to develop proposals for proper long-term resource management, and this work is already having important influence on sustainability efforts in countries including India and Mexico.

SEE ALSO The Prisoner's Dilemma (1950), The Common Pool Problem (1954), The Coase Theorem (1960), The Free-Rider Problem (1965), The Experimental Turn (1986), The New Institutional Economics (1997)

Elinor Ostrom traveled to rural Nepalese villages to study how these communities created rules and systems that allowed them to effectively manage their forests and irrigation systems, an example of which is shown here.

Natural Experiments

David Card (b. 1956), Joshua D. Angrist (b. 1960), Alan B. Krueger (1960–2019)

Everyone who has dealt extensively with statistical studies knows how difficult it can be to get clear-cut answers. For example, there are numerous studies finding that unions increase worker wages, and just as many finding that unions have no effect at all. The problem here is separating correlation from causation. Scientists evaluating, say, the efficacy of a new drug can avoid it by randomly assigning people to treatment and control groups. In the real world, separating the two is much tougher. In recent years, economists such as David Card, Joshua Angrist, and Alan Krueger have turned to "natural experiments" as a solution.

Natural experiments exploit rules, policies, or even geographical idiosyncrasies that can quasi-randomly assign people to different "treatments." An excellent example is the Mariel boatlift, which labor economist David Card used to examine the effects of immigration on the wages of unskilled workers. On April 15, 1980, Cuban president Fidel Castro suddenly announced that Cubans wishing to emigrate to the United States could do so at the port of Mariel. Over the next several months, more than 100,000 people left for Miami. Card's study, "The Impact of the Mariel Boatlift on the Miami Labor Market" (1990), found that, contrary to what economic theory would predict, this influx of immigrants barely affected local wages and unemployment rates. This suggested, against conventional wisdom, that some labor markets can absorb newcomers without negatively affecting native workers.

Normally, immigrants choose when and where to move, making it difficult to separate their effects from the factors that draw them to a community in the first place. By using Castro's unexpected announcement, and the proximity of Miami to Cuba (only 90 miles/145 km by boat), Card could isolate the effect of the Cuban immigration without needing to account for other factors that typically attract immigrants. Although natural experiments can't answer all questions, development, environmental, health, and labor economists have enthusiastically embraced them. For example, Angrist used Vietnam-era military drafts to show that time away from the labor market decreases earnings, while Card and Krueger found that increases in the minimum wage may have only negligible effects on employment.

SEE ALSO The Econometric Society (1930), Haavelmo's "Probability Approach" (1944), Economics Becomes Applied (1970), The Experimental Turn (1986)

Cuban refugees at Mariel wait for their ship to depart for the United States after Fidel Castro announced that those wishing to emigrate could do so at the Port of Mariel.

The New Institutional Economics

Ronald H. Coase (1910–2013), Douglass C. North (1920–2015), Oliver E. Williamson (b. 1932)

As economics became an increasingly mathematical science, the early twentieth-century analysis of institutions, which don't necessarily lend themselves to mathematical models, largely disappeared. A rebirth of institutional economics began in the 1970s when a small group of scholars started to examine how property rights and organizational structures influence economic performance. By 1997, Nobel Prizes had been awarded to Ronald Coase, Douglass North, and Oliver Williamson for their work in this area, and the International Society for the New Institutional Economics (now the Society for Institutional and Organizational Economics) had been formed.

Unlike their predecessors, the new institutionalists use modern tools to examine institutions and to design laws and policies that enhance efficiency. For example, the delineation of property rights significantly affects how markets function. If property rights aren't protected against invasion, there is little incentive to invest or pursue endeavors that create wealth, since that wealth can easily be taken away. This helps explain why, as societies develop, we see pressure for more comprehensive systems of law and justice and why corruption tends to inhibit economic growth. Legal rules also affect economic growth. North illustrated their role with his study of industrialization in Europe; he found that England and the Netherlands industrialized more quickly because they had fewer restrictions on work practices and entry into manufacturing occupations, and because guilds were less powerful.

New institutional economists have made important contributions to the study of business organization, showing how laws and transaction costs affect corporate governance and contracting practices. For example, Williamson's work has enhanced our understanding of why businesses operate and structure themselves in the way they do, and it has suggested that the large corporation is often an efficient response to market conditions rather than an inefficient market predator.

SEE ALSO Institutional Economics (1919), Coase's "Nature of the Firm" (1937), The Coase Theorem (1960), Cliometrics: The New Economic History (1961), Governance of the Commons (1990)

This stamp commemorates Ferdinand Marcos, president of the Philippines from 1965 to 1986, signing the Tenant Emancipation Decree No. 27, which came a few days after he declared martial law in 1972. Marcos often used his political power to launder money through illicit investments, an example of how corruption can inhibit economic growth.

The Euro

Robert Mundell (b. 1932)

A national currency can strengthen a country's national identity and allow it to control its own money supply. In 1999, however, many European nations adopted the euro, which meant eliminating their domestic currencies. As of 2019, the Eurozone consists of nineteen nations that use the euro as their official currency.

Though the European Economic Community (now the European Union) had wanted to establish a common currency since its inception in the 1960s, differing political and economic priorities created obstacles. Progress began with the creation of an exchange-rate system that kept the values of the members' currencies within a narrow range. In the early 1990s, plans for launching the euro were put into place, including the creation of the European Central Bank, which would manage monetary policy for Eurozone nations.

The intellectual groundwork for the euro came from a 1961 article, "A Theory of Optimum Currency Areas," by Canadian economist and Nobel Laureate Robert Mundell. Mundell suggested that there are geographic regions where it is efficient to have a common currency. An optimal currency area (OCA) should meet several criteria: It should be easy for labor and capital to move through the region, and wages and prices should be flexible enough to allow local markets to adjust to changing economic conditions. The OCA should have a risk-sharing mechanism that lets members transfer funds to assist areas experiencing economic difficulties, and it's also ideal for member nations' economies to have similar business cycles.

The euro's brief history has raised questions about whether the Eurozone meets these criteria. Language barriers have hampered the movement of labor between countries. During the European debt crisis, which began in 2009 at the height of the Great Recession, several countries, including Greece and Spain, couldn't repay or refinance their debts. Their requests for bailouts from the stronger Eurozone nations generated great resentment and were accompanied by what some considered punishing austerity measures. On the other hand, the euro has reduced the cost and risk associated with doing business within the Eurozone, integrated member-nation financial markets, and provided these nations with a stronger voice in the world's economy.

SEE ALSO Thornton's *Paper Credit* (1802), The Federal Reserve System (1913), The Bretton Woods Agreement (1944), Flexible Exchange Rates: The End of Bretton Woods (1971), The Great Recession (2007)

A one-euro coin (center) lies on top of coins from other countries, many of which are no longer in circulation because of the arrival of the euro.

Dynamic Stochastic General Equilibrium Models

Edward C. Prescott (b. 1940), Finn E. Kydland (b. 1943), Frank Smets (b. 1964), Raf Wouters (b. 1960)

Until roughly twenty years ago, macroeconomic policy analysis was the exclusive province of the large-scale macroeconometric models. These enormous models included thousands of variables and hundreds of equations that attempted to capture all manner of economic relationships and complexities. Things began to change when Finn Kydland and Edward Prescott introduced new ways to simulate the behavior of the economy. These new models, which became known as dynamic stochastic general equilibrium (DSGE) models, differ radically from their predecessors. They are incredibly simple, using just a handful of equations. Unlike macroeconometric models, the DSGE models revolve around the optimizing behavior of individuals, simulating how individual agents in the economy rationally respond to changes in economic conditions and tracing the effects of those responses over time.

By the mid-1990s, these simulation models had become the macroeconomists' laboratories. Because they rely on actual economic data, their forecasts can be evaluated against past economic phenomena, even if the data are highly aggregated to accommodate the simplicity of the DSGE models. By the mid-2000s, central banks and policy institutions, including the Fed, the European Central Bank, the Bank of England, and the IMF, began using these models alongside large-scale macroeconometric counterparts to forecast the economic activity and to guide monetary policy. DSGE models come in many varieties, including new classical and new Keynesian, though the latter, originally developed by Frank Smets and Raf Wouters in 2003, are preferred by central banks. Because of their extremely abstract nature, their use is controversial. Many saw their failure to forecast the Great Recession as a serious shortcoming, though macroeconometric models did no better on that score. Economists continue to tinker with these models to better capture the financial world's impact on economic activity and account for the possibility that individuals may not always respond to changing circumstances as rationally as these models assume.

SEE ALSO Large-Scale Macroeconometric Models (1955), The New Classical Economics (1972), The New Keynesian Economics (1977), Real Business Cycle Models (1982), The Great Recession (2007)

The European Central Bank, headquartered in Frankfurt, Germany, is one of the many central banks that use DSGE models to provide economic forecasts.

The Great Recession

The financial crisis that began in late 2007 plunged the world's economy into its worst recession since the Great Depression. It began with the collapse of the sub-prime mortgage market. Thousands of people with poor credit had taken out mortgages with adjustable interest rates when those rates were low. As market rates began rising in 2005, they found themselves unable to make their mortgage payments. Banks foreclosed, and the housing market cratered. The investment banks that traded risky financial instruments based on these mortgage loans were hit hard by the defaults. The situation worsened for the international financial system after investment bank Lehman Brothers declared bankruptcy in September 2008, plunging economies around the world into recession. In the U.S., unemployment doubled, home prices fell by nearly one-third, and stock markets lost more than half of their value. European economies experienced similar difficulties, and the spillover effects spread around the world.

Governments and central banks responded quickly, approving massive public-works programs and tax cuts to reduce unemployment and increase consumer spending. They also bailed out major corporations whose survival was deemed essential. Central banks tried to boost business investment with quantitative easing, which kept interest rates low and injected liquidity into the economy. Though the U.S. recession, as measured by the NBER, officially lasted from December 2007 through June 2009, its effects continue to linger. Unemployment has reached historic lows, but wage growth hasn't been consistent with what one would expect in a recovery. Some European countries are still grappling with the fallout as the economic collapse left governments unable to pay their debts.

Like the stagflation of the 1970s, the Great Recession saw criticism rain down on economists. Their sophisticated models had failed to predict the crisis and offer the opportunity for government policy to prevent or even deal with it. Just as important, it raised questions about the extent to which markets can be relied on to provide widespread benefits, and it prompted calls for governments to strengthen lax lending standards, increase financial market regulation, and enact policies—such as higher minimum wages and increased taxes on the wealthy—to reduce income inequality.

SEE ALSO Tulipmania (1636), The Federal Reserve System (1913), The Great Depression (1929), Keynes's *General Theory* (1936), The Keynesian Revolution (1947), The New Classical Macroeconomics (1972), The Euro (1999), Dynamic Stochastic General Equilibrium Models (2003)

During the Great Recession, many banks foreclosed on homes throughout the United States, including the three shown here, as many subprime mortgage owners defaulted on their payments.

Cryptocurrency

"Satoshi Nakamoto"

Money exists for several purposes. It is a medium of exchange, sparing people the hassles of bringing goods for barter; a unit of account, which makes different commodities comparable; and a store of value, meaning people can save it for future use—unlike, say, beans, which are perishable. As seen throughout history, almost anything *can* serve as money, including beads, coins made of precious metals, and paper. Today, most money takes a digital form. People regularly make payments using debit cards and digital payment apps. In fact, when the Federal Reserve transfers money to a bank, it is simply as a digital record that appears in the bank's accounts. The convenience of digital payments has led some people to design their own digital currencies, known as cryptocurrencies. The most famous of these is Bitcoin, which was created in 2009 by an unknown person or persons using the name Satoshi Nakamoto.

The name "cryptocurrency" derives from the fact that these currencies use cryptography, complex algorithms and secret codes that protect information and communication. Many of these currencies, including Bitcoin, rely on blockchain technology, which stores all transactions in an online ledger that is copied to the computers of all that currency's users. Cryptocurrencies are backed by their networks, rather than the government, but these systems are structured to maximize security and minimize fraud.

Cryptocurrency's supporters find its anonymity particularly appealing, since governments and financial institutions have no access to your funds or personal information. Because of this, these currencies have proven useful for those wishing to launder money or engage in other types of illegal financial transactions. Cryptocurrencies are also susceptible to hacking and theft and, because their prices are driven by supply and demand, their values fluctuate wildly. Governments are leery of the spread of cryptocurrencies because they limit a central bank's ability to control the money supply—a key macroeconomic policy tool—and many economists consider them a fad driven by speculators. However, their privacy features, the ability to help their users avoid bank fees, and the ease of fund transfer have made them attractive to many people.

SEE ALSO Debasement and Oresme's *De Moneta* (c. 1360), Gresham's Law (1558), The Quantity Theory of Money (1568), Tulipmania (1636), The Velocity of Money (1668), The Gold Standard (1717), Thornton's *Paper Credit* (1802), The Bullionist Controversy (1810), The Federal Reserve System (1913), *A Monetary History of the United States* (1963), The Personal Computer (1981)

Cryptocurrencies are "mined" using computers with specialized hardware and software. Those who mine cryptocurrency on a large scale sometimes keep their servers in rooms with cooling systems that prevent the equipment from overheating.

Notes and Further Reading

The literature on the topics covered in this book and that which I consulted during the research for it is voluminous and, in the case of topics in modern economics, often quite technical. Due to space constraints, I am able to provide only a single reference for each milestone. The references provided here are typically important secondary sources, with the latter selected with a general audience in mind. I have provided a much more extensive list of references, including both primary and secondary sources, on my Duke University website: https://sites.duke.edu/sgmedema/the-economics-book/.

General Reading

Backhouse, Roger E. *The Ordinary Business of Life*. Princeton, NJ: Princeton University Press, 2002. (Outside the U.S., this book is available as *The Penguin History of Economics*.)

Blaug, Mark. *Economic Theory in Retrospect*, 5th ed. Cambridge: Cambridge University Press, 1996.

Heilbroner, Robert L. *The Worldly Philosophers*, 7th ed. New York: Touchstone, 1999.

Spiegel, Henry W. *The Growth of Economic Thought*, 3rd ed. Durham: Duke University Press, 1991.

There are also a number of very useful reference works that explore the individuals and ideas dealt with in this volume:

Faccarello, Gilbert, and Heinz D. Kurz, eds. *Handbook on the History of Economic Analysis*. Cheltenham: Edward Elgar, 2016.

Durlauf, Steven N., and Lawrence E. Blume, eds. *The New Palgrave Dictionary of Economics*, 2nd ed. London: Macmillan, 2008. Online at dictionaryofeconomics.com.

Excerpts from primary sources can be found in:

Medema, Steven G., and Warren J. Samuels. *The History of Economic Thought: A Reader*, 2nd ed. London: Routledge, 2013.

There are also several online sources that allow one to access many of the writings noted in this book—and a wealth of others beyond that:

The Online Library of Liberty: oll.libertyfund.org

The McMaster University Archive for the History of Economic Thought: socialsciences.mcmaster.ca/econ/ugcm/3ll3/

JSTOR: jstor.org

Extensive amounts of information about the work of the economics Nobel Laureates can be found on the official website of the Nobel Prize, nobelprize.org.

c. 700 BCE, Hesiod's *Work and Days*

Gordon, Barry. *Economic Analysis Before Adam Smith: Hesiod to Lessius*. London: Macmillan, 1975.

c. 530 BCE, Pythagoras and Ordering Society

Lowry, S. Todd. "Pythagorean Mathematical Idealism and the Framing of Economic and Political Theory." *Advances in Mathematical Economics*, vol. 13: 177–199. Berlin: Springer, 2010.

c. 380 BCE, Plato, Aristotle, and the Golden Mean

Lowry, S. Todd. *The Archaeology of Economic Ideas: The Classical Greek Tradition*. Durham: Duke University Press, 1988.

c. 370 BCE, Xenophon's *Oeconomicus*

Xenophon. c. 370 BCE. *Oeconomicus: A Social and Historical Commentary*. Ed. and trans. Sarah B. Pomeroy. Oxford: Clarendon Press, 1995.

c. 340 BCE, Justice in Exchange

Lowry, S. Todd. "Aristotle's Mathematical Analysis of Exchange." *History of Political Economy* 1, no. 1 (1969): 44–66.

c. 1100, Scholasticism

Langholm, Odd. *Economics in the Medieval Schools*. Leiden: Brill, 1992.

1265, The Just Price

Baldwin, J. W. *The Medieval Theories of the Just Price*. Philadelphia: American Philosophical Society, 1959.

1265, Aquinas on Usury

Noonan, Jr., John T. *The Scholastic Analysis of Usury*. Cambridge: Harvard University Press, 1957.

c. 1360, Debasement and Oresme's *De Moneta*

Langholm, Odd. *Wealth and Money in the Aristotelian Tradition*. Oslo: Universitetsforlaget, 1983.

1377, Ibn Khaldun's *Al-Muqaddimah*

Soofi, Abdol. "Economics of Ibn Khaldun Revisited." History of Political Economy 27, no. 2 (1995): 387–404.

1517, The Protestant Reformation

Biéler, André. 1959. *Calvin's Social and Economic Thought*. Ed. Edward Dommem. Trans. James Greig. Geneva: World Alliance of Reformed Churches, 2005.

1539, Mercantile Policies

Viner, Jacob. *Studies in the Theory of International Trade*. New York: Harper and Brothers, 1937.

1544, The School of Salamanca

Grice-Hutchinson, Marjorie. 1978. *Early Economic Thought in Spain, 1177–1740*. Indianapolis: Liberty Fund, 2016.

1558, Gresham's Law

Roover, Raymond A. *Gresham on Foreign Exchange: An Essay on Early English Mercantilism with the Text of Sir Thomas Gresham's Memorandum: For the Understanding of the Exchange*. Cambridge, MA: Harvard University Press, 1949.

1568, The Quantity Theory of Money

Laidler, David. *The Golden Age of the Quantity Theory*. Princeton: Princeton University Press, 1991.

1620, Empiricism and Science
Letwin, William. *The Origins of Scientific Economics: English Economic Thought, 1660–1776.* London: Routledge, 1963.

1621, The Balance-of-Trade Controversy
Irwin, Douglas. *Against the Tide: An Intellectual History of Free Trade.* Princeton: Princeton University Press, 1996.

1636, Tulipmania
Goldgar, Anne. *Tulipmania: Money, Honor, and Knowledge in the Dutch Golden Age.* Chicago: University of Chicago Press, 2007.

1651, Hobbes's *Leviathan*
Schmitt, Carl. *The Leviathan in the State Theory of Thomas Hobbes: Meaning and Failure of a Political Symbol.* Chicago: University of Chicago Press, 2008.

1662, Rent and the Theory of Surplus
Goodacre, Hugh. *The Economic Thought of William Petty: Exploring the Colonialist Roots of Economics.* London: Routledge, 2018.

1662, The Equalization of Returns
Aspromourgos, Tony. *On the Origins of Classical Economics: Distribution and Value from William Petty to Adam Smith.* London: Routledge, 1996.

c. 1665, The Invention of Calculus
Bardi, Jason Socrates. *The Calculus Wars: Newton, Leibniz, and the Greatest Mathematical Clash of All Time.* New York: Basic, 2007.

1668, The Velocity of Money
Humphrey, Thomas M. "The Origins of Velocity Functions." *Federal Reserve Bank of Richmond Quarterly* 79, no. 4 (1993): 1–17.

1690, Locke's Theory of Property
Macpherson, C. B. *The Political Theory of Possessive Individualism: Hobbes to Locke.* Oxford: Clarendon Press, 1962.

1695, Laissez-Faire
Viner, Jacob. "The Intellectual History of Laissez-Faire." *Journal of Law and Economics* 3, no. 1 (1960): 45–69.

1705, John Law and Paper Money
Murphy, Antoin E. *John Law: Economic Theorist and Policy Maker.* Oxford: Oxford University Press, 1997.

1705, Mandeville's *Fable of the Bees*
Hont, Istvan. "The Early Enlightenment Debate on Commerce and Luxury." *The Cambridge History of Eighteenth-Century Political Thought.* Cambridge: Cambridge University Press, 2006.

1717, The Gold Standard
Craig, John Herbert McCutcheon. *Newton at the Mint.* Cambridge: Cambridge University Press, 1946.

1718, The Scottish Enlightenment
Hont, Istvan, and Michael Ignatieff, eds. *Wealth and Virtue: The Shaping of Political Economy in the Scottish Enlightenment.* Cambridge: Cambridge University Press, 1983.

1738, Bernoulli on Expected Utility
Bernstein, Peter L. *Against the Gods: The Remarkable Story of Risk.* Princeton: Princeton University Press, 1996.

1751, Galiani's *Della Moneta*
Cesarano, Filippo. "Monetary Theory in Ferdinando Galiani's *Della Moneta*." *History of Political Economy* 8, no. 3 (1976): 380–399.

1752, The Price–Specie Flow Mechanism
Schobas, Margaret and Carl Wennerlind "Retrospectives: Hume on Money, Commerce, and the Science of Economics." *Journal of Economic Perspectives,* 25, no. 3 (2011): 217–230.

1755, Cantillon's *Essay on the Nature of Trade*
Murphy, Antoin E. *Richard Cantillon: Entrepreneur and Economist.* Oxford: Clarendon Press, 1987.

1755, Rousseau's "Political Economy"
Gourevitch, Victor. *Rousseau: The "Discourses" and Other Early Political Writings.* Cambridge: Cambridge University Press, 1997.

1756, The Physiocrats
Vardi, Liana. *The Physiocrats and the World of the Enlightenment.* New York: Cambridge University Press, 2012.

1758, The *Tableau Économique*
Meek, Ronald. *The Economics of Physiocracy.* London: Allen and Unwin, 1963.

1760, The Industrial Revolution
Daunton, Martin J. *Progress and Poverty: An Economic and Social History of Britain, 1700–1850.* Oxford: Oxford University Press, 1995.

1766, Turgot's *Reflections*
Meek, Ronald L. *Turgot on Progress, Sociology, and Economics.* Cambridge: Cambridge University Press, 1973.

1767, Supply and Demand
Hutchison, Terence W. *Before Adam Smith.* Oxford: Blackwell, 1988.

1776, Smith's *Wealth of Nations*
Evensky, Jerry. *Adam Smith's Wealth of Nations: A Reader's Guide.* New York: Cambridge University Press, 2015.

1776, The Division of Labor
Foley, Vernard. "The Division of Labor in Plato and Smith." *History of Political Economy* 6, no. 2 (1974): 220–242.

1776, The Competitive Process
Berry, Christopher, Maria Paganelli, and Craig Smith, eds. *The Oxford Handbook of Adam Smith.* Oxford: Oxford University Press, 2013.

1776, The Invisible Hand
Winch, Donald. *Adam Smith's Politics: An Essay in Historiographic Revision.* Cambridge: Cambridge University Press, 1978.

1776, Productive and Unproductive Labor
Perrotta, Cosimo. *Unproductive Labor in Political Economy.* London: Routledge, 2018.

1789, Utilitarianism
Schofield, Philip. *Utility and Democracy: The Political Thought of Jeremy Bentham.* Oxford: Oxford University Press, 2006.

c. 1790, Classical Political Economy
Winch, Donald. *Riches and Poverty: An Intellectual History of Political Economy in Britain, 1750–1834.* Cambridge: Cambridge University Press, 1996.

1798, The Malthusian Population Theory
Winch, Donald. *Malthus: A Very Short Introduction.* Oxford: Oxford University Press, 1987.

1802, Thornton's *Paper Credit*
Murphy, Antoin E. *The Genesis of Macroeconomics: New Ideas from Sir William Petty to Henry Thornton.* Oxford: Oxford University Press, 2009.

1803, Say's Law
Sowell, Thomas. *Say's Law: An Historical Analysis.* Princeton: Princeton University Press, 1972.

1804, Underconsumption
Bleaney, M. *Underconsumption Theories: A History and Critical Analysis.* London: Lawrence & Wishart, 1976.

1810, The Bullionist Controversy
Selgin, George. *Good Money: Birmingham Button Makers, the Royal Mint, and the Beginnings of Modern Coinage, 1775–1821.* Ann Arbor: University of Michigan Press, 2008.

1813, Utopian Socialism

Cole, G. D. H. *A History of Socialist Thought, Volume 1: The Forerunners, 1789–1850.* London: Macmillan, 1953.

1815, Diminishing Returns

Brue, Stanley L. "The Law of Diminishing Returns." *Journal of Economic Perspectives* 7, no. 3 (1993): 185–192.

1815, The Stationary State

Eltis, Walter. *The Classical Theory of Economic Growth*, 2nd ed. London: Macmillan, 2000.

1816, *Conversations on Political Economy*

Forget, Evelyn L. "Jane Marcet as Knowledge Broker." *History of Economics Review* 65, no. 1 (2016): 15–26.

1817, The Machinery Question

Berg, Maxine. *The Machinery Question and the Making of Political Economy, 1815–1848.* Cambridge: Cambridge University Press, 1980.

1817, Ricardo's *Principles of Political Economy and Taxation*

King, John E. *David Ricardo.* London: Palgrave, 2013.

1817, The Theory of Comparative Advantage

Irwin, Douglas A. *Against the Tide: An Intellectual History of Free Trade.* Princeton: Princeton University Press, 1996.

1820, The Law of Demand

Smith, Victor E. "Malthus's Theory of Demand and Its Influence on Value Theory." *Scottish Journal of Political Economy* 59, no. 3 (1956): 242–257.

1821, The Political Economy Club

Henderson, James P. "The Oral Tradition in British Economics: Influential Economists in the Political Economy Club of London." *History of Political Economy* 15, no. 2 (1983): 149–179.

1821, The Labor Theory of Value

Meek, Ronald L. *Studies in the Labor The Theory of Value.* London: Lawrence & Wishart, 1956.

1826, Thünen's *Isolated State*

Samuelson, Paul A. "Thünen at Two Hundred." *Journal of Economic Literature* 21, no. 4 (December 1983), 1468–1488.

1830, The French Engineering Tradition

Ekelund, Robert B., Jr., and Robert F. Hébert. *The Secret Origins of Microeconomics: Dupuit and the Engineers.* Chicago: University of Chicago Press, 1999.

1832, *Illustrations of Political Economy*

Chapman, Maria Weston, ed. 1877. *Harriet Martineau's Autobiography*, 2 vols. London: Virago, 1983.

1836, The Abstinence Theory of Interest

Bowley, Marian. *Nassau Senior and Classical Economics.* London: Allen & Unwin, 1937.

1836, *Homo Economicus*

Persky, Joseph. "The Ethology of *Homo Economicus*." *Journal of Economic Perspectives* 9, no. 2 (1995): 221–231.

1836, The Positive–Normative Distinction

Colander, David, and Huei-Chun Su. "Making Sense of Economists' Positive-Normative Distinction." *Journal of Economic Methodology* 22, no. 2 (2015): 157–170.

1838, Cournot's *Researches*

Touffut, Jean-Philippe, ed. *Augustin Cournot: Modelling Economics.* Aldershot: Edward Elgar, 2008.

1843, The German Historical School

Tribe, Keith. *Strategies of Economic Order: German Economic Discourse, 1750–1950.* Cambridge: Cambridge University Press, 2007.

1844, Consumer Surplus

Ekelund, Jr., Robert B., and Robert F. Hébert. "Consumer Surplus: The First Hundred Years." *History of Political Economy* 17, no. 3 (1985): 419–454.

1848, *The Communist Manifesto*

Berlin, Isaiah. *Karl Marx: His Life and Environment*, 4th ed. New York: Oxford University Press, 1996.

1848, Mill's *Principles of Political Economy*

Reeves, Richard. *John Stuart Mill: Victorian Firebrand.* London: Atlantic Books, 2007.

1849, The Dismal Science

Jay, Elisabeth, and Richard Jay, eds. *Critics of Capitalism: Victorian Reactions to Political Economy.* Cambridge: Cambridge University Press, 1986.

1854, Gossen's Two Laws

Jolink, Albert, and Jan van Daal. "Gossen's Laws." *History of Political Economy* 30, no. 1 (1998): 43–50.

1857, The Falling Rate of Profit

Howard, M. C., and J. E. King. *A History of Marxian Economics.* Princeton: Princeton University Press, 1989.

1862, The Iron Law of Wages

Stirati, Antonella. *The Theory of Wages in Classical Economics.* Cheltenham: Edward Elgar, 1994.

1863, Index Numbers

Persky, Joseph. "Price Indexes and General Exchange Values." *Journal of Economic Perspectives* 12, no. 1 (1998): 197–205.

1866, The Wages Fund Controversy

Breit, William. "The Wages Fund Controversy Revisited." *Canadian Journal of Economics and Political Science* 33, no. 4 (1967): 509–528.

1867, Marx's *Das Kapital*

Brewer, Anthony. *A Guide to Marx's Capital.* Cambridge: Cambridge University Press, 1984.

1867, The Labor Theory of Value and the Theory of Exploitation

Singer, Peter. *Marx: A Very Short Introduction.* Oxford: Oxford University Press, 2001.

1867, The Theory of Crisis

Mandel, Ernest. *Marxist Economic Theory.* New York: Monthly Review Press, 1970.

1871, The Marginal Revolution

Collison Black, R. D., A. W. Coats, and Craufurd D. Goodwin, eds. *The Marginal Revolution in Economics: Interpretation and Evaluation.* Durham: Duke University Press, 1973.

1871, Jevons's *Theory of Political Economy*

Maas, Harro. *William Stanley Jevons and the Making of Modern Economics.* Cambridge: Cambridge University Press, 2005.

1871, Menger's *Principles of Economics*

Caldwell, Bruce, ed. *Carl Menger and His Legacy in Economics.* Durham: Duke University Press, 1990.

1871, The Austrian School

Boettke, Peter J., and Christopher J. Coyne. *The Oxford Handbook of Austrian Economics.* New York: Oxford University Press, 2015.

1874, Walras's *Elements of Pure Economics*

Jolink, Albert, and Jan Van Daal. *The Equilibrium Economics of Léon Walras.* London: Routledge, 1993.

1879, The Single Tax

O'Donnell, Edward. *Henry George and the Crisis of Inequality: Progress and Poverty in the Gilded Age.* New York: Columbia University Press, 2015.

1881, Edgeworth's *Mathematical Psychics*
Creedy, John. *Edgeworth and the Development of Neoclassical Economics.* Oxford: Basil Blackwell, 1986.

1883, *La Scienza della Finanze*
Buchanan, James M. "'La Scienza delle Finanze': The Italian Tradition in Fiscal Theory." In *Fiscal Theory and Political Economy: Selected Essays.* Chapel Hill: University of North Carolina Press, 1960.

1883, The Bertrand Model
Magnan de Bornier, Jean. "The Cournot-Bertrand Debate: A Historical Perspective." *History of Political Economy* 24, no. 3 (1992): 623–656.

1883, The *Methodenstreit*
Tribe, Keith. *Strategies of Economic Order: German Economic Discourse, 1750–1950.* Cambridge: Cambridge University Press, 1995.

1884, *Lectures on the Industrial Revolution*
Kadish, Alon. *Apostle Arnold: The Life and Death of Arnold Toynbee, 1852–1883.* Durham: Duke University Press, 1986.

1884, Fabian Socialism
Cole, Margaret. *The Story of Fabian Socialism.* Stanford: Stanford University Press, 1961.

1884, Böhm-Bawerk's *Capital and Interest*
Kuenne, R. E. *Eugen von Böhm-Bawerk.* New York: Columbia University Press, 1971.

1885, The Professionalization of Economics
Augello, Massimo, and Marco Guidi, eds. *The Spread of Political Economy and the Professionalisation of Economists.* London: Routledge, 2001.

1886, Economics Journals
Coats, A. W. "The Role of Scholarly Journals in the History of Economics: An Essay." *Journal of Economic Literature* 9, no. 1 (1971): 29–44.

1889, Opportunity Cost
Wicksteed, Philip. *The Commonsense of Political Economy.* London: Macmillan, 1910.

1890, Marshall's *Principles of Economics*
Groenewegen, Peter. *Alfred Marshall: Economist, 1842–1924.* London: Palgrave Macmillan, 2007.

1890, The Demand–Supply Model
Creedy, John. *Demand and Exchange in Economic Analysis.* Aldershot: Edward Elgar, 1992.

1890, *Ceteris Paribus*
Barrotta, Pierluigi. "On the Role of 'Ceteris Paribus' Clauses in Economics: An Epistemological Approach." *History of Economic Ideas* 8, no. 3 (2000): 83–102.

1890, Elasticity
Humphrey, Thomas M. "Marshallian Cross Diagrams and Their Uses Before Alfred Marshall: The Origins of Supply and Demand Geometry." *Federal Reserve Bank of Richmond Economic Review* 78, no. 2 (1992): 3–23.

1890, The Time Horizon
Whitaker, John K. "The Emergence of Marshall's Period Analysis." *Eastern Economic Journal* 8, no. 1 (1982): 15–29.

1890, Antitrust Laws
Freyer, Tony. *Regulating Big Business: Antitrust in Great Britain and America, 1880–1990.* Cambridge: Cambridge University Press, 1992.

1893, Ordinal Utility
Schmidt, Torsten, and Christian E. Weber. "On the Origins of Ordinal Utility: Andreas Heinrich Voigt and the Mathematicians." *History of Political Economy* 40, no. 3 (2008): 481–510.

1894, Tugan-Baranovsky and the Trade Cycle
Barnett, Vincent. "Tugan-Baranovsky as a Pioneer of Trade Cycle Analysis." *Journal of the History of Economic Thought* 23, no. 4 (2001): 443–466.

1896, The Benefit Principle of Taxation
Musgrave, Richard A. *Theory of Public Finance.* New York: McGraw-Hill, 1959.

1896, Unemployment
Freeden, Michael, ed. *Reappraising J. A. Hobson.* London: Unwin Hyman, 1990.

1896, The Real Rate of Interest
Humphrey, Thomas M. "The Early History of the Real/Nominal Interest Rate Relationship." *Economic Review* 69, no. 3 (1983): 2–10.

1898, Wicksell's Cumulative Process
Uhr, Carl G. *Economic Doctrines of Knut Wicksell.* Berkeley: University of California Press, 1960.

1899, Veblen's *Theory of the Leisure Class*
Tilman, Ric. *Thorstein Veblen and His Critics, 1891–1963: Liberal, Conservative, and Radical Perspectives.* Princeton: Princeton University Press, 1992.

1899, Clark's *Distribution of Wealth*
Henry, John F. *John Bates Clark: The Making of a Neoclassical Economist.* London: Palgrave, 2016.

1903, The Economics Tripos at Cambridge
Tribe, Keith. "The Cambridge Economics Tripos of 1903–1955 and the Training of Economists." *The Manchester School* 68, no. 2 (2000): 222–248.

1906, Pareto Optimality and Efficiency
Ingrao, Bruna, and Georgio Israel, eds. *The Invisible Hand: Economic Equilibrium in the History of Science.* Cambridge: MIT Press, 1990.

1906, Indifference Curves
Shackle, G. L. S. "The Indifference Curve." In *The Years of High Theory: Invention and Tradition in Economic Thought.* Cambridge: Cambridge University Press, 1967.

1912, Pigou's *Wealth and Welfare*
Aslanbeigui, Nahid, and Guy Oakes. *Arthur Cecil Pigou.* London: Palgrave Macmillan, 2015.

1912, External Economies and Diseconomies
Papandreou, Andreas A. *Externality and Institutions.* Oxford: Oxford University Press, 1994.

1913, Mitchell's *Business Cycles*
Biddle, Jeff. "Social Science and the Making of Social Policy: Wesley Mitchell's Vision." In *The Economic Mind in America: Essays in the History of American Economics.* Ed. Malcolm Rutherford. London: Routledge, 1998, pp. 43–79.

1913, The Federal Reserve System
Lowenstein, Roger. *America's Bank: The Epic Struggle to Create the Federal Reserve.* New York: Penguin, 2015.

1913, Luxemburg's *Accumulation of Capital*
Sweezy, Paul M. "Rosa Luxemburg's *The Accumulation of Capital.*" *Science & Society* 31, no. 4 (1967): 474–485.

1914, The Oxford Approach to Welfare
Cain, Peter J. *Hobson and Imperialism: Radicalism, New Liberalism and Finance, 1887–1938.* Oxford: Oxford University Press, 2002.

1915, Income and Substitution Effects
Barnett, Vincent. *E. E. Slutsky as Economist and Mathematician: Crossing the Limits of Knowledge.* London: Routledge, 2011.

1919, Institutional Economics
Rutherford, Malcolm. *The Institutionalist Movement in American Economics, 1918–1947: Science and Social Control.* New York: Cambridge University Press, 2011.

1920, The National Bureau of Economic Research
Fabricant, Solomon. "Toward a Firmer Basis of Economic Policy: The Founding of the National Bureau of Economic Research." New York: National Bureau of Economic Research, 1984. nber.org/nberhistory/sfabricantrev.pdf.

1920, The Socialist Calculation Debate
Lavoie, Don. *Rivalry and Central Planning: The Socialist Calculation Debate Reconsidered.* Cambridge: Cambridge University Press, 1985.

1921, Knight's *Risk, Uncertainty, and Profit*
Cowan, David. *Frank H. Knight: Prophet of Freedom.* London: Palgrave, 2016.

1924, *Legal Foundations of Capitalism*
Rutherford, Malcolm. "John R. Commons's Institutional Economics." *Journal of Economic Issues* 17, no. 3 (1983): 721–744.

1925, Kondratiev Waves
Barnett, Vincent. "A Long Wave Goodbye: Kondrat'ev and the Conjuncture Institute, 1920–28." *Europe-Asia Studies* 47, no. 3 (1995): 413–441.

1928, The Cobb–Douglas Function
Biddle, Jeff. "The Introduction of the Cobb–Douglas Regression." *Journal of Economic Perspectives* 26, no. 2 (2012): 223–236.

1929, The Hotelling Model of Locational Choice
Ridley, David B., "Hotelling's Law." *Palgrave Encyclopedia of Strategic Management.* Ed. Mie Augier and David Teece. London: Palgrave Macmillan, 2018.

1929, The Great Depression
Kindleberger, Charles P. *The World in Depression, 1929–1939,* 3rd ed. Oakland: University of California Press, 2013.

1930, The Econometric Society
Morgan, Mary S. *The History of Econometric Ideas.* Cambridge: Cambridge University Press, 1990.

1931, The Multiplier
Snowdon, Brian, and Howard R. Vane. *Modern Macroeconomics: Its Origins, Development and Current State.* Cheltenham: Edward Elgar, 2005.

1932, Scarcity and Choice
Backhouse, Roger E., and Steven G. Medema. "On the Definition of Economics." *Journal of Economic Perspectives* 23, no. 1 (2009): 221–234.

1932, The Cowles Commission
Christ, Carl F. "The Cowles Commission's Contributions to Econometrics at Chicago, 1939–1955." *Journal of Economic Literature* 32, no. 1 (1994): 30–59.

1932, *The Modern Corporation and Private Property*
Samuels, Warren J., and Steven G. Medema. *Gardiner C. Means: Institutionalist and Post Keynesian.* Armonk, NY: M. E. Sharpe, 1992.

1933, The Circular Flow Diagram
Patinkin, Don. "In Search of the 'Wheel of Wealth': On the Origins of Frank Knight's Circular-Flow Diagram." *American Economic Review* 63, no. 5 (1973): 1037–1046.

1933, Émigré Economists
Hagemann, Harald. "European Émigrés and the 'Americanization' of Economics." *European Journal of the History of Economic Thought* 18, no. 5 (2011): 643–671.

1933, *The Theory of Monopolistic Competition*
Samuelson, Paul A. "The Monopolistic Competition Revolution." In *Monopolistic Competition: Studies in Impact.* Ed. R. M. Kuenne. New York: Wiley & Sons, 1967.

1933, The Heckscher–Ohlin Model
Flam, Harry, and M. June Flanders, eds. *Heckscher–Ohlin Trade Theory.* Cambridge: MIT Press, 1991.

1933, *The Economics of Imperfect Competition*
Aslanbeigui, Nahid, and Guy Oakes. *The Provocative Joan Robinson: The Making of a Cambridge Economist.* Durham: Duke University Press, 2009.

1933, Mathematical Dynamics
Johansen, Leif. "Ragnar Frisch's Contributions to Economics." *Swedish Journal of Economics* 71, no. 4 (1969): 302–324.

1934, The Stackelberg Model
Niehans, Jürg. "Heinrich von Stackelberg: Relinking German Economics to the Mainstream." *Journal of the History of Economic Thought* 14, no. 2 (1992): 189–208.

1934, National Income Accounting
Vanoli, André. *A History of National Accounting.* Amsterdam: IOS Press, 2005.

1934, The Hicks–Allen Consumer Theory
Lenfant, Jean-Sébastien. "Complementarity and Demand Theory: From the 1920s to the 1940s." In *Agreement on Demand: Consumer Theory in the Twentieth Century.* Ed. Philip Mirowski and D. Wade Hands. Durham: Duke University Press, 2006.

1936, Keynes's *General Theory*
Skidelsky, Robert. *John Maynard Keynes: 1883–1946: Economist, Philosopher, Statesman.* New York: Penguin, 2005.

1936, Liquidity Preference and the Liquidity Trap
Boianovsky, Mauro. "The IS–LM Model and the Liquidity Trap Concept: From Hicks to Krugman." *History of Political Economy* 36, Suppl. (2004): 92–126.

1936, The Tinbergen Model
Jolink, Albert. *Jan Tinbergen: The Statistical Turn in Economics, 1903–1955.* Rotterdam: CHIMES, 2003.

1937, The IS–LM Model
Hoover, Kevin D., and Michel De Vroey, eds. *The IS–LM Model: Its Rise, Fall, and Strange Persistence.* Durham: Duke University Press, 2005.

1937, Coase's "Nature of the Firm"
Medema, Steven G. *Ronald H. Coase.* London: Macmillan, 1994.

1938, Logical Positivism
Caldwell, Bruce J. *Beyond Positivism.* London: Allen and Unwin, 1982.

1938, The Bergson Social Welfare Function
Feldman, Allan M., and Roberto Serrano. *Welfare Economics and Social Choice Theory,* 2nd ed. Berlin: Springer, 2005.

1938, Revealed Preference Theory
Hands, D. Wade. "Paul Samuelson and Revealed Preference Theory." *History of Political Economy* 46, no. 1 (2014): 85–116.

1939, Hicks's *Value and Capital*
Hagemann, Harald, and O. F. Hamouda, eds. *The Legacy of Hicks: His Contributions to Economic Analysis.* London: Routledge, 2013.

1939, The Harrod–Domar Growth Model
Easterly, William. *The Elusive Quest for Growth: Economists' Adventures and Misadventures in the Tropics.* Cambridge: MIT Press, 2001.

1939, World War II
Lacey, Jim. *Keep from All Thoughtful Men: How U.S. Economists Won World War II.* Annapolis: Naval Institute Press, 2011.

1939, The Multiplier–Accelerator Model
Heertje, Arnold, and Peter Heemeijer. "On the Origin of Samuelson's Multiplier-Accelerator Model." *History of Political Economy* 34, no. 1 (2002): 207–218.

1939, The Kaldor–Hicks Efficiency Criterion
Feldman, Allan M., and Roberto Serrano. *Welfare Economics and Social Choice Theory*, 2nd ed. Berlin: Springer, 2005.

1941, The Stolper–Samuelson Theorem
Deardorff, Alan V., and Robert M. Stern, eds. *The Stolper–Samuelson Theorem: A Golden Jubilee.* Ann Arbor: University of Michigan Press, 1994.

1941, Input–Output Analysis
Dietzenbacher, Erik, and Michael L. Lahr. *Wassily Leontief and Input–Output Economics.* Cambridge: Cambridge University Press, 2004.

1942, Creative Destruction
McCraw, Thomas K. *Prophet of Innovation: Joseph Schumpeter and Creative Destruction.* Cambridge: Belknap Press, 2007.

1943, The Fundamental Theorems of Welfare Economics
Blaug, Mark. "The Fundamental Theorems of Modern Welfare Economics, Historically Contemplated." *History of Political Economy* 39, no. 2 (2007): 185–207.

1944, Hayek's *Road to Serfdom*
Caldwell, Bruce J.: "Introduction." In *The Road to Serfdom—The Definitive Edition* by F. A. Hayek, 1–36. Chicago: University of Chicago Press, 2007.

1944, Game Theory Enters Economics
Leonard, Robert. *Von Neumann, Morgenstern, and the Creation of Game Theory.* New York: Cambridge University Press, 2010.

1944, Haavelmo's "Probability Approach"
Hoover, Kevin D. "On the Reception of Haavelmo's Econometric Thought." *Journal of the History of Economic Thought* 36, no. 1 (2014): 45–65.

1944, The Bretton Woods Agreement
Steil, Benn. *The Battle of Bretton Woods: John Maynard Keynes, Harry Dexter White, and the Making of a New World Order.* Princeton: Princeton University Press, 2009.

1945, Hayek's "Use of Knowledge in Society"
Caldwell, Bruce J. *Hayek's Challenge: An Intellectual Biography of F. A. Hayek.* Chicago: University of Chicago Press, 2004.

1946, The Council of Economic Advisers
Bernstein, Michael A. *A Perilous Progress: Economists and Public Purpose in Twentieth-Century America.* Princeton: Princeton University Press, 2001.

1946, The Chicago School
Emmett, Ross B., ed. *The Elgar Companion to the Chicago School of Economics.* Cheltenham: Edward Elgar, 2010.

1946, The Consumer Price Index
Stapleford, Thomas A. *The Cost of Living in America: A Political History of Economic Statistics, 1880–2000.* New York: Cambridge University Press, 2009.

1947, The Keynesian Revolution
Clarke, Peter. *The Keynesian Revolution and Its Economic Consequences.* Cheltenham: Edward Elgar, 1998.

1947, *Foundations of Economic Analysis*
Backhouse, Roger E. *Founder of Modern Economics: Paul Samuelson. Volume 1: Becoming Samuelson, 1915–1948.* New York: Oxford University Press, 2017.

1947, Linear Programming
Dorfman, Robert. "The Discovery of Linear Programming." *Annals of the History of Computing* 6, no. 3 (1984): 283–295.

1948, Samuelson's *Economics*
Giraud, Yann. "Negotiating the 'Middle of the Road' Position: Paul Samuelson, MIT and the Politics of Textbook Writing, 1945–55." *History of Political Economy* 46, Suppl. (2014): 134–152.

1948, The Factor-Price Equalization Theorem
Fenestra, Robert C. *The Impact of International Trade on Wages.* Chicago: University of Chicago Press and NBER, 2000.

1948, The Median Voter Theorem
Mueller, Dennis. *Public Choice III.* New York: Cambridge University Press, 2003.

1948, RAND and the Cold War
Jardini, David. 2013. *Thinking Through the Cold War: RAND, National Security, and Domestic Policy.* E-book.

1948, Computation: The Orcutt Regression Analyzer and the Phillips Machine
"The History of the Phillips Machine." In *A. W. H. Phillips: Collected Works in Contemporary Perspective,* edited by Robert Leeson, 89–114. Cambridge: Cambridge University Press, 2000.

1950, Non-Cooperative Games and Nash Equilibrium
Nasar, Sylvia. *A Beautiful Mind.* New York: Simon and Schuster, 1998.

1950, The Prisoner's Dilemma
Poundstone, William. *Prisoner's Dilemma: John von Neumann, Game Theory, and the Puzzle of the Bomb.* New York: Doubleday, 1992.

1951, Arrow's Impossibility Theorem
Maskin, Eric, and Amartya Sen, eds. *The Arrow Impossibility Theorem.* New York: Columbia University Press, 2014.

1952, Resources for the Future and Environmental Economics
Pearce, David. "An Intellectual History of Environmental Economics." *Annual Review of Energy and the Environment* 27, no. 1 (2002): 57–81.

1952, The Theory of Portfolio Selection
Brine, Kevin R., and Mary Poovey. *Finance in America: An Unfinished Story.* Chicago: University of Chicago Press, 2017.

1953, The Shapley Value
Hart, Sergiu. *The Shapley Value: Essays in Honor of Lloyd S. Shapley.* Ed. Alvin E. Roth. New York: Cambridge University Press, 2008.

1953, "The Methodology of Positive Economics"
Mäki, Uskali, ed. *The Methodology of Positive Economics: Reflections on the Milton Friedman Legacy.* Cambridge: Cambridge University Press, 2009.

1954, Proving the Existence of a General Equilibrium
Düppe, Till, and E. Roy Weintraub. *Finding Equilibrium: Arrow, Debreu, McKenzie and the Problem of Scientific Credit.* Princeton: Princeton University Press, 2014.

1954, Public Goods
Cornes, Richard, and Todd Sandler. *The Theory of Externalities, Public Goods, and Club Goods*, 2nd ed. New York: Cambridge University Press, 1996.

1954, Development Economics
Tignor, Robert L. *W. Arthur Lewis and the Birth of Development Economics*. Princeton: Princeton University Press, 2006.

1954, The Common Pool Problem
Hardin, Garrett. "The Tragedy of the Commons." *Science* 162, no. 3859 (1968): 1243–1248.

1955, Bounded Rationality
Augier, Mie, and James March. *Models of a Man: Essays in Memory of Herbert A. Simon*. Cambridge: MIT Press, 2004.

1955, Large-Scale Macroeconometric Models
Marwah, Kanta, Lawrence Klein, and Ronald G. Bodkin. *A History of Macroeconometric Model-Building*. Cheltenham: Edward Elgar, 1991.

1956, The Theory of Second Best
Mishan, Ezra J. "Second Thoughts on Second Best." *Oxford Economic Papers* 14, no. 3 (1962): 205–217.

1956, The Tiebout Model
Singleton, John. "Sorting Charles Tiebout." *History of Political Economy* 47, Suppl. (2015): 199–226.

1956, The Solow–Swan Growth Model
Boianovsky, Mauro, and Kevin D. Hoover, eds. *Robert Solow and the Development of Growth Economics*. Durham: Duke University Press, 2009.

1957, The Economics of Discrimination
Fleury, Jean-Baptiste. "Wandering Through the Borderlands of the Social Sciences: Gary Becker's *Economics of Discrimination*." *History of Political Economy* 44, no. 1 (2012): 1–40.

1957, The Permanent Income Hypothesis
Meghir, Costas. "A Retrospective on Friedman's Theory of Permanent Income." *Economic Journal* 114, no. 496 (2004): F293–F306.

1957, The Rational Voter Model and the Paradox of Voting
Caplan, Bryan. *The Myth of the Rational Voter: Why Democracies Choose Bad Policies*. Princeton: Princeton University Press, 1997.

1958, Human Capital Analysis
Teixeira, Pedro. *Jacob Mincer: Founding Father of Modern Labour Economics*. Oxford: Oxford University Press, 2007.

1958, Externalities and Market Failure
Papandreou, Andreas A. *Externality and Institutions*. Oxford: Oxford University Press, 1994.

1958, Cost–Benefit Analysis
Pearce, David W. "The Origins of Cost-Benefit Analysis." In *Cost-Benefit Analysis*, 2nd ed. London: Macmillan, 1983.

1958, The Modigliani–Miller Theorem
Miller, Merton H. "The Modigliani–Miller Proposition after Thirty Years." *Journal of Economic Perspectives* 2, no. 4 (1988): 99–120.

1958, The Phillips Curve
Forder, James. *Macroeconomics and the Phillips Curve Myth*. Oxford: Oxford University Press, 2014.

1958, Galbraith's *The Affluent Society*
Parker, Richard. *John Kenneth Galbraith: His Life, His Politics, His Economics*. New York: Farrar, Straus, and Giroux, 2005.

1959, Debreu's *The Theory of Value*
Düppe, Till. "Gérard Debreu's Secrecy: His Life in Order and Silence." *History of Political Economy* 44, no. 3 (2012): 413–449.

1960, The Coase Theorem
Medema, Steven G. "The Coase Theorem at Sixty." *Journal of Economic Literature* (forthcoming).

1961, Cliometrics: The New Economic History
Goldin, Claudia. "Cliometrics and the Nobel." *Journal of Economic Perspectives* 9, no. 2 (1995): 191–208.

1961, The Economics of Information
Stiglitz, Joseph E. "The Contributions of the Economics of Information to Twentieth Century Economics." *Quarterly Journal of Economics* 115, no. 4 (2000): 1441–1478.

1961, The Theory of Auctions
Hubbard, Timothy P., and Harry J. Paarsch. *Auctions*. Cambridge: MIT Press, 2016.

1961, The Rational Expectations Hypothesis
Sheffrin, Steven M. *Rational Expectations*, 2nd ed. Cambridge: Cambridge University Press, 1996.

1962, The Capital Asset Pricing Model
Harrison, Paul. "A History of Intellectual Arbitrage: The Evolution of Financial Economics." *History of Political Economy* 29, Suppl. (1997): 172–188.

1962, Public Choice Analysis
Medema, Steven G. *The Hesitant Hand*. Princeton: Princeton University Press, 2009.

1963, *A Monetary History of the United States*
Rockoff, Hugh. "On the Origins of *A Monetary History*." In *The Elgar Companion to the Chicago School of Economics*. Ed. Ross B. Emmett. Cheltenham: Edward Elgar, 2010.

1965, The Free-Rider Problem
Tuck, Richard. *Free Riding*. Cambridge: Harvard University Press, 2008.

1965, The Efficient Markets Hypothesis
Lo, Andrew W., ed. *Market Efficiency: Stock Market Behavior in Theory and Practice*, 2 vols. Cheltenham: Edward Elgar, 1997.

1966, Emissions Trading
Tietenberg, Tom. "Cap and Trade: The Evolution of an Economic Idea." *Agricultural and Resource Economics* 39, no. 3 (2010): 359–367.

1967, Rent Seeking
Congleton, Roger D. and Arye L. Hillman, eds. *Companion to the Political Economy of Rent Seeking*. Cheltenham: Edward Elgar, 2015.

1967, The Natural Rate of Unemployment
Stiglitz, Joseph, et al. "Symposium: The Natural Rate of Unemployment." *Journal of Economic Perspectives* 11, no. 1 (1997): 3–108.

1968, The Economics of Crime and Punishment
Freeman, Richard B. "The Economics of Crime." *The Handbook of Labor Economics*, vol. 3, part C. Ed. Orley C. Ashenfelter and David Card. Amsterdam: Elsevier, 1999.

1969, The "Nobel Prize" in Economics
Karier, Thomas. *Intellectual Capital: Forty Years of the Nobel Prize in Economics*. New York: Cambridge University Press, 2010.

1970, Economics Becomes Applied
Backhouse, Roger E., and Beatrice Cherrier, eds. *The Age of the Applied Economist: The Transformation of Economics since the 1970s*. Durham: Duke University Press, 2017.

1970, The Market for "Lemons"
Löfgren, Karl-Gustaf, Torsten Persson, and Jörgen W. Weibull. 2002. "Markets with Asymmetric Information: The Contributions of George Akerlof, Michael Spence and Joseph Stiglitz." *Scandinavian Journal of Economics* 104, no. 2 (2007): 195–211.

1970, *Collective Choice and Social Welfare*
Morris, Christopher W., ed. *Amartya Sen.* Cambridge: Cambridge University Press, 2009.

1970, The Atkinson Inequality Index
Sen, Amartya. *On Economic Inequality*, 2nd ed. Oxford: Oxford University Press, 1997.

1971, Regulatory Capture
Dal Bó, Ernesto. "Regulatory Capture: A Review." *Oxford Review of Economic Policy* 22, no. 2 (2006): 203–225.

1971, Flexible Exchange Rates: The End of Bretton Woods
James, Harold. *International Monetary Cooperation since Bretton Woods.* Washington: International Monetary Fund, 1996.

1971, Optimal Taxation
Kaplow, Louis. *The Theory of Taxation and Public Economics.* Princeton: Princeton University Press, 2008.

1972, The New Classical Macroeconomics
Hoover, Kevin D. *The New Classical Macroeconomics.* Oxford: Blackwell, 1988.

1972, Mechanism Design
Börgers, Tilman. *An Introduction to the Theory of Mechanism Design.* Oxford: Oxford University Press, 2015.

1973, The Economic Analysis of Law
Mercuro, Nicholas, and Steven G. Medema. *Economics and the Law: From Posner to Post Modernism and Beyond.* Princeton: Princeton University Press, 2006.

1973, Agency Theory
Eisenhardt, Kathleen M. "Agency Theory: An Assessment and Review." *Academy of Management Review* 14, no. 1 (1989): 57–74.

1973, The Black–Scholes Model
Mehrling, Perry. *Fischer Black and the Revolutionary Idea of Finance.* New York: Wiley, 2005.

1973, Signaling
Weiss, Andrew. "Human Capital vs. Signaling Explanations of Wages." *Journal of Economic Perspectives* 9, no. 4 (1995): 133–154.

1973, OPEC and the Arab Oil Embargo
Blinder, Alan. *Economic Policy and the Great Stagflation.* New York: Academic, 1979.

1974, Supply-Side Economics
Roberts, Paul Craig. *The Supply-Side Revolution.* Cambridge: Harvard University Press, 1984.

1975, The Policy Ineffectiveness Proposition
De Vroey, Michel. *A History of Macroeconomics from Keynes to Lucas and Beyond.* Cambridge: Cambridge University Press, 2016.

1976, Screening—or Pooling and Separating Equilibria
Riley, John G. "Silver Signals: Twenty-Five Years of Screening and Signaling." *Journal of Economic Literature* 39, no. 2 (2001): 432–478.

1976, The Lucas Critique
Snowdon, Brian, and Howard R. Vane. *Modern Macroeconomics: Its Origins, Development and Current State.* Cheltenham: Edward Elgar, 2005.

1977, The New Keynesian Economics
Galí, Jordi. *Monetary Policy, Inflation, and the Business Cycle: An Introduction to the New Keynesian Framework and Its Implications, 2nd Ed.* Princeton: Princeton University Press, 2015.

1979, The New Trade Theory
Neary, J. Peter. "Putting the 'New' into New Trade Theory: Paul Krugman's Nobel Memorial Prize in Economics." *Scandinavian Journal of Economics* 111, no. 2 (2009): 217–250.

1979, Behavioral Economics
Heukelom, Floris. *Behavioral Economics: A History.* Cambridge: Cambridge University Press, 2015.

1981, The Personal Computer
Backhouse, Roger E., and Beatrice Cherrier. "'It's Computers, Stupid!' The Spread of Computers and the Changing Roles of Theoretical and Applied Economics." *History of Political Economy* 49, Suppl. (2017): 103–126.

1982, Real Business Cycle Models
Young, Warren. *Real Business Cycle Models in Economics.* London: Routledge, 2016.

1986, The Experimental Turn
Kagel, John H., and Alvin E. Roth. *Handbook of Experimental Economics.* Vol. 2. Princeton: Princeton University Press, 2015.

1986, Endogenous Growth Theory
Warsh, David. *Knowledge and the Wealth of Nations: A Story of Economic Discovery.* New York: W. W. Norton, 2007.

1990, Governance of the Commons
Aligica, Paul Dragos, and Peter J. Boettke. *Challenging Institutional Analysis and Development: The Bloomington School.* London: Routledge, 2009.

1990, Natural Experiments
Angrist, Joshua D., and Jörn-Steffen Pischke. "The Credibility Revolution in Empirical Economics: How Better Research Design Is Taking the Con out of Econometrics." *Journal of Economic Perspectives* 24, no. 2 (2010): 3–30.

1997, The New Institutional Economics
Brousseau, Éric, and Jean-Michel Glachant, eds. *New Institutional Economics: A Guidebook.* Cambridge: Cambridge University Press, 2008.

1999, The Euro
Dyson, Kenneth, and Ivo Maes, eds. *Architects of the Euro: Intellectuals in the Making of European Monetary Union.* Oxford: Oxford University Press, 2016.

2003, Dynamic Stochastic General Equilibrium Models
Christiano, Lawrence J., Martin S. Eichenbaum, and Mathias Trabandt. "On DSGE Models." *Journal of Economic Perspectives* 32, no. 3 (2018): 113–140.

2007, The Great Recession
Bernanke, Ben. *The Federal Reserve and the Financial Crisis.* Princeton: Princeton University Press, 2015.

2009, Cryptocurrency
Ammous, Saifedean. *The Bitcoin Standard: The Decentralized Alternative to Central Banking.* New York: John Wiley & Sons, 2018.

Index